Royal Sovereign

Mars
Belleisle
Tonnant
Bellerophon
Collossus
Achille
Polyphemus
Revenge
Swiftsure
Defence
Thunderer
Defiance
Prince
Dreadnought

COMBINED FLEET, October 21st 1805.

dmiralty Novr 1805.

Nelson's Purse

Nelson's Purse

*An extraordinary historical detective story
shedding new light on the life of Britain's
greatest naval hero*

Martyn Downer

BANTAM PRESS

LONDON · TORONTO · SYDNEY · AUCKLAND · JOHANNESBURG

TRANSWORLD PUBLISHERS
61–63 Uxbridge Road, London W5 5SA
a division of The Random House Group Ltd

RANDOM HOUSE AUSTRALIA (PTY) LTD
20 Alfred Street, Milsons Point, Sydney,
New South Wales 2061, Australia

RANDOM HOUSE NEW ZEALAND LTD
18 Poland Road, Glenfield, Auckland 10, New Zealand

RANDOM HOUSE SOUTH AFRICA (PTY) LTD
Endulini, 5a Jubilee Road, Parktown 2193, South Africa

Published 2004 by Bantam Press
a division of Transworld Publishers

A catalogue record for this book is available
from the British Library.
ISBN 0593 051807

Typeset in 13.25/15 pt Perpetua
by Falcon Oast Graphic Art Ltd.

Printed in Great Britain by
Mackays of Chatham plc, Chatham, Kent

1 3 5 7 9 10 8 6 4 2

Papers used by Transworld Publishers are natural, recyclable products
made from wood grown in sustainable forests. The manufacturing processes
conform to the environmental regulations of the country of origin.

CONTENTS

For Sam

NELSON'S PURSE

The Immortality of Nelson, after Sir Benjamin West (1807).

VICTORY

100 GUNS,
CAPTAIN THOMAS MASTERMAN HARDY

WILLIAM HARDLY SLEPT; none of them did. The dull ache in his stomach had risen to his throat, bringing with it bile and the sour taste of fear. Men had told him about the morning of battle, bragging of their own bravery. They were lying, of course – it was the grog talking – but everyone went along with their swagger. The men who had fought at the Nile or Copenhagen never spoke of it. Now that day had dawned for him, and he simply felt hollow. He was cheek by jowl with a thousand men but felt as lonely as a lost child. He expected his bowels to open, and they did, and to be sick, which he was; but this awful sensation of helplessness in the face of a brutal, random death was startling.

His hand shook as he shaved, though it still paused instinctively as the ship rose and fell. William took longer than usual over the task, relishing the mundane routine. It was only when he gazed into his glass and imagined himself dead, his torn body sinking into a crimson sea, that he was, for a moment, overwhelmed by such dread that he had to hold himself from running wildly away. But he couldn't move and there was nowhere to run to. Only when his spiralling fears glimpsed Elizabeth asleep in London did he relax, clutching the image. His wife did not know what he was facing here, now, today. He was grateful for that. It would be days, weeks even, before she heard whether he was alive or dead. He vowed, if he survived, never to leave her again.

William, as a mere servant, berthed in the orlop deck, below the waterline, in the dank, fetid bowels of the ship. He watched as it was cleared for casualties. The loblolly boys were rolling bandages, counting out sponges and busily swabbing down the midshipmen's table in the cockpit. Beatty the surgeon was arranging his knives and saws, checking their keenness from time to time with his thumb. The men hid their thoughts, each absorbed in his task. William was thankful the edgy heartiness of the night before had gone. He was reassured by the sight of this orderly calm before the looming chaos. More than ever now he wanted to live.

In one involuntary movement, as if joined together by an invisible thread, all the men on the deck suddenly paused and glanced up. For a moment there seemed no reason for this. Then William realized that the familiar creaking and thudding sound of the rudder, the heartbeat of his wooden world, was changing. The noise rose to a roar as, heaving slowly at first and then with a sudden lurch, the ship slipped steeply to port to go about. The men clutched the beams above their heads. Beatty's tools crashed off the table, clattering chaotically across the deck. For several minutes the ship held this position, shuddering painfully, until slowly the deck straightened and the lanterns hung vertically again. High above the spot where William stood, the wind grabbed the vast sails of the ship and the familiar rolling sensation again surged through his body. His lordship had turned them towards the enemy.

There was no formal breakfast this morning. William was told to prepare bread and plates of ham instead. He would keep up a running supply of tea and coffee not only for his own officers but also for any last visitors to *Victory*. Going up through the ship to the staterooms, William paused at the galley to collect pots of hot water. Everywhere he saw preparations for action, though the guns were not yet run out and the ports were still down. Some of the men were clustered around their guns talking quietly, but the ship was unusually still and empty. When William reached the main deck he understood why. Most of the men were crowded together on the forecastle, the boys clinging to the masts. All of them were gazing silently east, into the flat, grey dawn.

At first William saw nothing. Then, as his eyes grew accustomed to the pale, watery light after the darkness below, he noticed a shadow on the horizon, then another and another. Straining his eyes, he counted thirty warships, maybe more, strung out on the seam between sea and sky, apparently motionless. Only the empty, rolling sea lay between him and them. Transfixed by this awesome spectacle, William was seized for a moment by the same cold dread that had paralysed him below. Struck by a sudden thought, he turned to search the faces of the officers gathered behind him on the poop deck, the weak morning sun glinting off their telescopes. Behind them were the ships following *Victory*, their masts rising and falling like the keys of a giant's piano. There was no sign of his lordship.

Then, from somewhere among the crowd of seamen pressed against the rails, the spell was broken by a lone, low voice singing softly. The words drifted back along the deck.

Farewell and adieu to you fine Spanish ladies,
Farewell and adieu all you ladies of Spain.

As the voice grew stronger and more confident, others joined it. William felt the men stir and rise as if awoken:

We'll rant and we'll roar like true British sailors . . .

He turned again to look back at the officers. They were unmoved, their telescopes still resolutely aimed at the enemy. But among them now William saw the slight figure of his lordship. He was not watching the enemy. He was looking at his men.

William tried to concentrate on his work as they were

carried inexorably towards the battle. Now and then he dared to glance over the rail, irresistibly drawn by the brooding presence of the enemy ships. Each time they looked bigger and more appallingly beautiful as the blanket of sea between the two fleets was slowly rolled up. Thankfully William was kept busy as the officers went about their rounds. Once he was startled by the clattering sound of the chicken coops being tipped over the side, to the cheers of the men. He tried not to remember that the livestock was being jettisoned to make room for casualties on the lower decks.

Captain Blackwood of *Euryalus* came on board early. He spoke quietly with Captain Hardy for a few minutes before John Scott, his lordship's secretary, ushered them both into the great cabin. They remained there some time. As William moved among the officers, serving drinks and clearing plates, he observed them closely. Most of the furniture in the staterooms had been cleared and the men – men he knew so well – stood, or perched, where they could. Many spurned the coffee he carried, preferring wine. Some of them, he noticed, the young midshipmen in particular, seemed as unconcerned as if they were going hunting on their estates in England rather than about to face the French guns. He supposed this display of nonchalance was deliberate; in any event, he found it highly unconvincing. Others stood quietly, lost in thought, sipping their coffee, ignoring the food. A few laughed a little too loudly or too long – among them John Scott; but when the secretary turned his flushed face towards the steward as he held out his glass for more wine, William saw the desperate pleading in his eyes. The chaplain, Dr Alexander Scott – no relation to the secretary – was nowhere to be seen. William assumed he was touring the decks, suddenly popular. Yet when his lordship appeared from the great cabin he looked entirely calm and – there was no other word for it – happy. He smiled warmly, taking a cup of sweet, milky tea.

By eleven o'clock the enemy ships loomed like a vast dark forest, casting a menacing shadow towards the British.

Spellbound, William stared across at them. He could see hundreds of brightly coloured figures, men like himself, moving on the towering decks. Their ports, he saw, were open and the guns run out. It would be soon now. Calmly he collected the plates, cups and glasses scattered around the staterooms. He rinsed them in his small pantry and stowed them neatly away, taking care to count them carefully first, as he always did. Remembering the fate of the chickens, he sadly threw the scraps overboard.

The last minutes before he went below passed like a dream. He heard music, shouts, the urgent beating of the drums. He shoved bread and cheese into the hands of the officers as they hurried past him to their posts. Turning towards the ladder to leave the deck for the last time, William saw his lordship, watching a signal go up. Beside him was John Scott, staring at the enemy, his face impassive but ashen with fear. The secretary's hands were clasped tightly behind his back, his papers beneath his arm. Even deep within the ship, as he pushed down through the packed decks, William heard the cheers that greeted that signal.

All the men were stripped to the waist, their hard bodies shiny with sweat. As he passed them, William smiled and wished the men well, forgetting that their ears were plugged against the roar of the guns. With the ports up, the decks were lighter and fresher than usual. William thought they looked as lovely as he had ever seen them; but the orlop was the same as usual, as if all the foulness of the decks above had sunk into it. Only a few dimly flickering lanterns broke the darkness, though the midshipmen's table was lit up like a waiting stage. Stoves were warming the surgeon's tools and his sickly-smelling oils, making the deck, which was always uncomfortably close, hotter than hell. William felt the sand through the soft leather of his shoes. The powder boys were clustered excitedly by the dampened curtain of the magazine. William's heart lurched at the sight of their pale, fragile bodies.

Beatty greeted William, shaking him solemnly by the hand. The chaplain, his work done, was talking with Burke the purser. Bunce, the carpenter, kept a respectful distance, waiting patiently with his crew. Dry-mouthed, William took off his coat, brushed it with his hand and placed it tidily on the hook by his berth, before rolling his sleeves up neatly. Then he, too, waited. Time stood still in that loathsome hole, the men all looking silently at one another, too tense for words.

It was hard to tell when it began. Gradually the sound of distant thunder filtered down to them, steadily growing stronger. Then the ship shuddered as if stopped dead in the water – and again, more sharply. Bunce and his men disappeared.

The first casualty to arrive walked calmly down. A splinter the size of a candlestick was sticking out of his arm. Beatty quickly inspected the wound before pulling the splinter free in one abrupt, skin-tearing movement. A loblolly rushed forward to dress the bloody hole and bind the flapping skin. The muffled rumbling of the guns was now constant and the ship was lurching violently. Deep in the lower decks, the grapeshot sounded like pebbles on a window. The orlop steadily filled with casualties, many carried there by mates or marines. Most were gravely hurt, their bodies torn open by round shot or ripped by flying splinters. William bustled about, helping where he could, holding beakers of water to bloodied lips, fetching bandages or simply clutching a man's hand as he died in wordless agony.

Then his life seemed to stop. First the feeling of being lifted as the air was sucked from his lungs; then, as quickly, being bent double by an enormous invisible weight. His ears roared, his body shook and the world around him plunged into darkness. Gasping and shaking, William looked up. The lanterns flickered back to life. The loblollys started moving again, more urgently. *Victory*, William realized with a terrible jolt, was fighting back. Only now had the battle truly begun.

In the carnage that followed William's head spun, his body clamped tight by the horror. The deck filled with hot, acrid, sulphurous smoke, so thick he could hardly see his own hand. His mouth burned and his eyes stung. Rancid, bloodied water seeped from the beams above his head. Choking, he lurched about the deck, slipping in blood and slivers of flesh, stumbling over dying men. Once his feet were caught up in the wet embrace of a man's guts tumbling from a torn belly. Occasionally, when the smoke was sucked out by the guns above, William glimpsed the gaping mouths and the staring eyes of the men around him, thankful that the pounding on the timber drowned their groans. At the heart of this dreadful pandemonium he saw Beatty bending over the midshipmen's table, his bloodied elbow frantically rising and falling as he sawed like a crazed automaton.

Amid all the confusion William was knocked to one side by a familiar figure in a black coat, his arms flailing wildly. It was the chaplain. His eyes were wide and white and staring madly about him. One hand was clamped over his mouth; vomit oozed between the long, elegant fingers. Then this demented creature was gone, swallowed up again by the murk. Blindly, William pursued him, almost careering into him at the foot of the ladder to the deck above. Here the chaplain had abruptly stopped as two seamen struggled awkwardly down the slippery steps with another wounded man. William recognized his lordship.

He was conscious and seemed more dazed and bewildered than hurt, yet his heavily bloodstained uniform indicated a terrible wound. He gazed up curiously at William. Seeing the men struggling to carry their one-armed burden over the gruesome obstacle course of the deck, William and the chaplain helped them find a way through. Alerted by the shouts of the men, Burke and Beatty, his apron smeared in blood, rushed forward. A place on the deck was cleared where a man had just died. William helped to strip away the bloodied coat, waistcoat, shirt and stockings. The breeches were briskly cut off. A green silk purse found looped over the waistband was passed to the chaplain, together with the gold medal hanging on a blue ribbon around his lordship's neck. The chaplain stuffed them both into his coat. A miniature of Lady Hamilton was found beneath the wet, red-splashed cotton shirt.

To William's surprise the thin, naked body looked unmarked. Only the ugly stump of his lordship's missing arm seemed suddenly, obscenely, shocking as it twitched uncontrollably. But Beatty soon found the small hole, no bigger than a guinea, in his lordship's left shoulder. It bled a little as Beatty inserted first his probe and then his fingers to search for the ball. At this his lordship became agitated and upset, as if shaken from a stupor. William noticed specks of blood on his lips. A glance at Beatty told him Nelson was dying. Nothing could be done.

The wound was washed and dressed. His lordship's nakedness was covered by a sheet of dirty sailcloth and the limp body propped against one of the great damp timbers in the ship's side, close to the capstan. William went for lemonade to quench the dying man's thirst. After his initial desperation Nelson became quieter, apparently resigned to his fate.

The chaplain, kneeling to the right of his lordship, began gently to rub his chest, which seemed to ease his suffering a little. From time to time the two men spoke, the chaplain leaning so close that their faces almost touched. Most of their words were lost to William, drowned by the cascade of noise around them. Burke knelt on the other side, his arm supporting Nelson. William stayed close, fetching sponges to wipe the sweat and the blood from the now tired, sad, smoke-blackened face. When his lordship soiled himself, William washed him. He was uncertain how long they remained there like that. At one point the captain came down, stooping beneath the beams, his face creased with fatigue and speckled with blood. Visibly moved, he bent over the dying man to say a few words. As Hardy rose to leave, Nelson clutched the captain's arm, lifting himself up. 'Pray let dear Lady Hamilton have my hair,' he pleaded in a desperate whisper, 'and all other things belonging to me.'

With Hardy gone, Nelson became weaker. He pleaded for water, his words now softly bubbling up through the blood that was drowning him. He looked frightened and lost. Beatty came when he could, his bloodied hands checking the fading pulse, testing the progress of the paralysis. When the captain returned with news of victory, his lordship rallied briefly, the spark of life flickering. Kneeling, Hardy held his friend's hand before gently kissing his cold, pale cheek. Then, rising to go, he gazed down a last time before quickly leaning forward to kiss him again.

It was hard to tell when Nelson died. After the captain had left he whispered a last order to William, asking his faithful steward to turn him to release a few precious last breaths from his blood-choked lungs. His pain seemed to increase at the end. He closed his eyes, wincing as his lips moved rhythmically, the words confused and indistinct. Only when they had stopped did William understand them. 'Thank God, I have done my duty. Thank God, I have done my duty. Thank God, I have done my duty.'

As William rose to go in search of Beatty, he noticed for the first time the men crowding around the lifeless body. Bunce was there. There was no pulse. It was over. His lordship seemed at peace. All the pain had left him. Before they covered his face, William thought he saw a single tear slowly roll away from his lordship's sightless right eye, catching the yellow light of the swaying lanterns. Then he noticed the silence. The guns had stopped.

SIX WEEKS LATER

SINCE BEFORE DAWN, people muffled against the sharp cold had been gathering to gaze out across a grey sea flattened by snow-swollen clouds. Those with telescopes occasionally pointed, causing a momentary flurry of excitement among the otherwise quietly expectant crowd. Some of the men carried children on their shoulders. The harbour was packed with all sorts of small boats. A number of battered, lifeless-looking warships were anchored at Spithead out in the Solent. It was Thursday 5 December, 1805. Young and old would remember this day for the rest of their lives.

The evening before, a boat pulled by seamen from *Victory* had arrived at the quay with a single passenger seated astern. The seamen, enjoying their celebrity, told the people their ship was anchored off the Isle of Wight, held back by the tide from

Jack and Poll at Portsmouth after the battle of Trafalgar: 'The people laughed and sometimes they cheered, but they fell silent when they heard how his body was sealed in a cask of brandy. Then some of them wept.'

reaching Portsmouth until the morning. They regaled eager lis-
teners with stories as the beer flowed in the taverns that night. The
people laughed and sometimes they cheered, but they fell silent
when they heard how his body was sealed in a cask of brandy. Then
some of them wept.

By that time the boat's passenger was miles away. A short,
thick-set man with curly, greying hair, clad in a long oilskin coat
and a wide-brimmed felt hat pulled low over his ears, he was a
servant; so no-one noticed or bothered him as he hurried to the
George inn to hire a post-chaise for London. Under his arm
William Chevailler, the steward in *Victory*, was clutching a leather
despatch case.

As the morning of 5 December wore on, it seemed the
whole town was crowding onto the platforms around the harbour.
Many people returned to where they had stood in September,
pressing forward to catch sight of Nelson as he was carried along
by the crowd towards *Victory*'s waiting barge. Towards nine
o'clock, the sharpest eyes in the crowd were drawn to a ship
emerging from the morning mist. As it approached, the warships
at Spithead lowered their flags. Gun salutes echoed around the
harbour, the doleful sound rolling lazily around the ramparts
before heading out to sea. A flotilla of small boats which had impatiently been waiting for this signal now streamed out of the
harbour.

Even from far away the onlookers could see the damage that
had been done to *Victory*. Shot was still lodged in her bows and the
shattered remnants of her masts were studded with bullets. The
first visitors on board were awed by the bloodstained decks. Many
commented on the eerie quiet and the pervasive gloom which
filled the ship, as if the men inside were in thrall to the ghosts of
their friends. Of the dead, only Nelson's body remained on board,
peacefully curled up in the brandy. All the other corpses, many
grotesquely mutilated, had been unceremoniously thrown into
the sea during the battle, as was the custom.

As *Victory* approached Portsmouth that morning, William

Chevailler reached 9 St James's Square after his overnight dash to London. Unlike its flat-fronted, red-brick neighbours, this house had a white stuccoed front decorated with Grecian pilasters, decorative banding and roundels in fashionable neo-classical style. In the windows of the house, as of many William had passed on his way into town, were coloured glass transparencies, lit from behind by candles. They spelled 'VICTORY' and 'NELSON'.

William was told to wait in the library. It was not a large room, but it was crammed with expensive furniture and exquisite objects. The walls were almost entirely obscured by bookshelves, prints and paintings, many of rural scenes. On the elegant tables and in the dimly lit cabinets all around him, William saw stone busts and antique black terracotta vases; jewel-like boxes decorated in mosaics, tortoiseshell and brilliants; and hardstones, carved in the Roman style. Medieval cups of ivory and crystal, mounted in gold and set with strangely shaped pearls and precious gems, glittered beside strange weapons from the East, their deadly blades hidden by rich crimson velvet scabbards studded with rare stones. Extraordinary guns with silver barrels and richly ornamented stocks lay beside miniature pistols, each as small as a woman's hand, kept in fruitwood cases lined with damask silk.

The bookshelves held volumes and folios bound in the finest green and red morocco, their titles chased in gold. *Daniell's Rural Sports* pressed against Darwin's *Zoonomia*, Roget's *Pleasures of Memory* against Smollett's *History of England*. Here were Shakespeare and Fielding, Plutarch, Milton and Goldsmith, Virgil and Dr Johnson. Around the room were numerous copies of the *Tatler* and *Spectator*, the *Annual Register*, *Quebec Almanack*, *Naval Chronicle* and the *Gentleman's Magazine*. Some lay open on a low mahogany table, as if just put down. Books from Italy and France stood beside books on America, Scotland and London. There were books on racing, parliament, law, farming, the army, roses, medicine, fashion, travel, trade and history. Most were quite recently published, with the notable exception of some very old volumes from Amsterdam, bound in blackened leather, their titles barely decipherable. Apart from the ticking of the magnificent gold and tortoiseshell clock on the carved marble mantle and the occasional sigh as the coals settled in the fireplace below it, the library was silent.

After a while the repose of the room was punctured by the sound of a female voice and the chatter of excited children elsewhere in the house. Then the door was thrown open and Alexander Davison entered in full army uniform, ready to take part in the parade of his own volunteer infantry corps, the Loyal Britons, at the service of thanksgiving in Westminster Abbey later that morning. As he headed towards William with an outstretched hand and a warm smile, the library seemed to fill with red and gold.

Now fifty-five, despite his age, lack of height and the years of gout which had stiffened his walk, Davison still exuded power and unspent energy. The watchful blue eyes above a thin nose and narrow mouth threatened a quick temper; when he was younger Davison's features – now softened by age and good living – had, like the man himself, been thought sharp. His hair, freshly powdered for the morning's service, was long and full and receded slightly from his brow. His teeth were poor, though he kept them. His complexion was good, with a healthy colour – unusual for London and more properly suited to a country squire, which in many respects he resembled. He gave off a comfortable smell of lavender oil, leather and horse sweat.

Davison showed concern as he sought reassurance that William was well and unhurt, listening carefully as the battle and the last hours of Nelson's life were recalled. Occasionally he interrupted with a brief question. Finishing his account, William gave Davison a letter dated 13 October which Captain Hardy had found in Nelson's desk. 'Some happy day', Nelson had written to his friend a week before the battle, 'I hope to get at their fleet and nothing shall be wanting on my part to give a good account of them.' William revealed that he was also carrying letters for

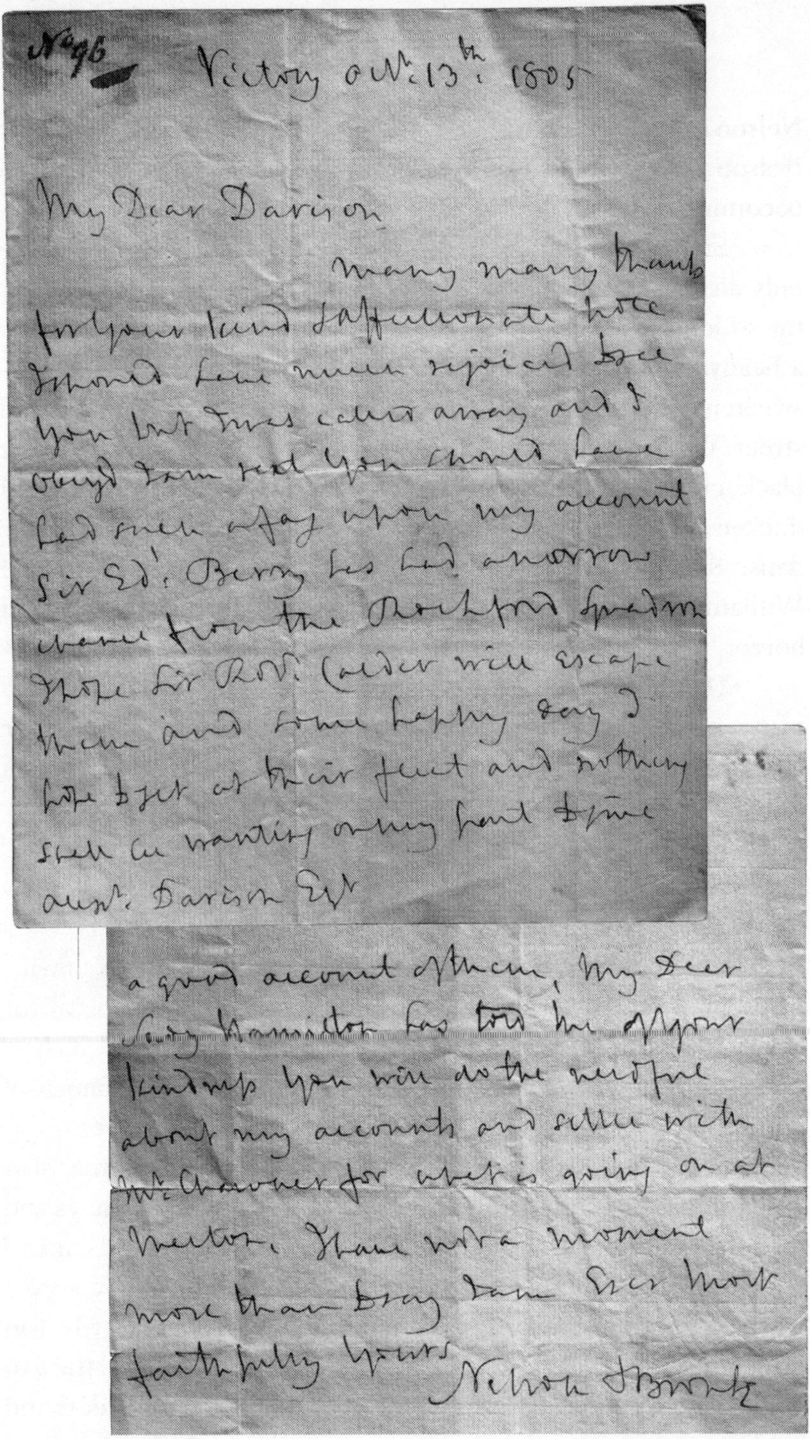

No 96

Victory Oct. 13th. 1805

My Dear Davison

Many many thanks for your kind & affectionate note I should have much rejoiced to see you but was called away and I ought I am not you should have had such a fag upon my account Sir Ed. Berry has had a narrow chance from the Rochefort squadron I hope Sir R. V. Calder will escape them and some happy day I hope to get at their fleet and nothing shall be wanting on my part to give a good account of them, my dear Lady Hamilton has told me of your kindness you will do the needful about my accounts and settle with Mr. Chawner for what is going on at Merton. I have not a moment more than to say I am Ever most faithfully yours

Nelson & Bronte

'Some happy day I hope to get at their fleet and nothing shall be wanting on my part to give a good account of them': Nelson's last letter to Davison, written a week before the battle of Trafalgar.

Nelson's mistress, Emma Lady Hamilton, and for his brother, Earl Nelson. Davison advised caution. He knew these two were becoming bitter rivals.

Emma Hamilton was at her town house in Clarges Street, only a short walk from St James's Square. After being cooped up for so long in *Victory*, William revelled in the odour of London – a heady mix of coal smoke, cooking, liquor and horse manure, sweetened by the scent of the fashionable people he passed in the street. Women gazed into the shops while the men, many wearing black crepe armbands, clustered around the coffee houses or ducked into narrow alleyways leading to brothels and gambling dens. Small boys raced up and down the street on errands. William, gazing on these familiar scenes after witnessing so much horror, felt strangely detached from them.

The door to the small, elegant house was opened by a footman who viewed William with all the disdain that only one servant can show to another. Here the visitor waited in the hall, which was full of antique marbles; portraits and prints of Nelson covered the walls. Eventually Mrs Cadogan, Emma's mother, appeared to conduct William to a pretty bedroom on the first floor, decorated in chintz and, despite the season, full of freshly cut flowers.

Nelson's mistress was propped on a mountain of plump white pillows. Scattered around her on the bed was the debris of her ceaseless letter-writing: discarded papers, pens and inkpots. Close to hand were a half-full wine glass and an empty burgundy bottle. Having delivered a short, carefully prepared speech, William gave Emma two letters. One was for her; the other was for Horatia, her four-year-old daughter. He looked away as she read them and wept.

William and Emma had met, briefly, before – in September, when William had packed the admiral's belongings at Merton Place, the house Nelson and Emma shared in Surrey. Then, she had scarcely noticed the steward; but now he was a physical link to the last hours of her lover's life, the first to arrive in London. Calling him closer, Emma implored William to reveal how Nelson had died and what, if anything, he had said. William, who had strict orders from Captain Hardy simply to deliver the letters and go, was no more proof against her entreaties than any other man; and so, as Emma clutched his hand, drawing him so near to her that he could smell the wine on her breath, William told her everything he knew. Then, realizing at once that he had said too much, he rashly asked Emma to keep his words secret.

In Portsmouth the tall figure of an officer, stooped with tiredness, pushed through the people on the quay, ignoring their demands for news on the landing of the body. Captain Hardy was looking for his friend Henry Blackwood, captain of the frigate *Euryalus*. The two men had last met in the great cabin of *Victory*, just hours before the battle, when Nelson had made them witness a statement in his pocket book. Hardy described this, in a letter he wrote to Davison from Portsmouth, as 'a kind of Codicil which he wrote on the morning of the 21st and read to me, desiring me to seal it up in the event of his falling. It does not in the least alter his will but recommends his family and Lady Hamilton to the protection of his Country.'

In fact, *Euryalus* had carried Blackwood home far faster than the limping *Victory*, and by the time Hardy was anxiously pacing the quay at Portsmouth, Blackwood was about to return to the town, having been in London for at least a week. There he had seen Davison and had already told Nelson's solicitor, William Haslewood, about the codicil in the pocket book. A cautious man, Haslewood decided to do nothing until he had read it. News of a secret final codicil would be unsettling for William Nelson, the admiral's brother and heir. William had just been made an earl by a grateful nation and was hopeful that great riches would follow his undeserved ennoblement.

Blackwood arrived back at Portsmouth before dawn on Friday 6 December and was taken out to *Victory* in heavy fog. Over breakfast with Hardy, Blackwood described his meeting with Haslewood; but Hardy, considering himself bound by the promise he had made to his dying friend to do all he could to see the terms of the codicil honoured, was reluctant to surrender the pocket book immediately to Nelson's family. He decided that, before sending it back to London with Blackwood, he would show the codicil to George Rose, a member of the government who was close to the prime minister, William Pitt, and who – unlike many in the cabinet – had always supported Nelson. Nelson had whispered Rose's name as he lay dying; so, by bringing the codicil to the minister's attention, Hardy could feel that he was insuring it against suppression by Nelson's family. Without further delay Hardy set off for Rose's country seat, half a day's journey along the coast from Portsmouth, leaving Blackwood to inform Lady Hamilton about the codicil – about which she may, in fact, already have heard from Davison, Haslewood or Chevailler. Blackwood gave the awkward task of writing to Clarges Street to his wife, who had joined him in the town.

In St James's Square, William slept late and breakfasted well, revived by his first night for months in a motionless bed. When Davison left for an important meeting at the Treasury, William plucked up the courage to visit Earl Nelson, his last task before catching the coach back to Portsmouth. After his brother's death, William Nelson had been thrust to the forefront of the national stage, in a role he assumed without the least surprise, his humble position in the church utterly forgotten. The new earl took a large house in Charles Street, close to Berkeley Square, filling it with a miserly mixture of old-fashioned and second-hand furniture and other people's portraits. Here he planned his brother's state funeral with military precision and ran his campaign for further titles – and money.

The earl was an overbearing, ruddy-faced man in his late forties, quite different in looks from his brother – not least in size, although they had shared the same heavily lidded eyes. Unlike Davison, whom he distrusted, the earl wore an old-fashioned wig. His collar was the only evidence of his calling; he was not a man handicapped by too much reflection or religious devotion. Chevailler had orders from Captain Hardy to give the earl 'every

William Nelson, Nelson's boorish brother, who reaped the rewards of Trafalgar. 'At that time you had always detested the present Earl Nelson,' Emma Hamilton later reminded Davison, 'nor would you let him come within your house.'

information relative to the effects of your ever to be lamented Brother and my Dear Friend'. This included delivering an inventory of Nelson's belongings in *Victory*. The earl was interested in the steward's account of the battle, but could scarcely be expected, he felt, to manage the business of his brother's effects himself. Instead, seizing some paper from his desk, he scrawled a note for Chevailler to take to Davison, a man he considered better suited to such a task. 'Send orders to Chevalier as soon as the Victory gets to the Nore,' he wrote, 'how he is to move the Goods, Wines &c to take charge of the whole of them & have them conveyed to London by water.'

Haslewood had told the earl about the codicil in the pocket book. Even so, the earl gave William a letter to take to Hardy enquiring after his dead brother's private papers. 'If there is any Will or Codicil or any paper of any sort entrusted to your care,' he wrote disingenuously, probing to discover who knew what,

> *I will esteem it a favour, if you will send a confidential person without loss of time, to bring it to me, with orders to deliver it to no other person — it would I think also be advisable as soon as possible to have his desk (containing his other papers & memorandums not of a public nature) carefully packed & sent by your stage wagon to me, as it may contain many things necessary for the executors to know.*

It was late and Hardy was tired when he returned to *Victory* after his long round trip to see George Rose; but he had cause to feel satisfied. Rose had assured him that he would discuss the codicil with Pitt, although the prime minister was currently ill at Bath; and in a letter to Emma Hamilton, Rose promised 'nothing but zeal' in seeing that Nelson's last wish was met. It was all Hardy could have hoped for. But William, who had reached *Victory* just before Hardy, seemed curiously unsettled, even furtive, when he delivered the earl's letter to the captain. The next day Hardy discovered why. He received a furious note from Emma, complaining bitterly about Chevailler's attempt to silence her and demanding that Nelson's personal possessions be delivered to her and to no-one else. By first revealing Nelson's dying words to Hardy and then making an inept attempt to cover his tracks by asking her to keep them to herself, Chevailler had spectacularly misfired in his attempt to soothe the grieving Lady Hamilton, who now suspected a conspiracy against her. It scarcely helped that the earl claimed to have detected 'something like a falsehood' in the steward. Chevailler's trip to London, it seemed, had stirred up a hornet's nest, and Hardy understandably now regretted sending a servant, even so trusted a one as Nelson's steward, on such an important mission.

'I am quite sorry to hear of Chevalier's conduct,' he apologized to Emma, 'I shall keep a strict look out over him and all the rest of the servants.' Despite the earl's imperious order that he should receive his brother's belongings, Hardy was determined to keep the promise he had made to Nelson. 'I have his hair, lockets, rings, breast-pin and all your Ladyship's pictures in a box by themselves,' he informed Emma; 'they shall be delivered to no one but yourself.' The box was entrusted to Henry Blackwood, who arranged to deliver it to Emma a week later. To avoid any later misunderstanding and for dramatic effect, Emma invited the earl, Haslewood and Davison to watch the trunk being opened.

Before *Victory* weighed anchor to begin the journey round the coast to the Thames, a shambolic new passenger joined the ship. His ill-fitting clothes were threadbare and old-fashioned. More intriguing was the ugly scar on his cheek, the result of an arrow fired by a native in the East Indies. This was Arthur William Devis: a painter of portraits and recent resident of the King's Bench prison for debtors. In his pocket was an advertisement torn from the *Morning Chronicle* offering 500 guineas for the best painting of the death of Nelson. Josiah Boydell, the printmaker who had placed the notice, wanted to emulate the commercial success of the prints made after General James Wolfe's heroic death capturing Quebec in 1759.

Devis, a man incapable of properly managing his affairs, had been dogged by debt for years. Hearing that *Victory* had reached England, he secured his release from the King's Bench, probably on the promise of Boydell's fee – which would have been easy enough as the printmaker held a sinecure at the prison. Quickly fetching his painting equipment from his lodgings in Hanover Square, Devis hurtled down to Portsmouth, trailing paint and brushes. By befriending the ship's officers in the taverns around the town he managed to secure a berth on *Victory*. It is likely that Davison, who at one point had been in the King's Bench with Devis, had a quiet word with Hardy on behalf of the artist.

To the disappointment of the people of Portsmouth, *Victory* sailed on 11 December with Nelson's body still on board. After checking with his own physician whether his brother might be infectious, the earl had decided that the body should be left undisturbed and landed in London without fanfare – 'not knowing whether it would be corrupted and produce any disagreeable smell by being kept out of spirits so many days before the internment'. As ship's surgeon, William Beatty was far better placed to judge how fast Nelson was decomposing; and so, like everyone else, Beatty ignored the earl. With *Victory* at sea and away from the gaze of the public, he set about removing the body from the cask and performing an autopsy 'to check the progress of decay which was taking place'.

Beatty's assistants prised open the cask, releasing a rush of putrid air. Many of the witnesses, who included Devis, gagged and turned away. The corpse, which was floating upside down in a foetal position, bobbed to the surface of the brandy. After being lifted and drained, it was placed on a board and slowly, very carefully, stretched out. Some of the bones had to be broken to do this. The corpse was naked except for a white cotton shirt which was cut off and discarded. The stink was appalling; nevertheless, everyone pressed forward to see the horrific sight. The corpse's roughly shaved head made it look vulnerable and childlike. The decomposition was advanced, the skin sticky and stained the colour of walnut by the brandy. After using a sponge to wash the body, Beatty gently rubbed the face with a soft cloth. Alexander Scott, *Victory*'s chaplain, who had kept a lonely vigil by the cask, noticed sadly that his friend's features could not, 'at this distant period from his demise, be easily traced'. Exposure during the lying-in-state, everyone agreed, would be impossible.

Wielding a large knife, Beatty opened the abdomen from throat to groin in a series of short, firm movements, releasing large quantities of rancid liquid. There was a tearing sound as he pulled the flesh away from the ribcage. Using a probe fed into the body through the neat hole in the shoulder, Beatty traced the line of the ball which had killed Nelson. He patiently explained how it had travelled diagonally down through the body, fracturing the scapulae and two ribs, slicing through the left lobe of the lungs and severing the pulmonary artery before fracturing two verte-brae and lodging in the muscles of the lower right back. Here Beatty extracted the ball with a slight theatrical flourish. Surprisingly, a small portion of Nelson's blue uniform coat and some gold lace from his epaulette remained stuck to the ball, which was passed to Devis to sketch. The contents of the body cavity, except for the heart, were removed, inspected and weighed. Beatty remarked, with approval, that the organs were in excellent condition: the result, he told the spectators – perhaps looking at Devis – of moderate habits. The gutted corpse was sewn up, wrapped tightly in bandages and placed beside its organs in a lead-lined pine coffin made by Bunce, the ship's carpenter. Before it was sealed, the coffin was filled with strong spirits, 'after the ancient mode of embalming'.

That weekend was bitterly cold – so cold, the Serpentine froze in Hyde Park. The royal family opened the Christmas season at Covent Garden. Mrs Siddons and Mrs Jordan appeared together at Drury Lane. Songs to Nelson were sung in the inter-lude. St Paul's Cathedral was a hive of activity, with labourers building galleries and enclosures for the state funeral. Daily bul-letins in the press reported *Victory*'s slow progress to London alongside advertisements for viewing positions along the funeral route.

Monday 16 December was the day appointed for the meeting at Clarges Street. William Haslewood woke with a cold, so he sent his brother to meet the earl and Davison at Emma's house, which the two men had visited often since the news of Nelson's death. They were joined there at two o'clock by John Tyson, one of Nelson's former secretaries and now a commissioner at Woolwich dockyard. Captain Blackwood had arrived earlier with the box from *Victory*. The first thing the earl and Davison noticed, as the bedroom door opened to admit them, was the blue uniform coat, stiff with blood, stretched across the mass of letters, papers, shawls and jewels strewn over the bed. Blackwood stood as they entered, acknowledging them with a nod.

Smiling bravely, Emma turned her large, green eyes towards each of the men in turn. Her mother, talking all the while, fussed about her, securing the curtains on the bed and arranging everybody on chairs with cups of tea. Emma had grown fat but she was still exceptionally beautiful. Her skin was very smooth, as pale and as perfect as the finest china, her face slightly flushed by wine and the warmth of the room. Her dark auburn hair fell in soft, loose curls across her large, full breasts. Two small crescents, the colour of rich chocolate, peeped above her thin shift. All the men tried to look elsewhere.

After some respectful words, and a stifled sob from Emma, Blackwood opened a red morocco box sitting on a table at the end of the bed. It was a moment of high drama. Reaching inside, he lifted out a group of papers and documents, some tied in bundles with pink ribbon, others sealed with wax. Everyone spotted the small flat parcel neatly wrapped and sealed in a sheet of paper. This was passed reverently to Emma, who broke the seal and tore off the wrapper, her tears falling silently. Inside was a slightly scuffed black leather pocket book. Pausing to recover her composure, Emma opened it and read the last words written in the book by Nelson. There was a prayer, followed by a statement of Lady

Hamilton's services to her country while married to the British ambassador in Naples. Finally, there was a bequest:

> *I leave Emma Lady Hamilton, therefore, a legacy to my King and Country, that they will give her an ample provision to maintain her rank in life. I also leave to the beneficence of my Country my adopted daughter Horatia Nelson Thompson, and I desire she will use in future the name of Nelson only. These are the only favours I ask of my King and Country at this moment, when I am going to fight their Battle. May God bless my King and Country, and all those who I hold dear. My Relations it is needless to mention they will of course be amply provided for.*

When Emma had finished speaking there was a long silence. Everyone knew that Nelson had been urging the government for years to give his mistress a pension; so, despite the drama attending its composition and transmittal, and despite all the conjecture surrounding it, the codicil was hardly unexpected, nor were its contents surprising. Hardy's interpretation that it did not change the will was right. Nevertheless, this codicil would obsess Emma for the rest of her life.

It seemed inevitable that William Pitt would grant the pension now that Nelson had saved the country from defeat. No-one in the room knew, however, that Pitt was dying. Davison offered to send a copy of the codicil to the prince of Wales to muster royal support. Emma's effect on the prince was well known – indeed, Nelson had once feared she would become 'a whore to the rascal'.

The remaining contents of the box were then examined and a list made. This list, which survives in the British Library, reveals a small and strangely affecting group of objects. Alongside a copy of Nelson's will, some old codicils and 'Papers unknown', were the seals from his desk used on the letters they had all received over the years. There were also a compass, a ring, some 'coins found in Sardinia', a picture and two pocket watches. 'A medal' may have been the gold medal taken from Nelson's neck as he lay dying. If so, it was passed to Davison.

There were also a worn banknote case holding £12 in cash and two purses holding coins. It seems from the surviving manuscript that, at first, 'contents unknown' was written beside the purses; but then, apparently, a quick tally was made, the coins spilling noisily across the polished table. One of the purses – presumably some form of pouch – was made of leather. It must have been tucked away in Nelson's desk rather than carried with him, for it contained no less than 79 gold guineas and one shilling, making £83 in total – a weighty sum worth over £4,000 today. But it was the other purse that attracted most attention. Later described as 'Nelson's pocket purse', this was made of woven green silk and was distinctly, and freshly, stained in blood. It held the far smaller sum of £17 5s 0d in an unspecified number of gold and silver coins. This purse and all the money were entrusted to Davison. The leather pouch disappeared for ever. Before the men headed back out into the snow, the earl arranged to call on Davison the next day with Haslewood to discuss his brother's estate.

As soon as he reached Charles Street, the earl wrote to Haslewood. 'The box', he revealed, with evident relief, 'contained duplicates of the will & codicils we had before, I don't recollect any thing new . . . the memorandum book, is a short account of his proceedings since he left England last, up to the day of battle & concludes with recommending L:H to Government – you will see all tomorrow.' The earl now knew that even if his brother's last wishes were honoured, they could not affect his new fortune. The issue of a pension for Emma was one for the government, not for his family. It was nothing to worry about after all.

Before the meeting at St James's Square Davison wrote to the prince of Wales as he had promised Emma. He enclosed a copy of Nelson's 'legacy . . . abstracted from his journal' and a note 'of a private nature' he had received that morning from Emma, 'whose sufferings poor woman are beyond expression'. Emma's note lavished praise on the prince and was clearly intended, with Davison's connivance, to be sent on to him at Brighton.

Davison received Haslewood and the earl in the back drawing room of 9 St James's Square, overlooking the narrow garden which stretched behind the house to the stables, offices and coach houses of Ormonde Yard. The garden was planted with small, bare fruit trees. A slow thaw made the whole scene look drab and grey, with piles of snow, blackened by soot, banked untidily against the walls. In brilliant contrast, the drawing room was filled with warmth and light. Nelson's purse lay on a table. After returning the pocket book to the earl, Davison asked a clerk to make a proper account of all the cash and coins found among Nelson's belongings.

The clerk called this document simply 'Money, Coins in Lord Nelson's Pocket Purse &c when Killed'. It reveals a total sum slightly larger than the one hastily calculated the day before, apparently combining the money found in both purses :

[Tue]sday	90 Guineas -	94	10	—
17th [Decembe]r 1805	9 Half do -	4.	14	6
St Jam[es's] Square	3 - 7/-	1.	1	
	Silver	2:	0	6
Contents of				
Lord Nelsons Purse in his Red		102.	6.	0
[Box]				
[Bank note case]		12		
		£114.	6	

Haslewood and the earl witnessed the document before hurrying off to prove Nelson's will, their concerns over the final codicil allayed. All the money was left with Davison, who folded the document and tucked it into the purse. He then carried the purse downstairs to his office, placing it in a large iron strongbox which he locked with an elaborate key kept in his waistcoat pocket. He had an important meeting to attend at the Treasury.

The next morning, Wednesday 18 December, Davison left the house early to cross the square. Again the fog was so heavy that he felt cocooned from the rest of the city. There was a soft yellow tear in the gloom where the financier Abraham Goldsmid had put up lamps to mourn his friend. No houses fronted onto the square on the south side; instead, the entrances led into the rear of houses facing onto Pall Mall. The unmarked door on which Davison tapped his cane was opened by a young footman, who bowed and took the visitor's coat. Striding through the house, past the clerks' room and the partners' room, Davison soon reached the main hall of his bank, Alexander Davison, Noel, Templer & Co.

Davison & Co. had been on Pall Mall for only two years, but in that short time it had acquired all the characteristics of the older, better-established banks in the West End. A feeling of timeless solidity, dependability and quiet industry permeated its rooms and the people within them. The banking hall had a polished wooden floor below a white plastered ceiling bordered by a simple classical pattern and supported on eight elegant oak pillars. The size of a comfortable drawing room, it felt smaller because running across it was a mahogany counter topped by a brightly polished brass railing and a row of oil lamps with dark green glass shades. Behind the counter were a desk for the chief cashier, stools for the clerks and wooden pigeonholes stuffed with papers. A large wall-mounted clock occasionally chimed sonorously. There were two fireplaces in the hall, one for the clerks and a better and larger one for the customers. On the other side of Pall Mall, Carlton House, the town residence of the prince of Wales, loomed through the fog.

After a brief discussion on business and the grave news of a victory for Bonaparte over the Austrians and Russians at somewhere called Austerlitz, Davison presented his chief cashier with a bill for £114 6s 0d drawn on himself. The cashier was told to credit the amount to Lord Nelson's account as 'cash found in his red box'.

Davison returned home to a letter from Brighton. The prince of Wales assured him that 'did it depend upon me, there would not be a wish, a desire of our ever-to-be-lamented and much loved friend, as well as adored hero, that I would not consider as a solemn obligation upon his friends and his country to fulfil'. In other words, the matter of Emma's pension was not his problem.

John Tyson searched the Thames estuary for three days in his yacht from Woolwich. Then, early on Sunday 22 December, the mist lifted to reveal *Victory* anchored peacefully near Sheerness, as if placed there gently overnight. When a strong gale blew up, however, it was only with the greatest difficulty, and some danger, that Tyson was able to clamber on board the towering warship. Lashed by squalls of freezing rain and with the ship pitching heavily, two coffins were winched across onto *Victory*, swinging so wildly on the ropes that they almost smashed to bits. Entering the great cabin, Tyson's eyes fell immediately on the long pine box. Around it, grim-faced and silent, stood the ship's officers, their shadows leaping about the cabin in the swaying light of the lanterns. William Chevailler stood a little behind them. Without ceremony, the box was prised opened and two marines lifted out the corpse, wrapped in its soaking bandages. It looked very small. As the marines paused to allow the bundle to drain, the cabin filled with the sweet smell of camphor.

The corpse and the parcels holding the organs were placed on the dining table, which William had draped with a Union Jack. Beatty stepped forward and started gently to remove the bandaging, careful to avoid lifting off the marbled, flaying skin. When naked, the corpse was dried. For the last time and with tears in his eyes, Nelson's Sicilian valet, Gaetano Spedillo, dressed his master in shirt, stockings, breeches and waistcoat. Alexander Scott, looking pale and tired, read a short prayer before the officers took farewell of their commander, each in his own way. Then the corpse was placed in the elaborate wooden coffin that had been made from the mast of *L'Orient*, the French flagship destroyed at the battle of the Nile. This was lowered into an outer lead casket which Bunce soldered shut, sealing it for ever.

On Christmas Eve, extracts from Nelson's will appeared in the London newspapers. 'The only legacies', noticed the *Morning Chronicle*, 'to persons not of Lord Nelson's family are to Lady Hamilton, to Mr Davison, to Mr Haslewood, Captain Hardy, to Miss Horatia Nelson Thompson, to Mr John Scott, [and] to the Rev. A. J. Scott.' Most interest was inevitably focused on Nelson's legacies to his estranged wife Fanny and to his mistress Emma. Few people noticed one intriguing detail buried deep within the document: 'I give and bequeath to Alexander Davison, of St. James's-Square, in the County of Middlesex, Esquire; my Turkish Gun, Scimitar and Canteen.'

II

TÉMÉRAIRE

98 GUNS,
CAPTAIN ELIAB HARVEY

M Y PART IN THIS STORY begins in June 2002 when I visited a Sotheby's office on the continent, as I often did in my end- less search for jewels to auction. There was nothing unusual about the trip; certainly no sign that I was about to come across some- thing that would change my life. The jewels I saw were the normal run-of-the-mill pieces: some old, some not; some precious, more not, though all of course priceless to their owners. Describing and valuing the jewels which were placed in front of me one by one, I tried to be as helpful and as tactful as I could. The owners responded as they did the world over, sometimes with surprise and pleasure but as often with disappointment, even resentment, their hopes of a fortune dashed. Nevertheless, as the hours passed, I steadily reaped a small harvest of jewels to take back to sell in London. So the company would be pleased in any event.

Late on, as my thoughts drifted towards my flight home, a pleasant middle-aged couple arrived with just one piece to show me. It was a large brooch designed as an anchor, sparkling with plump, watery white diamonds, all cut thickly in the old antique style. The diamonds were mounted in a sandwich of silver and honey-coloured gold. Dulled now by tarnish, the pure whiteness of the silver would once have flattered the diamonds, displaying them to their best glittering advantage, while the gold gave the jewel strength and richness. The diamonds, which I quickly gauged at over 17 carats, had the brilliance and the purity of the finest Indian stones, mined long before the great discoveries in South Africa in the 1880s. Turning the brooch over, I saw that its pin had an old lead repair. Otherwise the back was as beautifully finished as the front, a sign of excellence and rare in later reproductions. There were no maker's marks or hallmarks – but I would not have expected any on a jewel of that age.

The style of setting, the type and the cut of the diamonds, the *feel* of the jewel all told me it had been made early in the nineteenth century. As such it was undoubtedly a rare survivor, a glittering relic of a lost age. Most important diamond jewels from that far-off era have gone for ever, their stones recycled, recut and reset as fashions changed and fortunes fluctuated. I valued the brooch at over £100,000. But something else absolutely, uniquely, distinguished this jewel. Something which made me catch my breath. Something so improbable, impossible even, that it was hard to grasp, far too much to hope for. On either side of the anchor clung a small initial, each perfectly drawn in tiny diamonds. Two letters that promised everything yet revealed nothing. Two letters. *H* and *N*.

In the course of ten years as a specialist at Sotheby's I had seen thousands of jewels. Some were spectacularly valuable, some worthless; but the thrill of not knowing what might turn up next, the hope that a great discovery could be around the next corner, never diminished. Anyone in the auction business would say the same. Yet of all those jewels, those that I remember now I remember not because of their value but because of the stories they told. Jewels, especially the antique ones, carry an extraordinary emotional resonance. They hold the memory of cold metal on warm, scented skin; the candlelit gaze of a long-dead lover or a stolen kiss in a moon-drenched garden. Everyone it touches turns to dust, yet the jewel itself remains unblemished, an inviolable fragment of beauty, a silent witness to history tumbling through the centuries.

Now here I was on a warm summer's day, the faint noise of traffic and the happy babble of a café drifting through the open windows, stumbling towards the moment of discovery. Lying cold in my hand was a 200-year-old diamond brooch designed as an anchor and mounted with the initials of Britain's greatest naval hero. I tried to remain calm, professional, but my mind was racing. The tremor in my voice must have betrayed my excitement. How, I asked, turning the jewel over, its diamonds flashing brilliantly, did such a thing come to be in your family? Then, for the first time, I heard the name of the owner's English ancestor: Alexander Davison, 'Lord Nelson's best friend'.

The name Davison echoed in my head as, excited and intrigued, I returned to London. I knew the legend of Nelson, of course, as most of us do. The one arm, the one eye, the love affair, the death, the monument, the hero, the myth. But who was Alexander Davison? Where did he fit in? Why did he own such an extravagant relic?

I soon found him. He was in all the biographies, running like a thread through the well-worn story. Davison was described as a confidant, an adviser, an *homme d'affaires*, a banker, an agent – but yes, above all, as Nelson's friend, perhaps his closest. Yet he was overshadowed by the many more glamorous figures who surrounded Nelson, relegated, it seemed, to the status of a slightly roguish, even embarrassing, footnote. He was a remote, elusive figure. An outsider. A civilian in a military world. This unobtrusiveness was surprising, for Davison left a large legacy, far greater than most in Nelson's circle of friends.

Over one hundred letters from Nelson to Davison were published as early as the 1840s. Most are now in the British Library, while many of Davison's replies are kept in the National Maritime Museum at Greenwich. A cursory reading of them revealed no mention of the anchor brooch – nor could I realistically have hoped that it would. The NMM also holds a remarkable hoard of Nelsonian treasures from Davison's personal collection, bequeathed to the nation by his son in 1873. These are displayed in a gallery devoted to Nelson, the museum's busiest. They include a portrait of the admiral by an artist called Lemuel Abbott and a brass cannon captured at the battle of Copenhagen. Drifting round the gallery with the other tourists on my first visit there, I also noticed an exotic-looking sabre with a gold hilt designed as a crocodile. The scabbard was engraved:

This SCYMETER together with a GUN and CANTEEN were presented by the GRAND SIGNIOR to Horatio Viscount Nelson and by WILL bequeathed to his Friend Alexander Davison 10th May 1803.

The sabre looked uncomfortable in the scabbard, for it clearly didn't fit. These were disparate, isolated objects, the invisible cord of ownership that had bound them together broken and lost. I needed more. For the anchor to achieve its potential at auction, it needed to capture the public's imagination; and to do that, it had to tell its story. I needed to understand how Davison had acquired it, why he had it, why it had survived hidden away for so long. When the owners said they had a few of Davison's papers hidden away, I jumped at the chance to examine them. These might reveal a mention of the anchor in a family letter or a note of it in a dusty inventory. Something, anything. A few months later I went back; but this time I visited the owners at home.

The drive from the airport took over two hours, through a cold, empty landscape now dappled with snow. The village itself was undistinguished, much the same as the others I'd driven through and, like them, apparently deserted. Then, by an improbably large church, the clusters of small, neat houses parted to reveal an incredible fairy-tale castle with brightly painted turrets and sheer castellated walls. Its most striking feature was a gigantic white tower which rose up from the heart of this extraordinary spectacle like a great anchored rocket. The castle was protected by a wide moat and surrounded, in the English style, by a landscaped park. Only the cawing of the rooks, perched like black smudges in the bare branches of the beech trees, disturbed the complete wintry silence. It was spellbinding. Did Rosalie Davison feel the same as, newly wed, she stepped nervously out of her carriage after her long journey from England to stand where I stood now, to gaze as I gazed?

Inside I was led through a medieval stone-vaulted hall. On a wall above the stairs was a huge canvas of a red-coated officer on horseback. The officer was haughtily reviewing a line of troops. 'Respectfully presented', the plaque on the elegantly carved and gilded frame announced, 'to Lieut. Col. Alex Davison by the Loyal Britons Volunteer Infantry March 1806.' Hanging by Davison's side in the picture was the scabbard I had seen at the National Maritime Museum, though the sword in it was quite different. On a long, highly polished mahogany dining table in the next room was an old box brought down from the castle attics for me to look at. Covered in faded red morocco leather with scrolling brass handles at each end, it bore on its top, embossed in gold, the inscription: ALEX[R]. DAVISON ESQ[R]. COMMISSARY GENERAL.

The box was locked, but the small iron key turned easily enough. The inside was lined with rich green velvet and hand-coloured marbled paper. It was overflowing with letters and papers. I felt a rush of expectation, like a child the night before Christmas. I had no plan. I simply scooped the papers out, feeling the weight and grainy texture of their thick, creamy pages, and began to read them. As the minutes and then hours passed, the archive settled into two distinct parts. The first would loosely be termed the formal papers. There were legal and financial documents, full of incomprehensible numbers. There were also lists of the men in Nelson's warships, with long-forgotten names like John Jolly, Robert Dwyer, Luke Murphy, Jeremiah Reily, Joseph Murray and David Brady. On one, otherwise insignificant, roughly torn wrapper was written in a neat hand: 'Lord Nelsons last Memorandum Book up to the 21st of October 1805 containing a Codicil to his Will written a short time before the Commencement of the Action — Sealed up by Capt Hardy in

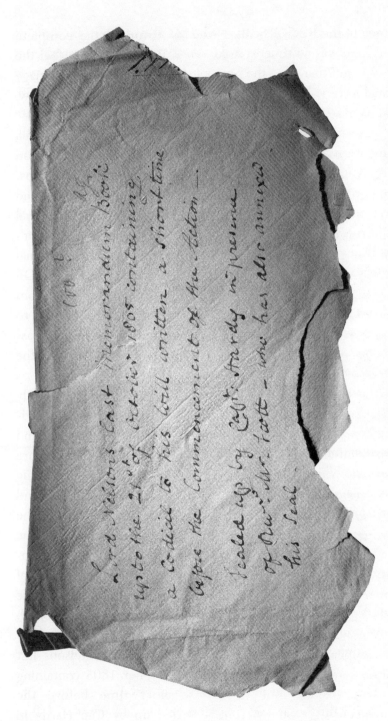

No. 1

Lord Nelson's last Memorandum Book
up to the 21st of October 1805 containing
a codicil to his Will written a short time
before the Commencement of the Action —

Sealed up by Capt. Hardy in presence
of Mr John Scott — who has also annexed
his Seal —

The wrapper which contained Nelson's pocket book when it arrived at Clarges Street on 16 December 1805.

presence of the Revd Mr Scott – who has also annexed his seal.'

There was no time to make sense of these documents, even if I could. So I turned to the remaining papers, which were largely personal letters. Most were written on thick sheets of paper with Britannia watermarks. Some were folded into envelopes, with their wax seals, smudged and pressed with a variety of crests, still clinging resolutely to them. The letters were in a variety of hands, all largely indecipherable at first to my inexperienced eye. I tried to arrange them by writer, scanning them for clues, looking at signatures and addresses. Small piles began forming on the table in front of me. As I grew familiar with the writing, scattered phrases began lifting off the pages to swim into focus, their meaning still a mystery.

> *My poor dear father is no more, god bless you . . . I am all to him in the world and god almighty knows he is all to me . . . I have not had a line from him this age I am sure he writes who can be so wicked as to take my letters . . . I am now distrustful and fearful of my own shadow . . . once the victory took fire near the powder magazine the whole of the terrified crew rund up the riggen . . . I hope to get at their fleet . . . I love him I would do anything in the world to convince him of my affection . . . one fortnight of joy and happiness I have had for years of pain . . . I am gone nor do I wish to live . . . this dreadful weight of most wretched misery . . .*

Voices released from their morocco-bound prison after two hundred years began to fill the room. They were hesitant at first but soon they pressed forward, each eager to be heard above the others. A glorious babble washed over me: a jumble of joy, laughter, love, pain, treachery, anger and death. Opening the box was like breaking a spell and eavesdropping on a conversation stopped long ago. I felt like an intruder and a little sad.

The park outside the windows had disappeared into darkness when I finally sat back, my eyes aching and my head full of broken fragments of speech. On the table were over seven hundred pages of letters and documents. The letters from Nelson to Davison were in a bold, open hand, the ink running thickly over the page. The last had been written in *Victory* just a week before the battle of Trafalgar. There were letters from Nelson's mistress, Emma Lady Hamilton. These were in a gratifyingly apposite style, her large, loose hand scattering the words across the page in lines sometimes so precipitously slanted that it seemed they might slide off the page altogether. They looked exactly what they were: letters written propped up in bed. Remarkably, there were also over seventy letters written to Davison by Frances Nelson, Nelson's wife. Fanny's hand was quite different from Emma's: small, neat and tight. She wrote with great care and attention. Yet this formal style disguised feelings every bit as passionate as those of her famous rival. Fanny's letters would be a revelation.

The papers in the box were just the beginning. Scattered around that remarkable castle, from top to bottom, hidden away in cabinets and drawers, was an astonishing treasure trove of Nelson relics, all preserved untouched from Alexander Davison's personal collection. There was another sword with a gold crocodile hilt set with a perfectly painted enamel of the battle of the Nile. Unlike the one at the National Maritime Museum, this sword was straight-bladed, its steel still razor sharp. There were also medals in gold, silver and copper, all in mint condition, all similarly decorated. On one side was a female figure standing on a cliff gazing out to sea holding a shield bearing a bust of Nelson; the other side depicted the battle of the Nile below the motto ALMIGHTY GOD HAS BLESSED HIS MAJESTY'S ARMS. Running around the edge of each medal was this inscription: FROM ALEX[R.] DAVISON ESQ[R.] S[T.] JAMES'S SQUARE – A TRIBUTE OF REGARD. Close to the medals was a small wooden snuff box. A gold plaque on its lid, no bigger than a postage stamp, told me the box was made from *Victory*'s main mast, 'close to which the immortal NELSON fell'. There were richly bound books from Naples, rare guns and a pair of magnificent wine-coolers from the Derby porcelain factory, flamboyantly painted with Nelson's coat of arms and a colourful profusion of Egyptian symbols: palm trees, pyramids, obelisks and sphinxes. Hanging on one wall was a heavy, dangerous-looking sabre. Beneath it was a label. 'This sword belonged to Lord Nelson', it read, helpfully. The hilt of the sabre was decorated with the head of Medusa and a cap of liberty. The dull, grey blade was etched to imitate watered silk, and decorated in gold Islamic script. It was unmistakably the sabre hanging by Davison's side in the painting on the stairs. Surely this sabre would fit the scabbard with the presentation inscription on display at the National Maritime Museum? What had happened here? How had sabre and scabbard become separated?

I knew I had stumbled into something quite extraordinary. This was not a lost collection, because no-one had ever looked for it or missed it. Somehow these papers and objects had slipped from history, lying undisturbed in that castle as time swirled past. Then, as I prepared to leave, my head spinning, one last thing was placed in my hand. It was a green woven silk purse, apparently stained with blood. The purse felt hefty with gold. With a lurch I knew what this had to be. I returned to the table. The purse was about 12 inches long and shaped like a tube with a tassel on either end. Coins entered it through a 2-inch horizontal slit halfway along. Two steel rings, each apparently covered in fine strands of hair, were then evidently slid down to the ends of the purse, gathering the material and capturing the contents. One end was clearly bulging with coins. The blood was dispersed across the purse but with a concentration in one large stain towards the middle, which the British press later described as tear-shaped.

Incredibly, the owners had never opened the purse. Very gently I parted the iron rings, opened the slit and felt gingerly inside. One by one I removed twenty-one gold coins with the tips of my fingers: eight guineas, six half-guineas and seven third-guineas. The earliest coin was dated 1772 and the latest 1804. Together the coins were worth £14 to Nelson. There was also a small, folded piece of paper tucked deep within the purse. I eased

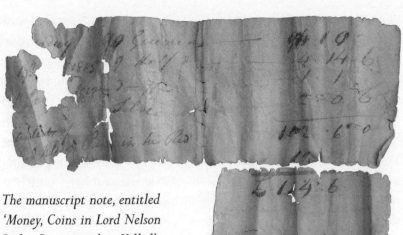

The manuscript note, entitled *'Money, Coins in Lord Nelson Pocket Purse &c when Killed'*, which was composed at St James's Square on Tuesday 17 December 1805. It was found in the purse two hundred years later.

this out very carefully using the steel tongs I always carried with me to examine loose diamonds. The paper left a trail of dust behind it. One-quarter of this fragile document was missing; but I could read the title: 'Money, Coins in Lord Nelson Pocket Purse &c when Killed'. There was an incomplete date: ' . . . sday 17th . . . 1805 St Jam . . . Square' and two names, presumably witnesses: 'Wm. Haslewood and Lord Nelson'. This was confusing. Wasn't Nelson dead? The manuscript was an account of the money in the purse. Yet it listed many more coins than were before me and a total sum of £114 6s 0d. What had become of the rest of the money?

The fragment of paper had barely survived its 200-year journey to me in the darkness of the purse. Yet, incredibly, it seemed to confirm that this commonplace object was with Nelson when he died in *Victory* at around four o'clock in the afternoon on 21 October 1805. Holding it felt like touching him. Why was the purse with Davison? Why had he been allowed to keep it? How did he get so close? Everything pointed towards a far deeper relationship between him and Nelson than had ever been hinted at. My visit to the castle had only deepened the mystery. At the heart of this puzzle, the key to it perhaps, was the enigmatic figure of Alexander Davison. Who was he?

III

N̶EP̶TU̶N̶E

98 GUNS,
CAPTAIN THOMAS FREMANTLE

ALICK DISEMBARKED AT Woolwich on Wednesday 29 April, 1767, four days after setting sail from Berwick and more than a week since leaving his family at Lanton. Already, as the wherry took him upriver to the city, the empty stillness of the Cheviot Hills, all he had ever known, felt a lifetime ago. The river was crowded with ships, boats and barges of all sorts. Through a confusion of masts crouched the dark mass of London, shrouded by a blanket of coal smoke punctured here and there by thin spires.

Sitting on Alick's head were an itchy new perruque and a felt tricorn hat which kept falling off. Under his heavy coat he wore a smart green silk waistcoat, bought in Newcastle, woollen breeches and cream-coloured cotton stockings which his mother had knitted. He felt hopelessly provincial, and his awkwardness was made worse when the boatman, a surly character, began mimicking his soft Northumbrian accent. He landed at Billingsgate, where foul-mouthed porters roared at each other in the oily air and his new stockings were instantly soiled by the muck on the wharf.

It was only with great difficulty that Alick found Moulls's house, hidden away down a subterranean alleyway. Ralph Moulls was a friend of his father, 'a good man', he said, but Mrs Moulls was a sour-looking woman who peered intently at the young man before reluctantly taking him up to a small, cold room on the third floor of her narrow house. The chamber was sparsely furnished: a stove, a couple of old cane chairs, a small looking-glass and a table with a battered iron candlestick on it. In the candlestick was a cheap, half-burnt, dipped candle. There were no pictures on the damp, peeling plaster walls. A truckle bed was pushed into one corner. Mrs Moulls disappeared without a word.

Alick felt slightly better when the stove was lit and he had eaten the last of the bread saved from his voyage. Slowly the feeling of excitement that had carried him down from Northumberland replaced his anxiety and loneliness. He had been seventeen years old for less than a month. 'You are now, my dearest Alick,' his mother wrote, when she heard he had safely arrived, 'in the gay part of the world in which you must unavoidably meet with many & great temptations let none of them ever be able to swerve you from the paths of virtue.'

In the morning Alick went out to look for work. His father could not afford to buy him an apprenticeship in the East India Company or the Bank of England, so Alick would have to rely instead on his own ambition and hard work, and hope to catch the eye of a patron. Some of the pavements, he noticed as he trudged the streets that first day, were laid with granite paving stones shipped from Aberdeen; but most were still cobbled and covered by a skin of slippery living filth, a foul combination of human and animal manure, straw and rotting vegetables. Alick soon discovered that most of the effluent of the overcrowded City ended up in the street – including the occasional decaying corpse. The stink was overpowering, far worse even than Newcastle. The noise, too, was ceaseless, from the sound of iron-bound coach wheels clattering over the cobbles to the yelling and cursing of the carters and the cries of the hawkers. Sedan chairs weaved through the bustling streets carrying severe-looking men in full wigs and rich velvet suits. Only the sheep and cattle going to the market in Smith's field reminded him of the life he had left behind.

Most of the houses in the City were quite new and built of

brick, the great fire a century before having obliterated the old wood-framed ones. But they still pressed uncomfortably against each other in the ancient manner, trapping a miasma of coal smoke and cooking smells which choked lungs and clung to skin and clothes. Two edifices loomed over everything else as a perpetual presence in the lives of the people below: the new dome of St Paul's Cathedral and, rising from the heart of the City, the Monument, a great Doric column crowned by gold which had been erected after the fire.

It took Alick until October to find a position at Hazard & Co., one of many small stockbroking companies populating 'Change Alley. His father, in the meantime, had grown anxious, concerned by stories of Alick visiting the gardens at Vauxhall, a renowned den of iniquity. 'Be sure to keep good company otherwise you will inevitably fall a victim to vice and debauchery,' he warned. He complained of his son's idleness, reprimanded him for not writing regularly and urged him to study his books. News that Alick had found a job was greeted cautiously. 'Convince them of your readiness, good nature and obliging behaviour,' his father wrote. When Alick arrived on his first morning the counting house was already busy with gaunt, pale-faced young men stooping over enormous suede-bound entry books propped up on long wooden counters. The partners briefly appeared much later before disappearing into one of the coffee houses surrounding the Royal Exchange – usually Jonathan's, at Temple Bar, where the hideous, desiccated heads of two rebels from the Jacobite uprising of 1745 were still spiked.

The Exchange opened at one o'clock. Alick was amazed by its colour and exoticism. The whole world seemed to be crowded into its elegant arcades and the air was full of strange words, sounds and scents. Clusters of dark-robed Jews with wide-brimmed hats and long beards consulted beside Mughuls and Muscovites, Armenians and Americans. There were Dutchmen and Frenchmen, Swedes and Japanese, their voices rising from the courtyard in a curious hubbub. Scattered among them were stockbrokers, bankers and merchants from the London companies conducting their business, recording transactions in tatty debt-books kept in voluminous pockets.

This first job was short-lived: complaining of ill-treatment, Alick left after no more than a couple of weeks. Undaunted, he soon found a new place at Taylor & Co., a company of gunpowder-makers in Old Broad Street. Here he learned basic book-keeping skills and acquired an understanding of bills, contracts, discounts, drawbacks and all the other complicated transactions of trading in the City. He may also have developed here the fascination with firearms that would last the rest of his life.

That winter was the worst that anyone could remember. The Thames froze and London suffered shortages of food and fuel. Violent protests broke out against high bread prices and low wages. The protests were led by the coal-heavers – a hard, belligerent breed of men who unloaded the sacks of coal onto the wharves from the colliers which arrived every day from the north of England. The coal-heavers were soon joined by the Spitalfield weavers, the coopers, the tailors and the hatters. Seamen rioted at Deptford. One day over two thousand watermen demonstrated in front of the Exchange. Every morning, Alick's fellow clerks gleefully reported the latest news.

In March 1768 London was swept by the riotous celebrations that greeted the election to parliament of John Wilkes, a popular radical who dared to challenge the corrupting vested interests of the aristocratic ruling elite. An excited mob surged through the narrow streets sporting blue cockades and shouting 'Wilkes and Liberty! Wilkes and Liberty!' Doorways were daubed and windows smashed. The duke of Northumberland's magnificent Tudor mansion at Charing Cross was saved only when the duke ordered the Ship alehouse to fill the rioters with beer. When Wilkes was imprisoned at the King's Bench prison in Southwark, a huge crowd gathered outside angrily demanding his release. Only a thin red line of frightened young foot guards prevented them from storming the famous old prison itself. When one of the guards opened fire, there was panic and confusion, the crowd fleeing chaotically over the river back to Westminster. Eleven torn bodies, including one of a pregnant woman, were left behind on the cold ground. Reports of the disturbances soon reached the north, prompting an anxious letter from Alick's father. 'Your mother', he wrote, 'joins me in begging you will take care of yourself as there is now such a mischievous mobbing spirit raging in the City.'

Keen to escape from Mrs Moull who, he told his sister, had 'use'd him ill', Alick moved lodgings several times that spring, staying first with George Moffatt, a cousin from Northumberland, before sharing rooms with his uncle, James Neal, at 3 George Lane. He found a new job, too, moving to Appleton & Wrigands, a company of merchants in Cloak Lane close by London Bridge. His position paid £30 a year, 'which', grumbled his father, 'will I suppose do little more than pay for your board'. Here, too, Alick complained of being treated like a 'slave'. His mother was full of sympathy. 'I hear the people you are with are a very wicked set,' Dorothy Davison wrote, worried by reports of excessive swearing; 'pray my dear lad take care of a bad example it is too, too often catching, pray is there no prospect of a better place?' In the meantime, she sustained him with deliveries of ham, hares, butter and goose pies sent by ship from Northumberland. When the Royal Exchange emptied in the summer and the merchants disappeared to their country villas, Alick returned to Northumberland for the first time, sailing from Woolwich on 2 July. After a night in Berwick he took a post-chaise to Lanton, arriving home late on 8 July.

Lanton House, where Alick had been born on 2 April 1750, was a comfortable-sized, solid-looking property built from the local grey stone earlier in the century. It had six bedrooms and a notably large hall. Similar houses occupied hillsides across the whole of the north of England in lasting tribute to the prosperous breed of minor gentry who farmed them. The house stood resolutely at the foot of Lanton Hill, on the sunny side of the river Glen. Cornfields and meadows carpeted the valley floor before rising gently into hillsides dotted with sheep and dark with the valuable plantations of oak so vital for building the warships of the Royal Navy. Three generations of Davisons had farmed Lanton as tenants until, after the recent war with France, Alick's father, also Alexander, had been able to buy the house and land. He was now improving his small estate by studying the latest farming techniques and investing in the best equipment.

History soaked the hills around the farm. Scotland was only nine miles away and Flodden, where King James IV had died, just three. This was a close-knit world populated by tough, independently minded people, united by an innate pioneering spirit that blurred the ancient cultural and religious divides between the Scots and the English. So although the Davisons were baptized, married and buried in the parish church of St Gregory's, a mile away in Kirknewton, they shared the nonconformist religious beliefs of their neighbours and supported the local Presbyterian chapel in Wooler.

At Lanton, Alick enjoyed a safe, loving but unconstrained childhood, free to wander the hills and to go fishing with his brothers. There were trips to the races at Kelso and to Holy Island for bathing. His upbringing gave Alick an instinctive knowledge of the wild vagaries of nature. 'You are such a good *calculator* of *wind* & *time*,' his wife wrote years later, full of admiration at his ability to predict the course and duration of long voyages. There is no record of his formal education. He probably attended a small church school or the grammar school in Morpeth. Alick's best friend from school, Johnny Cowley, appeared fifty years later as a character witness at his trial.

Lanton House still nestles beneath Lanton Hill, sheep still graze the slopes and the river Glen still bubbles along the valley floor. Less has changed here in two and a half centuries than perhaps anywhere else in this whole story. Walking those hillsides today, feeling the landscape that formed Davison, tasting the air which filled his lungs, was important to me. Did his childhood leave him with a natural affinity for a man who grew up on the empty Norfolk coast? It was certainly very fertile ground for breeding determined, successful men. Besides Davison, a lord chancellor, a lord chief justice and Nelson's second-in-command at Trafalgar were all born within a few years, and a few miles, of each other among those sweeping hills.

The Davisons were never rich – Alick's two sisters occasionally complained of shortages, particularly when their father was buying his 'hogs' – but they were growing prosperous; and, as they did so, Alexander Davison became ambitious for his children. Everyone knew that, in time, the farm would go to Jack, the eldest boy, who had just joined the Northumberland militia; but his brothers, Alick, George and Ralph, would need to develop business skills and find patrons. For this the Davison boys, with the rest of the local gentry, looked towards nearby Alnwick Castle, the daunting seat of the duke of Northumberland, whose land, and interest, dominated the north of England. Alick's sister Katty reported attending a 'grand' ball at the castle in August 1771 where she was introduced to the nine-year-old prince of Wales, a boy 'so affable & cheerful, that every person was in raptures with his manner'. It was well understood that the Davison boys' futures lay far from Lanton, leaving their sisters behind to marry well.

Alick stayed at Lanton that summer for just two weeks, no doubt helping with the harvest, before returning to London restored by the warm, clean air and eager to resume his new life. He moved lodgings again, this time to Black Raven Court off Seething Lane, close to the sprawling buildings of the Navy Office which Samuel Pepys had known so well a century before. At Appleton & Wrigands Alick caught the eye of Robert Hunter, who invited him to join Hunter & Baileys on £45 a year. Hunter & Baileys was a prestigious company with long-established and extensive contacts in the North American fur and fishing trades; 'a capital house', rejoiced Alick's father on hearing the news. Robert Hunter's family was originally from Kilmarnock, and his company purposely sought out bright, ambitious young men from Scotland and the borders – not simply to nurture and patronize them, but also to protect them from the hostility of their English peers.

The hub of Hunter & Baileys' global business was an imposing, double-fronted counting house at 54 Lothbury, a location that suitably reflected the firm's prosperity and prestige, within easy walking distance of both the East India Company in Leadenhall Street and the Hudson Bay Company in Fenchurch Street. Visitors entered through an imposing doorway raised from the dirt of the street by a short double flight of steps. To the left of the stone-flagged hall was the handsomely decorated partners' room, where a good fire was always kept. In this pleasant setting the partners entertained their clients, discussed deals and negotiated terms. The partners' room was the inner sanctum of a business that stretched around the world – but it was not a room that Alick would have visited often, certainly not at first. His life revolved instead around the clerks' room on the opposite side of the hall. This was equally substantial and well-proportioned, but was crowded with furniture and people. Unlike the orderly calm of the partners' room, the clerks' room was a place of constant, sometimes furious, activity.

The room was dominated by the merchant's bureau, a vast mahogany contrivance over eight feet tall which towered over everything else. Here, in a myriad of carefully arranged drawers and compartments, were the minutiae of Hunter's business. Some of the compartments were used for contracts and bills; others, arranged alphabetically, were for client correspondence; but everything, absolutely *everything*, had to be carefully and correctly filed. Arranged around the merchant's bureau were a bookcase, a library desk and a large wooden counter with five worn leather-covered stools for the clerks. The counter was populated by pewter inkstands, rulers, candlesticks, sandboxes and sheets of paper which during the day were in perpetual motion. The walls of the clerks' room were decorated, not in the fashionable chinoiserie paper of the next-door room, but with a large map of the world and complicated currency conversion charts. Each one of Hunter's interests around the globe was marked on the map with a pin. There were many pins.

Most of the clerks lived in, sharing bedrooms on the upper floors and living alongside the partners, their families and the servants. The house was comfortable but not grand. The furniture, objects and paintings that decorated it were all carefully, and prudently, purchased. Yet despite the house being principally a place of business there was also a relaxed domestic atmosphere, with the apprentice clerks enjoying high jinks away from the gaze of the partners. Alick soon moved in himself, passing his evenings playing cards and backgammon with the other clerks or studying in Hunter's small library. This was stocked with the latest books on trade and history, science and the arts, many in foreign languages. Some days Alick visited the New York coffee house, where the North American merchants gathered to discuss the market and to read newspapers.

Robert Hunter's family had been involved with the fur trade for over a hundred years, forging close ties with the Hudson Bay Company by purchasing valuable sealing, whaling and salmon fishing posts on the remote coast of Labrador. With the British conquest of French Canada in 1760, Hunter was able to extend his company's activities along the St Lawrence river to the trading posts of Lower Canada and, through Montreal, to the rich and largely unexploited hunting grounds in the west. He owned three of the eleven ships that regularly plied the Atlantic between London and Quebec. The ships were loaded at Gravesend with goods which, months later, would be exchanged with the Indians for their furs. For years the trade was characterized by rivalry with the French, but by the time Alick joined the company the British had established virtually complete control of the business – except for occasional smuggling by American colonists – having weaned the Indians off their diet of French goods to products from England and the colonies. So, every spring, the wharves at

Gravesend were piled high with vast bundles of Oxfordshire blankets, Yorkshire woollens, Irish linen, Manchester cottons, brass kettles and large sacks of coloured glass beads. Beside them were cases of those staple trading goods, guns and gunpowder, knives and hatchets. If it had been a successful hunting season, Hunter's ships returned in the autumn laden with bales of furs and skins of all kinds, including fox, mink, marten, caribou and bear. The most precious, however, were the beaver skins, the vital raw material for the valuable European felt market. The older and oilier the skin, the better the price.

At the counting house in Lothbury, Alick and his fellow clerks laboriously wrote up Hunter's books and copied his ceaseless correspondence. Hunter's emphasis on clear, concise letter-writing was to stand Alick in good stead throughout his long life. Generally the clerks worked nine hours a day, Monday to Saturday, with a couple of afternoons off during the week. Working for Hunter, Alick found himself among the small, largely nonconformist, Scots contingent in the City: men who, like him, were determined and clever, men who had grown resistant to the English merchants mocking their accents and blocking their path to positions in the large firms.

It was at Hunter's house that Alick fell in love for the first time. Mrs Norris was a young widow, a friend of his sisters, who was said to have an income of £400 or £500 a year and another £6,000 in stocks and cash. There was talk of marriage, though Alick's parents had understandable misgivings about such a hasty match. 'A. Davison fond of Mrs N,' wrote his mother;

> is it possible one who he hated as much as Turbot & who could not hear of his sisters coming to visit her, & now inordinately fond of her, a strange turn indeed! however to be grave, she is no doubt a very handsome fortune & very sensible & one I have a great regard for, but I must own I don't like her connections, particularly her mother, who I think you should know pretty well, & don't you think my dear, she is rather too old for you, & you rather too

young to enter into a married state, but there is no accounting for love & if your affections are so much engaged, as to be unhappy without the object of them, for my part shall leave it to your ownself.

His father was practical and businesslike.

For my part I have no objection. I think well of her father & your mother perfectly agrees with me but as marriage is a serious affair & for life, you are to consider well if the object suits your taste & will make you happy. This is your look out & I hope you will weigh it well. In point of fortune you may never have it in your power to do better . . . I do think she is good bait & may justly entitle her to a good match . . . if you are in earnest I have no doubt of your success as she seems to have a great attachment & a real affection for our family. But if you should proceed I would have you inform yourself well and particularly what her fortune consists of, I mean how much in stock and how much in cash not that I suspect any deceptions, but if a mistake of that kind should happen it may occasion discontent in case of union between you.

Regardless of all this good advice, it seems Alick misjudged Mrs Norris's affections, for she married someone else just three months later. 'I hope it gave you no pain,' wrote his mother, feeling her son's rejection. 'You have made a very narrow escape,' added his sister Katty.

Alick worked hard and learned fast. Hunter saw his protégé's ambition and late in 1772 introduced him to John Lees, an associate from Quebec. Lees, a Scot ten years older than Alick, was in London as part of a concerted, but so far unsuccessful, campaign by the Canadian merchants to persuade the government to relax its trading rules and to introduce a properly elected assembly into their province. It was agreed that Alick would join Lees in Quebec as his partner, replacing Lees's father who was retiring. There was time for a final, brief visit to Lanton and his family. George was now at the academy in Edinburgh, toying with a career in the church after abandoning, at his father's insistence, the idea of spending £400 on a commission in the army. Katty was engaged to Captain Roddam Home, a young naval officer who had been assiduously courting her for years. It was the last time Alick saw his other sister Meg, for she suddenly died only months later.

He sailed for Canada from Gravesend on 4 April 1773 in *Quebec*. The ship was uncomfortably packed with passengers, crew, provisions, trading goods and livestock. On this first transatlantic crossing Alick would have berthed in a three-tier bunk towards the stern, the closeness of his fellow passengers and the permanent damp gloom making it a fetid, depressing space. There was no privacy and little hygiene, and soon almost everyone suffered from lice. The food gradually deteriorated as the voyage went on and fresh provisions dwindled, until the diet was largely restricted to biscuits, soup and salt beef. Every day was much like the last, with life for the passengers settling into a routine of bells and meals, games of cards, backgammon and correspondence.

Quebec took three weeks to cross the Atlantic, Alick merely noting in his journal that the crossing was 'stormy'. Yet even when the ship reached the grand banks and great auks began circling the ship, she still had to conquer the dangers of the St Lawrence river, with its treacherous currents and hidden rocks; it would be a further three weeks before the ship could anchor safely at Isle-aux-Cordres. Finally, on 22 May 1773, *Quebec* sailed into the great basin spreading out in front of the sheer black cliffs of Cape Diamond, where the St Charles and St Lawrence rivers met. At the foot of the cliffs, Alick saw the old stone houses of the lower town of Quebec, clinging to the rocky ledge fringing the river. High above them on the summit, the silver domes and spires of the upper town, apparently prevented only by a great fortified wall from tumbling into the river below, flashed with the reflected glint of the bright morning sun. The sound of distant bells carried across the water.

The lower town moved with silent activity. The small harbour was full of ships, their tall masts moving together gently like swaying corn. More schooners and barges were moored along the wharves lining the river. Strange-looking boats which, Alick knew, were called canoes buzzed everywhere, paddled by Indians. At five o'clock in the afternoon *Quebec* moored in the river, close to a silent warship. The passengers were pulled across to the small harbour below the dark cliffs to disembark at a landing stage beside a marketplace. John Lees lived at 13 St Peter Street, a narrow, cobbled thoroughfare running the length of the lower town behind the wharves jutting into the river. After the conquest the British merchants had taken over the houses of their fleeing French rivals, and the street was now the backbone of their businesses, perhaps of the whole Canadian trade. These were tough, resourceful men with names Alick recognized from Hunter's correspondence: men like Adam Lymburner from Ayrshire, another Lothbury protégé who managed Hunter's fishing and sealing interests on the Labrador coast, and Brook Watson, who had lost a leg to a shark in Havana harbour and now dominated the fur trade in Nova Scotia.

Even now, more than ten years after the conquest, the British remained a minority in the town, outnumbered by the French Canadians, called *habitants*, who had lived and worked in the province for generations. Many of the *habitants* worked as cart-drivers on the wharves, living in miserable tenements in the bog of Sault-au-Matelot Street at the foot of the glistening cliff behind St Peter Street. The town was scarred by the British bombardment of 1759, many of the buildings still covered by wooden scaffolding. Most of the houses were built from the grey, rough-hewn local stone. This reduced the risk of fire in the lower town, where there was little hope of escape between the river and the cliffs. The houses were quite plain, echoing the villages in Brittany where the men who built them had lived, but constructed with steeply pitched roofs and narrow gabled windows to withstand the harsh Canadian winters.

On St Peter Street the houses were larger, and number 13 was typical, with three storeys and a painted tin roof. It stood close to the end of the street, facing the river, only a few steps from the harbour and the beach. Behind it was the Place Royale, where the sad ruins of the old French church of Notre Dame des Victoires, destroyed in the siege, were piled up in a corner. The house was arranged much like Hunter's in London, with a partners' room and a clerks' room on the ground floor and bedrooms on the upper levels. The deep, stone-vaulted cellar was used for storing goods and provisions. Most of the furniture was simple, in the French style, and made locally in cherry wood and pine; the better pieces, shipped from Europe, were in walnut. In the corner of every room was a heavy, ornately decorated, cast-iron stove which belched smoke throughout the winter. There was an occasional woollen tapestry, more for insulation than artistic effect, but only a few paintings hung on the walls. Large quantities of local earthenware, glass and faience were scattered throughout the house. The small windows and the narrowness of the street made the rooms gloomy, even on the sunniest day. A thick smell of old cooking, wood smoke and candles hung over everything.

Entertainment for the merchants in the lower town principally revolved around Simpson's coffee house on the quay. Alexander Simpson, known to everyone as Sandy, had arrived in Canada with General James Wolfe's army, although he took no part in the assault on Quebec. Like many veterans he stayed on after the conquest, setting himself up in the town as a tavern-keeper and marrying in 1766. His new wife Sarah came with a child, a six-year-old daughter called Mary; maybe she had lost a first husband with Wolfe on the Heights of Abraham.

In the evenings Simpson's coffee house was choked with tobacco smoke, still rare in London, and an extraordinary and colourful collection of people. *Habitants* wearing red caps above their strong, weathered faces sat playing backgammon beside

Indians decked out in brightly decorated calico jackets, scarlet leggings and amazing ornaments hanging from their noses and ears. Merchants huddled together discussing the latest news from London while red-coated soldiers from the garrison drank beside the blue jackets and checked shirts of the seamen from the warship in the river. There were many 'very wild songs'.

The upper town was far more spacious and elegant than the bustling streets below the cliffs. It was dominated by the citadel on top of the hill, the cathedral of Notre Dame and the famous Catholic seminary where priests gathered every morning before mass. One-horse buggies called *calashes* clattered around the wide streets, alongside the carts pulled by dogs which many merchants used to transport their goods. A man standing in the large square in front of the cathedral basilica could see the full sweep of the great St Lawrence river from Point Levy on the opposite bank down to the Isle d'Orléans and beyond, the whole vast, empty landscape encircled by distant snow-capped mountains. The quickest way of reaching the upper town from the lower was by Côte-de-Montaigne Street, a precipitous route perilous in winter.

Throughout the spring and into the summer, the warehouses lining the wharves filled with the furs which steadily arrived from distant trading posts. Immense log rafts, which had drifted for weeks from the forests in the west, began clogging the river. The rafts were marshalled into coves where they were broken up and the timber auctioned at Simpson's to shipbuilders from Quebec and England. As the months passed, every merchant felt the pressure of time. If a ship was delayed, or the wrong trading goods arrived from London, his whole season's trade could be jeopardized, allowing a rival to seize his business. Rather than risk everything in this way, most of the merchants diversified their businesses, developing a range of interests including property speculation, moneylending and importing luxury goods for the growing number of shops in the upper town.

When the first icy blasts came in October and the last ships disappeared past the Isle d'Orléans, taking with them the many merchants who returned to England for the winter, there was little for those who remained to do except take stock and balance their books. The relentless cold was astonishing even for a Northumbrian. For months the town lay wrapped in a deep blanket of snow, so deep that it sometimes came up to the bellies of the horses pulling the sleighs. The river froze, forming an ice bridge to Point Levy, which was quickly colonized by temporary taverns and wooden stalls selling all sorts of trinkets. Alick padded about town in his snowshoes with his beaverskin hat pressed firmly down around his ears. For entertainment there were dances at the garrison and candlelit sleigh rides to supper at Mr Menut's house, a tavern in the bleak countryside about a mile outside the town walls.

Some of the long evenings were filled by the meetings of the many masonic lodges which flourished in the town, as they did elsewhere in the small colonial communities of North America. The first masonic groups had arrived embedded in army regiments, but by 1773 there were at least a dozen local lodges in Quebec, including St Andrew's Lodge, for the Scots; Lodge No. 7, for the *habitants*; and the Grand Master's Select Lodge. The most prestigious was Merchant Lodge No. 1, founded in the year of the conquest. The lodge members met in taverns, as they did in England. The Provincial Grand Lodge, the local ruling body, met at Simpson's coffee house. A particularly popular venue was the Sun inn on St John Street in the upper town. This was owned by Miles Prentice, an ebullient Irishman who had served in Wolfe's army alongside his cousin Sandy Simpson. Merchant Lodge No. 1 met here, so it was probably in the room reserved for masonic meetings at the Sun inn that Alick, blindfolded, his breast bare, his buckles undone and his right knee exposed, was initiated into freemasonry. When the room was revealed he saw the floor cloth painted with emblems for the degree of apprentice: a staircase, a chequered pavement, a pair of columns and a rising sun.

The masonic principles of fraternalism, self-improvement, equality, charity, freedom of thought and religious toleration

Alexander Davison's
red morocco
dispatch box which
hid his Nelson
papers from the
world for two
hundred years.

Main pic: Quebec from Point Levy, painted by Maj.-Gen. Benjamin Fisher *c*.1790, showing the lower town and cul-de-sac harbour where Nelson stepped ashore in September 1782.

Left: A recently discovered oil sketch of Davison on his return to England from Canada, attributed to Sir Thomas Lawrence (*c*.1790).

Below: The Royal Exchange in the City of London, from Cornhill (1761).

Left: Captain Horatio Nelson painted by John Francis Rigaud (1777–81). This is the 'stern and erect' young officer who met Mary Simpson in Quebec. Davison visited Rigaud's studio in London with Frederick Haldimand on 15 February 1786.

Above: Hugh Percy, second duke of Northumberland, painted by Gilbert Stuart in 1785. Davison called the duke 'my best friend'.

Right: General Francis Rawdon-Hastings, second earl of Moira: 'his ample fortune absolutely sank under the benevolence of his nature'. Oil on canvas copy after Sir Martin Shee's 1804 painting.

Above left: William Henry, duke of Clarence (later King William IV) painted by John Hoppner *c*.1800. After the battle of the Nile, the prince proposed raising a naval pillar as a 'monument of British Glory & Pre-eminence'. Davison was appointed treasurer of the scheme.

Above right: Henry Dundas, first Viscount Melville, painted by Sir Thomas Lawrence *c*.1810. Down-to-earth with a famed sense of humour, 'Big Scotch Harry' had a gargantuan appetite for life and was William Pitt's most loyal supporter.

Right: George, prince of Wales (later King George IV) painted by John Hoppner *c*.1792. Nelson fretted that Emma might become 'a whore to the rascal'.

Main picture: A view of Swarland House painted from the Battle Park in 1828. The Palladian mansion at the heart of Davison's Northumbrian estate was acquired in 1795 using the vast profits from his work as a government contractor.

Left: Percy and William Davison painted by John Hoppner in 1802. At their sittings the twins must have seen the full-length portrait of Nelson on which Hoppner was working for the prince of Wales.

ght: Alexander Davison painted by
muel Abbott in March 1797, only
onths before the artist began his
nous series of portraits of Nelson.
is recently discovered picture, or a
rsion of it, hung at Merton Place
side portraits of Sir William Hamilton
d the Revd Edmund Nelson.

Right: Fanny Nelson's seal which she used in black wax following the deaths of Maurice and Edmund Nelson and again after the battle of Trafalgar.

Below: Fanny Nelson in an unflattering portrait from the 1790s that was no match for the lavish and loving attention afforded to Emma by artists across Europe.

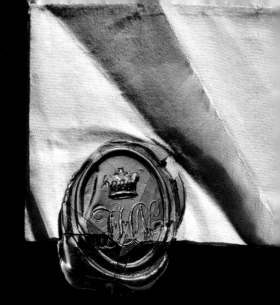

strongly appealed to the merchants. Freemasonry was tolerant and liberal, serving to bind the disparate religious and cultural elements in the town. But beyond these high-minded ideals, most members were attracted by the conviviality and mutuality of the lodges. Although the meetings at the Sun inn, which could last most of a day, had an important ritualistic element, they were principally an opportunity to debate philosophy and discuss arts and the sciences. Talk of politics and business was strictly prohibited. The merchants had quick, enquiring minds and, far from Europe, an insatiable thirst for knowledge. Processions of masons holding their trowels and wearing ankle-length white leather aprons would have been a familiar sight in the town. Their business over, the members dined together, sang songs and drank Brother Prentice's wine. Women were excluded from the meetings but enjoyed the Freemasons' Balls held each December at the Assembly Rooms.

After his first Christmas in Quebec, Alick visited the American colonies with John Halsted, a friend who managed a flour mill on Point Levy. Evidence of the growing unrest against British rule was unavoidable. They reached Boston just a few months after some rebels, dressed as Indians, threw a shipment of English tea into the harbour. Colonel Hugh Percy of the 5th regiment described the town and its environs in a letter to his father, the duke of Northumberland. 'It is', he wrote, 'as far at least as I have been round this town, most delightfully varied. The hills, rising from the valleys by gradual and gentle ascents, interspersed with trees give it a most agreeable appearance . . . Mr Browne [Lancelot 'Capability' Brown] here would be useless.' But he took a less favourable view of the local inhabitants. They 'are the most designing, artful villains in the world. They have not the least idea of either religion or morality.' Percy carried orders from London to crack down on the rebellious disorder. Like many British officers, he felt uncomfortable with his task, yet he understood its urgency. 'If Great Britain relaxes in the least,' he observed to his father, 'adieu to the colonies.'

Halsted and Alick separated at New York after falling out over a scheme to recover their expenses by selling some horses they had brought from Canada. Of the three horses, one died in Boston and the other two were sold in New York for a loss. Halsted was furious. Blaming Alick for the failure, he left him in New York to negotiate contracts to ship rum from the West Indies and stomped back to Quebec, lodging a claim for his losses in the Court of Common Pleas. Alick, who reminded Halsted that he had warned him 'that Canadian Horses were not in great esteem' in the colonies, was forced to pay his erstwhile friend £17 in compensation.

The Quebec Act, passed by parliament in April 1774, extended the boundaries of the province as far south and west as the Ohio and Mississippi rivers. English criminal law was introduced, but the act recognized the *habitant* majority and preserved many of the features of the *ancien régime* such as the French civil code, rights of the clergy and the seigniory system. It was a pragmatic solution to the cultural peculiarities of the province. But it confirmed the merchants' worst fears by establishing a legislative council in Quebec, rather than an elected assembly. The members of the council would be appointed by their new governor, a touchy, authoritarian Irishman called Sir Guy Carleton. In September 1774 Indian runners brought the dramatic news that the Americans had invaded Canada. The colonists hoped to prevent Britain using its northern province as a springboard for suppressing their rebellion. Carleton, who had earlier inadvisably despatched most of his regular troops to Boston, rushed upriver to defend Montreal. An irregular force of Canadian and British militia was left behind to guard Quebec.

Feverishly, the town prepared itself for attack. Houses were demolished to create barricades and the merchants' schooners requisitioned to patrol the river. Kenelm Chandler, who was in charge of the ordnance at the garrison, mounted cannons around the town walls and double-checked his armoury. Within days the ranks of the British militia swelled to include over three hundred men. This ragbag army was led by Lieutenant-Colonel Henry Caldwell, another veteran of Wolfe's army. A further two hundred Scots formed a regiment of Royal Highland Emigrants, while almost five hundred *habitants* created the French Canadian volunteer corps. Alick, who had returned to Quebec soon after completing his business in New York, John Lees and Adam Lymburner were all commissioned ensigns in the British militia. Miles Prentice enthusiastically became a sergeant-major again. During the emergency the militia officers met every day at noon in the parlour of the Golden Dog, Prentice's large new tavern at the top of Côte-de-Montaigne Street. Here guard rotas were agreed and daily patrols assigned before the officers left to drill their men on the Heights of Abraham.

As the Americans advanced down the river from Lake Champlain, the town gates were locked at night and a system of church bells and gun salutes developed to warn of attack. On 13 November, a day after Montreal fell, the first rebels were spotted landing at Wolfe's cove, below the Heights of Abraham. The following morning a few of them appeared about 800 yards from the town walls and gave three cheers. The militia guards on the walls responded in kind before letting loose some grape and canister shot. The Americans 'did not wait for a second round' and quickly melted back into the trees. More shots were fired to dislodge some of the rebels from Menut's tavern.

When the Americans reached Point Levy they occupied the flour mill run by John Halsted. According to Colonel Caldwell, who owned the mill, his manager 'turned out a great scoundrel, put me to great expense, and has proved to be in the rebel interest'. Halsted, who was quite prepared to betray his friends, promptly volunteered to be the rebels' commissary of provisions. On 15 November the Golden Dog was requisitioned as militia headquarters, the men were issued with twenty-four rounds each and Alick and Lymburner both gazetted lieutenants. Guard duties were more strictly enforced than ever, with anyone seen outdoors at night detained. With the prospect of an imminent siege, the movement of provisions or firewood away from the town was strictly prohibited. There were even rumours, which were swiftly dispelled, that all the men in the militia were going to be flogged to sharpen them up. When Carleton arrived back, having escaped Montreal dressed as a fisherman, he took charge of Quebec's defence, purging the town of 'useless, disloyal and treacherous persons'. Days later the last opportunity arrived to leave the town before the river froze and the siege closed in. Brook Watson had already sailed, and now Alexander Davison and Adam Lymburner followed him to London. The merchants probably judged, and Carleton must have agreed, that saving their businesses was more important to the future of the province than risking their lives in a siege.

In heavy snow on New Year's Eve the American rebels, by now badly outnumbered and severely weakened by the extreme conditions, launched a desperate assault on the town. They were eventually bloodily repulsed at the barricades on Sault-au-Matelot Street. Nevertheless, the crisis lasted for another four months. Davison's house on St Peter Street was badly damaged during the siege by shot lobbed over by the American guns on Point Levy. It was only on 6 May 1775, when three British warships and five troop transports appeared in the river after a heroic voyage through the ice, that the siege was finally lifted. The bedraggled, exhausted and starving Americans were pushed back west, with the British flushing out any sympathizers along the way. Quebec had survived; but to the south, the war that would see the British rulers ejected from their American colonies had begun in earnest.

Alick used his time in London well, forging valuable commercial and political friendships. He returned to Quebec in *Apollo*, arriving in early May 1777 determined to extend his interests into property, moneylending and ship-owning. Alongside him was his brother George, who had abandoned his lukewarm pursuit of a career in the church and now had hopes of farming in the province.

On 25 June 1778 a new governor stepped onto the quay in

the lower town. He was Lieutenant-General Frederick Haldimand, a Swiss mercenary who had been recruited by the British army during the Seven Years War. The streets from the landing place up to the governor's imposing chateau in the upper town were lined with troops for Haldimand's arrival. Salutes were fired from the frigates in the river.

The new governor was very different from his patrician predecessor, who had resigned in a fit of pique after being passed over to lead a counter-attack into the American colonies. Despite his obvious ability, Haldimand's accent and unconventional background cast him as an outsider in the army, feeding an insecurity that made him cautious and over-reliant on bureaucracy. Fearful of change, he refused to listen to the demands of the merchants in the reformist English Party for a more laissez-faire administration and an elected assembly, and instead surrounded himself with men who shared his dogmatic outlook. His legislative council was soon dominated by members of the reactionary French Party, a mixture of the more conservatively minded merchants and *habitants* who wanted to preserve the status quo. In return for their loyalty, supporters of the French Party were rewarded with the best contracts and positions. The Davison brothers sided with the French Party more, it would seem, for pragmatic than for ideological reasons, and began assiduously courting the new governor.

When the French joined the war in support of the American rebels, their warships started harassing the British merchantmen plying the North Atlantic. Few of the merchants burdened their businesses with insurance, preferring instead to organize their ships into convoys protected by the Royal Navy. In an unspoken quid pro quo for this protection, the government in London used the merchantmen to deliver secret documents to Haldimand. When one of his ships, *Lizard*, was chosen for the task, Alexander Davison gave instructions for the master to throw the papers overboard in the event of capture. The merchantmen also carried lavish presents to the Indians, whose loyalty to Britain was being tested by the war and the blandishments of the Americans.

Despite all the obstacles and the difficulties, business in Quebec boomed during the war. This expansion was fuelled by a policy of cheap credit, which flooded the province with money to meet the insatiable demands of the growing numbers of troops and loyalist refugees. Brook Watson was appointed commissary-general to the British forces in Canada, responsible for provisioning the army, while Davison developed a lucrative business as an agent victualler. The spring convoy of 1782, which sailed from Ireland on 26 April, consisted of about thirty ships including two owned by Davison, *Amazon* and *Maria*, both of which were carrying presents from the British government for the Indians. The merchantmen were escorted by *Daedalus*, Captain Thomas Pringle, and *Albemarle*, Captain Horatio Nelson. Nelson, who was twenty-three, was decidedly unenthusiastic about this 'd——d voyage' to Canada, dreading the prospect of spending the year chauffeuring convoys whilst freezing to death. It was an uneventful, if slow, crossing and all the ships arrived safely at the Isle of Bic, two days from Quebec, on 1 July. While the merchantmen continued upriver, Nelson sailed back into the Atlantic, hoping to catch a prize or two off the Boston coastline.

Among the bundles of letters for Haldimand that came with the convoy was a warning that the French were embarking six thousand troops at Brest for a possible raid on Quebec. Haldimand, already preoccupied by large numbers of American prisoners of war, thought that by the time the French arrived it would be far too late in the year for them to make an attempt on the town. Nevertheless he began discreetly to review his defences, 'cautiously avoiding to alarm the public'. He ordered his military secretary, Captain Robert Mathews, to inform London that three frigates were already moored at Quebec with two others, including *Albemarle*, 'cruising in the gulf'.

On 20 September 1782, a very cold day, *Albemarle* passed the Isle d'Orléans, sailed into the great basin in front of Quebec and dropped anchor alongside *Daedalus*, *Huzzar* and *Carnceaux*. Her hunt down the coast had not only been unsuccessful but had almost ended in the disastrous loss of most of the crew with scurvy. Having failed to take on fresh provisions at the Isle of Bic after the long Atlantic crossing, Nelson and his men were desperately short of supplies. Twenty-two seamen, their skin ulcerating in bloody sores and their teeth rocking in spongy gums, were sent forward to the general hospital outside Quebec. The dishevelled young captain who stepped onto the quay from the *Albemarle*'s boat later in the day was showing symptoms of scurvy himself. His gaunt body was bowed with exhaustion, his pale face was pinched and his breath was foul. People later also recalled the baggy, old-fashioned uniform and the long, lank pigtail.

The autumn convoy, which Nelson wearily expected to escort back to England, was being prepared as he arrived, so the wharves were piled high with bundles of furs, barrels of salted salmon and crates of nuts. The air rang with the clacking of clogs on cobbles, the rumbling of the wagons and the cries of the animals as they were loaded for the long voyage.

Nelson soon met Alick. Perhaps they were introduced by Thomas Pringle, whose Northumbrian family was well known to Davison, or at the governor's chateau or in one of the coffee houses in town. They became fast friends and Nelson, who in the absence of any hotel (apart from a few rooms at the Golden Dog) had the choice of lodging in the town or staying in his ship while it was anchored in Quebec, was often to be found at 13 St Peter Street during the following weeks. At Davison's house, Nelson recuperated on a diet of soup, boiled chicken and game followed by redcurrants in treacle and compôtes of blackberries washed down with sweetened milk and glasses of pitchy-tasting spruce beer. Meanwhile, *Albemarle* was repaired, repainted and stocked with fresh vegetables, fruit, beer and beef. On 23 September a salute was fired to celebrate the anniversary of the king's coronation.

The famous old town was full of noise and colour, its narrow streets packed with seamen and soldiers, many in the green coats of the German regiments which had landed to reinforce the British army. There were sightseeing trips, supper parties and dances to enjoy. Nelson must have made a pilgrimage to the spot on the Heights of Abraham where his hero James Wolfe had died capturing the town, the spot marked by a boulder rolled there after the battle.

Somewhere – over supper with Davison, perhaps, or at the Golden Dog – Nelson caught sight of a new and gloriously unexpected local attraction. Mary Simpson, Sarah Simpson's daughter, was now aged twenty-two and had grown into a notable beauty, counting Captain Mathews among her many admirers. Robert Hunter's son paid homage in his journal when he toured the province. Even the *Quebec Gazette*, generally a rather staid commentator, rhapsodized:

> *Sure you will listen to my call,*
> *Since beauty and Quebec's fair nymphs I sing,*
> *Henceforth Diana is Miss S——ps——n see,*
> *As noble and majestic is her air . . .*

Mary was living in Bandons Lodge, beside the St Louis Gate. The Simpsons had moved to the more genteel surroundings of the upper town in September 1779 after Sandy sold his coffee house to open a shop in Baude Street, opposite the basilica. Within just two years, however, he was dead, suffering a 'heavy stroke of the apoplexy' on 27 March 1781. The town was left to mourn 'a loving husband, a tender and affectionate father, a good master and a faithful friend'. Despite suffering ill-health herself, Sarah Simpson was determined to keep the business going, helped by her children and (until she ran away) by Mary Jeannevieve, the family's black slave. The advertisements for the shop which Sarah placed in the *Quebec Gazette* list an astonishing assortment of goods: stationery, paints, candles, china, earthenware, linen, shirts, beaver hats, ostrich feathers, silk petticoats, stays, spices, wines, porter, lemon juice, vinegar, barley sugar, tobacco, aniseed water, ketchup, dog-skin shoes and 'many other articles too tedious to mention'. Close in age, Mary and Nelson became good friends. He was infatuated with her and she grew fond of him, perhaps teasing this 'erect and stern' young officer with his out-moded uniform and old-fashioned views.

On Friday 27 September a cutter arrived in the river with urgent orders for Haldimand to prepare troop transports to evac-uate New York. Twenty-three vessels belonging to the merchants were requisitioned and hurriedly fitted with hundreds of berths. Nelson was told by Captain Mathews that, instead of returning to England with the convoy, *Albemarle* would accompany the trans-ports to New York. 'A very *pretty job*', Nelson described it in a letter to his father. The troop transports sailed on 10 October, anchoring at the Isle of Bic to wait for their escort. Nelson lin-gered in Quebec as long as he could, enjoying a few more precious hours with Mary. Growing impatient, Captain Worth of *Assistance*, who was at Bic waiting to accompany the merchant convoy to England, sent orders back up to Quebec early on 13 October for *Albemarle* to join the transports 'without a moments delay . . . in order to take charge and proceed with them to New York with all possible dispatch'. Shaken from his reverie Nelson took leave of his new friends, pressing three men on the wharves before leaving to replace those who had not returned from the hospital. At nine o'clock the same evening, in heavy rain, *Albemarle* moved the short distance to St Patrick's Hole, a deep cove on the Isle of Orléans.

Early the following 'dark and gloomy' morning, Monday 14 October, Davison, who was preparing for his return to London with the merchant convoy, was on the beach below the wooded Heights of Abraham. Looking up, he spotted *Albemarle*'s boat unexpectedly approaching the quay from across the basin. To his surprise Nelson was sitting in the stern. Assuming his new friend had forgotten something, Davison walked up to the landing place to meet him. Nelson appeared gripped by a steely determination, as if seized by a sudden and overwhelming desire. Alarmed, Alick asked him why he had returned.

'Walk up to your house and you shall be acquainted with the cause,' was the terse reply.

Years later, after the battle of Trafalgar, Davison was asked by John M'Arthur, Nelson's official biographer, to recall what had happened next on that morning long ago in Quebec.

'I find it utterly impossible', Nelson had exclaimed when the friends reached the privacy of the parlour at St Peter Street, 'to leave this place without waiting on her whose society has so much added to its charms and laying myself and my fortunes at her feet.'

Alick was astonished; he had had no idea of the strength of Nelson's feelings for Mary. But he knew that Nelson was risking everything in leaving his ship to return to town. He also knew Mary – had known her since she was a child – and, mindful perhaps of his own youthful disappointment over Mrs Norris, probably guessed that Nelson would be rejected. The next few minutes could destroy the young officer's career before it had barely begun.

'Your utter ruin', Alick said firmly, 'must invariably follow.'

'Then let it follow,' Nelson retorted angrily, turning towards the door, 'for I am resolved to do it.'

'And I also', Alick replied, grasping his friend's arm and pulling him back, 'positively declare that you shall not.'

There then followed what Davison later described as an unseemly 'mutual conquest'. Slowly and 'with no very good grace' Nelson was eventually led back to his boat as the rain began falling heavily again.

The troop transports left their anchorage at the Isle of Bic in 'thick and dirty' weather five days later, sailing down to the sea and New York. It was so cold that *Albemarle*'s sails froze to the yardarms. As they did so, Nelson turned to look wistfully back up the river towards Quebec and Mary.

'Health that greatest of blessings', he wrote to his father that evening, 'is what I never truly enjoyed till I saw Fair Canada. The change it has wrought, I am convinced is truly wonderful.'

On 29 October, the evening before he left to join the other merchants who were gathering at Bic before sailing to London, Alick called at the British coffee house on the quay. Kenelm Chandler, the ordnance storekeeper at the garrison, was there. A row broke out, possibly over some goods Davison had supplied the garrison. Davison could be hot-headed on occasion, and a challenge was made and accepted. At dawn the next morning the men met on the Heights of Abraham, which glistened with a 'fair frost'. The men chose their weapons and, ignoring the cold, removed their coats to prevent the cloth fouling their wounds. They then turned their backs and walked away a few paces. Moments later the sky darkened as hundreds of birds burst noisily from the trees with the crack of the pistols.

No harm seems to have come to either man, but honour was satisfied. Afterwards, with the smell of burnt gunpowder still hanging in the air and the last wisps of smoke drifting high away over the river, Davison walked quickly back to town. Hours later he followed Nelson downriver.

IV

BRITANNIA

100 GUNS,
CAPTAIN CHARLES BULLEN

Davison was in England by Christmas 1782. George, who had secured a seat on the legislative council in Quebec using the influence of Lord Percy, was there already, consulting his physician about his increasingly precarious health. The brothers lodged together at Lincoln's Inn, passing their days negotiating contracts in the City and 'being introduced to the first people in the Trade'. Davison's rooms, which he must have rented informally from a member of the Inn, were on chapel staircase beside the Old Buildings. They were lost when the chapel was extended in the 1880s.

Davison saw Nelson again on 12 July 1783, a few days after *Albemarle* was paid off at Portsmouth. Nelson had been presented to the king for the first time at a levée in St James's Palace and afterwards, flush with excitement and champagne, he walked the dusty streets to Lincoln's Inn rather than return alone to his lowly lodgings on the Strand. Amused, Davison called for wine and gave his young friend, who was stifling in his 'iron bound' heavy dress uniform coat, a dressing-gown to wear.

As the afternoon sank into evening, Nelson excitedly described the palace to Davison, recalling its remarkable treasures and the extraordinary men and beautiful women who filled its gilded rooms. Other guests had included the prime minister, Lord

North; the duke of Portland; Edmund Burke; and the unmistakable figure of Charles Fox. The king was shorter than he expected, sweated a lot and spoke with a strong German accent. The queen was charming.

With this story, coming after their fateful final meeting in Quebec, the impression grows of Nelson increasingly leaning on Davison, the elder of the two men by eight years, for advice and guidance. Similar figures fulfilled this role in Nelson's professional life, but, having been at sea since he was twelve, he was still largely untutored in the ways of the civilian world. It was a naivety which in many ways lasted until the end of his life.

Before Davison had left Quebec, Haldimand had given him a letter of introduction to Evan Nepean, the young under-secretary of state for home affairs. It was the beginning of a long and highly fruitful friendship for Alick. Nepean had served as purser to Sir John Jervis during the American War before joining the Home Office, impressing the pugnacious admiral with his 'superior talent for business, unremitting diligence, and integrity'. Nepean was currently embroiled in a row with Haldimand over the cost and quality of the presents London was sending to the Indians in Canada, which by 1782 were worth over £60,000 a year. The governor was a keen supporter of the programme of present-giving, believing it more important than ever now that the war had finished and some of the tribal lands had been ceded to the Americans. He was unhappy, however, with the cost of the goods that William Knox, the government contractor in England responsible for the presents, was sending over. Knox blamed the merchants in Quebec for the problems, accusing them of conspiring against him and of profiteering by trebling his prices before delivering the goods to the governor. Knox warned Haldimand 'against recommending traders to be employed in doing business for government; their own interest is their general guide, and that suppresses all feelings for the public service'. Knox's excuses were ignored and he was replaced by Davison, who never forgot the importance of present-giving when securing

Evan Nepean, Henry Dundas' loyal attendant and Davison's close friend. Nepean ran a network of spies in London informing on Jacobin activity during the 1780s and 1790s. He later became Nelson's principal contact at the Admiralty.

loyalty. Davison was also charged with supplying building materials to the thousands of loyalist refugees who were flooding into Canada from the newly independent American states.

'It gives me pleasure', Haldimand told Davison, when the contracts were confirmed, 'to find that my endeavours to serve you have not been ineffectual.' By now Davison was firmly in the governor's, and the reactionary French Party's, interest. But Haldimand's attempts to secure him the next vacancy on the legislative council failed – largely because, as Nepean pointed out, Davison 'had a brother in it already'.

Despite this political setback, Davison was 'indefatigable' in his work for the government. Knowing that his contract for supplying presents for the Indians would 'be of use in extending the credit of my House both here and at Quebec', Davison assured Haldimand, probably disingenuously, that he was completing the orders at 'no personal advantage to myself'. The first shipment of tools and Indian presents left Gravesend on 16 April 1784. Haldimand marvelled 'that he never saw packages arrive in such good order' when they reached Quebec three months later.

In October 1784 the governor returned to England on leave. His stubbornness had caused such difficulties in the council between the warring French and English parties that it seemed unlikely he would ever return to Canada. Robert Mathews, Haldimand's faithful military secretary, accompanied him. In a final act of patronage before he sailed, Haldimand proposed that the Davison brothers should be awarded the leases of five important trading posts called the king's posts and fisheries. These covered a vast tract of territory downriver from Quebec and had been brought under crown control by the French regime to prevent the Indians being corrupted by merchants trading rum. Worried that the trade in the eastern territories could collapse altogether, the French issued sixteen-year leases to the posts to their most trusted merchants in a system which the British continued after the conquest – 'it being the interests of the lessees', as Haldimand observed, 'to take care of the health of the Indians, and be vigilant against the abuse of spirits'. The first British leases to the posts were given to a consortium of three merchants called Thomas Dunn, William Grant and Peter Stuart. For an annual rent of just £400, the partners enjoyed a business worth as much as £2,500 a year.

Shortly before leaving the governor's chateau in Quebec for the last time, Haldimand discovered that the king's posts leases had expired six years before. This, he bitterly complained, 'has never been notified to me by the present possessors'. In a letter to Lord Sydney, the home secretary, Haldimand proposed the Davison brothers as the new tenants. 'These gentlemen', the governor assured the minister,

> *are well connected and deservedly supported – I say deservedly because their education and sentiments are such as it is much to be wished were more general here – and during my command I have experienced in them upon all occasions a great zeal in the support of government as well as a uniform disinterestedness in their conduct, I think that such persons particularly in a country like this are deserving of the attention and encouragement of government.*

Back in London, where he was compensated for the loss of the governorship with various sinecures, Haldimand – along with Evan Nepean – continued to press the Davisons' case; in Canada, the brothers had support within the legislative council from François Baby, a rich French merchant who had stayed on in Quebec after the conquest. So Davison sailed for Canada in May 1785 in high hopes, buoyed up by Sydney's provisional decision to grant him the leases to the king's posts. From Poole, in Dorset, while waiting for a favourable wind to carry his ship into the Atlantic, he wrote to his father in Northumberland telling him that he was returning to Quebec 'in a way that few if any in a commercial character ever did'. Word of his growing stature in Canada had spread quickly in the City, and he left England having 'laid a foundation to extend and do as much *good* business as any house in America'. Davison used his enforced delay in Poole wisely, introducing himself to 'the most capital Houses' in the town. He was amazed to find that at least two local merchants owned a hundred ships each. Through a combination of business skills and some tactical name-dropping, Davison secured 'not only the consignment of several ships annually but also commission to load them at Quebec'.

Dunn and Grant, however, were not about to surrender their valuable leases lightly. Stuart, the junior partner in the consortium, was not averse to co-operating with the Davisons; but Dunn, already 'a great enemy' of the two brothers, was a particularly powerful opponent. He was an influential voice within the English Party, which saw its fortunes revive after Haldimand left the province, and he had the ear of Henry Hamilton, the deputy governor. Like Davison, Dunn also had influential allies in London. These included George Rose, the secretary to the Treasury, and Brook Watson who was now a member of parliament. Watson was suspicious of Nepean's close interest in the matter of the leases, believing that, all along, the secretary's 'views had been the Posts of Tadousac for Davidson [*sic*] & a fingering of the Indian Presents', and was pressing Lord Sydney to recall Sir Guy Carleton to the province. By the time Davison landed at Quebec, Hamilton, blatantly ignoring Sydney's intentions, had given Dunn a one-year lease to the posts, enabling Davison's bitter rival to make his case in London.

Hamilton was dismissed for his action, paving the way for Carleton's return. In the meantime the struggle for the leases, which had become a conflict of political interests, moved to London with Dunn just as Davison left the city. There was little he could do in Quebec, except hope that Sydney would quickly ratify his decision; so, undaunted by the prospect of an immediate return crossing, he rapidly concluded his immediate business in Canada and set sail for England again, this time in a packet boat, the *Antelope*.

On 22 October 1785, a few days before embarking in the midst of this spiralling transatlantic dispute, Davison was raised to the status of master mason, the third degree of freemasonry, evidence of his deep commitment to the craft. His initiation ceremony was performed by Thomas Aylwin, the provincial grand master. 'Health, peace and good will to all the enlightened,' read Alick's certificate;

> We the principal officers of Merchant Lodge No. 1 by virtue of a warrant from the Grand Lodge in London, whose supremacy we carefully acknowledge, certify that the worthy and beloved Brother Alexander Davison Esquire was by us initiated into the first, passed to the second, and raised to the sublime degree of Masonry, and performed his work to our satisfaction. Therefore we recommend him to all the Royal Craft. May the peace of the Grand Architect of the Universe ever attend him.

With Davison on his way back to London, Nepean repeatedly pressed Sydney to settle the matter of the leases. In December he gave Haldimand a reason for the minister's prevarication. 'Mr Grant has been using his influence among his Scotch friends to counteract your intentions as well as mine in favour of Davison,' Nepean reported. 'I have explained my sentiments to his Lordship fully tonight, & should think that he would hardly oppose the granting the lease you have recommended.'

Davison was back in London by 15 February 1786, when he accompanied Haldimand to the studio of the painter John Francis Rigaud. Rigaud's portrait of Nelson, completed in 1781 and now at the National Maritime Museum in Greenwich, is one of the few images of the young man Davison met in Quebec. Over dinner with Haldimand three weeks later, Lord Sydney confirmed that the Davisons had won the leases. But there was still a hitch. William Pitt, the prime minister, was questioning the length of the leases. George Davison was 'much affected' by this delay, telling Haldimand that 'if the business failed it would destroy their credit in Canada'. Alick took solace in work, arranging ten shiploads of flour and biscuits for the army in Canada. The former governor was by now growing weary of the whole fraught affair and of the Davisons' incessant demands for him 'to interfere in Canadian affairs'. He confided in his journal that he thought Alexander Davison was a 'prater . . . who cannot be trusted'. Haldimand refused to plead with Pitt on the brothers' behalf, referring them to their patrons. It was sound advice. The 'exertions made by the Northumberland family' saw that Sydney's decision received royal assent in June. However, on Pitt's insistence the leases were reduced from sixteen to ten years, starting from October, with an option to extend by a further six years if all went well.

The leases gave the Davisons control of the trading posts at Chicoutimi, Malbaye, Tadousac, the Seven Islands and the Islets of Jeremie. Each of the posts was very remote, consisting of little more than a house for the trader, strengthened against Indian attack; stabling and a cowshed; and a wharf and a store for the trading goods and furs. The post at the Islets of Jeremie had a small church serving a small local community, but otherwise the traders lived solitary, sometimes perilous lives, cut off by the weather for weeks at a time.

Within months the Davisons' commercial status in Canada reached its apotheosis when they secured the crown lease to the St Maurice iron forge in Three Rivers, a fertile region between Quebec and Montreal. Benefiting from a plentiful local supply of excellent iron ore, the forge was the premier industrial business in Canada, possibly in the whole of North America. No fewer than five hundred people were employed making iron stoves, kettles, axes and hatchets for domestic use and export to Europe. Many of them could trace their ancestry to the Burgundians, imported with their iron-working skills by the French regime to work the forges. The pig iron that the forges produced was used as ballast in the merchantmen returning to Europe after exchanging their heavy cargoes of trading goods for furs.

When the lease to the forges suddenly became available in April 1786, following the unexpected death of the tenant, Alexander Davison, who owned the neighbouring seigniory of Gatineau, was given the chance of buying the remaining thirteen years of it for just £2,300. After the deal was signed, not only was unused iron ore worth at least £1,000 discovered at the forges, but the books revealed that Davison could expect to earn as much as £1,500 a year from the business.

George Davison, who was developing a model farm at nearby Rivière du Loup, could keep an eye on the forge for his brother. The farm was staffed by Northumbrians using – according to Robert Hunter's son, who visited George in 1785 – 'English principles of farming which were thought incompatible with this climate'. George lived in an elegant stone farmhouse called Lanton House with his cousin Jane Davison and her husband John Moffat. Hunter thought George 'quite lost there', although he carved out a considerable reputation as an agriculturist. Fragile health, however, which was evident in his letters as early as the 1760s, forced George back to the milder climate of England in winter with increasing frequency.

Davison cut his partner John Lees out of the deal for the king's posts. Lees was understandably furious, prising a share of the profits in the posts from Davison by 'threatening destruction to my friends, to whom we then owed money'. Nor did Thomas Dunn give up easily. He later sued the Davisons for £8,500 in compensation for over 21,000 beaver skins traded at the posts in their first year using goods the previous tenants had left behind. After arbitration, the Davisons paid out just £1,800.

Signature of the leases to the king's posts and the forge in September 1786 secured for Alick the key commercial interests in the province. Yet only two months later, barely speaking with his partner, his route to a seat on the legislative council blocked by his brother and by his enemies in the English Party, who were growing in confidence now Haldimand had gone, he sailed from Quebec for the last time, leaving George behind to look over his interests. Politics and commerce aside, there was another compelling reason to return to England. Harriett Gosling was the eighteen-year-old daughter of Robert Gosling, a prosperous Fleet Street banker living in Lincoln's Inn Fields, close to Davison's lodgings. In every way, Harriett was an eminently suitable wife for a successful 37-year-old merchant. She was, of course, young, pretty and affectionate; but also, more importantly, she came from a highly respectable family which was anchored in commercial society. She would bring Alick status, a good dowry and financial security. He in turn could offer her the possibility of great riches and future position. It was a shrewd merger. Davison proposed, she accepted, Robert Gosling happily approved and the couple married at St Leonard's Church in Shoreditch on a cold February morning in 1788.

After taking his wife on a whirlwind tour of Northumberland, Davison bought a house in Bloomsbury, an area of London colonized by successful merchants, bankers and lawyers. Number 4 Harpur Street, off Theobalds Road, was ideally situated for both the City and the West End and was only a short walk from Harriett's parents. It was here, before dawn on 19 December, after months of nervous anxiety, that Davison's new household doubled in size when first Hugh Percy and then, fifteen minutes later, his twin William were born. Hugh Percy, known as Percy, was loyally named after Davison's patron Lord Percy, who had by now succeeded his father to become the second duke of Northumberland. The same evening, with Harriett resting upstairs, Evan Nepean and Frederick Haldimand joined Alick and his parents-in-law for a celebration at Harpur Street. Haldimand recalled that before the happy party settled down to play whist, 'the two children were brought in who seemed to give pleasure to the grandfather etc.' Within five years three daughters followed the twins: Elizabeth, Harriett and Dorothy or 'Doddy'.

Like other successful men, Davison took a villa in the countryside west of London. It was a place to escape the city and a stepping-stone to the planned country seat. Sipson House in

Middlesex was a small, elegant house standing in its own grounds off the Bath road, midway between the duke of Northumberland's splendid seat at Syon House and Langley Grove, the Goslings' villa in Colnbrook. The house, which was leased from a Mrs Barnsley, would become a valuable retreat for the family in the frequently turbulent days ahead. It survives today, close to the perimeter fence of Heathrow airport.

When Davison dined with Nepean and Haldimand on 12 July 1790 he confided 'that probably he would never go back to Canada'. His partnership with John Lees, which had never been the same since 'that Gentleman's extraordinary and irritating conduct to me in 1786', was dissolved the next year when Lees, disillusioned with the cut and thrust of business, retired from commercial life to concentrate on politics. Matthew Bell, one of Davison's Northumbrian protégés, was given control of the remaining businesses. In London, Davison maintained a close eye on Canadian affairs by running errands for John Simcoe, the lieutenant governor of the newly created region of Upper Canada, a friend of Northumberland and a longstanding freemason. Simcoe had been appointed in place of Sir Guy Carleton's preferred candidate, causing Davison to hope that the influence of his formidable old opponent was now 'dwindling to nothing'.

Davison's diverse tasks included sending the London newspapers over to Simcoe and arranging for two hundred silver medals to be struck for the garrison in Quebec. In effect, he became Simcoe's eyes and ears in England, a role he was to revive later in partnership with Nelson. It was a good strategy. Although Davison was thousands of miles away, William Smith, the chief justice in Quebec, assured Nepean that his interests were kept well in mind: 'we look for Davison every moment. He shall have every good office within my small sphere.' Simcoe rewarded Davison's loyalty in 1793 by naming him sole agent of supply to the army in North America. Davison was delighted, promising to 'feed the king's soldiers well'. The dinner he enjoyed that evening at Harpur Street with Nepean and Haldimand would be one of the last occasions on which the three friends were together. Soon afterwards Evan Nepean, who Lord Grenville thought was 'killing himself by his labour', was sent to the West Indies to recover his health; and within a year Haldimand was dead, falling ill on a visit to Switzerland in June 1791.

Davison's business activities were expanding fast. Using his contacts with Lord Sydney, he acquired the contract to supply goods, including hospital stores, clothing and tools, to the new and rapidly growing convict colony in New South Wales, a business worth over £80,000 to him between 1789 and 1793, or almost one-quarter of the total cost of establishing the colony, including shipping the convicts, during those years. 'Having had so much to do with the settlement of New South Wales,' Davison boldly proposed, in a letter to the home secretary, Henry Dundas, that he set up a post on Madagascar with a view to the more economical supply of the colony, 'so as to lighten the burthen of the present expense of it to government'.

Davison's influence was now such that George Matcham, who was married to Nelson's sister Kate, even approached him in the course of his attempt to secure 'ten or twenty thousand acres' of land in New South Wales: the first recorded instance of a member of Nelson's family looking to Davison for help. After making a fortune with the East India Company, Matcham was turning his attention to farming; and, having bought an estate in Hampshire to improve, he wanted the farm in Australia for his younger son, George (another son was later named after Davison), though he was briefly tempted to settle there himself. Matcham confided to his other brother-in-law, Maurice Nelson, that 'I had much rather enjoy the abundance of a country life under a fine sky in a distant part of the British Government than hazard the precarious profession of a merchant in the city, and an attachment to our Empire and Government has alone prevented me from buying land in the new settlement of Kentucky.' Maurice was probably roped into the scheme because he worked at the Navy Office, which was responsible for settling the colony; he thought Matcham's idea was 'visionary'. The land was secured and twenty years later Matcham's son George eventually went out to farm it.

In a rare setback, Davison's tender to transport the convicts in the second fleet to sail to the colony failed after he stipulated that the East India Company should charter his ships to carry tea as 'back freight' on the return journey. The contract was awarded instead to a consortium of slave merchants who undercut Davison's price of £25 a head by £2 15s without demanding the promise of back freight. One of the slavers' ships, *Neptune*, was captained by Evan Nepean's younger brother Nicholas. The government would come to regret its parsimonious decision. One in four of the convicts died en route in a shameful episode embarrassing the administration and causing bitterness to this day. The next contract issued after this shocking news reached London was given to Davison, who charged £2,400 to ship an unknown number of convicts and settlers out to the colony in *Bellona* in June 1792.

Davison's defeat over the contract for the second fleet indicates his steadfast refusal to countenance uncommercial activities, such as returning empty ships from the Far East. When his transport the *Daedalus* was leased to the Admiralty in July 1792 he made sure to ask its commander, Captain New, to do some trading on the side. The home secretary, Henry Dundas, sent *Daedalus* to Nootka Bay on the north west coast of America. On board was a Lieutenant Hergast who carried orders from Dundas to take possession of several territories ceded to Britain by Spain in a recent treaty. *Daedalus* would also deliver provisions for *Discovery*, a ship which was surveying the Pacific coast of America in an expedition planned by the famous botanist Sir Joseph Banks. An astronomer called Gooch was invited to join *Daedalus* to take observations during the voyage. From America Captain New would continue to New South Wales with a cargo of livestock for the colony. *Daedalus* would then be placed at the disposal of the governor, Arthur Phillip, who would use the ship to collect supplies from China and India. It was here that Davison saw an opportunity to take greater advantage of the voyage. He asked New to load his ship with furs in Canada to trade with the East India Company in Canton. As *Daedalus* was going to China anyway, this would show Davison, as he remarked to Thomas Parry, the Company's supercargo in Canton, 'a considerable saving to me in the freight'. The voyage was quickly overwhelmed by tragedy, however. Six months after leaving England, before even reaching Nootka Sound, Hergast and Gooch were murdered by natives while collecting water on Woahoo in the South Seas. The ship limped on, eventually completing its three-year round journey using Spanish sailors. There is no record of a successful trade in China.

The French Revolution barely interrupted Davison's smooth rise to commercial power. Restrictions on trading with France could be bypassed with a bit of imagination, and the chaos in Paris offered global opportunities to British merchants at the expense of their French rivals. To a man of Davison's Whiggish outlook, clipping the wings of an absolutist monarch echoed the success of the Glorious Revolution in England a century before. But as the revolution gathered bloody pace, more radical societies, with distinctly republican tendencies, started to spring up in England, drawing inspiration from the populist views of writers like Thomas Paine. Paine's *The Rights of Man* not only espoused conflict between society and state but attacked the sanctity of personal property, the rock upon which Davison had built his life. By 1792 the rise of republicanism in England, reports of massacres in Paris and an upsurge of rebellious activity in Ireland had swung opinion strongly against the ideals of the French revolutionaries and their sympathizers.

'The affairs of Ireland and even those of Great Britain are taking a very serious aspect,' Davison reported to Simcoe in November:

that epidemical spirit for mischief which has been operating under the mask of reform, or a moderate application for redress of grievances, is growing fast into disorder and rebellion. The stupor which had lulled those in power is however now going off and all ranks of people who have any penetration and regard for the tranquillity of these countries are actually alarmed at the heights the frenzy for innovation and change has and may rise to . . . The writings of Paine and all the inflammatory Societies would have probably been harmless had not the dreadful lesson been given in Paris which a desperate and numerous rabble can do against the efforts of a Government united with the general sense of those inhabitants who possessed the chief part of the property, commerce and character in the country. I hope at the meeting of Parliament to see a manly and truly patriotic spirit on all sides, upon the interesting question of the state of the country, with respect to the tranquillity of the people and the means of establishing good order on a permanent basis.

Davison hoped that the prime minister, William Pitt, and Charles Fox, the popular leader of the Whigs, would bury their bitter differences and

come forward with a plan of granting relief to the people of the three Kingdoms in certain admitted hardships, and on the other hand settle and proceed on a vigorous system of procedure towards those miscreants who have offended against the laws and peace of society. Nine tenths of the Nation would applaud such conduct in Parliament, and support Government and good order against the schemes of a banditti of zealots who may hope to succeed in schemes of rapine and plunder under the specious and insinuating terms of liberty and equality.

The government did act. It established the police department under the aegis of Dundas, the home secretary, and an Aliens Office was set up to keep an eye on foreigners. The management of both departments was given to Evan Nepean, who had been gathering intelligence on revolutionaries for years through a network of informers in London's taverns and coffee houses. Seeing Nepean back in harness after his brief sojourn in the West Indies,

Davison commented that his friend was again so overstretched that 'it is melancholy at times to see him . . . I may without exaggeration say almost the whole official business is now thrown upon his shoulders and it is the astonishment of every person how he holds it out.'

From his suppliers, Davison heard reports of bulk buying by French contractors, a sure sign of a coming conflict. Many were struggling to complete their orders. John Maitland, who made blankets and greatcoats, exclaimed that 'our House is crowded with French men every day who buy anything at almost any price'. France declared war on Britain on 1 February 1793. Three days later Davison sent Simcoe the *Morning Chronicle* containing an account of the 'extraordinary' execution of King Louis XVI. Davison regretted the war – 'it would have been better could it possibly have been prevented' – but he was supremely confident of a swift victory. 'We cannot fail being very successful,' he assured Simcoe; 'we are far advanced in preparations, I hope sufficient in a short time so to destroy their fleet as will require a century to reinstate it.' In the event, with barely a respite, the war lasted twenty-two years.

Within days of the declaration of war an expeditionary force commanded by the duke of York, the king's younger son, was ordered to Flanders. The duke was confident that he could quickly overwhelm the dissolute and disorganized republicans, reach Paris and win the war. The only obstacle was getting the army to Flanders in the first place, as the Navy Board was quite unable to cope with moving so many men overseas at such short notice. When, on Nepean's advice, the navy commissioners turned to Davison for help, the necessary transports were found in just five days. It was a good time to be a military contractor. The demand for supplies rose so steeply on the outbreak of war that Davison soon happily complained that 'the business which the Government has given me fully occupies my time'.

Large numbers of royalist émigrés began arriving on the south coast of England, fleeing the Terror in France. The British government was encouraged, however, by the numbers of royalist insurgencies which were flaring up in the French provinces. In October Lord Moira was appointed to lead a force to aid the most hopeful of these uprisings, in the Vendée in western France.

Moira was another close political ally and friend of the duke of Northumberland. They had served together during the American War where, according to the duke, Moira 'distinguished himself in a most remarkable manner' at the battle of Bunker Hill. In America Moira earned a reputation as a martinet, with a dark, brooding presence which terrified his troops but fascinated women. Lady Bessborough commented that, 'if Lord Moira would shave off the black whiskers that grow just under his eyes and almost across his nose, he would be quite handsome'. His most persistent fault was his wilful extravagance, which kept him teetering on the edge of ruin, and eventually dependent on Davison, for most of his life.

Moira and Northumberland were bonded by their shared opposition to Pitt and regard for the prince of Wales, whose confidence they both enjoyed. When the prince was installed as grand master of the freemasons in England in 1790, three years after his initiation, he asked Moira – the 'don' – to be his acting grand master. The prince's involvement with freemasonry typified the fascination the craft held for royalty and, predominantly, the Whig aristocracy at the time. These powerful men were drawn to freemasonry not simply by its patriotism and emphasis on civic responsibility and law and order, but because the source of its ideological strength was the Bible, which – as they interpreted it – taught that all men were equal before God but that some were more equal than others on earth. This ideology uniquely allowed the aristocracy to fraternize with members of a lower rank while still claiming the greatest respect.

Moira struggled to build a force he considered large enough to be effective in the Vendée. He pressed the government to give him more troops and artillery, insisting that a commissariat be established as soon as possible on the south coast to manage his army's supplies. In the circumstances the choice of Davison as commissary-general (possibly recommended to Moira by the duke of Northumberland) was unsurprising. Moira testified later that they had never met, but that Davison was ideally suited for the role, being reliable, well connected and highly regarded as a contractor and agent at the Treasury and the Navy Board. Brook Watson had gone to Flanders as commissary-general for the duke of York's army. The duke of Northumberland was in Spain with a small expeditionary force; it achieved little, and by August 1793 he was enjoying court life in Lisbon with the duchess, though he kept his eyes open, complaining that the Portuguese were playing 'fast and loose' with the trading embargoes imposed by the war.

Davison's pay was a handsome £5 a day. The position also brought him further valuable commercial influence, notwith-standing the Treasury's insistence that a commissary-general should not profit from his position. Yet although he carried the authority of an officer, the commissary-general, caught as he was between the imperative of economy and the demands of the sol-dier's stomach, enjoyed the same low reputation in the army as a purser in a warship. He worked under the constant suspicion, shared by troops and Treasury alike, that he was, at the very least, on the make and probably fraudulent. The duke of Wellington later observed that 'the prejudices of society against a commissary almost prevent him from receiving the common respect due to the character of a gentleman'. William Windham, the secretary for war, compared the commissariat to the 'Cinderella of the fable, which is sacrificed in every instance to her more favoured sisters; but which may prove like her, in the end, the only one deserving of favour and attention'.

Davison's attachment to Moira's army received royal assent on 21 November 1793. His first task was to order equipment and to hire his staff. One of the first people he approached was Maurice Nelson, Nelson's eldest brother, whom he asked to be his assistant. Maurice, a quiet, diligent man of forty, was languishing

Maurice Nelson, Nelson's unprepossessing eldest brother, who abandoned the Navy Office to work alongside Davison on the commissariat.

as a clerk in the Navy Office. He lived with his blind wife Sukey in a small house in Rathbone Place, close to Oxford Street and convenient for the Navy Office's magnificent new premises at Somerset House on the Strand. Despite over twenty years' service, Maurice's annual salary was still no more than £60 – just enough for him to rent a cottage as well, by the Thames at Laleham in Surrey.

Davison liked Maurice, whom he must have met often within the corridors of Somerset House, and welcomed this unexpected opportunity to improve his prospects. Disillusioned with his stalled career, flattered by the invitation and lured by a wage of £1 5s a day, Maurice overcame his natural caution and resigned his position to take up the new offer. He was immediately despatched to Exeter to buy hay for the commissariat. Maurice's father, the Revd Edmund Nelson, warmly welcomed his eldest son's bold move. 'I do heartily rejoice,' he wrote to his son on Christmas Eve 1793, 'and that with every tender feeling of a parent, that you have been at last successful in your solicitation for some appointment.' Maurice's younger brother, who had resumed his naval career after five years 'on the beach' in Norfolk, was more sceptical. 'I wish Maurice may have exchanged his place for a better,' he confided to his wife Fanny, 'but am fearful these temporary appointments are not of much use.' Nelson recognized Davison's growing political and commercial connections, however, consoling himself by conceding that if his brother 'made himself useful to Mr Davison, he can do something for him'.

'The confusion here is incredible,' Moira stormed in a letter to the prince of Wales in November, having arrived on the coast to embark his army for France. His troops were tangled up with another force about to sail for the West Indies escorted by Sir John Jervis, who had 'monopolized' all the boats at Portsmouth. Moira's army was still chronically ill-equipped and undermanned, forcing Davison, who remained in London, to buy fourteen thousand muskets for the troops himself 'upon his private credit as a merchant'. Three thousand of these promptly went missing, turning up, after a frantic search, with 'Badger the carrier' in Southampton. Badger claimed he had become confused by so many wooden cases marked AD. To make matters worse, five thousand Hessian troops airily promised by Henry Dundas, recently appointed new secretary of state for war, failed to materialize. So when Moira sailed on 1 December, unable to delay any longer for fear that 'we shall find the Royalists beaten', he took fewer than five thousand men with him, less than a quarter of the army he wanted.

Davison, reaching the coast himself a few days after Christmas, discovered a chaotic and miserable scene. Moira and his pitiful force were already back, having failed even to make contact with the royalist insurgents in the Vendée. With the government hesitating over how to redeploy his troops, who remained on their transports in appalling conditions, a despondent Moira returned to London, 'ignorant of what is destined in regard for us'. To make matters worse, fifteen thousand bedraggled royalist evacuees had arrived following the fall of Toulon to the republicans, stretching to breaking point the limited resources of the towns and villages on the English south coast.

Davison, billeted in Cowes on the Isle of Wight and crossing daily to Southampton on a sloop provided by the Navy Board, worked efficiently and energetically. He pressed the Treasury for money and resources, set up stores, requisitioned equipment and ordered supplies of coal, hay and straw for Moira's hapless army. When typhus broke out among the troops marooned in the Solent, Davison purchased tobacco to fumigate their transports. Porter was bought for the men in hospital at Southampton. In February a transport from Deptford finally arrived carrying the materials Davison had ordered for the commissariat before Christmas. Accompanying all the tarpaulins, scales, funnels, camp kettles and stationery were over sixty people, including bakers, coopers, bricklayers, wagon drivers and clerks. A month later Maurice arrived from Exeter, having shipped more than 140 tons of hay to Portsmouth and the Channel Islands. 'I live with Mr D,' he wrote enthusiastically to Sukey from Cowes, '[and] if I may be allowed to judge his friendship increases.' Davison's efforts soon made an impact. When Moira returned from London some weeks later, he commented to the prince, with evident surprise, that his camp was now 'in very good order'.

Growing fearful of a French invasion, the government decided to leave Moira's army where it was, and the troops were disembarked into temporary barracks at Cowes, Lymington and Southampton. The stores on the Channel Islands, which Davison had so carefully prepared for Moira's aborted expedition, were recovered and the commissariat moved closer to army headquarters at Lyndhurst.

As well as providing for the everyday needs of the army, Davison was increasingly called upon by Moira to pay lavish gratuities to the many émigré officers arriving from France as refugees or for deployment in various unspecified 'secret services'. Discreet payments were made to royalist secret agents like 'Le Père Elizée' and 'Elias Cabot'. These monies were generally delivered by Moira's military secretary, Captain John McMahon of the 87th Foot, 'an Irishman of low birth and obsequious manners' whose red face was covered in pimples. Moira, who spent much of his time in London or at Donington Park, his seat in Leicestershire, made little effort to rein in the excessive costs of his headquarters. The finest food and best wines were expected at supper, and there were frequent balls at which the prettiest girls from Hampshire were distracted by the sophisticated charms of the aristocratic émigré officers. Davison himself was viewed by the officers merely as a necessary civilian functionary, held, as so often in his life, slightly at arm's length. He was, however, very rich, and many of the officers, especially the commander-in-chief, Moira, took advantage of his eagerness to ingratiate himself with them by borrowing money at interest rates as high as 15 per cent.

Davison did not allow the onerous work of the commissariat to interfere with his other enterprises. He returned on leave to London whenever he could, breakfasting with John Maitland at the Gower Hotel in Bloomsbury to discuss their tenders for the clothing contracts that were constantly advertised in the *London Gazette*. When his efforts were rewarded by the lucrative contract to supply clothing to the marines, the comptroller of the navy, Sir Andrew Snape Hamond, commented that 'Mr Davison took the contract (his price being considerably lower than the rest) at a price which surprised the Navy Board very much, for it was considerably lower than that at which clothing had been supplied.' To meet these growing demands on his business, Davison established his own clothing factory in Bedford Street beside Covent Garden market, poaching Mungo Shedden from one of his suppliers to run it. The new factory hit Maitland's business hard and he grew jealous of Shedden, unfairly accusing him of dishonesty. The relationship between Maitland and Davison deteriorated still further when Davison later embroiled his associate in a dubious scheme to circumvent the ban on trading in French goods by shipping brandy to America, where it could be exchanged for tobacco to sell in Britain. Davison saw nothing 'morally wrong' with the scheme, which he openly described as 'smuggling'. He was furious when Maitland had qualms and withdrew, punishing his erstwhile partner by withholding payment on other goods.

'Whatever epithet the Brandy Speculation deserves,' he stormed at Maitland, 'you were perfectly acquainted with its nature and object before you engaged in it.'

The outraged Maitland replied: 'My God Davison is this treatment I have deserved from you who has assured me that every advantage he gained from Government Business was through me.'

The dispute, which echoed Davison's falling out with John Halsted over the American horse-trading scheme, lasted until 1805 when it was settled by arbitration.

In May 1794 Moira was ordered to embark a force as quickly as possible to reinforce the duke of York who, despite his early optimism, faced losing his whole army in Flanders. As Moira's army broke camp, Lord Howe's fleet returned to

Portsmouth after its great victory out in the Atlantic on the 'Glorious First of June' – the first sea battle of the war. Trailing behind the British ships were six shattered French prizes, full of the dead and dying, an image which surely impressed itself on Davison. On 27 June King George himself visited the town to inspect the prizes and to present Howe with a sword and a gold medal.

With Moira gone at last, Davison moved the commissariat to join the Royal Artillery, the 5th, 7th and 9th Heavy Dragoons and the Irish Cavalry at Netley, outside Southampton. He was facing increasing difficulties. After months of supporting mounting numbers of troops, the whole region was becoming 'drained of its natural supplies'. Davison's local suppliers were struggling to cope with his orders because of the shortages. Their profits were also being squeezed by the high labour costs caused by the summer harvest and inflated prices in the winter when the cavalry demanded increased hay rations. Furthermore, Davison was becoming inundated by compensation claims from local landowners for broken fences and damaged crops, while his stores of beef, pork and biscuits on the Isle of Wight were constantly being robbed. Much of the flour being stored in transports on the Solent turned sour before it was shipped to Flanders.

At Netley Davison became more closely involved with the various émigré corps camped around Lymington, Lyndhurst and Iron Hill. The government in London had finally woken up to the potential of these bonus troops which, bolstered by French prisoners of war, could be used to spearhead an invasion of France without resorting to yet another major expedition by the British army. Encouraged by intelligence reports of renewed royalist guerrilla activity in western France, the government started planning a raid on Brittany. Nepean asked Davison to arrange 'an immediate supply of money' for the émigrés. 'Look about you,' he advised his friend, 'and see if some barracks can not be appropriated to their use – at any rate whatever may be absolutely necessary to them ought to be furnished.' By now the broadening of the commissariat's role, the late accounting and the rash of large, unauthorized payments were ringing alarm bells in Whitehall. In November, Davison was summoned to explain himself before the lords commissioners of the Treasury in an attempt to re-establish 'harmony'.

While in London Davison received a letter from Lieutenant-General Oliver De Lancey, the barrackmaster-general. De Lancey, the scion of a New York family whose cousin Stephen had been inspector of loyalists in Quebec, was in charge of an ambitious and innovative programme of barrack-building that Pitt had initiated at the beginning of the war. In his letter De Lancey, frustrated by 'the uncertainty arising from trusting to contractors', invited Davison to become the sole agent of supply to the barracks in Britain. Using agents on commission to source supplies, rather than relying on contractors to meet the needs of the military, marked a shift in policy from previous wars. It not only reduced the administrative burden on an already over-stretched government but it also put the business of supply into the hands of those most able, and experienced, to complete it.

De Lancey proposed paying Davison a 'moderate commission' for sourcing and purchasing all the goods necessary to fit out the new barracks, including a regular supply of coal. Davison's account with his suppliers and his commission would be settled by the Treasury, which could, 'if required', check that Davison was buying the goods at the best possible market price. De Lancey conceded that 'In the course of conducting the business, there will be many circumstances which will require more particular explanation and arrangement, but which will of necessity be made the subject of further instruction.'

'My house', Davison replied on 10 January 1795 after careful consideration, 'is disposed to undertake the business on the footing which you state, of an Agent upon Commission.' He suggested a commission of $2\frac{1}{2}$ per cent 'upon the whole amount', which included his costs of insurance, packing and shipping, because it 'will require my house to be devoted to the business, which from its minuteness, in every measure, will render a continued application absolutely necessary'. Anticipating the need to stockpile goods against 'a bare or speculative market', Davison insisted that he should be allowed to draw down cash advances from the Treasury whenever necessary and to act on 'verbal orders' when written ones would take too long.

The terms agreed solely by this exchange of letters, Davison took a large warehouse next to his clothing factory in Bedford Street to handle the barrack-office business. John Lodge, who had worked for Davison since 1784, was employed as chief packer. Within a year Davison had supplied the barrack office with more than £230,000 worth of goods.

Davison soon realized that the business of delivering coal to the barracks would have to be handled differently from the supply of clothing. A single warehouse to store coal for the whole country would be completely impractical; instead, depots would have to be built in several different locations. Unsurprisingly De Lancey baulked at the expense that would involve and was no doubt grateful when Davison offered to supply the coal as a contractor, working with a network of coal dealers to deliver supplies through their existing arrangements, rather than as an agent. 'I can', he assured the barrackmaster-general, 'from the connections I have in the best coal countries, execute the business upon as favourable terms as any person.' To secure the contract, and to prevent De Lancey putting it out to tender, Davison volunteered to supply the coal to the barracks at a price no higher than the local market price at each place. Under this arrangement, only one coal depot would have to be built to service the barracks clustered around London. Millbank, opposite Lambeth Palace and a short distance upriver from the Palace of Westminster, was chosen as the site of the new depot. The river was less choked here than closer to the City, and the site was within easy reach of the open roads of Chelsea which led to the barracks at Knightsbridge and beyond.

The subtle distinction between Davison's functions for the

barrack office is worth dwelling on; for disagreement over it later cost him his freedom. Davison himself defined it as follows:

> *by the engagement of general supply I was to act as an agent upon commission; whereas by the engagement for the supply of coal, I was not to act as agent on commission but to supply the article at what might happen to be the price of the day, at the place of delivery, whether more or less than what I paid for it. The second distinction is to support my charge for coal, I was* bound to produce *a certificate of the price of the day, at the place of delivery, whereas by my engagement as to general supply I was bound to produce a certificate of the price being fair and reasonable* only in the event of the Barrack Office requiring it.

Throughout May 1795, amid chaotic scenes, the émigré forces gathered at the ports on the south coast. 'We are very busy preparing for a secret expedition,' Maurice excitedly revealed to his sister-in-law Fanny Nelson. Finally, in fine hot weather on 17 June, a force of 3,500 émigrés, the vanguard for the much larger invasion army, sailed for Brittany escorted by a squadron from the Channel fleet under Sir John Borlase Warren. There was great jubilation when the news reached Southampton a few days later that the émigrés had successfully landed on the Quiberon peninsula. William Pitt invited the comte d'Artois, the brother of the executed French king, to lead the invasion army in person on board *Jason*. The émigrés would be supported by a force of British troops commanded by Moira, who had returned to England 'out of delicacy' to his superiors in Flanders. But royalist dreams of a breakthrough were tragically short-lived. Before the invasion army could land, blue-coated troops of the republican army swooped on Brittany and executed over six hundred of the émigrés who had sailed in such high hopes from Cowes just weeks earlier. 'The unhappy emigrants could gain no footing in their native country,' Edmund Nelson reported to 'dear Hor' in September:

the hearts of some recoiled and could not support the trial of
fighting against their own household, laid down their arms or
turned against their leaders, others fell into the hands of their
cruel foes and are destroyed, some returned to British asylums,
and are again embarked to join the Royalists . . . it will be the
language of many that this Pittian Minister will not attend to
the loud calls of his countrymen 'Give us Peace'.

The invasion was abandoned. Undaunted, d'Artois returned to Portsmouth and persuaded the British government to escort his force to the Vendée instead. Moira's role was reduced to keeping the émigrés' lines of communication open. Nelson, who was cruising off Italy in *Agamemnon*, was dubious about the plan. 'The people say the army is true to the convention,' he wrote to Fanny, 'and they do not think the Comte d'Artois will be successful. If he is to be, I pray God it may be soon and let us have peace.' There was naturally no mention in his letter of the sexual dalliance he was openly enjoying with an opera singer called Adelaide Correglia in Leghorn. Nelson's blatant affair embarrassed many of his fellow officers. 'Dined with Nelson,' Captain Thomas Freemantle wrote to his wife one evening; 'Dolly aboard, who has a sort of abscess in her side . . . he makes himself ridiculous with that woman.'

While waiting to sail, d'Artois enjoyed his celebrity status. Unable to land in England for fear of being arrested for debt, the comte entertained a stream of politicians and society figures in *Jason*, all of them curious to meet the brother of the executed French king. At George III's personal request, Henry Dundas ordered Moira to arrange a gratuity of £10,000 to be paid to the royal exile. On 22 August Moira passed the request to Davison, reminding him to ask for a receipt and 'to keep this article separate from ordinary charges'. No record exists of the meeting in *Jason*, but Davison must have revelled in attending the brother of Louis XVI.

On 26 August d'Artois sailed for the Vendée at the head of

a fleet of sixty vessels. The émigrés were accompanied by a British force of four thousand – not including Lord Moira, who had resigned when he heard that he would not be involved in the invasion itself. *The Times* mused that Moira's resignation would be 'severally felt by the emigrants. Pine-apples and the Donington venison must be changed for economical broth and cutlets.' They would also miss the blank cheques Moira habitually left in their bedrooms when they stayed at Donington Park. Unsurprisingly, Moira's debts were now rising steeply. Davison lent him £15,000, £5,000 of which was secured against the Loughborough Navigation, an ambitious scheme to cut a canal across Moira's estate in Leicestershire, the remainder by bond. Davison lodged this bond with William Smart, his banker in Lombard Street, alongside the deeds of his marriage settlement and 'Lines of Mrs Davison which I value more than all the rest', presumably love letters.

With d'Artois and the army gone, Davison set about winding up the commissariat. His staff was disbanded and the surplus stocks of flour and oats sent for auction in Ireland. Maurice, who according to Fanny 'had grown stout' at the commissariat, was asked by the Treasury to return to the Navy Office 'to execute some business the commissioners of the navy wish to employ him in'. Edmund Nelson was told in the Pump Room at Bath that the business in the Navy Office had 'stood still' without his son. Nelson was 'glad' when he heard this news; but he was concerned that Maurice was returning to Somerset House in a lower position than before, and hoped his brother had saved up during his time with the commissariat. Politely, he wrote to Davison, thanking him for 'the kind method you have taken for effectually serving my dear brother'.

Davison stayed behind in Southampton to embark Sir Ralph Abercrombie, who was replacing Moira as commander-in-chief of the British element of the invading force. Abercrombie, like Moira and Sir John Borlase Warren, was an active freemason. When d'Artois reappeared in November, having failed to make any advance in the Vendée, it seemed for a time that Davison might even have to accompany Abercrombie's army on a hastily rearranged expedition to the West Indies, which would have been extremely inconvenient for him. Only when an alternative commissary-general was found in January 1796 was Davison released. He left as soon as he could for his new country house in Northumberland.

Swarland House near Morpeth was a substantial four-storey mansion built some thirty years before in the fashionable Palladian style and commanding, the sale agent had boasted, 'an extensive view of the sea coast, rich cultivated plains, and barren mountains'. The main building was a solid square, with rectangular windows on the principal floor and square windows on the bedroom floor, all within plain mouldings. The half-sunk ground floor was distinguished by roughened stonework. Two short wings on the north side of the house enclosed a small courtyard and a covered carriageway, while on the south side there was a three-bayed pillared portico with steps leading down to the gardens and grounds. 'These and the woods are thriving,' continued the agent in timeless fashion, 'which with the hedges are well adapted for breeding and preserving game.' On the surrounding estate were a home farm, a sawmill and a small coal mine, one of the many that dotted the Northumbrian coastline. Swarland was convenient both for Lanton, which Alick's brother Jack was now farming, and for Alnwick Castle, the daunting seat of Davison's 'best friend', the duke of Northumberland.

Davison had purchased Swarland House in March 1795, raising a mortgage of £12,500 against its price of £27,250 and paying the balance in cash. Within a year another £4,500 was spent doing the house up in the latest fashion under Harriett's direction. Cases packed in London with expensive linen, glass, china and paintings became a familiar sight as they arrived by sea at Alnmouth for forwarding to Swarland.

The hall, with its grand staircase, was at the heart of the house, leading from the main entrance on the north front through to the drawing room, the dining room, Davison's writing room, the 'farmers' waiting room' and the library. Beside the hall was a small water closet, reserved for women. Beneath the 'grand stairs' was a substantial cellar which soon filled with the very best wines. Above the drawing room were Harriett's bedroom and her dressing room, overlooking the gardens which soon became her passion. Davison's bedroom, with double bed, was on the opposite side of the house, with a water closet for his private use outside it in the east passage. The kitchen was next to 'Mr Davison's armory' in the east wing. The servants' bedrooms, the 'boot rooms, fish rooms, root and vegetable rooms' were all in the west wing. Fourteen servants lived in when the family were in residence including May the cook, Stephen the butler, Robert Tenwick the steward, the under-butler, the upper footman, the under-footmen and sundry housemaids, laundry maids and kitchen maids. The gamekeeper, coachmen, grooms, woodmen and gardeners all lived out. The tasks of the servants appear frequently to have overlapped. The grooms were occasionally expected to double up as footmen, for instance, or even help the gardeners (which they probably resented). The footmen wore yellow morning coats with striped waistcoats and black woollen breeches. They put on olive brown top coats when they rode behind the Davisons' carriage to church.

Davison insisted on discipline and order. He expected his servants to be 'kind, civil and polite' and neat and clean at all times. Bad language and gaming were strictly prohibited. The male servants were expressly ordered never to frequent public houses or – and Davison was quite insistent on this point – 'to interfere with the maid servants'. 'No man servant is permitted to enter the apartments of any female servant – nor allowed to go into the laundry – this article to be strictly obeyed – under the greatest displeasure.' All the servants had a duty of ensuring that no strangers or, worse, beggars, approached the house. Davison prized his privacy.

He was also a stickler for punctuality, and the house ran to a strict routine. The day began for the under-footmen at six o'clock with the 'dirty work' of cleaning knives and bringing in coal for laying the fires ('I forbid heaping on coals and that the fires never appear above the bars as they did last winter when the house had been nearly set on fire by the quantity of coals put upon it'). In the stables the grooms and coachmen cleaned the carriage and the harnesses and fed and dressed the horses. Davison was very particular about his horses. 'I do not allow any horse of mine to be mounted or any way used during my absence,' he ordered, insisting that 'no strangers be permitted into my stables or meddle with my horses'. The family breakfasted at nine o'clock, dining at six in the summer and half-past five in the winter: a much later hour than had been usual when Davison was young. Bells were rung for the family half an hour before each meal and again when the food was on the table. 'When the family has taken their seats,' Davison instructed the under-footmen,

> you will keep your eyes about you ready and alert on waiting and sharply removing dirty plates and replacing them with clean ones carefully avoiding awkwardness and on no account holding conversation with any one in the room, nor allow your voice to be heard – and when going to the kitchen for any dish or message, not to wait a moment but return to the dining room – this rule to be strictly obeyed – look how you set down your feet, lest you hit against a plate or any thing else to the annoyance of the company – avoid rattling the knives and forks upon the plates – let your voice never be heard above your breath.

After the family retired, Davison expected the house to be locked up and the servants in bed no later than ten o'clock.

Swarland House was pulled down in the 1950s. No physical trace of it survives, and it exists now only in the memory of a few elderly residents in the village and a handful of fading photographs. Bindweed, nettles and grass quickly reclaimed the ground once occupied by Davison's library, his elegant drawing room and his 'private wine cellar under grand stairs'. Harriett's hothouses and vines, her mushroom beds and carefully tended fruit trees are long gone. Silence and emptiness now fill that previously bustling space. But the 'extensive view' remains, and a palpable emotional charge lingers in the footprint of Davison's lost mansion.

The family's excitement at their new house was overwhelmed by tragedy in April 1796 when little Harriett died of whooping cough 'after a long lingering illness'. She was four years old. Her tiny body was interred beside her grandfather in the Goslings' family vault at St Mary-the-Virgin in Langley, Buckinghamshire.

Celebrations were therefore muted when the family gathered to spend that Christmas in Bath. They stayed in Great Poultney Street, close to Edmund Nelson's lodgings at 17 New King's Road. Edmund had arrived in the town in November with his daughter-in-law Fanny, who had led a peripatetic life since her husband's departure from England, flitting between London, Bath and Norfolk, sporadically house-hunting. Despite suffering frequent bouts of ill-health herself, looking after Edmund appealed to Fanny's sense of duty, while he was a source of comfort and support to her. They were rarely apart now, and would remain constant companions until his death. There was ample polite entertainment in Bath to keep Fanny occupied, but her thoughts were elsewhere. 'I long for to be with you,' she wrote to her husband in February 1797.

LEVIATHAN

74 GUNS,
CAPTAIN HENRY BAYNTUN

THE GOVERNMENT WAS EDGY. The campaign in Europe was going badly, with the collapse of the first anti-French coalition leaving Britain isolated against the revolutionary forces; British efforts to make peace had failed and the fear of a French invasion hovered like a dark cloud over the country. In December 1796 an attempt was made to land in Ireland, where, according to Davison, rebels promised 'mischief and destruction'. The war was unpopular in the country at large, and it was costing a fortune. The combination of military and economic menace was causing banks to fail and government stocks to crash; in February 1797 the Bank of England itself was even forced to suspend cash payments, albeit briefly.

The emergency soon rippled even the genteel waters of Bath, where that same month, according to Fanny Nelson, 'everybody are full of the talk of an invasion'. 'Scarcity of money is very great,' she reported anxiously a few weeks later; 'one hears of nothing but banks stopping.' She tried hard to get rid of any banknotes as soon as she got them, although one at least 'stuck fast'. The town, she noticed, was filling up with county families, who believed themselves safer there than in the country (the opposite of twentieth-century experience).

Everywhere volunteer military corps sprang up in response

to the mood of national emergency. The Percy Tenantry, raised by the duke of Northumberland from his estates in the north of England, was typical of many – except in that, whereas most such groups financed their own equipment and uniforms, its members ('a numerous and hardy race of men') were kitted out entirely by the duke. Davison, who supplied the corps with everything from swords to horses, calculated this cost his patron £20,000 a year. Soon the Percy Tenantry were one of the largest, certainly the grandest, corps in the whole country, with over six hundred infantrymen and four hundred cavalrymen. Davison, marvelling at the duke's munificence, confided to his friend Admiral Sir John Jervis that he thought it 'was the most princely thing ever done in this or perhaps in any other country'.

Despite all the dire omens, Davison remained positive about Britain's prospects. The diarist Joseph Farington commented that he was London's 'only comforter'. Davison steadfastly refused to talk of defeat, insisting instead that the English remained 'more rich and powerful than any other people'. This confidence seemed vindicated when Jervis smashed the Spanish fleet off Cape St Vincent on 14 February – which happened to be Fanny Nelson's birthday. Jervis was awarded an earldom in honour of his victory, but it was the daring of his subordinate, Horatio Nelson, which caught the eye of the commander-in-chief during the action and captured the public's imagination afterwards. Nelson was promoted to rear-admiral and knighted by the king.

One of the first people to hear of the victory and to send his congratulations to Nelson was his brother Maurice. To everyone's relief, Maurice had been reappointed to the position at Somerset House he had abandoned to join the commissariat – but only, he confided to his brother, after 'the most violent contest that almost ever took place at the Navy Board' and possibly a quiet word from Davison in the ear of Sir Andrew Snape Hamond, the comptroller of the navy. Maurice's salary was increased to a healthy £300 a year.

The afterglow of the victory off Cape St Vincent was

short-lived. In April 1797 the Channel fleet mutinied, first at Portsmouth and then at the mouth of the Thames, plunging the government into a potentially fatal new crisis. The dispute was ostensibly over food and conditions, although Maurice voiced the fear of many when he wrote of 'artful people behind the curtain'. The government faced insurrection not only in the fleet but also in parliament. Several MPs who, according to Davison, were 'virulent against Pitt, though they vote with him', began rallying behind Lord Moira in an attempt 'to save the country from the evident ruin into which it is most rapidly running'. Moira invited Northumberland to help him 'prevent this country from being reduced to the very lowest rank', although he conceded that 'to propose office to any man at present is nearly the same thing as proposing to him to be crucified'.

The duke, who was in Bath suffering from gout, heartily agreed that the country was running into the 'mire'. He blamed 'the French revolution and imbecility and arrogance of our present premier'. Yet he declined to take an active part in Moira's plan, citing in excuse his ill-health. The real reason, as he confided to Davison, was his towering pride: 'I feel that my own situation in this country is much above what any office in the kingdom can give me.' Northumberland urged Moira to involve Charles Fox, the popular leader of the Whigs in parliament. 'No administration', he warned, 'will last through two whole sessions of parliament with Mr Pitt & Mr Fox both in opposition to it.'

In fact, Northumberland had already received similar overtures to Moira himself, and was furious to be approached again – and in so indiscreet a manner. 'A more unsatisfactory & unconfidential one [letter] our good friend could not have wrote to his apothecary if he was a member of parliament & wished for his vote,' he stormed at Davison. 'Good God! Can our worthy friend conceive that I would thus pledge myself to act & join in office with persons without ever knowing their names, or being at all entrusted with the plans they wish to adopt, or the measures they wish to pursue? Does our good friend really think I am so greedy for office as to accept it in such a manner?' Moira was unimpressed by the duke's fulminations. 'The plan may go to the devil for what I care,' he retorted when he heard about Northumberland's letter from Davison: 'I am enough accustomed to rough weather to bear the impending storm.'

Davison was soon embroiled in Moira's political manoeuvrings himself. The Northumberland papers reveal a furious flurry of correspondence on the subject between the duke, Moira and Davison during May. Eventually Davison, stressing the need for secrecy, began shuttling in person between London and Bath – while remaining concerned, as his own leaking of the duke's intemperate letter about Moira shows, to avoid being compromised by either party. His strength, and his usefulness to both the duke and Moira, lay in his commercial and political connections, his independence and his ability to move easily between ranks. Moira, whose outlook was almost entirely dictated by the attitudes of the aristocratic clique surrounding the prince of Wales at Carlton House, was constitutionally unsuited to the role of conspirator. Davison knew his involvement with Moira's political cabal was risky, and was careful to avoid being seen publicly opposing his paymasters in the government; however, he took Northumberland's advice and acted as an intermediary with the Foxite Whigs. Charles Grey, Fox's great friend with whom Davison must have been familiar through their shared Northumbrian background, told him the Foxite Whigs were planning their own coup. Grey was trying to organize a petition 'for the removal of ministers'.

In May 1797 Charles Fox secretly met Moira to impress on him the need for them to combine their strengths for the assault on Pitt, united as they were in their desire for peace. Fox even offered to step aside in Moira's favour if necessary. But there was little realistic chance of success, whatever deal they cut between themselves, for the king's dislike of both men was intense and well known. Fox had been a royal irritant for years, and Moira was a close associate of the king's loathed son and heir, the prince of

Wales. Besides, the king was in no mood to ditch Pitt just yet. The royal will, the critical factor in any change of administration, was unmoved. On 26 May, following a heavy defeat in the House of Commons, Fox withdrew from active politics.

For a while Moira pressed on alone. He even sent Davison to Bath to ask the duke for names for his cabinet. The duke retorted that 'I have lived so long out of the world that I scarce know anybody,' surely prompting a loyal denial. But the game was up. After a last-ditch appeal to the king in June, Moira declared his hopes 'completely extinct'. Aware of whisperings that he had caused Fox's downfall, Moira retired to Donington Park to pen a long vindication of his recent actions. This he sent to John McMahon, his former military aide who was now private secretary to the prince of Wales, who, as Moira no doubt wished, passed it to *The Times*. Having read this rambling, self-righteous document, Earl Cornwallis, the master of ordnance, commented wearily on Moira's 'excess of vanity and self-importance': 'I am sure', he sighed, 'there was a time when he had sense.'

This episode illustrates Davison's mercurial skill at slipping easily between warring parties – a talent facilitated by his lack of social position. The duke later called upon the services of his 'ever devoted' friend when he became embroiled in a row with the government after resigning the lord lieutenancy of Northumberland in a fit of pique: in recruiting Davison as his 'lieutenant' in the highly charged negotiations to find a replacement, he happened on a good definition of the role Davison was to play for Nelson and others.

After the battle of Cape St Vincent, Davison wrote to Nelson offering to manage the sale of the Spanish ships, or prizes, that Nelson had captured during the action, and the distribution of the proceeds. Davison, always keen to diversify his business interests, considered himself ideally qualified for the role of prize agent. He was well connected at the Navy Office and the Admiralty, critical qualifications for steering prize work through the courts, while as a commissary-general he had mastered the labyrinthine world of government bureaucracy. He was also very rich, which might ease the traditional suspicions of the captors that their agent was on the make.

Prize money was the single most persuasive factor in luring the younger sons of the gentry into the navy in the first place and the one that, above all, kept the seamen to their duty. Before 1797, after some twenty-seven years' service, Nelson had received only about £2,000 – a sum he considered a 'trifling' amount, though it was probably about average at the time, bearing in mind his rank and the ebb and flow of war and peace during his career to date. Much of this money had been looked after by William Marsh, Nelson's navy agent at Marsh & Creed in Norfolk Street off the Strand. Not unusually, Marsh also doubled up as his client's banker. But although Marsh handled Nelson's prize proceeds he was not his prize agent, a role that required specific skills. For his small captures as a captain, Nelson had generally given the business to one of the large Mediterranean firms.

The situation was now very different. Nelson carried the authority and influence of a flag officer, and had been involved in a successful fleet action. His agency was suddenly very valuable and highly sought after. But Davison was not alone in wanting to become a prize agent. Maurice had long hankered after his brother's agency. Many of his colleagues at the Navy Office moonlighted as agents, exploiting their privileged position to supplement their meagre salaries. Trusting to family ties Maurice, knowing of Davison's offer, refused to be drawn into a competition for the agency. 'I shall say nothing about it,' he loftily informed his brother. He had every reason to feel confident. There is little evidence that Davison and Nelson stayed close in the years following their meeting in Quebec. Indeed, it fell to Maurice to forward Davison's congratulations to his brother after the battle of St Vincent.

Yet both Davison and Maurice forgot that Nelson was a stickler for custom. Despite his seniority, the right to appoint the prize agents still resided with the captains of the individual ships that had taken the enemy vessels and, as Nelson reminded Davison, now that he was a flag officer, it was unseemly to involve himself in the business. Moreover, following a large action involving several ships, such as the battle of St Vincent, it was usual for the captains to pool their prizes and to appoint a joint agent, making a complicated business simpler and more efficient. The captains wielded this valuable act of patronage carefully, generally flattering their commander-in-chief, who had power over their futures, by naming his secretary or another of his close associates as their sole agent.

So no-one should have been surprised when the agency for prizes captured during the battle of St Vincent was given to George Purvis, Sir John Jervis's secretary. Nelson estimated, to Davison's chagrin, that Purvis might earn £10,000 in commission. Davison realized that two factors had contributed to the failure of his approach on this occasion – and that both would also influence future decisions. One was Nelson's rank and seniority in the Mediterranean fleet, which was outside his control. The other was the nature of their relationship, and he began working on this immediately.

In Bath, while the rector rhapsodized about his son's success, Fanny fretted over his safety. Accounts of her husband's dramatic exploits unsettled her, bringing to the surface the deep-seated fears shared by every navy wife. Nelson's own colourful account of the battle may have deliberately fed his growing public fame, but it terrified his wife. 'What can I attempt to say to you about boarding,' she pleaded; 'you have been most wonderfully protected. You have done desperate actions enough. Now may I, indeed I do beg, that you never board again. *Leave* it for *Captains.*' She begged him to return. He had done enough. His reputation was secure. 'Rest satisfied,' she implored. Yet, homesick, tired and ill as he was, he could not, or would not, stop.

Fanny received letters erratically from her husband when he was at sea. These now began to be forwarded to her by Davison, who made a point of collecting them on his visits to the Navy

Office. For the most part, Nelson's letters at this time describe the stressful, dangerous task of blockading the Spanish fleet at Cadiz. Cooped up in his cabin for days on end, he had plenty of time to gripe about his lack of recognition or to mourn lost opportunities to capture rich prizes. He complained bitterly when Jervis, now ennobled as Earl St Vincent, not only ignored his claim to chase down some Spanish treasure ships but left him vulnerable when others were sent to do it instead. 'It is impossible to conceive', he seethed in a letter to Davison, 'the ill-blood it has created in this fleet . . . one of our *Task-Masters* attempting to rob us of our harvest [and] leaving us very *handsomely* to spend our blood in opposing so superior a force.'

Nelson cherished the long, chatty letters he received from Bath, filled as they were with trivial gossip and family news. Through the summer his idea of home and of his wife probably crystallized into an impossible fantasy. Then in July his letters pause. 'You must not expect to hear very soon from me,' he wrote to Fanny, 'as I am going on a little cruise.'

In Britain the programme of barrack-building was in full swing. By June 1797 Davison had supplied stores totalling more than £380,000 to forty-three new barracks across the country. Each day a clerk in his employ visited Whitehall to collect De Lancey's latest orders. The goods were then procured by Davison through a network of suppliers whose wagons arrived all day long in Bedford Street teetering with piles of bedsteads and boilers, iron stoves and urine tubs, bedding and clothing. By now hundreds of men were employed at the warehouse, unloading, sorting and packing the goods for delivery to the barracks under the watchful eye of John Lodge, Davison's chief packer. Clerks scuttled everywhere, checking and signing the suppliers' delivery vouchers. Next door to the warehouse for barrack supplies was Davison's clothing factory, where bedding and clothing were made for the marines, the convicts at Botany Bay and several army regiments. It employed another thousand men, still managed by Mungo Shedden.

Davison's position as agent on commission to De Lancey prevented him supplying his own manufactured goods to the barracks, a situation which struck him as absurd. Late in 1797, with the demand for supplies escalating as the fighting intensified, Davison warned De Lancey that his suppliers could no longer meet the growing demand. De Lancey gratefully accepted Davison's offer to bolster the barrack supplies from his own factory, without pausing to consider upon what terms these goods would be supplied by his agent.

Davison was at Swarland with his family when Nelson returned to England in September, earlier than expected. News of the dreadful wound his friend had sustained during an attack at Tenerife soon reached him, but he stayed in the north of England and it was not until 11 October, when he visited the Nelsons at their lodgings in Bond Street, that he saw the shocking sight of the empty sleeve for himself. It was the first time, too, that he noticed the opaque milkiness of Nelson's right eye, sightless since 1794 when it was damaged during an attack on Corsica; the horrible contrast with the unnatural brightness of the other made him feel uncomfortable. Nelson looked like an old man, weary of life. His tangled shock of unpowdered hair was almost completely white. The skin on his face, burned by months at sea and glistening with fever, was stretched painfully across hollow cheeks. When he spoke his voice was heavy with laudanum.

Fanny bustled protectively about her husband: arranging refreshment, plumping up the cushions on his day bed and occasionally pausing to touch his brow tenderly with a cool flannel. Physical intimacy between them, after four years apart, seemed to have been reduced to the miserable, unpleasant business of dressing his wound. The room was uncomfortably warm and stuffy, for Fanny had closed all the windows against the autumn chill, muffling the sound of the street below. The stifling atmosphere was made worse by the smell of decay issuing from the suppurating stump hidden by Nelson's dressing-gown. From time to time, as he spoke, Nelson's body jerked painfully as his brain forgot his arm was gone. When Davison arrived he had been labouring over a letter, which Fanny took to another room to finish, leaving the men alone to talk.

When Nelson was strong enough, he drove to Suffolk with Fanny to look at a house. Fanny had been house-hunting for months without success, rejecting a series of properties which failed to meet her exacting standards in respect of size and location. But Roundwood, outside Ipswich, looked ideal. It was a small, modern farmhouse with four principal bedrooms and two 'genteel parlours'. Surrounding the house were outbuildings and 50 acres of land, which were let to a tenant. It was convenient for Norfolk and close to the road for the eastern ports. The house was an appropriate property for a gentleman of comfortable means. Fanny saw how to improve it and was delighted when Nelson's offer of £2,000, the most he could afford, was accepted.

By now Nelson was attracting attention wherever he went. People gathered outside the small house on Bond Street to wait, sometimes all night, for a glimpse of their distinctive new hero. Their presence worried Fanny, who feared they might disturb her husband, but Davison saw that his friend enjoyed the attention and indeed thrived on it. Nelson's growing celebrity was fuelled by the press, but although his disfigurement made him instantly recognizable – even in a city full of men mutilated by war – there was no recent mass-market image available to his fans in the print shops on the Strand. A new portrait was needed.

Before Christmas 1797, while still recuperating from his wound, Nelson visited Lemuel Abbott, an artist living close to Davison in Bloomsbury. Abbott was not as renowned, fashionable or expensive as Lawrence, Beechey or Hoppner, but he had built a sound reputation as a portrait painter, particularly among naval officers. This was despite a chaotic lifestyle, which left unfinished canvasses scattered around his studio in Bloomsbury, and an odd manner which startled people. He would end his days in an asylum. Abbott had completed a portrait of Davison only a few months before Nelson's visit. In this painting – recently rediscovered – Davison looks content and prosperous in a favourite blue coat with a brown velvet collar and double row of large, gilded buttons. Nelson sat to Abbott twice, gazing past the artist's left shoulder, impassively pondering his return to sea while trying hard to ignore his aching, burning wound. From the oil sketches he made on these occasions Abbott finished a number of half-length portraits of Nelson, one of which was soon hanging at Harpur Street.

Nelson returned to sea in March 1798, joining *Vanguard* (one of only three ships in the Royal Navy granted a warrant to hold lodge meetings on board) at Portsmouth. He was in a tetchy mood, frustrated by his disability and exasperated by the domestic failings of his wife. 'At half past five I arrived here,' he complained, 'and what you will be surprised to hear, with great difficulty found one pair of raw silk stockings . . . I suppose in some place or other I shall find my linen, for there is scarcely any in this trunk.'

'I assure you I rejoice to see you so exact,' Fanny retorted. This tone, of a mother indulging a rebellious child, appears frequently in Fanny's letters to her husband. Likewise Nelson, despite his often bullying manner, often approaches his wife warily and with overt deference. Having lost his mother at a young age and passed much of his life thereafter in an isolated, all-male environment, Nelson may have felt not only disconnected from women but instinctively subordinated by them. This is not to say he took them lightly; far from it. He placed them either on a pedestal, as with Mary Simpson and Fanny, or in bed, as with Adelaide Correglia. It is not surprising, then, that he was overwhelmed when, within a few months of this departure, a beautiful woman of perceived rank would, quite literally, throw herself at his feet. Nor is it surprising that when it came to making his choice between his lover and his wife, he lacked the courage to tell Fanny in person.

Nelson sailed from England in unsettled mood. His leave, overshadowed by the pain of his wound, had changed his perception of his wife from lover to nurse; and her increasingly maternal attitude towards him contrasted starkly with the adoration he was getting in the streets of London. Fanny was now over forty, and any hopes that she might have children were fading fast. For a man like Nelson, the thought of dying childless was unbearable. Fanny sensed this change and felt her husband pulling away. Fearing a rift that could leave her isolated and alone, her declarations of love and gratitude in her letters became more frequent and urgent, exacerbating the confusion of his emotions.

As spring turned to summer that year, the sense of a looming national catastrophe grew stronger in Britain. 'Everybody is gloomy,' Fanny wrote to her husband from Suffolk; 'how very fortunate your time is so much taken up, that it must prevent you from thinking. We have little else to do.' In June she heard from Nelson that he was in hot pursuit of the French fleet in the Mediterranean. 'Everyone', Davison (who saw the letter) reported to Northumberland, 'is of the opinion Nelson must come up with them . . . the result may be easily guessed.'

Fanny tried to keep her mind on the improvements to her new house, but, starved of news and relying on rumours from newspapers and the Navy Office, her fears naturally multiplied. 'No one period of the war have I felt more than I do at this moment,' she wrote in July. Louise Berry, the wife of Nelson's flag captain and 'a very mild good young woman', came to stay at Roundwood, and the presence of another woman in the same anxious situation as herself gave Fanny some small comfort. The women passed their days in embroidery, reading and whist. Visits were made to Fanny's neighbours, though almost without exception they proved a bitter disappointment. An afternoon was spent touring Sir Robert Harland's new house. Sir Robert was 'a very gay young man' and the women 'were not at all gratified by the indecent ornaments of a gay young man, fine, naked figures' in his bedroom. They were puzzled too by the 'very handsome looking glasses at the bottom of the bedstead'.

Louise left Roundwood on 30 July 1798. Three days later and two thousand miles away, in the bay of Aboukir at the mouth of the Nile, her husband Edward Berry was summoned by Captain James Saumarez to *Orion*. That evening thirteen captains, whom Nelson had christened, in strongly masonic terms, his 'band of Brothers', met to dine in Saumarez' cabin. An empty place was laid for George Westcott, the fourteenth captain, who had not survived the battle the previous night. Nelson himself was recuperating from a head wound in *Vanguard*. The captains toasted their survival and their victory, while bloated corpses and debris drifted around *Orion* bathed in the light of a million stars and the large limpid moon. The previous evening these men, daringly led by Nelson, had achieved an astonishing victory over the French fleet which, anchored close to the Egyptian shore, had seemed impregnable. At a stroke, the unlikely victory crushed Bonaparte's ambitions in the east. It cut off his army in Egypt, lifted the threat of a French invasion of Turkey (and, more seriously, of India) and returned control of the eastern Mediterranean to the British.

After supper, when the table was cleared and the steward had retired, the captains discussed their prize agency. They agreed that to deal with the proceeds of such a battle, a sole agent would be best. Several candidates were discussed, but the captains failed to reach agreement. Instead, they resolved to ask their commander-in-chief for a name. The business concluded, a proposal was made, possibly by Saumarez, that the captains form themselves into a fellowship to be known as the Egyptian Club, in tribute of their great victory. The first act of the Egyptian club would be to present their chief with a precious sword and to have his portrait painted for a room set aside for their meetings. Elsewhere, deep within the *Orion*, the exhausted tars looked at each other with puzzlement as they heard the cheering from the great cabin.

Evan Nepean was the first man in England officially to hear news of the battle of the Nile. Nepean's ceaseless work had been rewarded by his appointment as secretary at the Admiralty Board, a position once occupied by Samuel Pepys. This paid Nepean £4,000 a year, more even than the first lord, Earl Spencer.

Nepean was now Nelson's principal contact at the Admiralty, as he was for every flag officer in the navy.

Rumours of a major engagement in the Mediterranean had been circulating in England for weeks before a post-chaise clattered into the courtyard of the Admiralty late on 2 October, bringing Captain Capel of *La Mutine* with Nelson's dispatches. Nepean read quickly by the light of the lantern in the hall. 'Almighty God has blessed his Majesty's arms by a great victory over the Fleet of the enemy, who I attacked at sunset on the 1st August, off the mouth of the Nile.' An express was sent right away to Suffolk.

At half-past four the following morning, a letter from Egypt arrived at Harpur Street, forwarded by Nepean from the bundle Capel had delivered. A servant sleepily explained to the messenger that the house was deserted and the family gone to the country. But he took the letter anyway promising to send it on. It reached Swarland two days later.

> *My dear Davison, this fleet have unanimously appointed you sole Agent for the capture at the Battle of the Nile. It is a great concern, and they rely on your established character and abilities for a speedy payment of their Prize-Money, which all Agents hitherto so studiously endeavour to keep from them . . . Best respects to Mrs. Davison. God bless you. H.N.*

There was also a letter for Davison from Maurice in London. Unable to wait any longer to send him the extraordinary gazette announcing the battle which was being rushed off the presses in London, Maurice breathlessly gave Davison 'the first tidings' of his brother's victory.

> *He is but slightly wounded and was well when Captain Capel left him . . . I now think he has done enough and I hope the country will think so too. The prizes are on their passage home under convoy of the ships that have suffered most . . . 9 sail of the line*

and 2 frigates are taken, 2 sail of the line & 2 frigates escaped. The French admiral & his captain are killed — we have lost Captain Westcote of the Majestic . . . we have not lost a ship.

When the momentous news reached Henry Dundas at Arniston House, his family seat near Edinburgh, he expressed the feeling of relief universal in the country. 'Having no words adequate to express the sentiments I feel upon the subject of your victory,' he wrote to Nelson, 'I must content myself with saying that in the present state of this country, and of the world at large, Providence has made you the instrument of performing the most signal service that ever was done to any country.' In a letter to Earl Spencer, Dundas was more candid. Commenting on Nelson's earlier blind pursuit of the French, he remarked that 'it is a much pleasanter predicament to be the panegyrist of his glory and utility, than to be the defender of an unintended mistake'.

Such considerations did not trouble the majority of his compatriots. Everywhere, joy was unbounded. After all the months of pent-up anxiety, this sudden, unexpected, wonderful news triggered wild, jubilant scenes. London and provincial towns alike were lit up, echoing to the sound of bells, gun salutes and cheers for Nelson.

Fanny's pleasure in the news, however, was muted. Any feelings of happiness were mixed with concern for Josiah, her eighteen-year-old son by her first marriage. Josiah was also serving in the Mediterranean, in *Bonne Citoyenne*, and from him there had been no news. The stress brought on a heavy cold. 'Withal your joy there is a damper,' sympathized her sister. It was a further two weeks before Maurice told her that Josiah was safe. Only then did she relax and celebrate her husband's victory, attending the queen's drawing room at St James's Palace and going to a ball in Suffolk as guest of honour. A stream of well-wishers visited Roundwood. Even so, she felt patronized by all the sudden attention. 'The great in this neighbourhood', she remarked primly, 'ought to have found their way to the cottage before.'

In contrast, Maurice enjoyed his brief moment in the lime-light. The prime minister even invited him to dinner. But it was small consolation for the terse letter he had received from his brother in Capel's bundle (though the anger it must have caused him was magnanimously absent in his letter to Swarland): 'The fleet have appointed Davison *sole* agent for the ships captured at the battle of the Nile . . . Whatever assistance you may give Davison, or whatever he may wish to serve you in, I beg that you may never be considered, directly or indirectly as having anything to do with the Agency.'

Nelson confided to Davison that he had 'the strongest reasons' for excluding his brother from the agency. Whatever these were, they were certainly informed by Nelson's desire to protect his own reputation and to leave no opportunity for accusations of favouritism. He might also have been aware of a shift in official attitude towards clerks moonlighting at the Navy Office which could compromise him later. Nelson's fastidiousness cut little ice with Maurice. He had just heard that it was unlikely he would ever become a commissioner on the Navy Board, a humiliation which contrasted painfully with his younger brother's public triumph. Maurice's pain flooded his reply.

> I am free to confess to you that I feel myself not a little hurt at
> my not having been named with Mr D as one of the agents to
> your squadron. It might have put something in my pocket, at least
> it would have stopped people's mouths who repeatedly say there
> must have been some misunderstanding between me and you . . .
> I have no doubt you have sufficient reason and content myself in
> present degrading situation, degrading I call it because I cannot
> reach the top of my profession.

'I am truly sorry,' Nelson answered, stung by his brother's words and shaken for a moment from the seductive charms of the court at Naples into which he had gratefully sunk after the battle, *you should think I had neglected you about the agency, but it was no more in my power to name an agent than an Emperor. All the captains had brothers, cousins or friends. As all agreed this could not be done, they agreed for me to name a man who I thought could serve them best and with responsibility. Davison was the only man I knew who answered the description.*

This letter probably made Maurice feel even more resentful. It also shows that, in the short space of time they were together in London, Davison had secured a remarkable grip on Nelson, re-establishing that position of authority evident during their fateful meeting on the quay at Quebec. Nevertheless, the episode made an impact on Nelson, and from now on he tried to use his growing influence to advance his brother within the Navy Office. Davison suggested offering £3,000 to a commissioner whose 'affairs were in a deranged state' in return for his resignation in Maurice's favour. Maurice was horrified. 'I verily believe the First Lord would not suffer such a negotiation to be carried on,' he exclaimed upon hearing the plan.

For himself, Davison was elated by his appointment as prize agent. 'I will not attempt to describe the sensations I felt on receipt of your letter,' he replied to Nelson from Swarland;

the honour done me by your Lordship and the officers of the fleet in unanimously appointing me sole agent for the prizes imposes on me a duty which every effort of mine shall be strained to fulfil, with credit to my Reputation and with advantage to their Interests. Your Lordship may rely no pitiful consideration of private advantage shall ever induce me to delay the distributions a day longer than absolutely necessary.

Nelson's shock decision to award such a high-profile task to a man unknown in the prize business left a trail of disgruntled agents in its wake. Davison flatly refused all their offers of help. None the less, he would need assistance in the Mediterranean because the six surviving prizes were being taken to Gibraltar to be assessed. John Campbell, Nelson's secretary in *Vanguard*, and George Purvis, Earl St Vincent's secretary, were both given shares in the business. As Nelson's squadron was operating within St Vincent's command at the time of the battle, Purvis might have expected rather more.

To the victor, the spoils. As Davison in London began the laborious task of sorting out the prize money, Nelson in Naples was basking in his newly burnished fame. Gifts and titles rained down on him from grateful monarchs throughout Europe. King Ferdinand IV of Naples gave him a 'richly ornamented sword' and the dukedom of Bronte, a small estate on Sicily. The tsar of Russia and the king of Sardinia each sent exquisite snuff boxes. Sultan Selim III in Constantinople – who had more reason than most for thanking Nelson for destroying the French threat in the eastern Mediterranean – plucked a diamond aigrette or *chelengk* from his own turban and sent it, its rays sparkling like the rising sun, to Naples, along with a diamond star and a sable-lined pelisse. In England, the committee that had been set up at Lloyd's coffee house to raise money for the wounded and bereaved voted Nelson £500, 'to be laid out in plate'. Another 200 guineas was set aside by the City of London to pay for a magnificent jewel encrusted presentation sword.

Davison, who was eager to cement his relationship with Nelson and to bathe publicly in his friend's glory, launched into a truly spectacular round of present-giving. First he arranged for prints to be made after his portrait of Nelson by Lemuel Abbott. Copies were presented to the king, the royal princes, Nelson's 'gallant' captains and the heads of all the official departments: 'to show them the sense I have of your friendship towards me'. Cheaper versions sold like hot cakes on the Strand.

Davison then proposed a far grander scheme, one which appealed in equal measure to his patriotism, his philanthropy and his self-interest. He approached the government with an offer to pay for medals to be struck for every man – all six thousand of

The HERO   of the NILE.

The Hero of the Nile, *by James Gillray, published in December 1798. Nelson is wearing the* chelengk *and the pelisse given to him by the sultan of Turkey and carrying a captured French sabre, similar to the one later bequeathed to Davison. Note the bulging purse in Nelson's satirized coat of arms; the motto above reads '£2000 per annum' — a reference to the government pension he was awarded.*

them – who fought in the battle alongside Nelson. This novel and eye-catching idea was attractive to a government keen to make political capital out of Nelson's victory without setting an expensive precedent for future actions; so Davison's offer was accepted, on condition that the government was involved in the design of the medal. The project fell within the remit of the secretary of state for war, Henry Dundas, who gave the task of liaising with Davison over the matter to his private secretary, William Budge, a man of 'inflexible integrity'. On the face of it this arrangement seemed to consign Davison to the role of mere paymaster. But it gave the medals valuable official standing while enhancing Davison's own reputation by publicly binding him closer to government, the fount of his wealth. He hoped, too, that so extravagant a gesture might purchase loyalty in the fleet the next time a large agency was awarded.

Budge asked the pioneering steam engineer Matthew Boulton to consider 'the very liberal ideas with which Mr Davison is now animated'. Boulton was the obvious choice to make the medals. His state-of-the-art steam presses at the Soho manufactory outside Birmingham already supplied the government with much of its coinage. When business was slack, Boulton used the presses to strike speculative medals. At least one of these, commemorating the assassination in 1792 of Gustavus III, the king of Sweden and grand master of the Swedish Grand Lodge, was in Davison's collection.

Boulton and Davison were perfect partners in such an enterprise: both were determined self-made men; each had a marked flamboyant streak; neither suffered fools. Boulton was enthusiastic about the idea, readily accepting the commission and promising Davison he would make the medals at cost. He had never known 'such a popular act of an individual', he proclaimed.

Keen to ensure his own ideas were incorporated into the medal, Davison wasted little time in preparing a detailed description and preliminary drawing of his preferred design:

[obverse] Hope crowned with Oak and Laurel with the Olive Branch in her right hand and the medallion of Lord Nelson supported by her left, as it appears in the design, and her forefinger pointing to his bust. The anchor should appear exactly also as it is sketched; the foot of the figure, in a sandal, should also be seen, and the drapery to fall in the most graceful manner. Hope should also appear to be standing on a rugged shore. Round the circumference is to be placed 'R. Admiral Lord Nelson of the Nile'. *Round the medallion the words* 'Europe's Hope – Britain's Glory and Defence.'

The reverse would depict 'the French fleet at anchor in the Bay of Bequeire and the British fleet under sail advancing to the attack'.

The design was sent to Downing Street for approval. Budge raised no objections to it and sent it on without delay to Birmingham by the overnight coach. A black basalt bust of Nelson by Wedgwood, which was considered 'a very good likeness except that the forehead is rather too high', was also sent to Boulton for his engraver to copy.

Boulton, admitting he was not 'a connoisseur in naval subjects', sent Davison's sketch straight back to London to be improved upon by Robert Clevely, a marine artist living in Millbank. Boulton gave the task of cutting the medal's die to Conrad Küchler, a German émigré who was Soho's best engraver.

Davison's design was loaded with masonic iconography, presumably with the tacit approval of Henry Dundas, himself a prominent freemason. Hope was one of the three principal theological virtues of freemasonry, together with faith and charity. On Davison's medal she is reinforced by the symbolic use of an anchor and has her breast bare in imitation, perhaps, of the masonic initiation ceremony. Davison's insistence to Boulton that 'the anchor should appear exactly also as it is sketched' leaves its stock appearing like a coffin from behind the figure of Hope, another strongly masonic allusion. Additional familiar masonic motifs appeared in

The battle of the Nile Thanksgiving medal, struck in November 1798, anticipates the masonic iconography on Davison's medal and the wine coolers. The obverse (top right) depicts: 'Religion supporting the bust of Admiral Nelson, with her right hand resting upon a cross and skull, by her is the British lion defending the Irish Harp. In the background a Pyramid and Palm Tree to mark the country where the Victory was obtained. Legend, "Nothing can oppose Virtue and Courage"'. The reverse (top left) depicts: 'An Anchor, with a shield, on which is the Royal Arms of England, surrounding with laurel . . . above, The Eye of Providence denoting its influence and favour. Legend, "Under this Sign you shall conquer"'. Robert Clevely's final design for Davison's Nile medal (above) did not include the symbol of a rising sun.

the use of laurel, signifying immortality, and olive, representing peace; both also shared an association with the idea of victory.

It was a timely moment for a mute demonstration of masonic loyalty. For some time there had been widespread suspicion that the lodges were harbouring revolutionaries. More seriously, laws prohibiting secret oaths and secret societies, introduced by Pitt in the wake of the naval mutinies to counter the Jacobin threat, threatened the freemasons with extinction. Their predicament was made the more difficult because their very constitution prevented them from defending themselves in public. So while Lord Moira, as the acting grand master, discreetly lobbied Pitt to exempt the freemasons from the acts, Davison arranged for his allegorical medal design to be published, suitably acknowledged, in the *Anti-Jacobin Review and Magazine*. Sponsored by the government and edited by Pitt's young acolyte George Canning, the *Anti-Jacobin* was a satirical magazine with serious propaganda intent. By placing his design here, Davison was making a coded statement, and currying favour.

Davison's medal was not unique, however. Symbols of freemasonry were used even more blatantly on a medal speculatively struck ahead of 29 November, the day designated by the government for general thanksgiving at Nelson's victory. This medal, which was advertised in *The Times* as 'The Thanksgiving Medal', incorporated a number of images drawn from ancient Egypt, a fashionable masonic preoccupation which providentially dovetailed with the site of the battle. The images on the obverse included a skull, a cross, a pyramid, a palm tree and a sphinx-like winged creature, entitled 'Religion', which supported, like the figure of Hope in Davison's medal, a bust of Nelson. The reverse, which bore an anchor and shield entwined with laurel, was dominated by the persuasive presence of the masonic All-Seeing Eye or 'The Eye of Providence denoting its influence and favour'. The All-Seeing Eye was accompanied by the motto SUB HOC SIGNO VINCES, meaning 'under this sign you shall conquer'. The medals were available in silver, bronze, copper and gilt from a 'Dealer in

The Earl of Moira in his regalia as the acting grand master of the freemasons in England, a position he held from 1790 to 1813. Admiral Sir Peter Parker was the deputy grand master.

Coins, Jewellery &c' called M. Young at 16 Ludgate Street. Versions in 'Lattin' (tin-plated iron) were available to the masses as souvenirs at just 1s each.

Boulton was not at all convinced by the use of so much complicated iconography on Davison's medal. 'One of the most learned and classical men in this Kingdom', he brusquely informed Budge, 'says it is very bad taste and highly improper to attempt to record historical facts by allegorical emblems when it can be done by plain and simple means.' He was also unhappy that the image of Nelson was subordinated to Hope's shield. 'The brave tars', he believed, 'will be better pleased to recognise the features of their noble admiral than to see a figure that may require to be explained to them.'

As an example of what he meant, Boulton sent Budge the medal struck after 'The Glorious First of June' in 1794, the obverse of which was occupied entirely by a bust of Earl Howe, the victorious commander. But Budge, a dogged civil servant, would not budge. His firm reply indicated that the matter was settled. Wary of Nelson's growing celebrity and concerned to avoid upsetting his fellow officers, the government did not want the medal to worship the hero of the hour but rather to celebrate the fleet as a whole. Moreover, the principal political message of the medal was not intended to be triumphalist but to convey the nation's overwhelming desire for peace. It was in this context that Nelson was 'Europe's Hope – Britain's Glory and Defence'.

Davison may have intended the medal to be a propaganda tool for the freemasons, but the government was not slow to take advantage of it on their own account. Nelson's image was manipulated by Budge throughout the development stage. As Wedgwood's bust was the officially approved likeness of the admiral, Boulton's complaints that Küchler found it difficult to copy were ignored. Even when Küchler did achieve a good copy, Budge fiddled with it – to Boulton's obvious annoyance – by insisting that the Order of the Bath, awarded to Nelson by the king, be shown to better advantage and that the 'medal of merit' be added.

Even the hairline was changed. Nor was Budge's meddling limited to ensuring that the medal showed the government in the best light. The waves in Aboukir Bay, on the reverse of the medal, were deemed too 'regular'; Budge ordered them to be 'broke a little'. There was also one other distracting but telling detail. 'I should be glad', Budge asked Boulton,

> if you would call Mr Kuchlers attention to the following objects
> – viz on the obverse the nipple of the breast of the allegorical
> figure is not visible and as this may certainly be considered as the
> crown to one of the most enchanting Beauties with which Nature
> has adorned the female sex, I have no doubt therefore that not
> only you but Mr K will be inclined to do her justice.

In his drawings, Robert Clevely, remembering that the battle took place at night, left the sky blank over Aboukir Bay. Yet by the time the medal was struck a sun had appeared above the battle. This poses one of the medal's most abiding mysteries, one on which the meticulous Budge, who otherwise complained that the sun was too large and then too small, was silent. It has always been thought, because the battle was at night, that Davison added a setting sun to the design. If so, and here is the mystery, with the Egyptian coastline to the right of the battle the sun is shown setting in the east. Why was this glaring error allowed to pass without comment? Was it perhaps because the sun is not *setting* but is *rising*? Did Davison introduce into his medal, at the last moment, the masonic leitmotif for wisdom?

Davison soon moved from such recondite imagery to more immediately important matters. 'As these medals are for presents expressive of my sense of their bravery,' he wrote to Boulton from Swarland,

> I wish to have round the rim or edge of the medal something sig-
> nifying its being given by me. As you are so well versed in such
> things, I must submit it to yourself what would be proper. I was

thinking some words to this effect 'In token of Alex^r Davison's respect' *or other words as you judge best applicable to the occasion.*

On 17 November Davison called at the Soho manufactory to check on the medal's progress. Unfortunately Boulton was in London, so it fell to William Cheshire, one of his managers, to show the important visitor around the factory. Davison must have loved his tour. The manufactory hummed with industry, its hundreds of workers producing thousands of articles every day using James Watt's up-to-the-minute steam engines: everything from cut steel buckles to coloured glass bowls and intricate scientific instruments. It was the thrilling, exuberant heart of a new age. With his acquisitive instincts Davison could hardly have passed through the factory without placing several large orders for luxury goods. He also collected a pair of elaborate silver candlesticks for the duchess of Northumberland.

Intrigued and excited as he undoubtedly was by this extravaganza, Davison was in Birmingham principally to see Boulton's mint. This was housed in a smaller building behind the manufactory, next to the tea rooms for visitors. Inside were eight steam-driven coining presses, all brilliantly engineered and interconnected. Working harmoniously together they could strike tens of thousands of coins and medals a day. The presses were run by young boys wearing crisp white linen trousers and matching cotton shirts. The building shook with the thumping of the vast presses which, wreathed in steam, whirred, knocked and sighed over Davison's head like giant clockwork toys. Sometimes, Cheshire told him, the presses worked for days on end, the boys working ten-hour shifts as they fed the insatiable machines with thin sheets of Cornish copper or Mexican silver and collected the endless stream of coins that magically spewed out of the other end. As a souvenir, Cheshire gave Davison a medal struck in honour of Lord Cornwallis.

Davison reached London in time for Mary Simpson's marriage to Robert Mathews. The wedding was held at St George's,

Hanover Square, on Thursday 22 November. Mathews had admired Mary since he first laid eyes on her on his arrival in Quebec as Frederick Haldimand's military secretary in 1779. But after Nelson's aborted proposal in 1782, which Davison must have revealed to her, Mary informed Captain Mathews that she could not 'think of accepting anyone belonging to the army whose rank was below that of colonel after having been sought by a captain of the Royal Navy'.

Haldimand raised eyebrows in army circles by reserving a vacant majority in the 53rd Foot for his secretary, but it was not enough to secure Mary's hand. Undeterred, Mathews bided his time. He travelled to England on Haldimand's retirement as his patron's amanuensis. Then, shortly before Haldimand died in 1791, Mathews returned to Quebec as aide-de-camp to Sir Guy Carleton. On the outbreak of war with France he sailed with his regiment to Flanders, where he distinguished himself in the duke of York's campaign. In 1795 Mary moved with her mother to England, where the women settled in a modest house in Clapham, a prosperous village in Surrey. Mathews followed her and eventually, after he was finally promoted to lieutenant-colonel in 1798, again pressed his claim. Mary kept her word and accepted him. She was thirty seven and he was fifty-three.

Davison was returning to a far more glamorous address in London. In 1798, only three years after buying Swarland, he paid another £25,000 for a 'more convenient and better' house in St James's Square in the heart of London's fashionable West End. Nevertheless, he kept Harpur Street, which his family and his status had outgrown, as a counting house and prize agency office – a decision which reveals the scale of his wealth by this point. It was a timely move. Harriett returned from Northumberland pregnant with their sixth child.

St James's Square was populated almost exclusively by the aristocracy, giving it a tone and atmosphere quite different from the mercantile and legal tenor of Bloomsbury. Davison's thirty-one new neighbours included four dukes, eight earls, a viscount, a marchioness, a baron, a baronet and the bishop of London. By joining them Davison was making a bold statement of his ambition. Number 9, the house he bought, was by general opinion the gaudiest in the whole square. Twenty years earlier, the architect John Adam had stuck a new façade onto the house in modish classical style, covering it with a confection of 'pilasters and corresponding ornaments' using 'Mr Liardet's stone paste' that made the house shine out like a new tooth beside its flat-fronted, red-brick neighbours.

Number 9 is now number 11 St James's Square. Cement replicas have replaced the stone statues of the four Muses that once topped the façade, but otherwise Davison would feel instantly at home. The house is anonymously squashed between two more famous addresses, each commemorated by plaques. William Pitt the elder lived at number 10 St James's Square (then number 8) in his last years – the thought of which must have pleased Davison – while Lord Byron's daughter Ada, countess of Lovelace, later moved into what is today number 12. There is no plaque on number 11, nor any indication that in the years before Trafalgar this particular house became the fulcrum of Nelson's private world.

CONQUEROR

74 GUNS,
CAPTAIN ISRAEL PELLEW

'HOW VERY MUCH I am pleased with the appointment of Mr Davison. Had I the whole of England to choose, I should say "this is the man".' So wrote Captain Edward Berry to Nelson upon arriving back in London after the battle of the Nile: 'he has universal good character, indeed from what I hear, his responsibility is only equalled by his honour and integrity.'

Writing to Davison on 28 November from quarantine at Spithead, Captain James Saumarez was equally effusive in his praise. 'It afforded me real satisfaction in concurring with the wishes of our gallant and worthy admiral to appoint you sole agent to our prizes knowing they could not be in better hands.'

Saumarez and Berry were the first Egyptian Club captains to reach England after the battle of the Nile and they brought with them the order for Nelson's presentation sword. It seems they gave the task of arranging the sword to their new prize agent, who was ideally suited to the role. The obvious choice of goldsmith to make such an item was Philip Rundell of Rundell & Bridge, the royal jewellers on Ludgate Hill. Rundell was fifty-five years old, an astute man of business with a sharp tongue and a quick temper. His shop 'at the sign of the leaping salmon' was a favourite haunt of the *beau monde*, who peered through the small windows of the ancient building hoping to catch sight of the prince of Wales,

Rundell's best customer. Inside the shop, the counters shimmered with rare and precious gems, jewels, plate and *objets d'art*.

Rundell was anyhow already preparing a silver centrepiece for Davison to give Nelson in honour of his victory. Davison had ordered a column crowned by the figure of Britannia and entwined with laurel and lotus flowers: 'a celebrated Egyptian Plant which also has an allusion to the water'. At the foot of the column, prefiguring a later, more famous monument, he envisaged 'three *Lions* copied from the celebrated *Egyptian Lions* at Rome [which] are emblematic of British *Generosity* and *Valour*'.

The comments of Berry and Saumarez, though inevitably coloured by respect for their chief, must have reassured Davison. He valued his 'honour and integrity' very highly. The beautiful things with which he surrounded himself, from his London mansion with its growing collection of art to his Palladian country seat, were all acquired to purchase the good opinion of his peers and to secure his status. Yet he knew that various 'insinuations' had greeted his unexpected appointment as sole agent for the Nile prizes. Most of these came from the courtyards surrounding the Strand, driven by the jealousy of other prize agents. But some influential figures in the navy were also uncomfortable with Nelson's decision. For the time being they kept their views to themselves. Two years later, however, when the euphoria of the battle's immediate aftermath had faded, Sir John Orde, third-in-command of the Mediterranean fleet, felt sufficiently emboldened to speak out. On behalf of his 'brother admirals' Orde asked Nelson why George Purvis, a 'very worthy agent', had been ignored after the Nile, 'in favour of a man unknown to most of them and little acquainted with the nature of the employment'. Despite a well-known rivalry with Nelson and, surviving family correspondence indicates, at least a passing acquaintance with the Davisons in Northumberland, Orde must have echoed the opinion of many.

From the start Davison knew he was under close scrutiny. He was keen to complete the business as quickly as possible, both to impress Nelson and to confound his critics. However, he could not even begin until he received some vital papers from the Mediterranean. These were the power of attorney documents signed, or marked, by all the men in the British ships naming Davison as their agent and 'letters of condemnation' from the Admiralty court in Gibraltar establishing the prize status of the six captured French ships. By December these papers were on their way to England with George Purvis in *Colossus*.

While Davison waited impatiently for Purvis to arrive, two unforeseen problems needed disentangling. The first concerned three other French ships, *L'Heureux*, *Le Mercure* and *Le Guerrier*, which Nelson had destroyed after the battle rather than delay by repairing them. The loss of the ships made them worthless to the Admiralty, but Nelson was determined that they should still be recognized as prizes and sent Davison a petition to present at the Admiralty, in which he argued that only urgent sailing orders from Earl St Vincent, the commander-in-chief of the Mediterranean fleet, had prevented him saving the three ships and sending them to Gibraltar with the other prizes. Nelson even went so far as to suggest that he had done the Admiralty a favour. 'I am bold to say', he wrote, 'when the services, time and men with the expense of fitting these three ships for a voyage to England is valued, that government will save nearly as much as they are valued at.' Nelson considered £60,000 fair compensation for the lost ships, and – unashamedly prodding the Admiralty towards the right decision – he claimed he had already promised the money to his men.

Nelson then went even further. He ambitiously proposed that the French ships destroyed *during* the action should also be considered prizes. This claim – an unprecedented suggestion running counter to the whole basis of the prize money system – was made following reports that *L'Orient*, the French flagship, was carrying £600,000 in looted treasure when it spectacularly exploded at the height of the battle. Sensibly, Davison sought out Nepean's advice before submitting the petition. Nepean urged him to seek a private audience with Earl Spencer, the first lord, 'to gauge reaction before it is sent to the admiralty'. Unsurprisingly, Spencer thought Nelson was pushing his luck. Even so, the Admiralty might consider paying out on the three lost prizes, bearing in mind the exceptional circumstances, if Nelson dropped the claim to the French ships destroyed during the battle. Davison revised the petition, suggesting that the three lost prizes should each be settled at the average value of the six prizes that reached Gibraltar. As this figure was £19,000, Nelson's claim for £60,000 was not, he suggested, unreasonable.

It was a good try, but Davison's calculation ignored the wide disparity in value between the prizes. The most valuable ship, Le Franklin, which was only ten months old, was valued at over £30,000, or £14 a ton, whereas Le Peuple Souverin, of unknown age, was valued at just £5,000 or £3 a ton. Even Davison admitted privately that the Admiralty would be unlikely to settle the lost ships much above the lowest value obtained in Gibraltar for one of the prizes – 'under the impression', he confided to Nelson, 'that you would give orders for the worst ships to be destroyed'. He was right. The Admiralty offered to pay £20,000 for all three ships, the commissioners making it abundantly clear that this sum was not negotiable. 'Lord Spencer's plan is not fair to the captors,' fumed Nelson when he heard about this 'mean and unjust' settlement; 'I shall know better another time and will, from this very hard conduct, fit out at any expense all my prizes.'

The other pressing matter Davison had to address was the issue of head money. This was a bounty paid out to the victorious crews after an action, based on the numbers of enemy seamen in the ships 'sunk, burnt or otherwise destroyed' during the battle. Unlike prize money, head money was shared out equally, so every man from flag officer to the lowest seaman received the same amount. But before the head money could be calculated and approved by the Treasury, the enemy numbers had to be sworn by at least three prisoners of war before an appropriate British civilian authority, such as a consul or vice-consul.

The certificate Saumarez gave Davison on his return to London claimed that the French had lost 2,949 men at the Nile (compared to just 218 British casualties). It was soon pointed out, however, that the numbers had been sworn before British officers on board *Alexander*, and not in front of a civilian authority as they should have been. As all the prisoners had long since been released there was no chance of repeating the process in the correct form. The irregularity jeopardized the head money, but left Nelson untroubled. 'This must do,' he replied dismissively when Davison raised the matter, 'for the complement of men, and the number of ships destroyed, will not, I fancy, be disputed . . . you must settle this.'

This time Davison sought Maurice Nelson's help. Maurice was far less sanguine than his brother that the Treasury would pay out on the flawed certificate, for he knew of at least one similar recent case when head money had been refused. Still stinging from the slight over the agency, Maurice nevertheless obeyed his brother's injunction to lend Davison 'assistance' in the business, agreeing to help resolve the problem. He persuaded Sir Andrew Snape Hamond, the comptroller of the Navy Office, pre-emptively to admit the mistake in a letter to the Treasury, and told Davison to plead the special circumstances of the victory in an appeal to George Rose, the secretary to the Treasury. The strategy worked and the Treasury agreed to pay the victors of the Nile over £45,000 in head money. Maurice's prompt action had saved the day.

As Christmas approached, Davison was not alone in hoping for rather more than simply the prize business paperwork. 'I must now, my dear friend, tell you how much I regret your stay in the Mediterranean. You have done enough, more cannot be effected and your object now ought to be that of contributing to the tranquillity and comfort of your inestimable wife, whose anxiety may be conceived but never expressed by words.'

Since recovering from the alarm over Josiah, Fanny had waited anxiously for her husband to return home. In one of his first letters to her after the battle he suggested he might be back as early as November. As the Egyptian Club captains started to arrive home one by one, Fanny grew first mystified and then concerned at Nelson's prolonged delay in the Mediterranean. Such letters as she received dwelt more and more on the talents and superior qualities of Emma Lady Hamilton, the wife of the British ambassador in Naples. Nelson considered her 'one of the very best women in this world . . . an honour to her sex and a proof that even reputation may be regained'. Fanny must have been already well aware, through gossip and titbits in her periodicals, of the infamous Lady Hamilton. The woman was a *bête noire* to polite society, yet there was an appalled, prurient fascination in her extraordinary career and marriage to Sir William Hamilton. For Fanny, reading her husband's letters in the chill emptiness of Suffolk, all the talk of the lavish balls and hero-worship in Naples must have been distinctly unsettling; mention of Emma Hamilton even more so. Yet, despite her nagging worries, Fanny kept up a civilized and relaxed demeanour. When, out of the blue, Emma herself wrote, Fanny replied in amiable fashion, sending her husband's new friend a number of Davison's prints.

Like most of her female friends, especially those married to naval officers, Fanny would have held few illusions about the desires of men. She had been married before and was well travelled. She must have known, and accepted, that he would seek sexual release when he was away. She also knew that he was a more sensual person than she was. The occasional discreet liaison was not an obstacle to a loving and harmonious marriage. Yet any such licence was given on the understanding that Fanny would never have to hear about her husband's affairs. When she returned to London in late November 1798, it seemed no-one was talking about anything else.

The gossip confirmed her worst fears. By December she could bear it no longer, and one morning called unexpectedly at St James's Square, 'in good health but very uneasy and anxious'. Dropping her public demeanour, Fanny told the Davisons that she was planning to go to her husband in Naples. She was quite pre-pared to endure a hazardous journey across war-torn Europe to reach him. There was nothing keeping her in England.

When a startled Davison revealed that he was in the middle of writing to Nelson, Fanny insisted that he repeat her threat in the letter. Perhaps to make sure he did, she stayed with Harriett while Davison returned to his office to pick up his pen again. 'Your valuable better half writes to you,' he continued tentatively, choosing his words carefully; 'she begs me say, that unless you return home in a few months, she will join the *Standard* at Naples. Excuse a woman's tender feelings – they are too acute to be expressed.'

Davison would have found this situation embarrassing and uncomfortable. He would have been well aware of the rumours – and the Navy Office version would have been far more explicit than that circulating in the West End drawing rooms. Davison himself was not immune to the playful glance of a pretty girl – later he is spotted flirting with the daughter of an associate – but, Mrs Norris notwithstanding, there is no record of any sexual adventures before he met Harriett, though it is hard to believe that he reached the age of thirty-eight without indulging, at least, in the use of prostitutes. Once married, an iron will and deter-mined self-control would have protected him from the destructive sexual urges that afflicted many of the men around him. His outlook and upbringing dictated that his marriage would be based on affection, loyalty and trust; it was the pursuit of money and status that drove him forward, not sexual desire. Even so, he was a worldly man and a tolerant one who rarely passed judgement on the private behaviour of others. This made it more painful when others later came to judge him.

William Budge signed off the Nile medal at Christmas. The king was said to be 'much pleased with the novelty of the idea'. Davison was unhappy with the final design, though the reasons for his disappointment are lost. The medal certainly meets all his orig-inal directions. Budge and Davison wanted to show Nelson the design, but as Küchler had begun cutting the die there was no time for that. A veil of secrecy now fell across the project. 'The famous Mr Boulton', Davison teased Nelson, 'is as tenacious as myself of the design being known till I am in possession of the medals.'

Beside the very public project of his medal, Davison now embarked on a series of more intimate gifts and gestures. The latter included naming one of his ships *Lady Nelson*. 'She stays well and is to be depended on in all kinds of weather,' reported the ship's master. Many of the gifts came from the Derby porcelain factory, which had a shop on the corner of Henrietta Street and Bedford Street, next to Davison's clothing factory. Derby made the most exclusive, the most elegant and the most costly china in the whole of England. The shop shone with an intoxicating opulence. Countless chocolate cups, vases, teapots and jugs jostled on the shelves, all brilliantly painted in pinks, greens and blues and finished in the purest, brightest, gold leaf. Davison was already a good customer. Buying Derby was more patriotic than buying Sèvres, and he loved the miniature world that the Derby artists painted onto their pieces. Recently Davison had excelled himself in the shop even by his own increasingly lavish standards. Guests at St James's Square ate from a 212-piece Derby dinner service, decorated with a 'richly gilt and diamond border'. Their champagne was cooled in Derby ice pails as they gazed at a pair of 'sumptuously gilt' Derby vases, each 'inimitably painted with birds', sitting on the sideboard. Dessert was presented on yet another Derby service, painted in 'botanical subjects, (each piece varied) rich pink and gold border'. Yet another service decorated with nautical scenes appeared in Davison's collection two hundred years later.

One day before Christmas 1798, Davison walked into the Derby shop to discuss a very special commission. The order was for a pair of magnificent wine-coolers gilded with oak and acanthus leaves. One side of each was painted with Nelson's coat of arms, the other with a tableau celebrating the victory on the Nile.

These were replete with Egyptian and masonic symbolism, for Davison shared the voguish masonic conviction, encouraged by recent architectural discoveries in the Middle East, that the craft could be traced to the ancient world. Nelson's providential victory at the mouth of the Nile – a victory of order over chaos, of good over evil on the doorstep of that world – seemed to validate this belief.

Under Davison's careful guidance, the Derby artists produced an astonishing blend of imagery. Familiar allusions to naval victory such as anchors and tridents were placed in a landscape populated by sphinxes, obelisks, pyramids, crocodiles, palm trees and lotus flowers. An ibis bird sits on a flag-draped gun. An educated eye would identify the geography and recognize the symbols of victory, but would be puzzled by the incongruous use of a Roman Corinthian column at the heart of one tableau. An initiated observer, however, would decipher the masonic code behind these obviously Egyptian motifs, for each is a hieroglyph loaded with allegorical meaning. The column, for instance, the dominant image on the coolers, is a principal emblem of freemasonry, a symbol of strength and wisdom. To dispel any remaining doubt of the message Davison intended his coolers to convey, alongside the column is the unmistakable figure of a mason, the date of the battle written on his apron.

The coolers offer the most vivid physical proof of Davison's guiding philosophy. Their deliberate symbolism is knowing, even conspiratorial, part of a sophisticated game Davison was playing within his social circle – and with posterity. They were found in his collection, but the prominent and proprietorial use of Nelson's coat of arms makes it inconceivable that they were intended for St James's Square. If, as I believe, they belonged to Nelson, they give a dramatic and intimate insight into the backdrop to his life. A tantalizing clue to their ownership is buried deep within a letter Fanny wrote Davison from Bath in February 1799. 'I have to offer you my thanks for some of the most beautiful china I have ever seen, we spent the day in admiring them and disposing of them in various parts of the room.' If, as seems likely, Fanny was referring to the coolers, they would have been far more ostentatious than anything she would ever consider buying herself, even if she could afford it. Davison's extravagance brought unintended consequences. 'One expense brings on others,' Fanny complained good-naturedly, 'for I shall exert my judgement in forming a plan for something quite out of the ordinary for them to stand on.' She assured Davison that 'the Bath talkers' would know who had given her this magnificent gift. She awarded the china her highest compliment. 'The devices', she wrote, 'are elegant.'

Davison's lavish gift cheered Fanny. She had been unwell since Christmas and her letters, while remaining impeccably restrained and polite, betray a persistent anxiety. James Saumarez was so struck by her unhappiness when he saw Fanny in Bath that he mentioned it to Davison, who was spurred into an unplanned 'flying visit' to see her. Maurice tried to help as well, reprimanding his brother for his lack of attention to his wife. It was not simply a feeling of neglect that troubled Fanny, nor even solely her nagging suspicions about Lady Hamilton. Nelson's letters, when they did arrive, revealed a growing impatience, antagonism even, towards her son and his stepson, Josiah. There was talk of the boy's 'bluntness' and his 'roughness'. More serious still were reports that Josiah was squandering his advantages and that his behaviour was costing him promotion. Even so, the letters hid many of the worse complaints. Stories of Josiah's drunkenness and disobedience were circulating the fleet, even reaching the ears of Earl St Vincent.

Fanny must have found these comments about her only child very upsetting. Like any mother, she would have rallied to his defence. In Fanny's case the relationship with her son was particularly intimate, for they had bonded closely in the years spent alone together after the death of her first husband. Criticism of one deeply hurt the other. It was a private world from which Nelson was excluded, and one he threatened at his peril. Fanny corresponded frequently with Josiah who, as a staunchly loyal witness, must have been a valuable – if, out of delicacy, not entirely candid – source of information on events at the Neapolitan court. They would remain close through thick and thin, parted only by Josiah's death in 1830.

There was little doubt that Josiah had fallen in with a bad set of dissolute young officers in the Mediterranean, men who were attracted to him by his reflected celebrity. But his drinking and boorishness were the symptoms of far deeper ills. Complex tensions between a still adolescent boy and his stepfather had erupted in the stifling and sexually charged conditions of Naples. For in Naples they both met Lady Hamilton.

Emma lavished attention on Josiah, in a strategy clearly designed to flatter Nelson. Josiah – like half the fleet – would have felt strongly attracted to this alluring woman; and, knowing of her past life as a prostitute, probably felt he had cause to hope for a sexual relationship, despite her current position. His friends may have egged him on; he may even have mistaken her interest in him for genuine affection. Even Nelson observed that Josiah 'likes Lady Hamilton more than any female', remarking that her influence seemed good for the boy. The realization, when it dawned, that Emma was merely using him as bait to catch his stepfather must have crushed Josiah. His humiliation and shame were then compounded by Nelson's progressively more embarrassing behaviour in the company of Lady Hamilton – so much so that one evening Josiah had to be led away after shouting drunken abuse at his stepfather.

This crisis over Josiah was very damaging at a critical moment in the Nelsons' marriage, thrusting them into opposing positions as stepfather and mother. Fanny was a long way from the dangerous undercurrent of fermenting emotions swirling around the Neapolitan court, but she felt her son's pain. All the same, hiding her own thoughts, she remembered her duty and reprimanded Josiah gently. 'Disappoint us not,' she wrote, 'you are very young and cannot know the *world*.' And, she reminded him, 'you are more conspicuous than you imagine. Be assured you are much envied from having such a father to bring you forward.'

Davison's new career as a prize agent was not going well. In December *Colossus*, with George Purvis and the prize papers on board, foundered off the Scilly Isles. Purvis saved himself and most of the papers, but some letters of condemnation and the powers of attorney for *Goliath* and *Zealous* were lost. This caused Davison further delay and irritation; but the loss of *Colossus* was a personal catastrophe for Sir William Hamilton. Deep in the hold of the ship had been his spectacular collection of antique vases, which were being sent home, ironically, to keep them safe from the French. The prize papers I subsequently found in Davison's despatch box, including the power of attorney for *Alexander* signed by the ship's officers and crew, give no clue of their eventful journey to England two hundred years before.

Forced to wait for John Campbell in Gibraltar to replace the missing documents, Davison busied himself drumming up trade for his new agency, dropping Nelson's name into the letters he sent out. Hearing that Nelson had saved the Neapolitan royal family from the grasp of the French by evacuating them to Sicily, Davison even offered to act for King Ferdinand IV and his 'unfortunate and unhappy family', pointing out that whatever the embattled king sent him 'will at least be *safe* in my hands'.

Davison's original proposal was to make his Nile medal in five different metals, one for each of the four classes of officer plus one for the tars. The order he gave William Budge on 12 January 1799 to pass to Boulton followed this scheme. Of 7,000 medals, 25 would be in gold, 150 in silver, 300 in copper gilt, 525 in copper and 6,000 in 'bronze' (meaning copper applied with Boulton's special purple-brown 'bronzed' finish). The order took into account a surplus of medals for Davison's personal use. Only fifteen gold medals would be needed, for instance, for the Egyptian Club captains.

The scheme was further simplified by the time Davison revealed it to Nelson in March, medals in plain copper having been abandoned. 'The medals that I have had struck for your Lordship and the captains of your fleet are of gold, those for the

Lieutenants and Officers who rank with them are of silver, those for the warrant officers and inferior officers are of copper gilt and those for the men are of copper bronzed.' The order placed, the government dropped out of the project, leaving Davison preoccupied by the all-important wording on the medals identifying him as their patron.

Boulton, irritated already by Budge's endless dithering, rejected Davison's more florid suggestions, insisting that the inscription be as simple as possible. 'A man may be a Johnson, a Pope or a Dryden and yet he may not be a critic in the language of medals,' he pointed out to his client. Nevertheless Davison fretted over the wording, which evolved from 'In token of Alex^{r} Davison's respect' via 'As a mark of Alex^{r} Davison's Esteem Soho 1799' to 'From Alex^{r} Davison Esqr – a Tribute of his Respect'. Just when the matter seemed finally to have been settled, Davison insisted that his 'residence in London' be inserted. This forced Boulton to alter 'Respect' to 'Regard' to save space. Only then was the final version agreed: 'FROM ALEX$^{R.}$ DAVISON ESQ$^{R.}$ S$^{T.}$ JAMES'S SQUARE – A TRIBUTE OF REGARD'. It was not quite the end of the matter. Davison later made Boulton change the spacing of the letters. Before and after versions were both found in his private collection.

By February, Davison was 'vexed beyond conception' by the prize business. Without all the papers from Gibraltar, the distribution of the money might be delayed indefinitely, doing fatal damage to his reputation for efficiency. 'My being without these essential documents', he chafed, 'is actually being without *everything*, for the Navy Board, however well disposed they are, cannot take notice of my powers, nor indeed pay a *shilling* till the condemnation arrive.' He could feel his rivals watching him, waiting for him to fail. He confided these fears to Nelson in terms that suggest Davison was already building defences ahead of the attack. 'I feel most sensibly and hurt to the greatest degree, for those who do not know the cause of the procrastination in settling the prize money will readily blame me.'

Davison's gout had forced him back to bed, which hardly helped his temper and gave him plenty of time for morose pondering on the matter. He suspected some 'secret underhanded work in this business' and shared his frustration with Nelson. 'It is cruel upon the captors and I hope and trust to god, who is the cause of keeping from me the necessary vouchers and documents will meet the reward they deserve'. Davison fingered George Purvis as the prime suspect; acutely aware of Purvis's resentment, he had even sent a copy of his letter of appointment to St Vincent's disaffected secretary because 'you seem to think I have arrogated it to myself'.

Davison's gloom deepened with the death in London, on 21 February, of his brother George. The news, he wrote, though surely not unexpected after years of ill-health, 'occasions me much affliction'. He had lost more than a dear brother. Good, sensible George, who had shared in his triumphs and trials for twenty-five years, had been a vital check on Alick's vaulting ambition. That restraint gone, Davison grew careless in his dealings. The results would be devastating.

The first delivery of neat oak packing cases from Birmingham arrived towards the end of March 1799. In a state of high excitement, Davison called for his carriage to drive the short distance to the Queen's House (now Buckingham Palace). In his pocket were one gold and one silver medal. The medals were received 'with much Joy & Pleasure'. 'I was *alone* with the King a full hour,' he breathlessly recalled in his next letter to Nelson, 'when much of the conversation was about *you*. It is impossible to express how warmly he spoke of you and asked me a thousand questions about you.' He returned the next month to present one of his prints of Nelson to the king, who 'speaks of you with the tenderness of a father'. And, like a concerned father, the king quizzed Davison on the hero's whereabouts. 'I said a great deal (but not too much) regarding my idea of your situation,' Davison reported archly. The next gold medal was given to Earl St Vincent, who had returned early from the Mediterranean suffering from ill-health. Two years later the earl reciprocated Davison's gift with a gold medal of his own, struck by him as a 'testimony of approbation' to his brother officers. Below the motto, 'Loyal and True', a seaman and a marine make what could be a masonic handshake. Davison sent another gold medal by express to Bath. Fanny thought it 'elegant' and 'an heirloom to my *son*'. She sent it out to Josiah at Naples with a letter for her husband, asking her son to deliver it to his stepfather in person, 'fearing it might fall into other hands'. 'I never had a secret from him,' she wrote desolately.

Davison was hoping to present Nelson with his medal in person. So he was 'truly mortified' to learn, on 6 April, that Nelson was marooned at Palermo, having committed himself to restoring Ferdinand to his throne. An alternative plan was hurriedly put into action. A box of the medals, '15 Inches long, 11 Inches wide and 1½ Inches Deep', was despatched to Portsmouth after a tip-off from Evan Nepean that *Queen Charlotte* was about to sail for the Mediterranean. Admiral Sir Peter Parker, the shore-based commander-in-chief at Portsmouth and an old friend of Nelson's from the West Indies, ensured that the medals safely reached the ship before she sailed. In return for this help (and, no doubt, because he was the deputy grand master of the freemasons in England), Sir Peter Parker received a silver medal.

The box held twenty-two medals. Eleven of them were gold: two for Nelson and nine for the Egyptian Club captains remaining in the Mediterranean. John Campbell, Nelson's former secretary in *Vanguard* and a partner in the prize business, was recruited to distribute the gold medals from Gibraltar. The other eleven medals were in silver, including one for Campbell himself and ten for Nelson, 'to be given to whom you please'. Each of the medals was cased in its own red morocco box and arrived with a short printed testimonial from Davison.

Nelson was delighted when the medals eventually reached him in August. Like his wife he thought them 'elegant', thanking Davison on behalf of the 'brethren of the Nile'. Nelson gave one of the two gold medals intended for himself to Sir William

Hamilton and the other to his flag captain, Thomas Masterman Hardy, who Davison, momentarily ill-informed, thought had already returned to England. As Captain Ralph Miller of *Theseus* had been killed in an accident, Nelson kept his medal for himself as a substitute. The government was not slow to take advantage of the medal for some strategic gift-giving itself. In July the foreign secretary, Lord Grenville, asked Davison to send gold medals to the emperors of Russia and Germany, the sultan of Turkey and King Ferdinand. Davison happily obliged, waving aside all offers of payment.

The news that Nelson would not be home in the near future was inconvenient for Davison but devastating for Fanny. The crisis of December, when she had threatened to go to her husband, had blown over, and she had resigned herself to waiting just a few more months. So the report that he was staying in Palermo was a terrible blow, reigniting Fanny's fear, fuelled by the constant rumours, that Emma Hamilton had ensnared her husband. In public Fanny kept up an appearance of dignified stoicism. Her letters to her husband remained dutiful and chatty. Only to Davison did she feel able to voice her anger and bewilderment. 'What recompense has government to offer my dear Lord for being a Slave to the State,' she wrote on 11 April. 'I am truly disappointed . . . Lord Hood always expressed his fear that Sir W and Lady Hamilton would use *their influence* to keep Lord Nelson with them: they have succeeded.'

The strain made Fanny ill. 'Upwards of eighty oz. of blood' was bled from her and she was ordered to rest in Clifton, near Bristol. This seemed to help as by May she was back in London, taking lodgings with Edmund Nelson in Sloane Street. Edmund, now almost eighty, was confused by this unexpected turn of events, his behaviour giving Fanny yet another cause for concern. 'His extreme agitation upon hearing a carriage or a knock on the door is quite distressing,' she anxiously reported. As the letters from her husband dwindled, Fanny leaned heavily on Davison for practical and emotional support. In April she wrote to him six times. Davison was now running errands for both Fanny and Edmund: sorting out Fanny's tax return, managing her post to the Mediterranean, paying her bills and storing her china. When Nelson ordered Fanny to find them a house in London, she asked Davison to be 'master of the subject'. Davison promised not to take 'too splendid a mansion', vowing in a letter to Nelson that 'the chief and principal object now with me is to see that your income be such as to enable you to support the dignity and titles so gloriously won'.

When Harriett's baby, a boy, arrived on 25 June, Fanny volunteered her husband as godfather to the 'little hero'. Maurice stood as proxy in his brother's absence; Fanny herself, to whom the baby was another silent rebuke of her own failure to conceive, missed the christening of Alexander Horatio Nelson Davison, pleading the lack of a suitable gown. She sent a small present instead.

The Nelsons' growing dependence on Davison made William Marsh resentful. Nelson's faithful banker knew that Davison's interest in official circles was far greater, and better cultivated, than his own. This contrast was thrown into sharp relief when Davison effortlessly secured an award of £10,000 for Nelson from the East India Company, using his influence with the chairman of directors, Henry Dundas. 'This money will enable you to do many things,' Davison suggested tellingly, 'which I am sure you are desirous of contemplating in regard to your dearest wife.' 'Ten thousand thanks' came from Palermo. The money was sent to Marsh, who was left looking out of touch and ineffectual.

Davison was not alone in wishing to celebrate the battle of the Nile in a 'most durable manner' or in trying to make political capital out of it. In June he was invited to join a committee formed by the duke of Clarence, the king's third son, to examine proposals for a 'national monument of British Glory and Pre-eminence'. The duke claimed a personal interest in Nelson's victory, having served in the navy alongside him back in the 1780s. Like his brothers the duke was a freemason, having been initiated into the aristocratic Britannic Lodge by Lord Moira himself. Freemasonry gave him the urge to build.

Sitting alongside Davison on the duke's hand-picked committee were the most powerful men in the country, including the first lord, the prime minister, and the chairmen of the Bank of England and the East India Company. Davison, who was made the treasurer, was now unquestionably close to the very heart of the establishment.

After long deliberation the committee settled on building a 'grand naval obelisk' costing over £15,000 on Portsdown Hill, overlooking Spithead. With typical enthusiasm Davison began soliciting subscriptions. He opened an account at Goslings & Sharpe, Harriett's family bank on Fleet Street, placed advertisements in *The Times* and sent circulars 'to the mayors and chief magistrates of the principal cities and towns throughout Great Britain'. He even asked Nelson whether Ferdinand would make a donation, 'no man having derived greater security by our victories than His Sicilian Majesty . . . But you know best – and how his heart beats.'

The duke's scheme was received with great enthusiasm by a population brimful with patriotism. Money and pledges poured in. All the principal figures in public life subscribed, their pledges in proportion to their rank: from £21 for the duke of Northumberland and members of Pitt's cabinet to £26 5s 0d for a royal prince. Within weeks, half the cost of the obelisk was secured.

Despite the delays and accidents, the Navy Office, on behalf of the Admiralty, bought the six Nile prizes from Davison in April, paying him £117,465 11s 5d for *Le Franklin*, *Le Tonnant*, *Le Peuple Souverin*, *L'Aquilon*, *Le Conquérant* and *Le Spartiate*. The prizes themselves were escorted into Plymouth by James Saumarez in July. According to the instructions he passed to Maurice, Davison received the prize money from the Treasury in eleven ninety-day bills which were scheduled to fall due at five-day intervals from 16 June to 12 August. As each bill became due it incurred interest at

3½ per cent a day, which Davison promised – he was not obliged to do this – to add to the final distribution. Davison was prevented by law from distributing the money to the victors within a year of the battle, to allow counter-claimants to the prizes to come forward. Even so, 1 August 1799 came and went with no sign of a distribution. Some vital documents were still missing. 'I am quite vexed and out of humour about it but it has been no fault of mine,' Davison confided to Nelson; 'yet I feel sensible how few there are that will take the trouble to investigate the cause of the procrastination.' He offered to advance money to any officer suffering hardship because of the delay and appealed for Nelson's help in countering the rising tide of complaints by stating 'the precise situation I am placed in'.

At least the Egyptian Club sword was ready. 'I have had [it] sent here,' Davison wrote on 8 August, 'from the makers Messrs Rundell & Bridge, the sword ordered by your captains intended for you as a present from them in commemoration of the glorious 1ˢᵗ August 1798 – I shall keep it till I receive their orders about it – It is very handsome.'

The sword was extraordinary. Its grip was made of pure gold and shaped like a crocodile. There was a rumour that the eyes of the crocodile were set with diamonds and its scales with amethysts, emeralds and other precious gems. In fact the crocodile was set with two enamel plaques, one showing Nelson's coat of arms and the other allegorical figures of Britannia and Africa. The guard of the sword was set with another enamel depicting the battle and was engraved with a dedication to Nelson from the Egyptian Club captains.

It seems a number of the wealthier captains, such as Samuel Hood of *Zealous*, arranged similar swords for themselves, possibly using Davison's services. Another was presented to the prince of Wales. These copies were in ormolu rather than gold. Davison, who inveigled himself into the Egyptian Club, owned at least two versions of the sword himself, confirming his pivotal role in its production. One, bearing Davison's crest, was bequeathed by his

son to the Royal Hospital at Greenwich in 1873; the other, perhaps left uncollected by a captain or retained as a 'spare', I found
in his lost collection.

Nelson was impatient to see his new sword, which he
thought 'an uncommon mark of brotherly regard'. Fatalistically
believing he might never return to London and keen to show it off
in Naples, he pressed Davison to send it out with the presentation
sword from the City of London. Eager to please and hearing that
Superb was about to sail, Davison sent for the City's sword. It was
refused. He was loftily informed that the Lord Mayor wanted to
present it in person if or when Nelson arrived back in England.
The Egyptian Club sword would have to go by itself.

Fanny suffered from ill-health throughout the year, plagued
by a persistent cough and low fever. She tried to concentrate on
improving Roundwood and caring for her 'very feeble' father-in-
law, but her thoughts were inevitably drawn towards Naples.
Edmund, who thought it 'fifty to one' he would live to see his son
again, tried to be reassuring. 'I am sure', Edmund told her, 'he will
do everything he can to make you happy.' The old man then inadvertently gave a glimpse of his son's motivation, the constant
pressure that fed his ambition and his campaigns. 'Others expect
more of him than he can perform,' he said.

Fanny still dutifully wrote to her husband every week, filling the pages with the usual 'chit chat'. By now she was getting
few letters in return, which stretched her endurance to breaking
point. 'I am sure he writes,' she exclaimed from Bath in July; 'who
can be so wicked as to take my letters.' Back in London, she and
Edmund moved to lodgings on St James's Street to be closer to
the Davisons, and her petite figure became a familiar sight as she
walked to the square every day to collect her post or to discuss
domestic business with Davison. Her house became a Mecca for
officers returning to England, all of whom were anxious to pay
their respects to Nelson's wife. She dined with the Nepeans and
the Marshes; and she ostentatiously attended court, 'most magnif-
icently attired in a superb embroidery of silver, in drapery of

stripes, with a robe of silver'. Her head-dress was made from ostrich feathers. Fanny later revealed to Davison that at St James's Palace she had been 'openly' asked about her husband's affair with Emma Hamilton. Earl St Vincent had even sought her out to discuss it.

Davison was holidaying in Northumberland when it was announced in the *London Gazette* that the first distribution of the Nile prize money would take place at his offices on Millbank on 25 October. With the £20,000 wrestled from the Admiralty for the three lost prizes and interest from the Navy Office bills, the prize money had risen to £139,269 16s 1d. This was reduced to £131,161 0s 8d after deducting Davison's costs and his 5 per cent agency commission, some of which, annoyingly, had to be given to Campbell and Purvis in recompense for their role in bringing the documentation back to England. This sum was divided into eight equal shares of £16,395 2s 7d. The first share, or flag share, was given to Earl St Vincent, the commander-in-chief of the Mediterranean fleet. The earl was obliged to distribute half this share, or £8,197 11s 0d, among the six flag officers under him in the fleet. Each received £1,366 5s 2d, although only Nelson had actually fought the battle.

The next two shares of the prize money, totalling £32,790 5s 0d (2d appears to have gone astray), were for the fifteen captains at the battle: the fourteen Egyptian Club captains plus Thomas Capel of *La Mutine* who carried Nelson's dispatches to London. Each received £2,186 5s 2d – the equivalent of about five years' pay. The shares for Captains Westcott and Miller, both now dead, were sent to their families. The others were collected in person or, most probably, by the captains' navy agents. William Marsh collected Nelson's share.

It may seem surprising that the captains earned far more from the battle than Nelson. But prize money was specifically designed to reward the captains and *pour encourager les autres*; not to enrich the flag officers, who anyway enjoyed a share in all the actions in the Mediterranean. The real winner, as usual, was the commander-in-chief of the fleet – for the battle of the Nile, the absent Earl St Vincent. It was not a perfect system, but it was one that rewarded ambition. Most men accepted it, though it grated on Nelson.

A share was then given to each of the three remaining classes of officer: a total of 866 men. A second-class officer, such as a lieutenant or master, received £167 5s 1d, while an officer of the more abundant fourth class such as a midshipman was paid £26 13s 2d. The final two shares of prize money were reserved for the 6,947 'gallant tars'. Each received £4 14s 4d: a sum equivalent to about a quarter of his yearly pay.

The distribution at Millbank was handled by Henry Cutler, one of Davison's former suppliers who had been employed to manage the agency. The Nile medals must have been handed out at the same time, stopping the 'gallant tars' pestering Davison for them. In the end Boulton struck 7,216 medals, not including 100 struck in error. This was more than enough for all the survivors. Küchler's die was given to Davison and destroyed. Boulton's bill, which took another two years to arrive, showed 25 gold medals at just under £11 each, 154 silver medals at 11s 6d each, 506 in copper gilt at 4s each and 6,531 in bronzed copper at 2s 6d. The total came to a little over £1,200, far less than the £2,000 generally quoted by historians. After Davison complained about the lateness of the bill and reminded Boulton that he had once airily promised to make the medals at cost, the amount was reduced by a further £100. Boulton had met his match.

Only *Defence*, *Leander* and *Orion* were in home ports when the distribution was announced. The payments to the other men would be made in their ships as they reached England. Failing that, the money could be collected at Millbank on the last Wednesday of every month for the next three years. Any money still unclaimed after that time would be passed to Greenwich Hospital. Many men never saw their prize money at all, having mortgaged it to the slopsellers and tavern-keepers who preyed on them in the ports. Some were simply robbed.

After his head-money payment and a share in the sale of the stores and ordnance in the prizes, Nelson's proceeds from the battle rose to over £2,300 – still only a fraction of Davison's commission. More galling still was Earl St Vincent's windfall, even though he had done nothing except allow Nelson to pursue the French to Egypt in the first place. Then, in November, an unexpected and glorious opportunity was presented to redress the balance. After the earl left the Mediterranean because of ill-health, one of the ships under his command, *Alcmeme*, was involved in the spectacular capture of two Spanish treasure ships, *Santa Brigida* and *El Thetis*, laden, it was rumoured, with nearly a million pounds' worth of silver. It was Maurice who alerted his brother to the possibility of claiming *Alcmeme*'s flag share in the earl's absence. Without a moment's hesitation, Nelson asked Davison to look into the matter. 'Custom will give it me,' he predicted confidently.

While Cutler struggled with the agents, tars and slopsellers at Millbank and Nelson brooded over prize money in the Mediterranean, Davison embarked on his last great tribute to the victory: a modern landscape re-enacting the battle in the park at Swarland, using trees as warships and gorse as the hidden sandbanks of Aboukir Bay. It was not an entirely unique idea. Further down the Great North Road, Charles Herbert, Earl Manvers, erected a pyramid in the grounds of Thoresby Hall, his Nottinghamshire seat, surrounding it with trees named after the Nile captains. Yet for scale and boldness, Davison's creation was matchless.

First a great wood of beech, chestnut, elm and pine trees was planted to the west of the mansion under the supervision of Joe Lloyd, the head gardener at Swarland. The sweeping edge of this wood was bordered with gorse bushes which, in late summer, would burst into a mass of golden colour, imitating the sandy Egyptian coastline. More plantations, fringed with gorse, represented shoals and islands within the bay.

The battle was laid out in front of the wood, to the south of

he French flagship *L'Orient*
xplodes during the battle of the
ile. An Egyptian Club captain
resented Nelson with a coffin made
om *L'Orient*'s shattered mainmast,
hile snuff boxes were made from
e smaller fragments – as Davison
ould do after Trafalgar using wood
ken from *Victory*.

Above: Davison's Egyptian Club sword indicating his close involvement with Nelson's 'band of brothers'. Davison owned two such swords, his other example mistakenly passing to Greenwich Hospital in 1873 with the scabbard to Nelson's sword.

Below and right: The Nile wine coolers. These were decorated with Nelson's coat of arms and symbols of freemasonry, including the figure of a mason displaying the date of the battle on his apron.

Above: Davison's medal for the battle of the Nile. The mysterious late inclusion of a rising sun on the reverse (*top right image*) may have been another veiled masonic reference. This example was described in 1866 as 'The *Gold* medal worn by the immortal Nelson when he fell 21st October 1805 at Trafalgar'.

St. JAMES'S SQUARE.

The PARISH of St. IAMESS Westminster, taken from the last Survey, with Corrections.

N°. B¹ For Hannover Square See St. Martins in the Fields.

PART OF St. MARTINS PARISH

MARTINS PARISH

PART OF St. ANNS PARISH

T. BORN ROAD

Great Marlborough Street

Carnaby Market

Burying Place

Broad Str.

Golden Square

PORTUGALL STREET

PICCADILLY

Ger-man Street

Ger-man Street

Stable yard

St. James

Hay Market

Coventry Street

St. James's Street

King Street

James Square

Charles 4ᵗʰ Street

PALL MALL STREET

St. James's Palace

The KINGS GARDEN

St. JAMES'S PARK

500 Yards

Publish'd According to Act of Parliament 1725 for Stows Survey.

References to the near Buildings
1 Benjamin Street
2 the Riding house
3 Taylor Street
4 Little Marlbr. Street
5 S. Iames Gravel pitts
6 Little windmill Street
7 Gravil Lane
8 Little Silver Street
9 Little Peter Street
10 Kemps Court
11 Cock court
12 Hopkins Court
13 Husband Street
14 Maidenhead passage
15 Greens Lane
16 Prices Alley
17 Walkers Court
18 Red Lyon Yard

24 Soltons Court
25 Windmill yard
26 Trumbull yard
27 Browns Court
28 Hunts Court
29 Condé Court
30 Black horse yard
31 Crown yard
32 George yard
33 Salters Court
34 Floces yard
35 Boar Alley
36 Black horse yard
37 Davids yard
38 Nags head Inn
39 Cock yard
40 Salters Court
41 Sue Bell Ally
42 Whi. horse yard
43 Phenix Inn
44 Unicorn Inn
45 Stone Cutters alley
46 Pal Mal Court
47 Paved Alley

173

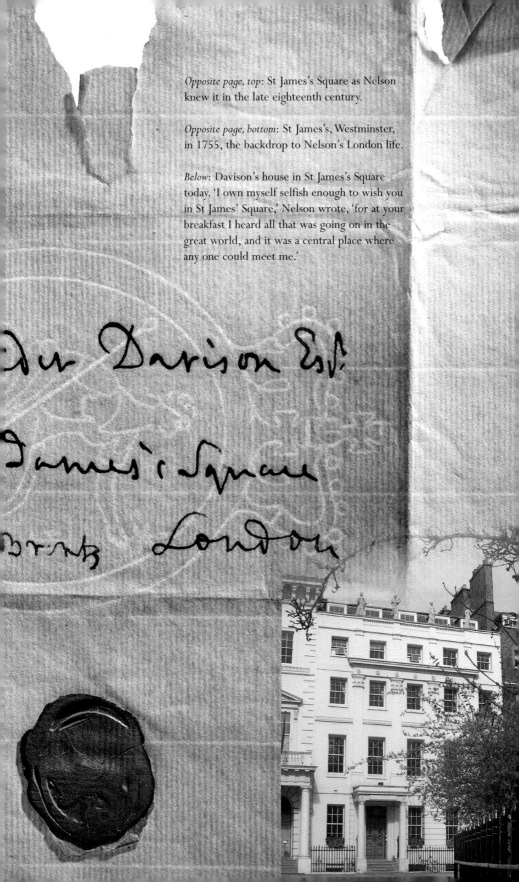

Opposite page, top: St James's Square as Nelson knew it in the late eighteenth century.

Opposite page, bottom: St James's, Westminster, in 1755, the backdrop to Nelson's London life.

Below: Davison's house in St James's Square today. 'I own myself selfish enough to wish you in St James' Square,' Nelson wrote, 'for at your breakfast I heard all that was going on in the great world, and it was a central place where any one could meet me.'

Nelson, 1800. This is the only contemporary image of the admiral out of uniform; one Davison would find familiar.

Opposite page, top: Merton Place, Surrey. Emma and Davison almost fell out over the alterations to the house and grounds, but by September 1805 she could write that 'Nelson is so delighted with Merton & now he is here 'tis a paradise . . .'

Opposite page, centre: Emma Hamilton as she looked when Davison first met her in November 1800.

Opposite page, bottom: Sipson House today. Davison's elegant country villa stood on the London to Bath road close to the Goslings at Langley, the duke of Northumberland at Syon House, and Maurice Nelson at Laleham.

The Revd Edmund Nelson was painted by Sir William Beechey in March 1800 at the lodgings he shared with Fanny in St James's Street, where the old man would hear 'the chat of the day' from Davison. The finished portrait was intended as a surprise for his son. Nelson became a particular friend of Beechey, who was one of the many freemasons at the Royal Academy.

Right: The brief but poignant note Nelson scrawled to Davison after hearing that his father had died.

the house and stretching away towards the North Sea in the far distance. It covered almost 100 acres. Small clumps of oaks were placed in the positions of the British warships at the height of the action. A gravel pathway was cut through the clumps, tracing the line of the anchored French fleet. The 'seaward' side of the park was enclosed by a ha-ha and a deep belt of purple flowering gorse. Behind the ha-ha was a raised carriage drive, giving visitors a panoramic view of the Battle Park as they approached the mansion. On warm summer nights they could walk the gravel pathway, assailed on both sides by the British 'warships', while Davison enthusiastically described the battle.

Davison's park was a bold, visionary gesture in keeping with his enlightened times. On a bleak, windswept hill on the northern coast of England he had recreated Egypt itself. The ensuing two centuries washed most of it away. Little evidence of the Battle Park remains today and no memorial survives. The wood has been built over and the gravel pathway replaced with a road. But much of the park is still open ground and it still sweeps down towards the distant sea. There are few, if any, 200-year-old oaks left, but clusters of younger trees have sprung up here and there, perhaps where *Leander*, *Goliath* and *Minotaur* once stood. Closing your eyes on a still Northumbrian evening you can still imagine the roar of the battle.

VII

AGAMEMNON

64 GUNS,
CAPTAIN SIR EDWARD BERRY

B<small>Y</small> 1797 TROUBLE WAS brewing at the Millbank coal depot. William Wilkinson, the managing clerk, was nursing a grievance. Despite endless promises, Davison had failed to increase Wilkinson's lowly salary, which the clerk complained was 'scarcely enough for my family expenses'. Wilkinson's discontent soon reached the ears of George Walker, an unscrupulous coal merchant in the Channel Islands who was fiddling the barrack office by mixing cheap, poor-quality coal into his supplies. Sensing an opportunity – and possibly also a threat if he failed to act – Walker offered Wilkinson a cut of his profits in return for turning a blind eye to his fraud. Seeing the dangers of this illicit arrangement, Wilkinson's son, who also worked at Millbank, dissuaded his father from getting involved with Walker. He was too late, however, to prevent him writing to Walker, who was on a buying trip in the north of England. In his letter the embittered clerk warned the merchant 'to be upon his guard': Davison was on his way to Newcastle and 'Mr Davison was of a very suspicious disposition'.

Unfortunately for Wilkinson, Walker's own clerk, a man called Robert Edington, thought he should have been given a cut in the swindle and, out of pique, leaked Wilkinson's careless letter to Walker to Davison, hoping to incriminate both of them. It half worked. As Edington expected, Davison was outraged at

Wilkinson's insinuation, dismissing him instantly; but he took no action against Walker, the instigator of the frauds.

Then, one warm summer's day in June 1800 Mungo Shedden, the general manager of Davison's clothing factory, sent for John Allen, one of his junior book-keepers. Allen was to go immediately to the common office at St James's Square and present himself to John Bowering, Davison's principal clerk. There the terrified young clerk was given a bundle of papers to sign. Eager as he was to return as quickly as possible to the factory in Covent Garden, Allen could not help noticing that he was counter-signing receipts for payments from Davison. Some of the receipts dated back as far as 1797, and all of them, Allen saw, were in the name of George Watson. This confused Allen because he knew Watson was one of the apprentice clerks handling the goods coming into the warehouse for the barrack office. Watson was certainly not supplying the goods himself and nor, as far as Allen knew, was Davison allowed to make anything for the barracks in his own factory. The receipts were for more than £40,000. When Allen had gone, Bowering sent the accounts to the barrack office for reimbursement. As usual, he added Davison's agency commission of 2½ per cent to the total.

Davison had far more important things to consider than the local shenanigans of his coal merchants, which left him untroubled. He was at the pinnacle of his career, engaged 'in commercial transactions, general agency, prize agency, clothing concerns, contract with the navy board, public loans & private concerns with the trusts which were confided to him by some of the most eminent persons in the kingdom'. The money was flowing into St James's Square. All this wheeling and dealing enabled Davison to acquire the trappings and attitudes of the great Whig landowners he courted and admired at his masonic meetings. Through their influence he metamorphosed into a great benevolent figure, one close to the vibrant cultural and scientific heartbeat of the age. He befriended a fellow freemason, dramatist and Whig MP, Richard Brinsley Sheridan, buying shares in his theatre on Drury Lane.

Improving his family's status entailed sending the twins to Eton; improving himself made him a charter member of the Royal Institution. He was patron to at least three London hospitals: St George's at Lanesborough House, the Middlesex (where Fanny used his influence to get one of her maids treated for 'scorbutic rheumatism') and the Magdalen in St George's Field, which purged and reformed young female prostitutes. As the Magdalen was colloquially known as the Asylum, and the duke of Northumberland was a vice-president, it seems likely that Davison was referring to it when he accepted a vice presidency in 'the Asylum' on Nelson's behalf. 'It was intended as a mark of respect for you, and my knowing the other vice presidents I conceived you would not refuse.' The irony was surely not lost on Nelson, who was at the time on the verge of an affair with Emma Hamilton, herself a reformed prostitute.

The evidence for Davison's enhanced status was visible at both ends of the country. He gained power and prestige by extending and improving his estate at Swarland, while his mansion in St James's Square became the showcase for a growing art collection. Without the benefit of the conventional European grand tour enjoyed by the sons of grandees, in the course of which they would be introduced to the art and architecture of the continent, he had an eclectic taste veering towards the showy. Dutch masters hung alongside Italian landscapes; but, as he grew in confidence, he focused on his taste for the rural and sporting pictures of the British school (he also owned at least one painting by Gainsborough). As in everything he did, once hooked Davison was a compulsive consumer, and he rapidly acquired almost forty paintings by George Morland, a leading exponent of the genre. Ten years later, his passion spent, he dumped the lot into auction at Christie's.

Davison's social ascent received royal recognition when the prince of Wales came to dinner at St James's Square on 15 April 1800. The prince drank from the very finest diamond-cut Bohemian wine glasses and ate off Derby china using silver with an elegant threaded pattern and engraved with Davison's crest. 'If you are entitled to bear your crest on an *Earls* coronet,' the *roi d'armes* commented tartly when Davison later applied to paint the crest onto the doors of his carriage, 'it should have no *cap tassel* or *lining* – such were never worn with Crests on helmets – Every nobleman & every Gentleman who understand the least of Heraldry laugh at the absurd & ridiculous assumption & affectation of a modern Earl's coronet cap &c'. Other guests in the glittering party included the prince's brother, the duke of Cumberland; the prime minister's brother, the earl of Chatham; and the duke of Northumberland's brother, the earl of Beverley. Alongside them were close friends like Lord Moira, Evan Nepean and William Huskisson, the young under-secretary of state for war who had secured the parliamentary seat of Morpeth in 1798 by renting land from Davison. Like Nepean, Huskisson was an acolyte of Pitt's boon companion Henry Dundas, the secretary of state for war who bestrode the political scene. Nelson was unavoidably (though presumably not unwillingly) detained in Naples, though within the year he would be guest of honour when the dinner was repeated. Skilled at public relations, Davison ensured that his dinner received a good press. *The Sun* called it 'sumptuous'; and three months later it even received a mention in the *Quebec Gazette*, proof, if proof were needed, to the *Gazette*'s envious readers of Davison's stratospheric rise since his return to London.

Nelson's thoughts at this time were a long way from the dining table. He was brooding over the spectacular capture of the Spanish treasure ships the previous November. As soon as the silver was landed at Plymouth it was loaded into no fewer than forty-four wagons and escorted under armed guard to the Bank of England, where it was sold for over £600,000 – equivalent to £30 million today.

As expected, Earl St Vincent, despite having been absent from the Mediterranean at the time of the capture, laid claim to the *Alcmene*'s flag share of the treasure. Nelson was outraged, calling the earl 'dishonourable'. 'I beg', he beseeched Davison, 'that you will show your friendship for me, and not sacrifice my right to any person, however elevated his rank. Right is right. I only want justice, and that I will try and obtain, at the expense of everything I am worth.' The earl was astonished when he heard Nelson was counter-claiming. It was preposterous, he stormed at Davison, that he should be accused of 'taking from his Lordship . . . when the whole world, and he in particular ought to know, that I have in every thought & deed contributed to his aggrandizement'.

At first Davison, who was uncomfortably caught in the crossfire, was confident that an embarrassing quarrel between Nelson and the earl could be avoided. He arranged a meeting with Benjamin Tucker, who had replaced George Purvis as the earl's agent and secretary. Tucker gave the impression that the earl knew his claim was weak, telling Davison they wanted to avoid a dispute with Nelson. Both sides agreed to take legal advice; in the meantime, the *Alcmene*'s flag share, estimated at £12,000, stayed firmly in the Bank of England.

Weeks passed and it became obvious that the earl would not retract his claim. When Tucker presented a memorandum outlining the earl's case – dismissed by Davison as 'feeble and defective' – Nelson responded in kind with a vigorous rebuttal. Tempers were fraying fast, though for the sake of propriety the two protagonists ensured that, throughout the ordeal, their public utterances and letters to each other remained scrupulously correct. With litigation now inevitable, Davison spent several days in April 'shut up' with his lawyers preparing Nelson's case. He assured Fanny, who took a keen interest in the matter, that 'I shan't lose one farthing that I can get.'

Fanny was by now almost entirely confined to the house in St James's Street caring for Edmund, whose health was fast deteriorating. The old man was installed in the back drawing room, sustained on a diet of fish, game and injections of laudanum. Fanny prepared cordials and helped the physician with Edmund's catheter. Twice during February Fanny persuaded her father-in-law to take a walk, but each time they were forced back inside after Edmund complained that the fresh air was irritating his bowels. He preferred to stay by his fireside and hear 'the chat of the day' from Davison, though he rallied to sit for Sir William Beechey, the famous portrait painter and another freemason.

Fanny coped, but her own health, never robust, suffered under the strain not only of nursing Edmund but also of trying to ignore the persistent stories of her husband's affair with Emma Hamilton. The chronic cough was now accompanied by a 'troublesome' rash. Even the servants fell ill 'one after the other', causing further difficulty. The occasional 'cheerful' dinner with the Davisons relieved the dreary monotony of Fanny's life, but she longed for 'hot sea bathing and the warmth of the summer'. Most of all, she wanted her husband back. By April 1800 she had heard nothing from him for over four months.

When the spring arrived, and the blossom burst from the cherry trees in St James's Park, Fanny took Edmund to Roundwood, away from drawing-room whispers and newspaper innuendo. So she might have been in her Suffolk garden admiring her improvements, or watching the skylarks circling over the cornfields, when the letter arrived out of the blue in June. 'He is coming home,' Davison scrawled in a hurried, excited note; 'his letters have set me to work, and will keep me fully employed for seven days.'

But Nelson was not returning alone from Naples. He was travelling overland through Europe in a party which included Sir William and Lady Hamilton. The reason for this unusual arrangement was inescapable even to the most loyal and dimmest of minds. Nelson's elder brother William, a humble rector in Norfolk who was already badgering his newly famous sibling for help in advancing his church career, tactlessly asked Fanny whether she had any objections to his meeting his brother before she did. 'I said no, none, what objections can I have?' Fanny tetchily wrote to Davison.

Nelson expected to arrive in London in mid-October. Writing from Vienna, he asked Davison to 'take either a house or good lodgings for me – not too large, yet one fit for my situation, to be hired by the month'. Davison gave this task to his own general factotum, a man called James Dodds whom he had known since first coming to London in the 1760s and with whom there was a Northumbrian connection. Nelson also ordered Fanny to meet him in London, warning her to expect a 'worn out old man'. Fanny might have wondered why. Nelson, who had not seen or spoken to his wife for two and a half years, expected to be in England for less than a month before returning to sea.

Fanny would have preferred to stay in a hotel in London rather than waste money on a house. Nelson's command also entailed moving linen and servants from Suffolk to town, which was a complicated, tiring business. However, she let Davison decide the matter, insisting only that she would meet her husband and the Hamiltons in Suffolk before they all travelled to London together. A note to this effect was sent to meet Nelson at Yarmouth. Fanny must have dreaded the prospect of Nelson making a highly publicized return to London on the arm of another woman. This way, too, she would have the chance to assess the nature of her husband's relationship with Emma Hamilton on her own terms, possibly forestalling the humiliation that threatened.

But events were not within Fanny's control. At this pivotal moment in her marriage, Fanny's letters to Davison reveal muddle and confusion. Worried that this change of plan might not reach Nelson in time, Davison urged her to stick to the original instructions and to meet her husband in London. Trusting Davison's judgement, Fanny left Suffolk on 23 October. Another note was sent to Yarmouth in which she looked forward to meeting her husband in London as planned. As insurance against a mix-up, Fanny left Edmund behind at Roundwood to greet his son if he should still call at the house. In the meantime, no doubt acting on good intelligence of Nelson's expected date of arrival, Davison managed to squeeze in a trip to rejoin his family for their annual holiday at Swarland. Fanny was given the run of St James's Square in his absence. 'I would prefer a bedroom up stairs,' she wrote rather ungraciously, 'and my woman servant very near. Samuel and the coachman can sleep out.' When there was still no sign of the admiral or a house by the time the Davisons returned in early November, Fanny moved to rooms at Nerot's hotel in King Street.

Nelson landed at Yarmouth on 6 November. Among the bundles of letters waiting for him there were the two notes from Fanny dated 20 and 22 October. Her heart must have sunk reading the reply which was forwarded to her from Roundwood. 'I have only had time to open one of your letters,' her husband wrote; 'Sir and Lady Hamilton beg their best regards and will accept your offer of a bed.' Sitting beside Fanny as she read this at Nerot's hotel was Edmund who, rather than waiting any longer for his son at Roundwood, had turned up in London. Only the servants remained in Suffolk to welcome her husband and his new friends. It was not a propitious start.

The meeting seemed doomed. London woke on Sunday 9 November, 1800, to gales and lashing rain. Tiles were torn off, trees were uprooted, even the gate to Hyde Park was blown down. Towards three o'clock in the afternoon, a foreign-looking carriage clattered through the gloomy, rubbish-strewn streets towards St James's, its blinds firmly drawn down. Alerted by the commotion outside, Fanny went nervously down to the hall of the hotel. There stood her husband, in full dress uniform, looking very thin and very wet and probably very sheepish. Standing behind him, unmistakably, were Sir William and Lady Hamilton. Fanny could hear the huzzas of the small crowd gathered outside. It is one of the great set-pieces of Nelson's life. Emma said later that Fanny's reaction at that moment sent a 'petrifying chill' through Nelson's heart.

The uneasy party then dined together, everyone no doubt grateful for Emma's incessant chatter. Afterwards the Hamiltons left for Grosvenor Square to stay with the exotic aesthete (and freemason) William Beckford – reputedly the richest man in England – while Nelson escaped to meet the first lord of the Admiralty, Earl Spencer. Fanny later joined her husband at Spencer House for supper, so it was only much later in the evening that the Nelsons were finally alone together. There would have been a lot to talk about; whether they did talk about it we do not know. In the morning Nelson, wearing undress uniform, was spotted walking with a friend to the Admiralty in Whitehall. The friend must have been Davison, because when the two men reached the Navy Office later in the morning Davison called for his carriage for the return journey to St James's. The day ended with a splendid banquet at the Mansion House where, with elaborate ceremony, Nelson was at last given the sword voted by the City of London.

Nelson was mobbed wherever he went. George Matcham, who was recovering from a drunken fall off his horse, warned his brother-in-law that 'every description of persons, especially the young women, have the serious intention to eat you up alive & God knows (the barbarians) your physical, corporal substance will not go much further than a sprat but I suppose they mean to intoxicate themselves with the spirit'. No wonder his head was turned. But behind the glittering public celebrity there was private turmoil. Unable to be with Emma, Nelson did everything he could to avoid being alone with Fanny. He plagued the Admiralty and Navy Office and visited the Royal Exchange, the East India Company and the Turkey Company. Davison was at his side throughout, even accompanying Nelson to a 'large dog shop' in Holborn to buy Emma a fox terrier, which she promptly christened Nilus. Maybe she had heard the ditty that circulated after the battle:

Where Nilus pours his hallow'd flood,
Discolour'd with Egyptian blood,
By Frenchmen basely shed,
Brave Nelson, with indignant pride,
Beheld their impious squadron ride,
A gallant band he led.

162

Eager to spend the £500 given to him by Lloyd's coffee house to spend on plate, Nelson called at Rundell & Bridge on Ludgate Hill, the makers of the Egyptian Club swords. Philip Rundell prepared an estimate of £570 for a service of first- and second-course dishes, each piece engraved with Nelson's crest. Flush from the Nile awards, for the first, and only, time in his life Nelson probably felt he had money to burn; and in Davison, who was given the task of arranging the commission, he had a past master in the art of luxury shopping. The Nile service, which would eventually cost over £620, was sent out to Nelson the following April in 'a strong iron bound wainscot chest partitioned & lined with green baize'.

When Nelson had last been in England he was sick from the loss of his arm, the time before he had lived quietly with Fanny in Norfolk; but fame, life in Naples and principally Emma had transformed him into a bon vivant, enjoying an endless round of late-night supper parties and boisterous trips to the theatre. This relentless social programme, which enabled Nelson to delay addressing the crisis in his marriage, threw Emma and Fanny painfully together night after night. At one of these parties, possibly at a dinner hosted by the Hamiltons on 20 November, Alick and Harriett must surely have seen Emma perform her renowned 'Attitudes', sexually charged poses taken from antique models – or, as Horace Walpole described them, her 'gallery of statues'. When the pace got too hot, or the strain on the women became too great, or his situation became too uncomfortable, Nelson reverted to male type, asking Davison to arrange a stag party, or 'man party', to the Royalty theatre.

On Saturday 30 November, Davison hosted his own 'grand entertainment' in honour of 'the hero of the Nile'. It was a glittering occasion. The finest 'champagne, burgundy and cape wines' flowed all evening as Davison's liveried servants glided among the dazzling guests. The prince was back, this time accompanied by the prime minister, William Pitt, his brother the earl of Chatham and the top echelons of government. Pitt's presence was no doubt responsible for Lord Moira's absence, though William Huskisson

Emma Hamilton strikes an 'Attitude'.

and Evan Nepean returned, joined on this occasion by William 'weathercock' Windham, the secretary for war, and his chief Henry Dundas. The navy was represented by the first lord, Earl Spencer, and Admirals Parker and Payne. Nelson and Sir William Hamilton completed the party. Admiral Payne claimed to have deflowered Emma on her arrival in London twenty-five years earlier; assuming this to be true, then, as one of Nelson's biographers has pointed out, no fewer than three men around Davison's dining table that evening had slept with Lady Hamilton, with at least one other, the prince, desperate to make a fourth.

Despite all the evidence of her husband's affair, Fanny maintained the appearance of a dutiful and affectionate wife. A mother herself, she surely noticed Emma's pregnancy, though she kept the knowledge of it to herself. She immersed herself in routine, as people do when they are grieving. She managed the move to a house that 'Davison's man' James Dodds found for the Nelsons on Dover Street. Fanny made a list of her husband's Nile jewels, which were lodged for safekeeping at St James's Square during the upheaval. Two glaring omissions from this list, which was found in Davison's papers, were the *chelengk*, which Nelson had adopted as an ornament for his hat, and the sultan's diamond star, which was probably with Emma. Nelson's other personal belongings, which trailed after him from Naples, were put into store at Dodds's warehouse in Soho. These comprised a miscellany of souvenirs, pictures, furniture and coffee, including a 'Large piece of the wreck of a ship' and a section of the mast from *L'Orient*, the French flagship at the battle of the Nile. The coffin in which Nelson would one day come to rest had already been made from the mast – a mawkish gift from an Egyptian Club captain – as had a smaller box, a snuff box. Davison would imitate this latter gesture after Trafalgar, using wood from the mast of *Victory*. The wines that Nelson had ordered on his travels were laid down in the cellars at St James's Square.

Nelson, his status as their hero secure, enjoyed great acclaim from the lower ranks; but polite opinion remained firmly on

Fanny's side. Writing to Nepean, Earl St Vincent had predicted 'much brouillerie' would greet the Hero of the Nile, and he was right. When Nelson appeared at court, ludicrously bedecked in his foreign orders, his reception was 'cold and repulsive'. More seriously, Lady Spencer, the wife of the first lord, cut him dead. Fanny was welcome to the queen's drawing room, while Emma was most decidedly not. These slights hurt Nelson, though for the most part he suffered in silence; the gossips must have lapped them up.

Aware that his public image was a little tarnished, Nelson set about refreshing it. In between visits to the Admiralty, where he continued to press for the sanctuary of an appointment at sea, Nelson trailed around artists' studios. In the few weeks he was in London he sat for at least seven, including William Beechey, Lemuel Abbott (again) and John Hoppner, the prince of Wales's 'Principal Painter'. Their portraits fed the growing market on the Strand for cheap prints of the hero, the eighteenth-century equivalent of teenage pop idol posters. Earl St Vincent commented scathingly that 'that foolish little fellow Nelson has sat to every painter in London'.

Nelson's strategy of avoiding Fanny culminated in her spending Christmas alone in London while he passed the holiday with the Hamiltons at William Beckford's phantasmagorical gothic mansion in Wiltshire. He returned to orders to join the Channel fleet as second-in-command to Sir Hyde Parker, an admiral with fifty years' experience of the navy but whose old-fashioned views and methods were viewed with some disdain by his bumptious subordinate. An expedition was being planned to Copenhagen to confront the 'Armed Neutrality', an aggressive confederation of Scandinavian countries led by Russia. A new flagship, a Spanish prize called *San Josef*, was waiting for him at Plymouth. Nelson took advantage of his imminent departure to set in motion the formal and, as far as he was concerned, final separation from his wife. Divorce, though theoretically possible, was an impossibly long and expensive option requiring an act of parliament, so instead his marriage would die by a thousand cuts. To carry out his plan Nelson would need Davison's help, though the latter was at first an unsuspecting accomplice. Nor was her husband's intention obvious to Fanny when she went to Lincoln's Inn with him on 10 January to arrange the sale of Roundwood, which they agreed had never been a satisfactory property. The town house in Dover Street was also let go after barely a month. As ordered, Davison had found a house 'fit' for Nelson's situation, but unfortunately not one suitable for his pocket. 'The best thing for Lady N when she is in town', he was now informed by Nelson, 'is good lodgings, next to that to hire a very small ready-furnished house.' Nelson was preparing the ground for a new life, and a new home.

Fanny must have assumed they were simply tidying up their affairs before Nelson returned to sea, when in fact she was helping to loosen the ties that bound her to her husband. It seems he gave no indication of his motives, and discussion of a separation was not one she would have broached herself, because the prospect was too grim. She was praying things would blow over, while he was hoping she wouldn't notice what was going on. The situation left Fanny in the dark, clinging desperately to her marriage.

William Marsh was instructed to pay Fanny £500 quarterly during Nelson's 'absence'. The allowance was generous, representing a little over half Nelson's income at the time. In addition, Davison was told to discharge Fanny's debts and to purchase a £200 annuity for her using £4,000 she had inherited from an uncle on Nevis. Fanny asked Davison and Maurice Nelson to be her trustees. There was no legal requirement for Nelson to settle any money on his wife or even to allow her use of her own inheritance, but to ignore his moral obligation would have had a devastating effect on his reputation. The size of the settlement ensured that Fanny would be able to live comfortably – and, it was no doubt hoped, silently – while Nelson, with his escalating outgoings, would struggle financially for the rest of his life. But it was a price worth paying for finishing his marriage and assuaging his feelings of guilt.

Early on 13 January, before leaving for Plymouth, Nelson called on his wife at Dover Street, evidence that they were already living apart. Fanny was still in bed, tortured by thoughts that, despite all the evidence to the contrary, she might be responsible for the crisis in her marriage. When Nelson entered her bedroom, she held out her hand.

'There is not a man in the world who has more honour than you,' she said; 'now tell me, on your honour, whether you have ever suspected or heard from anyone anything that renders my own fidelity disputable?'

For the first time in many months, Nelson looked his wife in the eye. 'I call God to witness there is nothing in you, or your conduct, that I wish otherwise.'

And then he was gone, taking with him a promise from Davison that he would follow him to the west country as soon as he could get away from London.

Emma felt Fanny's 'tristesse'. She apologized for not visiting Dover Street in person, 'but I am not well'. It was the last superficially friendly contact between the two women, the only reason for their remaining cordial having left London. Days later, Emma secretly gave birth to Nelson's daughter, Horatia.

When Davison called on Fanny on 22 January, he urged her to go to Brighton, where he had taken a house for her. Did Nelson tell Davison to bundle Fanny out of town? Fanny was certainly reluctant to leave London, or at least to do so alone. She asked her sister-in-law, William Nelson's wife Sarah, to accompany her or, if not, to give her an excuse to stay in town at Nerot's. 'I *will stay* on purpose,' Fanny declared. But Sarah, who was drifting over to Emma's side, made excuses and said that she too thought it best that Fanny leave town. On 24 January, with no-one left to turn to, Fanny took the coach to Brighton, leaving London to Emma. 'Let her go to Brighton or where she pleases,' remarked Nelson to his jubilant mistress on hearing this news: 'I care not; she is a great fool and thank god you are not the least like her.'

Before leaving London, Nelson took the momentous step of

asking his solicitors, Booth and Haslewood, to start proceedings for recovering the *Alcmene*'s flag share of the disputed Spanish treasure ships, worth about £14,000, from Benjamin Tucker, Earl St Vincent's prize agent. This sum, Davison discovered, had been paid to Tucker as early as January 1800 – the high profile and spectacular nature of the capture apparently negating the restriction on early payout – long before their meeting at St James's Square and the exchange of testimonials. Although Nelson was suing Tucker, the die was cast for a damaging dispute between Nelson and the earl. Neither of them mentioned the subject, however, when they met in Devon. But the strain of it on Nelson, coming on top of the clandestine birth of his child and the betrayal of his wife, was all too obvious. Writing to Fanny, Lady St Vincent archly commented that 'I cannot say I think Lord Nelson looks well or in spirits'. This letter was found among Davison's papers, as if passed to him by Fanny as proof of her husband's confused state of mind.

In private both Nelson and the earl were more candid about their dispute. The earl described Nelson to Evan Nepean as 'devoured with vanity, weakness, and folly'. He thought Davison's role in the affair was 'offensive', prompting Davison to retort 'that my conduct is actuated by the love of justice, which perhaps may be "offensive" to his nice delicate feelings'. Nelson was equally forthright. 'I will support him as a great sea officer,' he wrote to Davison, 'but was he forty times as great I will not suffer him to rob me with impunity.'

The stakes were raised still further when William Pitt's administration fell over the question of Catholic emancipation in Ireland and the earl replaced Lord Spencer at the Admiralty. Nelson's opponent was now the most powerful man in the navy and the keeper of his destiny. On taking office the pugnacious new first lord signalled his determination, in a letter to his friend the duke of Northumberland, to clean up the 'the flagrant abuses which pervade the naval service, both civil and military'. In this, he meant the activities of contractors and prize agents.

Davison reached Torbay in gales and driving rain on Friday

6 February. There he found a note from Nelson urging him to take advice from the boatman before risking the journey out to *San Josef* to avoid 'risk drowning'. Undaunted, Davison made the journey and survived, clambering onto the magnificent 120-gun ship later that afternoon to interrupt Nelson's dinner. Here he took over from William Nelson, who had accompanied his brother down from London; Nelson, clearly emotionally vulnerable in the wake of his affair, the birth of his child and the breakdown of his marriage, wished to keep a civilian confidant close at hand for as long as possible. Only the pressure of his work at the Navy Office kept Maurice Nelson from making the journey as well.

The staterooms in *San Josef* were larger and more elaborately decorated than in a British warship, with heavily carved and gilded hardwood panelling. It was very dark in the great cabin itself, where the windows were draped against the pale wintry light outside. On the dining table was the silver centrepiece Davison had given Nelson after the Nile victory. Davison noticed that Britannia's trident was bent and askew. In the midst of all this gloomy splendour sat Nelson eating a simple meal. A green felt eyeshade was stitched to the brow of his hat. Sitting beside him was Lieutenant Edward Parker, one of Nelson's young protégés, helping his disabled chief to cut his meat. Coming closer to greet his friend, Davison saw that Nelson's left eye, the remaining good one, was bloodshot and almost closed with a yellowy sticky discharge. Nelson brushed his concern aside, blaming the infection on excessive letter-writing. Davison delivered a bundle of letters from Piccadilly, commenting that Emma looked 'handsomer than ever'. This made Nelson wonder (as I do) whether Davison secretly admired Emma himself. Davison also mentioned that Emma seemed thinner, proof that Horatia's birth was kept even from Nelson's closest friend.

Over that weekend there was ample opportunity for Nelson to open his heart to Davison. Davison would have been pragmatic and efficient, a necessary foil to Nelson in the latter's highly charged state. He recommended, for instance, that his friend make out a will. Nelson revealed the depth of his 'attachment' to Emma but gave little else away, uncertain perhaps of Davison's trustworthiness and wary of his familiarity with Fanny. Only Emma knew Nelson's true intentions, if he even knew them himself: 'rest quiet,' he told her; 'you know that everything is arranged in my head for all circumstances'. Fanny's correspondence with Davison over the coming months indicates that he was giving her hope even when, with hindsight, there was none. Either Davison was being wilfully cruel, which is unlikely, or he was receiving contradictory messages himself.

Nevertheless the sense of emergency was palpable by the time Davison returned to London on 10 February. The attitudes of both Fanny and Emma had hardened considerably during his flying visit to *San Josef*. One reason for this sudden change was revealed in a letter waiting for him at St James's Square. 'I will relate to you', wrote Fanny, 'a thing which seems nothing, but coming from Lady Hamilton I am certain some mischief is brewing.'

Rumours had reached Fanny in Brighton by way of the servants' kitchen and Mrs Mills, her housekeeper, that Emma was trying to poach the Nelsons' French butler, Bartimelle. To make matters worse, during her attempt to lure Bartimelle to Piccadilly, Emma had disclosed Fanny's £2,000 annual allowance. She also expressed surprise that Lady Nelson should have left town during the Season. 'It looks very *odd*,' Emma told the baffled butler, confident no doubt that her words would soon reach Brighton along the servant grapevine.

The disclosure of her allowance horrified Fanny. Not only was it an unforgivable breach of propriety, but it showed the intimacy between Emma and Nelson. 'None of us', she wrote to Davison, 'like the servants to know our incomes – I can only say that no woman can feel the least attention from a husband more than I do.' Mrs Mills then went on to reveal an even more remarkable conversation she had had with Nelson himself, shortly before he left for Plymouth. Describing his wife as 'an exemplary woman',

Nelson had spoken 'of your *want of health* your great *dejection of spirits*, in short that you looked *miserable*. It made him unhappy, but he could not tell the reason for it.

'*I* could have told him,' continued the loyal housekeeper to Fanny, her face flushing with anger, 'but I did not know how he would like the truth.'

Davison was in a quandary. On *San Josef*, Nelson had given him a bundle of letters to deliver to Piccadilly, but none for Brighton. Davison also returned with strict orders to seal up the mahogany box containing the Nile jewels which Fanny had delivered to St James's Square in November. 'I have further to desire', insisted Nelson, worried that his jewels might fall into his wife's hands during the impending separation, 'that the Box may not be opened or delivered to any person but by my order or in case of my death when they will be disposed of by my Will.' On the accompanying list, now in the British Library, Nelson mentions the sultan's diamond star, omitted from the inventory Fanny made of the jewels at Nerot's hotel. Did Emma deliver it to St James's Square herself?

At their house in Piccadilly the Hamiltons greeted Davison like a long-lost friend. Sir William was mournfully arranging the sale at James Christie's salerooms of much of his lifetime's collec tion of paintings and antiques – those that had avoided the catastrophe of *Colossus*. The sale was being forced upon the Hamiltons by the harsh financial reality of life back in England after their dreamlike existence in Naples. Even Emma had surrendered most of the jewels she had accumulated, though any good this sacrifice achieved was soon undone by her lavish lifestyle. Emma pressed Davison to tell her about his trip to the *San Josef*, sitting close to him to weave her spell. This calculated intimacy was a tactic she was using on Nelson's family with great success while waiting impatiently for the final breach between Nelson and his wife. She had discovered widespread resentment of Fanny's haughty manner, and was working this rich and surprisingly vindictive seam to her advantage. William and Sarah

Nelson were easy recruits, Sarah and Emma soon becoming thick as thieves. They dubbed Fanny 'Tom Tit', after the precise, pigeon-toed way she walked, while poor, guileless Josiah was labelled 'the cub'.

Possibly to make up for an uncomfortable feeling of guilt, Davison wrote several times to Brighton over the next few days. Fanny had heard nothing from her husband since a perfunctory letter of 3 February from *San Josef* complaining that Dodds had damaged his furniture. Davison's letters to Fanny are lost, but from her replies it is clear he tried to be reassuring. 'I hope in God all you say is true,' Fanny replied on 20 February; 'my mind has not recovered its natural calmness, nor do I think it ever will. I am now distrustful and fearful of my own shadow.'

Hearing from Davison of her husband's eye infection, Fanny offered to go to the *San Josef* herself. 'My affection, my anxiety, my fondness for him all rushed forth,' she confided to Davison, 'and I wrote him last Wednesday week and offered to nurse him and that he should find me the same I had ever been to him, faithful, affectionate, and desirous to do everything I could to please him.' Fanny's desolate plea had provoked a fierce response.

> *I only wish people would never mention my name to you, for whether I am blind or not, it is nothing to any person, I want neither nursing nor attention, and had you come here, I should not have gone on shore nor would you have come afloat. I fixed as I thought a proper allowance to enable you to remain quiet and not be posting from one end of the kingdom to the other. Whether I live or die, am sick or well I want from noone the sensation of pain or pleasure and I expect no comfort till I am removed from this world.*

Her husband's brutal rejection of her dazed Fanny. 'I have not answered this letter,' she wrote to Davison, 'will take some time days to consider.' It was clear everything was slipping away. She grew withdrawn, submissive. 'I think you had better not mention my name,' she finished the letter, 'leave me to my fate.'

Nelson arrived in London on leave on 24 February, grabbing the chance to spend two precious days seeing Emma and his daughter while his flag was shifted from *San Josef* to the 'dreary, dirty and leaky' *St George*. Nelson's hopes that he, rather than the antiquated Sir Hyde Parker, might command the expedition to attack Copenhagen were dashed when Davison reported that Parker's appointment had been confirmed during dinner among Earl St Vincent, Evan Nepean and Sir Andrew Snape Hamond. The new first lord was in no mood to show Nelson any favours.

In contrast to the frenzied public attention he courted in November, this time Nelson was keen to remain incognito while in town. He stayed at Lothian's hotel, in Albemarle Street, swapping his uniform perhaps for the pale blue wool jersey, dark blue coat and plain neckcloth he was painted wearing in Vienna on his journey back to England. He was equally desperate to avoid an unpleasant and possibly disruptive encounter with his wife at this delicate moment — so much so that he softened his tone when he wrote to Fanny in Brighton, asking her to 'rest quiet where you are', and signing himself 'as ever your affectionate Nelson'. Fanny obeyed, describing the letter as 'upon the whole rather milder'. It certainly gave her hope that reconciliation was not impossible. Her reply was carried by Josiah, for whom Nelson had secured a command. Josiah told his mother that he was received by Nelson and Emma at Piccadilly in a 'most affectionate manner'. The letter is lost, but from her comments to Davison it is clear that in it Fanny ignored her husband's latest cruel rebuff. Instead she thanked him for using his influence on Josiah's behalf and held out a hand of forgiveness. 'Tell me honestly,' she asked Davison, 'if you think silence is the best way sometimes to answer harsh & severe letters *Undeserved*.'

Nelson haunted St James's Square during his two-day stay in London. In between endless meetings to discuss his shaky finances and the litigation with Tucker, he found time to describe to Davison, while poring over a chart of the Kattegat bought at Faden's, the famous map shop in Charing Cross, how *he* would attack Copenhagen given the chance. Davison later recalled how, by shuffling various precious ornaments seized from around the drawing room at St James's Square, Nelson predicted exactly how the battle of Copenhagen would unfold.

Before leaving London on 26 February to join *St George* at Portsmouth, Nelson arranged to meet Davison again at Yarmouth, where the Channel fleet was massing on the Norfolk coast before the Baltic expedition. Davison, who would travel to Yarmouth overland, would probably have made the trip in any event. His young nephew, William Home, his sister Katty's son, was a midshipman in *Blanche*, a frigate attached to the fleet. Furthermore, William's father, Admiral Roddam Home, had died in Scotland just two weeks before, leaving the Davisons in England to rally around the boy. So Harriett and one of Davison's daughters, probably Doddy, also made the journey to Norfolk. It seems that Davison also dangled the exciting prospect of a tour of *St George* before his family.

The *St George* reached Yarmouth on 6 March, a day before the Davisons in their carriage. Nelson was pleased that his friend had come but distinctly unhappy at the thought of seeing Harriett, a known close ally of Fanny, let alone allowing her in his ship. There is again that feeling of discomfort, intimidation even, in front of women. Davison sensed this. 'I know your determination about women,' he told his friend, 'therefore I would not ask the favour of you.' So, soon after he arrived, Davison was pulled out alone to *St George*, no doubt leaving a furious wife and tearful daughter behind on the quay.

Before dinner in *St George* Nelson made out his will, naming Davison as his executor. This was the final, formal act in separating from his wife. In the will, which was given to Davison to safeguard, Nelson gave instructions for a further annuity worth £1,000 to be purchased for Fanny after his death. A sum of £3,000 was left in trust for Lady Hamilton, together with the diamond boxes in safe keeping at St James's Square. Emma would also receive the sultan's diamond star. The business over, guiltily

The obverse of a prelate jewel from the Ancient Order of Gregorians, one
of many friendly societies with links to the freemasons which flourished in
the late eighteenth century. Nelson was elected a member of the Gregorian
Lodge at Norwich in November 1800; Fanny later acknowledged the safe
receipt of his regalia. Note the pyramid and the image of a sun rising
above the sea, elements echoing the reverse of Davison's Nile medal.

remembering his broken promise, Davison took Nelson's flag captain Thomas Hardy to one side to ask him whether he could arrange a tour of another warship for Harriett and Doddy. Hearing of this subterfuge, Nelson relented. He arranged to stretch his legs with Davison on the quay the following morning, ordering Hardy to bring the women on board during his absence. This also gave Davison the chance to introduce his star-struck nephew to Nelson.

The friends parted on 10 March. Nelson sailed for the Baltic two days later; but not before acknowledging his election to the little known Ancient Order of Gregorians in Norwich. The Gregorians were one of a number of quasi-masonic friendly societies, such as the Oddfellows, which flourished during the eighteenth century, sharing the masonic emphasis on loyalty and fraternalism. Like the freemasons, the Gregorians in Norwich ritualized their ceremonies during their weekly meetings at the White Swan tavern in St Peter's Street. It was said the members of the Norwich chapter, who included the king's nephew Prince William of Gloucester, 'were memorable for their deep potations of Port wine'. Intriguingly, surviving medals and jewels illustrate a pervasive 'left-handedness' at the order's initiation ceremony, in contradiction to the masonic practice. This would make an admiral who had lost his right arm an ideal candidate. Another common element on the medals, which strongly link them to Davison's Nile medal, is that of a sun rising over a sea, its rays reaching to heaven beside the image of a pyramid. Nelson's elaborate regalia was sent to Fanny but is now lost, leaving the letter he wrote to William Gooch Pillans, the grand master of the Gregorians, on 11 March as the only proof that he ever formally belonged to a fraternal association.

Again Davison returned to London with a bundle of letters for Emma. But this time there was one for Fanny as well. This was Nelson's response to his wife's latest tentative attempt at *rapprochement*. It had taken him over a week to write, indicating that Emma might have had a hand in it. It was another brutal diatribe,

Fanny Nelson by Daniel Orme, 1798. Her letters to Davison reveal her heartbreak at the destruction of her marriage.

'. . . I love him I would do anything in the World to convince him of
My affection — I was truly sensible of My good fortune in having such a
Husband — Surely I have angered him . . . I still hope — He is affectionate
and possesses the best of hearts — He will not make me miserable — I hope
I have not deserved so severe a punishment from him': Fanny Nelson to
Alexander Davison, Friday 26 June, 1801.

Nelson railing against the condescending and pitying tone of his wife's letter. He was fed up with Fanny and irritated by Josiah, his comments revealing the simmering tension between him and his stepson. 'I have done *all* for him, & he may again, as he has so often done before Wish Me to Break my Neck,' he wrote. 'I have done my duty as an honest generous man, & I neither want or wish for any body to care what becomes of me, whether I return or am left in the Baltic. Living I have done all in my power for you, and if Dead you will find I have done the same, therefore my only wish is to be left to Myself.'

Fanny was bewildered by this fresh assault, describing it as her 'letter of dismissal'. Her shocked reaction was to send it to Maurice Nelson and Davison for their opinions. Maurice thought his brother had 'forgot himself' and Davison, who had a better insight into events and who must already have known at least the gist of the contents, was equally comforting. Their confidence calmed Fanny. After all, she could find no fault in her conduct as a wife – the reason, she believed, why so many marriages foundered. So perversely, rather than despairing, she forgave her 'dear deluded Lord', put her trust in God and resigned herself to waiting for her husband's brainstorm to pass. 'Whatever has passed,' she vowed, 'shall never pass my lips.' The weight of social opprobrium and Nelson's zealous regard for his own reputation would surely crush the affair. He would come back. This fatal misunderstanding of her husband sealed Fanny's fate.

By now, Davison was acting as both confidant to Fanny and go-between for Nelson and Emma. He was as integrated into the lives of the Hamiltons at Piccadilly as he had been into those of Fanny and Edmund Nelson in St James's Street. At the heart of this conundrum was Nelson, who by now was leaning on his man of business more heavily than ever, giving him increasingly diverse tasks. One of these was arranging a monument for Ralph Miller, the American-born Egyptian Club captain killed in an accident in the Mediterranean the year before.

Nelson wanted Miller's monument to be in St Paul's

Cathedral, where a Hall of Fame was being developed, under the supervision of the Royal Academy, by a government keen to honour the nation's heroes. It appears there was little chance of Miller's monument receiving public funding, probably because he was a relatively minor figure killed in an accident and not in action. The dean of St Paul's did, however, grant Davison permission to mount a memorial high on a pillar in one transept; but it would be 'unofficial' and so would have to be paid for privately. Davison gave the commission to John Flaxman, a sculptor working in the neo-classical style who had met the Hamiltons in Naples and whom Nelson greatly admired. Flaxman was fascinated by masonic culture, responding to the duke of Clarence's proposal for a naval pillar to celebrate the Nile victory by submitting his dream of building a colossal statue of Britannia, 240 feet high, at Greenwich. Flaxman sent a model of his vision to Davison.

Nelson envisaged Miller's monument as a tribute from the surviving Egyptian Club captains; but when they struggled to raise enough money, the subscriptions were thrown open to include the captains who had fought alongside Miller at the battle of St Vincent. Yet despite causing comment in naval circles by subscribing to the monument himself, Davison still failed to raise the necessary £500, and eventually most of the cost fell on Nelson, who had underwritten the project. Possibly for this reason, Nelson insisted that the monument be as simple as possible, telling Captain Edward Berry that he wanted an unfussy inscription 'as if flowing from the heart of one of us sailors who have fought with him' – sentiments which would have pleased Matthew Boulton.

The monument Flaxman prepared, in the form of a bas-relief panel, shows Britannia hanging a portrait medallion of Miller on a palm tree, assisted by a figure of Victory. A lion and Miller's ship *Theseus* are in the background. Unlike Davison's medal and Nile china, the monument was unambiguous and conventionally patriotic and heroic. Earl St Vincent was among those who approved the design. Moreover, the wording was, indeed, kept straightforward: 'Capt. R. Willett Miller. This Monument is raised by his companions in Victory.'

Davison's next challenge was more clandestine. Nelson asked him to secure a much-coveted painting of Emma by the artist George Romney before Sir William Hamilton put it under the hammer at Christie's with the rest of his collection. Nelson, failing to understand that Sir William had always viewed his wife merely as another ornament in his collection, to be admired and enjoyed by others as such, had been outraged to hear of the painting's impending sale. 'I see clearly, my dearest friend,' he wrote to Emma, 'you are on SALE.' Emma may have tried to prevent her husband sending her portrait to Christie's rooms herself; if so, she failed. So, as a last resort, Nelson turned to Davison, asking him to visit James Christie and buy the painting before the sale: 'for I could not bear the idea of Sir William selling his wife's picture'. Ten days before the auction, on 6 April, Davison, stricken by gout, persuaded Christie to sell him the painting (without naming the purchaser) for £300. Christie's receipt was still in Davison's papers two hundred years later. The painting was carefully wrapped and 'placed in *private*' at St James's Square, 'because', as Nelson warned Davison, 'it may make talk'. Mission accomplished, Nelson was delighted. He declared to his mistress that 'if it had cost me 300 drops of blood I would have given it with pleasure'.

VIII

AJAX

74 GUNS,
LIEUTENANT JOHN PILFOLD

IF SIR WILLIAM, a master of studied indifference, was aware that the portrait of his wife was hidden in Davison's mansion when he called there on 15 April 1801, he made no sign of it. As he had sold another of his portraits of Emma by Romney for only £25 in March, he was no doubt both grateful for the extravagant offer he had received and aware that it would be prudent to remain quiet about it. After all, there was really only one man in the world who would have paid so much for such a painting.

Sir William found Davison in bed, still afflicted by gout. The tears in his eyes were caused, however, not by pain but by joy. By Davison's hand was a letter with a familiar red wax seal, dated 4 April. He passed it to his visitor. 'The job is done,' Sir William read, 'and I know you will not like it the worse for having been done by me.' Nelson had won a great victory at Copenhagen.

Fanny seized the excuse of the battle to write to her husband. She was now in Bath, having moved there after her husband's latest snub to suffer in silence while searching her conscience for reasons behind his behaviour. The more she did so, the more she blamed herself for the crisis. This gave her renewed hope that it was within her power to save the marriage and may account for her heroic persistence in the face of such harsh rejection. It also suggests that the Nelsons had weathered similar problems in the past and that this may not have been the first time that Fanny had endured such treatment.

'I cannot be silent in the general joy throughout the Kingdom,' she wrote;

I must express my thankfulness and happiness it hath pleased God to spare your life . . . What my feelings are your good heart will tell you. Let me beg, nay intreat you, to believe no wife ever felt greater affection for a husband than I do. And to the best of my knowledge I have invariably done everything you desired. If I have omitted any thing I am sorry for it . . . What more can I do to convince you that I am truly your affectionate wife?

The reaction to the news of Nelson's victory was less dignified in Stafford Street, where William Nelson was seen rubbing his hands together at the prospect of further fame and riches for his family. But he celebrated too soon. In the wider world, reaction to Nelson's victory was subdued. The government had not properly consulted parliament before the expedition, and the reasons for attacking the Danes, when England faced imminent invasion by France, were obscure to the public. The mood was very different from that which had greeted the victory on the Nile. There were no wild scenes of celebration on the streets this time, no votes for lavish awards at East India House, no sparkling swords, no speeches at the Mansion House – and no gold naval medals from the king, a decision which outraged Nelson.

Before properly gauging the prevailing mood, and before the prize agency was awarded, Davison proposed repeating his act of largesse after the Nile by declaring in the *Morning Post* on 17 April that he would again give out medals: 'in like handsome manner to the brave tars who have distinguished themselves so nobly under their gallant leader, Lord Nelson, at Copenhagen'. The idea was later quietly dropped.

Nelson's material reward was limited to another £500 from Lloyd's coffee house to spend with Philip Rundell extending the

Nile service. Davison, whose reputation in such matters was now secure, was given *carte blanche* 'to make what you think necessary to add to the rest to make a complete set, such as plates, or whatever you may think right'. Six dozen silver plates and eighteen 'soop' plates were duly ordered, though their cost of £719 2*s* 0*d* was again over budget.

The government merely compensated for the lack of a medal with a derisory viscountcy. '*That* you ought to have had long ago,' huffed Davison; 'any thing short of an earldom I think would be deficient, if not degrading.'

While Nelson and his brother in London fulminated about an ungrateful nation, railing against the City merchants who only two years before had loaded him with money and ornaments, from Laleham there was only silence. Anxious enquiries revealed that Maurice Nelson was seriously ill with head pains. Most likely he had suffered a stroke. Fanny felt 'real uneasiness' when the news reached Bath, hiding it from Edmund. Deeply concerned, Davison sent his own physician to examine his friend. Sir John Hayes was a freemason, friend of Lord Moira and physician extraordinary to the prince of Wales. Hayes diagnosed an 'inflammation of the brain' and warned Davison to prepare for the worst.

This calamity had struck just as things seemed at last to be improving for the unfortunate Maurice. Only ten days before, on 4 April, Davison had reported to Nelson that his brother was 'contented', having been promoted to first clerk at the Navy Office, a position worth an extra £400 a year. It was not the seat on the Navy Board that Maurice craved but it was still, he declared, 'one of the things I have always been looking up to'. And, in an age when position relied so heavily on patronage, it was 'made more gratifying to me as there was not any interest made for it, but devolved upon me as a matter of right'.

Shaken by Hayes's grim prognosis and unable to visit Maurice because of gout, Davison was spurred into making an urgent and 'Most Secret' appeal to Earl St Vincent. In asking for a favour, when in the current circumstances the earl owed him nothing, Davison unashamedly invoked the need for reconciliation between the earl and Nelson. 'Give Maurice Nelson a seat at the Navy Board or make him an Extra Commissioner,' he pleaded,

> and let the Act be your own, without the suggestion of any person, and send Lord Nelson a single line acquainting him that you have done it. This Act I well know would be more gratifying to Lord Nelson than any mark of attention that possibly could be bestowed . . . to revive stronger if possible that Friendship, that Attachment between You two which I wish from the bottom of my Heart never to see intercepted – but that your Greatness may be excelled only by Affection for each other.

After discussing the matter over breakfast with George Rose on 22 April, the earl decided to offer Maurice the next available place not on the Navy Board but on the less prestigious Board of Customs. Nevertheless it was encouraging news which, added to a report that Maurice had rallied, enabled Davison to adopt an upbeat tone when he reported it the same day to Nelson, enclosing a letter from Emma on 'how matters *stand* in Piccadilly'.

It was all too little, too late. Maurice died during the night of 23 April, with Sukey by his side. He died as he had lived, quietly and politely, 'without any apparent struggle or uneasiness'. The news, which seemed suddenly shocking and unexpected, reached St James's Square before eight o'clock the next morning. Davison was badly affected by Maurice's death – more so, it seems, in the absence of proof otherwise, than he would be by Nelson's four years later. 'I have lost', he wept, 'my bosom and sincere friend!'

He blamed himself for deserting Maurice in his hour of need. 'It distresses my mind beyond expression,' he bemoaned, 'the thoughts of my confinement when I should (however distressing and painful the scene) have been with my friend in his last moments.' Sir William Hamilton offered to break the news to William Nelson, leaving Davison to summon up the courage to write to old Edmund in Bath.

Davison had known Maurice at least since their time together on the commissariat and probably longer. He was much closer to him than to Maurice's more glamorous, but usually absent, younger brother, with whom, in any event, there was always an edge of mutual exploitation. When in town Davison probably saw Maurice most days. Maurice even appears to have become integrated into the Davison family for, as Fanny recalled, 'Maurice loved Mrs Davison, his character of *her* was a charming one and what she richly deserves.' Davison had admired his friend's honesty, his loyalty, his generosity, his quiet determination and above all else his 'open frank manner', a rare quality within the circles in which Davison moved. Six months later, when an unexpected vacancy did appear on the Navy Board, it was given to Benjamin Tucker, Earl St Vincent's sidekick.

Maurice's body was taken to Burnham Thorpe, the small village in Norfolk where he had grown up. Davison asked Dodds to handle the necessary arrangements, settling the funeral costs of £184 himself. Despite his incapacity, Davison accompanied the coffin on its long journey from London. The funeral on 2 May was, he reported, 'the most awful scene I ever witnessed'. Poor, blind Sukey was 'a truly distressing object'. At his father's insistence, Maurice was buried as close to the church as possible 'in a most decent frugal manner'. His simple slate gravestone, paid for by Davison, is still clearly visible. Only the chancel wall separates him from his mother, whose body was placed in a vault inside the church in 1767.

Maurice's death deepened the wounds opening up in the Nelson family. Although William Nelson went to his brother's funeral, he failed to visit him before he died and refused to wear mourning, considering it an unnecessary expense. Fanny, rightly suspecting that William was in the 'party forming against *me*', was appalled by his heartless conduct. 'We none of us thought an opportunity would so soon *offer for William Nelson to show himself* in his *right colours*. He *never, never* had a spark of affection for his *brother* Maurice,' she wrote to Davison.

Fanny's loathing for William reached such a pitch that 'when I hear his name mentioned I give an involuntary movement'. In a move designed to secure his loyalty, she told Davison of William's 'contempt' for him. Kate Matcham, Nelson's younger sister, told Fanny she feared that William was trying to drive a wedge between Nelson and his agent, 'then he [Nelson] will have no one to tell him the truth'. Kate stuck by Fanny longer than the rest of her family, with the exception of Edmund. Fanny told Davison that Kate was 'determined not to know anything of my Lord Nelson's conduct towards *me*', though in fact this important ally was already being actively courted by Emma and would soon turn viciously against her sister-in-law. Davison was certainly no admirer of William, recoiling from him, perhaps, because he saw many of his own worst faults crudely represented in his fat, self-satisfied face. Davison deliberately avoided William when he called at St James's Square after Maurice's death, tolerating his constant hankering for preferment solely for Nelson's sake.

Someone in the family, probably William, had certainly stirred things up by suggesting to Nelson that Davison was looking to buy a house for Fanny rather than rent lodgings as he had been instructed. No doubt as its instigator had intended, this malicious piece of gossip, with its implication that Davison was siding with Fanny, caused an explosion:

'I do not believe Lady Nelson can have desired such a thing,' Nelson had stormed at Davison, 'for where am I to get the money?'

'Such reports could only have been fabricated for the vilest of purposes,' came the hurt reply,

and none would have dared to have said such a thing but those who are alternately both our enemies. I should have felt still more grieved had you given the slightest credit to them, trusting you have known me long enough to be assured I could have no other motive than your interest and happiness at heart and that I could never be such an egregious fool as to go and do that which I knew would be diametrically opposite to your wish and intention.

Edmund tried to remain aloof from his warring family, politely thanking Davison for his steadfast help in arranging Maurice's funeral. The old man had a delicate question, however, one which had been troubling him for some time. 'Are you assured', he asked Davison, 'that my late dear son was ever legally married?' Davison was not, soon discovering that Maurice had never actually married Sukey Field. But, as he noted in a pointed remark to Nelson in a letter written on the journey back from Norfolk on 3 May, 'it would be happy to civil society were all wives to conduct themselves with the same attention, fidelity and affection toward their husbands as this poor disconsolate woman'. Nelson attached no opprobrium to this startling discovery about his brother, nor was he in a position to do so. Like his father, he must always have suspected this to have been the case. Sukey simply became Maurice's 'honor'd wife', while her affairs, like so much else, were entrusted to Davison.

Waiting for Davison at St James's Square on his return from Norfolk was Edward Parker, the young, humbly born officer who had sat beside Nelson at Torbay. Parker, whom Davison thought 'a very excellent young man', had returned from the Baltic on the promise of a command only to discover when he reached London that he had lost out. Davison urged the unhappy young man to return to Nelson, promising to use his influence in getting him a position on the admiral's personal staff. In return the grateful Parker agreed to smuggle the portrait of Emma bought at Christie's out to Nelson. A previous attempt to get the painting to the Baltic with Lieutenant-Colonel William Stewart, who had commanded the troops from the 49th Regiment on board the British squadron sent to attack Copenhagen, failed dismally when Stewart had been unable to collect the painting from Piccadilly, where it had been surreptitiously moved. From his later correspondence with Davison, it appears Parker was also recruited at this meeting to be an informer in the *St George*, feeding St James's Square with information on Nelson's activities. It was a discreet method of intelligence-gathering that would be repeated by William Chevailler, Nelson's steward during the Trafalgar campaign.

Parker had brought with him to Davison's house a bundle of letters from Nelson. These betrayed the feelings of a man ill at ease, unwell and desperate to get home, 'for my *health*, and to take care of my *private affairs*'. As so often before, Nelson was brooding over prize money. With Fanny's generous settlement and Emma agitating for a house to be bought in which they could live together, Nelson knew that his outgoings were about to increase dramatically, and painfully.

According to custom, the Copenhagen captains offered their prize agency in the first instance to Sir Hyde Parker's secretary. In Nelson's eyes the man was as useless as his commander-in-chief, and after just two weeks the agency was taken away from him and, with Nelson using his influence on the captains, given to Davison instead. No-one bothered to tell Sir Hyde about the change. In a rather unseemly way, Nelson began collecting prize lists and preparing accounts of the goods seized in the enemy's ships. 'I am now working for you,' he assured his agent, apologizing for once again inflicting this 'troublesome office' on him.

Davison was grateful, but the business would be far less rewarding than the corresponding task after the Nile. Only one prize, a Danish warship called *Holstein*, was sent back to England intact: four other ships had been destroyed after the battle on Parker's orders, to Nelson's fury. 'The wanton waste which has been made of our prizes, which, God knows, we fought hard to get, has been hard upon the captors. Admirals etc may be rewarded, but if you destroy the Prizes, what have poor Lieutenants, Warrant Officers and the inferior officers and men to look to? Nothing!'

In this black mood, Nelson longed to escape to Emma. The thought of living with her occupied his waking moments and the memory of her body filled his dreams. By now he was receiving a stream of angry letters from Piccadilly which revealed Emma's rage at Fanny's strategy of blithely continuing her life as if nothing untoward were happening. This even included looking for a house to replace Roundwood. The ceaseless pressure from Emma for him to put an end to all the prevarication forced Nelson into writing to Davison again on 23 April, by chance the day Maurice died. Wanting Emma's approval of its content, Nelson ensured his letter reached St James's Square via Piccadilly.

My dear Davison you will, at a proper time and before my arrival in England, signify to Lady N. that I expect, and for which I have made such a very liberal allowance to her, to be left to myself, and without any inquiries from her; for sooner than live the unhappy life I did when I last came to England, I would stay abroad for ever. My mind is fixed as fate: therefore you will send my determination in any way you may judge proper.

'Depend upon it,' Davison promptly replied, hiding the unease he must have felt,

I shall implicitly obey and execute your wishes at the proper time and before your arrival in England for it is totally out of the question that you should suffer so much as I have seen you and, in my mind, you had better be out of this world altogether than endure the misery. It was a heartbreaking business to me to be witness to your daily unhappiness. I will break the subject in the most delicate manner I possibly can and in a way to give least offence to Lady N.

With the shock of Maurice's death reverberating, now was not the 'proper time' for Davison to drop his bombshell, and he did nothing. Perhaps he hoped the affair would still blow over; perhaps he shared with the upper echelons of the navy, government and society the almost uniform disapproval of Nelson's conduct; perhaps he was loath to do Nelson's dirty work; or perhaps Harriett simply stayed his hand. Either way, he did not relieve Fanny's agony of apprehension.

Fanny's 'congratulatory letter' to her husband after Copenhagen went unanswered. She had heard nothing directly from him since his 'terrible' letter from Yarmouth. Feeling increasingly ostracized by him and his family alike, Fanny's resolve finally began to crumble, and she returned to Bath to care for Edmund. Oblivious to the axe he was uncomfortably holding over her, she saw Davison as her only friend, writing to him no fewer than six times in May, her letters growing longer and increasingly forlorn.

Her confidence shattered and feeling 'more circumspect and cautious than even any young Miss of 16', Fanny begged Davison not to discuss her moribund situation with Nelson, believing it could only harm her cause further. 'So much has been said to him that I believe it has angered *him* instead of doing *good*.' She made one proviso for sharing her innermost thoughts with Davison. '*Never*', she insisted, 'mention me at 23 Piccadilly.'

Fanny emerged from exile to make her dutiful attendance at court in June. She would not surrender a valuable privilege denied her rival. 'I *assure* you I *did my very best*,' she reported. Otherwise, throughout her brief stay in town, she remained quietly at Nerot's hotel, fearful lest she 'run her head against any of them'. She called at St James's Square but Davison still baulked at his unpleasant task, leaving Fanny to return to Bath still 'ready willing & desirous' to live with her husband.

Reports of Nelson's imminent return once again filled Fanny with joyful relief. Then 'a moment's unwelcome and intruding reflection made me truly a miserable and pitiable being'. She took up her pen to Davison and in a letter of startling intimacy revealed her turmoil. She was submissive, repentant, abject, wretched and confused.

I love him I would do anything in the world to convince him of my affection – I was truly sensible of My good fortune in having such a husband – surely I have angered him – it was done unconsciously and without the least intention – I can truly

say, my wish, my desire was to please him – and if he will have
the goodness to send for me – I will make it my study to obey him
in every wish or desire of his – and with cheerfulness – I still
hope – He is affectionate and possesses the best of hearts – He
will not make me miserable – I hope I have not deserved so severe
a punishment from him . . . if you find that you can mention me
– I will esteem it the greatest favour you can confer on me . . .
you or no one can tell my feelings . . . My poor mind is so
distressed and disturbed that I dare not write – and particularly
of what makes me wretched – If you do not think I have expressed
My feelings, My affection and My sincere desire to do everything
he wishes me I am willing to say More – if possible. Should he
receive me with affection I will do everything he desires and in
gracious Manner he shall have no reason to regret his goodness,
to me I give you my honour.

Nelson arrived at Yarmouth on 30 June 1801, travelling to
London in a carriage decorated with ribbons and with the postilions dressed as seamen. Edward Parker, by now a firm favourite,
was in tow. Despite his showman's entrance, the triumphalist
mood of Nelson's welcome back to London the year before was
absent. Now the people were subdued, fearful of defeat and invasion by Bonaparte, who since the end of 1799 was no longer
simply the leading enemy general, but in effect dictator of France
– and a dictator with apparently imperial ambitions. On the
streets Nelson must have seen the bright uniforms of the many
volunteer corps springing up in the city to resist the threat. Even
Davison, the eternal optimist, was feeling down, having been
thrown from a buggy he was driving – one imagines recklessly –
when the shaft broke. The horse then kicked Davison's prone
figure 'so violently', *The Times* reported, 'as to confine him to his
house since'. Edmund Nelson, who was full of sympathy, blamed
the accident on 'some *nasty* hack post chaise'. Perhaps Davison
thought he was back in Quebec, madly driving a *calashe*.
As Nelson arrived in London at the same time as Fanny's painful

letter, he might have been grateful for even this uncomfortable means of avoiding explaining to his friend why his task remained undone.

London in its present condition was no fun, and Nelson escaped it as soon as he could, taking Parker and the Hamiltons on an excursion into the country. He called on Sukey at Laleham and in a letter to Davison renewed his refrain about lack of recognition. On his return to London he dined with Davison and the Hamiltons at Piccadilly on 11 July – and received another tentative note from Fanny. 'I could say more but my heart is too full,' she wrote. Nelson ignored it.

The following morning Davison plucked up the courage to write to Fanny himself. He felt awkward, apologetic. Yet in spite of all he knew he still held out the hope that her marriage could be salvaged, as if half-believing it himself. 'I have long wished to write to you,' he began,

> which nothing but the want of something to say to you prevented. I have nothing to relate particular, yet it is with unspeakable pleasure I can assure you, that Lord Nelson is in better health than I had ever reason to expect . . . I hardly need to repeat how happy I should have been to have seen him with you, the happiest. His heart is so pure and so extremely good that I flatter myself he never can be divested from his affection. I have the same opinion I ever had of his sincere respect for you. I have no right to doubt it.

Nelson's leave was broken by orders to take charge of the defence of the English coastline from Suffolk to Sussex. In many ways it was a humiliating assignment for the victor of the Nile, although Earl St Vincent dressed it up as one essential for the country's protection. Nevertheless, the appointment would keep Nelson employed and close to Piccadilly, so he accepted it, throwing himself into the job of deploying the motley defences with customary enthusiasm. 'I never witnessed more wonderful alacrity,' an awed Parker reported from Deal on 29 July; 'he filled everyone with admiration, emulation, and set everyone on the *qui vive'*.

Furthermore, Nelson's naturally aggressive instincts would not allow him simply to wait for the French to make their move. Early on 4 August he launched a daring raid on Boulogne, where Bonaparte's invasion army was massing. At ten o'clock Edward Parker sent Davison a breathless eye-witness account of the action.

> *We commenced our bombardment this morning. One brig, 3 luggers, and a flat boat are sunk . . . the Church is this moment knocked down. Some of the bombs are now firing carcases and I hope in the course of the day to see the rest of their flotilla destroyed . . . Lord Nelson energetic as usual, has been rowing about in his boat and is full of spirits, some of which he has given to all.*

The report was forwarded to the north of England, where Davison was staying at Castle Barnard with the antiquarian William Hutchinson, a man described as the 'father of masonic symbolism'. Yet despite Parker's enthusiasm, Nelson's raid on Boulogne was not a success, and for the first time he received a critical press: lobbing bombs from a safe distance was hardly Nelsonian, after all. Many newspapers had even begun to doubt whether Bonaparte was planning an invasion at all. Parker loyally dismissed all the 'fuss' in the newspapers, defending an action which, if nothing else, had eased the tension on the English coast and created alarm in the French. The people of Sandwich were so relieved that they gave Nelson the freedom of their town, though 'not in a box', joked Parker.

Parker was not so loyal towards Lady Hamilton, who was pressing Nelson to return to her. 'That B[itch] will play the deuce with Him, she is endeavouring to persuade him that the Ministry are jealous of the proceedings at Boulogne and it is her alone who is persuading him to go to London to purchase her a villa.' This impassioned comment, which is particularly powerful coming from an acolyte like Parker, offers a rare insight into the attitude of Nelson's brother officers to his affair with Emma. They reveal an assumption, which must have deeply hurt Nelson, that he was a good man being led astray by a woman who was no better than a whore. Moreover, the discovery of the letter in the Davison papers indicates that Parker knew, or thought he knew, that Davison shared this conventional view.

Assailed by Emma's demands, suffering from toothache and a fever, and worried that he might have badly damaged his reputation, Nelson's spirits began to sink as surely as the French batteries at Boulogne. He moaned that he felt 'very much fagged' and wanted to be 'quiet in my nest again'. Davison spoon-fed sympathy. 'I wish to heaven we had a peace and that you were quietly settled somewhere,' he replied; 'you have already gained *everything* and nothing is left to be acquired.'

He had pressed the right button. 'I agree with you,' came the swift response, Nelson having worked himself up into a lather, 'this is not a service for me, beyond the moment of alarm, but I am *used* and *abused* . . . *none* of the Ministry care for me beyond what suits *themselves*.' In this mood, perhaps to spite his detractors, Nelson launched another, more audacious raid on Boulogne.

The attack was a shambles. The French were fully expecting the assault and had thoroughly prepared their defences. The boats which guarded the harbour were mounted with iron spikes, then chained and netted to prevent boarding. Armed with pikes, cutlasses and tomahawks, the British seamen faced volley after volley of concentrated musket fire. Parker, who led one of the divisions, was among the first to reach the French boats, yet he faced an impossible task. Every man in his boat was either killed or wounded. Parker was hit high up on one leg, the ball ripping through his flesh and smashing his thighbone. Only quick thinking by a captain in a neighbouring boat saved him from death or capture.

At dawn the British began straggling back to their ships in boats full of the dead and the dying. Nelson was horrified. Stung by the dark mutterings among his men, he took full responsibility for the disaster, visiting the wounded in hospital and moving Parker to a small house in the town to recuperate at his own expense. At first the signs were encouraging. 'My wounds severe as they are, are thanks to providence in a very fair state,' wrote Parker to Davison on 28 August,

> *and I hope with the assistance of the Almighty to be restored with the salvation of my limb to my country and friends. My noble patron's attentions and parental conduct to me under my afflictions are almost alone sufficient to ensure my recovery; they are a balm that soothes all my pains, to ease and heal the sensible feelings of my wounds.*

After several urgent entreaties the Hamiltons, Emma demurely escorted by Sarah Nelson, joined Nelson at Deal. On arriving, Emma and Sarah took charge of Parker's recovery. By now, the injured leg had swollen to a grotesque size, and the unmistakable stink of decay filled the small, hot bedroom. The skin on the leg was mottled and turning blacker every day, with the wound discharging so much greenish pus that the sheets had to be changed regularly, causing Parker terrible distress. A month after the attack Dr Andrew Baird, the physician of the fleet who assumed personal charge of the case, took the inevitable decision to amputate the gangrenous leg. Only the awkward position of the wound, high on the leg close to a main artery, had prevented him doing so earlier.

Parker was heavily dosed with alcohol before being held down as Baird cut and then sawed his leg off. It was a gruesome scene. Emma stayed by 'poor dear little' Parker's side throughout the 'long, painful and difficult' operation, telling William Nelson that the boy's screams 'were heard far off'. Afterwards the foul-smelling, horribly deformed and blackened leg was hurriedly buried.

Parker lingered between life and death for a few more days, his agony torturing Nelson. On 20 September, as Baird had always feared would happen, Parker's 'great artery burst', spraying the room with blood and drenching his bed. The Hamiltons left for London the next day, believing it all over. But even in extremis Parker briefly rallied, taking a little 'milk and jellies'; it would be another week before he finally sank into death at nine o'clock in the morning of the 27th. In a fetishistic ritual that would be repeated at his own death, Nelson asked for the boy's hair. He then paid for a funeral in Deal with full military honours, disgusted by the Admiralty's refusal to foot the bill.

Davison stayed away throughout this drama, 'arranging and regulating matters against an invasion' as a deputy lieutenant of Northumberland, playing with 'your god son [who] is every hour becoming more interesting and is as wicked as any boy need be' and making a doleful visit to Edinburgh to see his sister Katty Home. Katty's son William, the bright-eyed, eager young midshipman whom Davison had introduced to Nelson at Yarmouth before the battle of Copenhagen, had died in *Blanche* off the Hebrides on 22 July, within just six months of his father's death. So Davison was already grief-stricken when he heard from Nelson, himself 'grieved almost to death', that Parker too had been lost. 'If there be a better world,' he bleakly commiserated, his words betraying a modern agnosticism, '*which we are taught to believe there is*, he must be gone there to enjoy it.'

The gloom was lifted in October by an armistice with France which released Nelson on leave. Without delay he left behind the unhappy memories of Deal and headed for London. On 23 October he stood in front of the house Emma had found for them to live in together. Merton Place was in the golden triangle of gentlemen's villas west of London. Nelson rhapsodized to Davison about his 'little farm', though the surveyor described the house as 'an old paltry, small dwelling of low storeys . . . altogether the worst place, under all circumstances, that I ever saw pretending to suit a gentleman's family'. It was not at all the sort of property that Fanny would have settled for.

Merton Place would cost £9,000. This was a substantial sum but one that, with his pay, pensions and prize money, Nelson should have been able to afford. After all, as he ruefully remarked, 'Everybody knows that Lord Nelson is amazingly rich!' The real picture was quite different. Nelson's generous allowance to Fanny eased his conscience but badly hurt his purse. This commitment together with a lifestyle designed to keep 'pace with my rank and position', seemed to make buying Merton Place an impossibility. Davison, who knew the true state of Nelson's affairs better than anyone, was surprised he was even considering it. 'You must have more money than I knew of,' he wryly commented, adding, 'whilst I have the means, you shall command them.'

Nelson was determined to buy the house. Emma had found it, and she was not to be disappointed. 'If I cannot', he exclaimed, 'after all my labour for the country, get such a place as this, I am resolved to give it all up, and retire for life.' So he sold his government stocks and arranged a two-year mortgage for £2,000 from the owner of the house at interest of 2½ per cent. Another £2,000 was borrowed from his brother-in-law George Matcham, who had appealed to Davison for help over a land purchase in New South Wales ten years before. Still Nelson was £3,000 short. While he was worrying over this shortfall, another nonchalant letter arrived from Northumberland.

> If you have settled for the house in Surrey you write me about, I am sure you must be in want of money to pay for it; and, lest that should be the case, I have written to my bankers, Messrs. Vere, Lucadou & Co., to honour whatever bills you may draw on them, with orders to those gentlemen to charge the same to my account. You may draw at sight on them whenever you please.

'Can your offer be real?' Nelson replied, 'can Davison be uncorrupted by the depravity of the world?'

The house was secured, Nelson making Emma 'Lady Paramount of all the territories and waters of Merton'. But it came at a high price. Buying it left Nelson in greater need of prize money than ever before and uncomfortably indebted to his agent. The halt in the war with France meant he could not win it at sea; so instead he would have to take it from Earl St Vincent in the courts.

Nelson intended to share Merton Place with Sir William Hamilton. It was a means of living with Emma within a *ménage à trois* that just about kept within the bounds of decorum, though it would fool nobody, least of all Fanny or Sir William. He insisted, however, that he should own the house and everything in it. Since his untidy separation from Fanny and the sale of Roundwood, most of his furniture and effects had been stored in Soho with Davison's man, Dodds. In a depressing and timeless ritual familiar to every broken marriage, Fanny and Nelson now began the process of sharing out their personal belongings.

Egged on by Emma, Nelson took the precaution of sending Dodds explicit instructions not to release anything without his permission. 'You will not permit the smallest article to be removed or taken away by any person without an order from *myself*,' he thundered. Fanny, who was living in Somerset Street, smartly evaded this attempt to frustrate her by going straight to Davison and coolly asking him to tell Dodds to deliver her linen, china and glass to her lodgings. 'No great quantity,' she said, 'but of great consequence to me – I look upon these things as mine although nothing passed on the subject.' She is unlikely to have considered the Nile wine-coolers her property, and if they were with Dodds they probably went to Merton with the pictures and plate that were being stored for Nelson at St James's Square. Fanny also made sure she got her rightful share of her husband's collection of wine. Nothing was overlooked during this miserable division of the spoils of the Nelsons' marriage. 'The wardrobe is hers,' Nelson reminded Davison, 'and if any of her clothes are at Mr Dodd's they had better be separated from mine.'

Nelson had returned from the south coast to an uncertain future. Peace with France had released him to join Emma; but it had also removed his livelihood. For some time he had been assiduously courting Henry Addington, who had replaced Pitt as prime minister earlier in the year. Now, encouraged by Emma, he decided to exploit his high public profile by turning his hand to politics. Encouraged by hints that there might be a role for him in the administration, Nelson was happy to be Addington's stooge when the House of Lords debated the peace terms with the French on 3 November. The draft treaty recognized British gains in the West Indies and French gains in Europe while returning Minorca to Spain, the colony at Cape Hope to the Dutch and Malta to the Knights of St John.

Nelson's patrons, new and old, were ranged against one another during the debate. Earl Spencer and Lord Grenville thought Addington's terms were a 'calamity'. Lord Moira, serving as mouthpiece for the prince of Wales, 'gave ministers credit for having made the best peace they were able to obtain and it should have his cordial support', a view endorsed by the duke of Clarence. Earl St Vincent pointed out that by gaining Trinidad and Ceylon, Britain held sway over 'two of the most valuable islands in the habitable globe'.

As the earl sat down, Nelson rose to his feet. The house was hushed as the nation's hero spoke, his short speech betraying a scarcity of experience and political sophistry but no lack of self-confidence. The peace terms, he declared, were 'honourable and advantageous to this country'. Minorca was anyway 'an island of little value' and Malta 'of no sort of consequence', while the Cape of Good Hope was 'merely a tavern' on the passage to India. Nelson then astonished the house by apparently lending Bonaparte's 'evil empire' legitimacy: 'Could any man say that the republic of France was not as permanent as any other state governed by one man?'

William Huskisson, the under-secretary of state for war, who managed the procurement of goods for the Cape colony, was outraged by Nelson's comments. 'I was much obliged to Lord Nelson', he scathingly told his patron Henry Dundas, 'for giving me anything that would create a smile on such a grave and awful subject.' 'How', Huskisson wondered, 'can Ministers allow such a fool to speak in their defence?'

Davison, whose carriage pulled into St James's Square from Northumberland whilst Nelson was on his feet in the House of Lords, probably shared his friend's jaundiced view of Nelson's enthusiasm for the peace terms. Through Huskisson's carefully nurtured influence he had developed a useful line of business supplying various goods to the Cape, including £55,000 worth of lead piping and pump equipment in one year alone, so the loss of the colony was a serious blow to him.

Davison just missed Fanny, who had called at the square on her return from visiting Edmund Nelson in Norfolk. The old man, shocked by his son's behaviour, remained her staunchest friend. 'My Horace', he told her, shaking his head, 'was always a good boy – but he is gone a little out of the straight road. He will see his error and be as good as ever.' Fanny found the visit upsetting; she knew that Edmund's loyal support for her was causing a 'cruel' breach between father and son. With tears in her eyes, she urged him to abandon her. But, alone among his family, Edmund would not desert Fanny. 'Be assured I still hold fast my integrity,' he wrote on 17 October; 'the opinion of others must rest with themselves and not make any alteration with us. I have not offended any man and do rely upon my children's affection that, notwithstanding all that has been said, they will not in my old age forsake me.'

Emma heartily blamed that 'wicked false malicious wretch' Fanny for the problems between Nelson and his father. She feared, however, the influence of the old man 'who protects this woman'. For her lover's sake she welcomed Edmund when he visited Merton in November, though he would not have been so warmly received had either she or Nelson known that he came to them from staying with Fanny in London.

Davison himself delayed visiting Merton Place, of which he

could claim one-third ownership, until December. The seven-mile drive from St James's Square took about an hour. Leaving London by Westminster Bridge, his carriage traversed Clapham Common and passed through the small farms and villages beyond. After it had crossed the Wandle River, close to the ruins of Merton Abbey, a high brick wall began running beside the road on the left. Soon afterwards, before reaching the turnpike outside the village of Merton itself, Davison's driver turned into a simple gateway beside a small lodge.

Through the bare trees, the dark shape of the house was visible against the grey morning sky. To reach it, Davison's carriage passed over a simple stonework bridge in Italian style which spanned a narrow, frozen canal cut from the nearby river. Merton Place was a two-storey residence, built of red brick about a hundred years before. The front was in a restrained classical style, with a five-bay pedimented centre between single-bay wings. The roof was crowned by four stone urns. As Davison crunched across to the front door, the house seemed deserted beneath a heavy blanket of snow. This impression was magically transformed when the door was opened by James Price, a black servant who used to work for Maurice at Laleham. James was in smart new livery, but more surprising was the brightness of the sparkling light and the warmth of the air that tumbled out from behind him into the cold winter morning.

To his left in the hall, hanging above a fireplace, Davison saw three portraits. One was of himself, possibly the one painted by Lemuel Abbott in March 1797. (In an act of some vanity, he had prints taken after this portrait in 1804, the original painting disappearing until it resurfaced in 2003.) Alongside Davison's portrait were those of Sir William Hamilton and of Edmund Nelson. Hamilton's is unidentified, but Edmund's must have been the one completed by Sir William Beechey the year before which is now in the National Maritime Museum at Greenwich. Maybe the relative positions of the portraits were shuffled depending on who was visiting. A glass door beside the fireplace led to a drawing room overlooking the grounds to the east of the house. On the other side of the hall, to his right, Davison would have glimpsed the library. As Sir William's extensive collection of books on history, sport, philosophy, travel, mineralogy and volcanology remained firmly at Piccadilly, the shelves were probably nearly bare, for Nelson was not an avid reader.

Ahead of Davison were the stairs, which led to five bedrooms. The staircase was lined with prints of Nelson, his ships and his battles. At the foot of the flight stood, rather incongruously, a French masthead lightning-conductor. This trophy of war is now also at Greenwich. In the centre of the stone floor, dominating the hall, was a large marble statue of the figure of the Nile, her ample naked figure surrounded by adoring children, a tribute perhaps to Davison's hostess. There was no great art in the house. Much of Sir William's famed collection had now gone under the hammer, and Nelson had neither the money nor the inclination to build his own beyond the things he was given. The interior decoration was part stolid Norfolk parsonage, part Neapolitan chic – not unlike that of a rock star moving to the country today. Like Fanny at Roundwood, Emma was about to launch into a comprehensive round of improvements to the house and gardens, encompassing extensions, tunnels, terraces and glasshouses.

Davison found the house full of people: friends, family and various hangers-on, all of whom enjoyed lavish dinners of dressed turtle, lobster and venison washed down by champagne and the best wines. Such profligacy could not last, of course. Unlike the insouciant Lord Moira, Nelson was tortured by his growing debts, particularly those to his man of business. With no sign of the Copenhagen prize money, no prospect of new prizes and no likelihood of an early settlement to his dispute with Earl St Vincent, there was nothing else for it: Nelson asked Davison to sell the jewel-encrusted pictures and boxes held at St James's Square. But the London jewellers were not very impressed by these foreign baubles, which glittered a little too brightly, and Davison struggled to find buyers. Expecting to raise a small fortune, Nelson was horrified by the 'shameful' offers he received. 'I would sooner beg', he exclaimed, 'than give those fellows my diamonds.' But there was no option. By Christmas most of the jewels were gone, leaving only one or two boxes, the *chelengk* and the sultan's diamond star.

An emergency summit to discuss Nelson's failing finances was called for 19 December 1801 at St James's Square. The same morning Davison received a letter for Nelson, its black wax sealed with a distinctive coronet and the monogram *FHN*. He passed it wordlessly across the table.

My dear husband — It is some time since I have written to you. The silence you have imposed is more than my affections will allow me and in this instance I hope you will forgive me in not obeying you. One thing I omitted in my letter of July which I now have to offer for your accommodation, a comfortable warm house. Do, my dear husband, let us live together. I can never be happy till such an event takes place. I assure you again I have but one wish in the world, to please you. Let everything be buried in oblivion, it will pass away like a dream. I can now only entreat you to believe I am most sincerely and affectionately your wife, Frances H. Nelson.

Nelson paused before giving a brief order and turning back to more pressing business. That evening Fanny got her letter back. Puzzled, she noticed it had been resealed, this time with a smear of red wax impressed with Davison's distinctive crest of a dove rising from an earl's coronet. Below the seal was a note written neatly and precisely in a very familiar hand, like a short stab to the heart: 'Opened by mistake by Lord Nelson, but not read. A. Davison.'

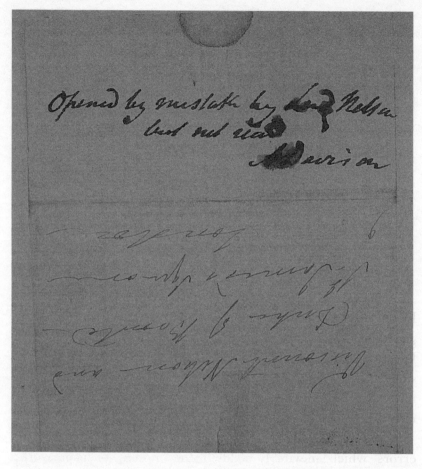

Davison's brutal annotation on the letter Fanny sent Nelson on 18 December 1801 in a desperate last effort to save their marriage.

IX
ORION

74 GUNS,
CAPTAIN EDWARD CODRINGTON

Looking back, it was in January 1802 that the trouble began. The Treasury was still doggedly, but rather aimlessly, pursuing loose ends in Davison's accounts from his days as commissary-general to Moira's army. This was not unusual: the accounts were long and complicated, and the Treasury wheels could turn very slowly. Then the auditor-general, the agreeable Charles Long, who might have closed the accounts, was replaced by a tenacious young man called James Chapman.

As well as noting the many straightforward accounting errors which inevitably riddled the mound of paperwork, Chapman started asking questions about missing invoices from Davison's forage suppliers. He also wanted to know the nature of the 'special payments' Davison made to Moira's headquarters for undisclosed 'secret services'. For most of these there were no receipts at all. At first none of this caused Davison particular concern. He knew that for matters involving the commissariat he could shelter behind the formidable figure of Lord Moira, who was just then being heavily courted by the prime minister Henry Addington.

More potentially serious was something the audit office turned up, quite by accident, while separately examining the barrack office accounts to 1795. Buried among a mass of questions for Oliver De Lancey, the barrackmaster-general, was query number 24. Query number 24 was a time-bomb for Davison. On the face of it, it dealt with a perfectly normal order from the barrack office to Davison asking him to supply a large quantity of bedding. But it was not clear to the auditors whether Davison had purchased the bedding in his role as agent to the barrack office, as he should have done, or supplied it himself from his own factory. Wherever the bedding had come from, Davison had undoubtedly charged the barrack office his standard 2½ per cent agency fee on the value of the order.

'In this transaction', the auditors noted,

> Mr Davison must have acted in the character of a merchant or as an agent employed by the Barrack Master General. If in the former it will not be necessary to produce the under bills and receipts of the parties but then the commission of 2½ per cent taken by him on the purchases (a charge which could only be made as an agent) must be disallowed. If considering him in the light of an agent, the charge of commission be persisted in, then the Bills and receipts of the parties must be produced.

John Bowering, the principal clerk at St James's Square, saw the danger of the situation immediately. Eighteen months earlier Bowering had compelled John Allen, an apprentice clerk from the Bedford Street house, to counter-sign receipts for bedding supplied in the name of another clerk called George Watson. The bogus receipts disguised the supply of goods to the barrack office from Davison's factory, enabling him to charge an agency commission on top of his manufacturing profit. Bowering, who must have been tipped off about query number 24 by someone in the barrack office, called an urgent meeting with Davison, telling him 'I thought he had better not let the commission stand as a charge upon the barrack supplies from Bedford Street.'

'Well then,' was Davison's nonchalant reply, 'get the accounts back and make the proper alteration, if I am to err, I would rather err the other side.'

But it was too late. The barrack office had already submitted the accounts to the Treasury, and when Bowering discreetly asked to have them back, he was told to make good any mistakes in a later account. This Bowering would fatally forget, or fail, to do. Besides, the peace with France, which was confirmed by the treaty of Amiens in March 1802, brought with it a sharp downturn in Davison's business. The Bedford Street house supplied nothing to the barrack office after June. Davison was told to hang onto the considerable cash advances he had negotiated from De Lancey and to wait for further orders.

The peace made Addington feel secure enough to call an election for July. Despite his political ambitions, Davison was prevented by law from becoming a member of parliament himself because he was a government contractor. The next best thing was to secure the election of hand-picked candidates who could further his commercial interests in parliament. Opportunities to do so were few and far between, however. There were now 658 seats in the House of Commons following union with the Irish parliament, but a web of patronage, interest and ownership ensured that few of them were ever contested. In the forthcoming election only 97 seats would be contested. To make an opening for himself, Davison would have to either buy a borough, and so effectively purchase its parliamentary seats, or persuade an electorate somewhere to vote against their local interest. To achieve his aim Davison needed an election agent or, more prosaically, a borough-monger. Such a man was Tom Oldfield, a former bankrupt, 'rank atheist' and brandy smuggler, and the author of a three-volume history of the boroughs.

Davison was introduced to Oldfield by a 'person of high rank'. The two men met several times at Davison's house during January 1802. Each time Oldfield's fifteen-year-old son John waited in the square outside, sketching in his notebook, skimming stones in the pond, peering through the windows of Wedgwood's china shop and gazing wistfully at the elegant women in their carriages.

Several boroughs were discussed as possible targets. Eventually Oldfield and Davison settled on Ilchester, a small Roman town in Somerset with about 160 voters, all house-holders, who sent two members to parliament. Control of the borough had see-sawed between competing interests over the past twenty years and Oldfield had discovered that it was about to become available again. During a visit to the town in December, a local solicitor called John Welsh told him that the present owner, a Colonel Wallis, was selling the borough to pay off his debts – but also that there might be a cheaper way of securing the seats. Welsh introduced Oldfield to John White Parsons, a farmer in the nearby village of West Camel, who was keen to gain influence over the new interest.

After his meetings with Davison, Oldfield set out for Somerset on Friday 19 February. Sitting in the coach alongside Oldfield, who had £10 in his pocket from Davison for his travel-ling expenses, were his son John and Thomas Hopping, a young lawyer from Ilchester who had been sent to London for news by White Parsons. The three men stayed the night in Salisbury before continuing to West Camel. John White Parsons was stooped over a table examining a list of names with Tom Lye, a plasterer from Ilchester, when he heard the commotion of the post-chaise out-side. Lye was hurriedly bundled into the kitchen to be joined, a few minutes later, by Thomas Hopping. Young John Oldfield went riding, leaving his father alone with White Parsons to discuss busi-ness. At about the time their meeting began, Davison followed Oldfield out of London, travelling incognito on the coach to Wincanton, where he was spotted later in the parlour of the Greyhound inn.

The following morning Davison joined the others for break-fast at West Camel. Oldfield introduced him to John White Parsons as a 'gentleman who had great interest' in the borough. Davison quizzed White Parsons about the borough and was told that on the rare occasions when Ilchester had been contested in the past it had always gone to the party prepared to pay the voters £30 each, even if it meant their voting against the local interest. No money, however, had been paid during the previous two elections, in 1796 and 1799, leaving the seats in the hands of the owner of the borough. Davison shrugged off the expense, telling his associates 'he should be happy to give that sum of money, if that would carry the election'.

White Parsons thought that paying about a hundred voters £30 each would secure the seats, but he warned Davison of 'a great deal of danger' in distributing the money himself. He proposed that Thomas Hopping, 'a very confidential young man' who knew the voters, should actually make the payments. The meeting broke for refreshments at one o'clock. While stretching his legs outside, Davison bumped into John Oldfield, who had remained outside during the meeting. Mistaking the boy for White Parson's son, Davison revealed he had just made his father an offer to place him in the East India Company. The slip gives a glimpse of how Davison liked to do business.

In the afternoon the men discussed where the money should be sent. Turning to Tom Oldfield, Davison asked whether he had 'any friend he wished to serve' in a local bank. Oldfield muttered about the bank at Shaftesbury, but in the end it was settled that Davison's £3,000 should be sent to the bank at Yeovil, where White Parsons had an interest. At dinner (served at four o'clock) Davison met Thomas Hopping for the first time. Hopping, who had been lurking all day in the kitchen with the servants, produced a list of one hundred voters in Ilchester who he staked his life could be relied upon to 'do the usual thing'. It was the list White Parsons and Lye had been working on before Oldfield arrived the day before. Davison glanced down at the names before tucking the list 'into his right hand breeches pocket'. He asked White Parsons to sort out Hopping's fee, which after a quick assessment of his client, Hopping raised from £300 to £500.

The conversation then turned to what would happen to the voters after the election. As almost every house in Ilchester belonged to the owner of the borough, any householder voting against his landlord would almost certainly be evicted. White Parsons told Davison that he would have to promise to rehouse them after the election. It just so happened that White Parsons owned a couple of acres outside the town where up to forty houses could be built. Without hesitation Davison agreed to buy the land for £400; this would be a shrewd move, as building houses would also secure him a long-term interest in the borough. Moreover, White Parsons' wife, who had been hovering around the men all day, had a relative in Weymouth called Mr Gear who could manage the building project. Gear was steward to Sir William Pulteney, a close political friend of Lord Moira's. Everything arranged, an express was sent to Ilchester to fetch John Welsh, the solicitor who had first brought the borough to Oldfield's attention. Welsh would act for Davison during the election.

By now Davison was in a boisterous, munificent mood, excited by the plot to win the two Ilchester seats at a fraction of the cost it would take to buy the borough outright. The mistaken identity resolved, he discussed India with White Parsons' son and promised his daughter, Fanny, that he would dance with her at a grand election day ball. He played his trump card on White Parsons himself, dangling the prospect of dinner with Nelson before the eyes of the awestruck farmer.

When Welsh arrived around teatime the Ilchester election was barely discussed. The solicitor was grilled instead on the condition of the neighbouring borough of Milbourne Port. Davison revealed that not only did he have two hand-picked candidates earmarked for Ilchester, he had two more lined up for Milbourne Port as well. Welsh promised to look into the possibilities, claiming later he insisted he would have nothing to do with any bribery.

The meeting at West Camel broke up at eight o'clock that evening, twelve hours after it had begun. After another night at the Greyhound, Davison continued to Portsmouth to attend to other business, leaving Mrs White Parsons, her daughter Fanny and the Oldfields to set out for Weymouth to fetch Gear. Tom Oldfield accompanied them to Dorchester, where he left the party to go deeper into the west country, travelling as far as Land's End in the search for more boroughs for Davison.

White Parsons met Oldfield again at West Camel in March. The farmer had just returned from seeing Davison's lawyer, Richard Wilson, at his chambers in Lincoln's Inn. Wilson, known as 'Morpeth Dick', was a colourful character who figured prominently in the Whig theatrical circle surrounding Richard Sheridan at Drury Lane. His dinners at Craven Cottage, his villa in Fulham, were legendary. Wilson was the fixer for a network of powerful Northumbrians in London which, Davison aside, included Lord Eldon, the lord chancellor, and Eldon's brother Lord Stowell, judge of the high court of Admiralty and a vital ally for any prize agent. He was also the duke of Northumberland's principal *homme d'affaires*. Wilson would have urged the utmost caution in proceeding with the Ilchester plot. White Parsons had returned from London with orders for Oldfield to leave Ilchester as soon as possible to avoid a 'bustle' which could arouse suspicion. The plan had changed. Instead of using Thomas Hopping, who was well known in Ilchester, a 'stranger' from London would hand out the money to the voters. Hopping's role was reduced to escorting the stranger around town.

In the light of these precautions, Oldfield was astonished to be told by Davison at St James's Square a few days later that he was 'great deal alarmed about the bribery' and was abandoning the plan altogether. Davison's dramatic change of heart was confirmed in person by the same 'gentleman of high rank' – possibly Moira – who had introduced them in the first place. Forgetting Davison, Oldfield briskly turned his attention to another client called Sir William Manners, the wealthy son of a notorious moneylender with a large estate in Lincolnshire. Manners had been agitating for a seat in parliament for years, and with Oldfield's help had already unsuccessfully contested Grantham in 1796 – causing a breach with his patron, the duchess of Rutland, in the process. Buying Ilchester outright would realize his long-held ambition while avoiding a repeat of that catastrophe.

Oldfield brokered the deal and on 3 April 1802 Manners purchased the borough from Colonel Wallis. His £53,000 bought land, property and, most importantly of all, interest in two parliamentary seats. Manners laughed off Oldfield's warning that he might also have bought himself a contest. But the borough-monger's suspicion that something was going on was well founded. Unknown to Manners and Oldfield as they shook hands with Wallis was the appearance in Ilchester two days before of a tall, 'thinnish' man dressed 'like a gentleman'. John Harvey, a local plasterer, first noticed the stranger drinking in the Swan inn with Thomas Hopping. Hopping had gestured at Harvey to join them in the small room at the back of the inn where, without a word, the stranger gave the plasterer three £10 bills. A short time later Bill Cheney, the local stonemason, found the stranger on his doorstep. While Hopping waited in the garden, the stranger silently handed Cheney £30 in new Bank of England bills. This, the guileless Cheney said later, was 'a very good thing in a poor house'.

It was a scene repeated a hundred times over that day. The lucky recipients included Nat Pigeon, a labourer, Tom Pipe, the blacksmith, Jim Bowditch, a carpenter, George Masters, a thatcher, Edward Norris, a liquor merchant, and Solomon Turner, the town's gingerbread baker. Sometimes the £30 was accepted by a voter's wife, but no-one refused it and no-one asked the stranger what the windfall was for. Later they all vehemently denied receiving *money*, though they readily admitted they had each been given three £10 *bills*.

The last person to be paid was old Jim Oswald, who kept the turnpike on the Ilchester to West Camel road. That evening two people approached his turnpike, riding wearily away from the town. As they reached the gate, one of the men leaned over, 'so much', recalled Jim, 'that I thought he would fall from his horse', to pay the toll. Jim would swear that it was only when the men disappeared into the fading light and he checked the payment by the light of his lantern that he realized he had £30 in his hand.

No-one seems to have asked how he could confuse three large paper bills with a shilling coin, even in the dark. In the morning Clement Pool, the town's surgeon, awoke to find a queue of people outside his door, all of them patiently waiting to settle their accounts. Some of their debts went back to 1790, the last time the 'bag had been cut'. They all paid Poole with new £10 bills issued by the Bank of England on 15 March.

The stranger who carried out the bribery was probably a trusted clerk from St James's Square – possibly John Bowering, the one man who shared the innermost secrets of Davison's business empire. Davison himself was in St James's Square that day, meeting Nelson, though his thoughts must have been elsewhere. Nelson had tried to live quietly since Christmas, taking his nephew Horatio, William Nelson's son, back to Eton and making only the occasional foray into town for meetings at the Admiralty or to breakfast with Davison. He needed to be prudent because both he and Sir William Hamilton were becoming increasingly financially stretched. Yet there was still no real effort in trimming costs at Merton; indeed, with Emma in charge, quite the reverse. With no sign of the Copenhagen prize money, no end in sight to his dispute with Earl St Vincent and peace with France, though uncertain, as yet also unbroken, Nelson's future looked unclear.

He was still considering a career in politics. He dined with the prime minister and from time to time attended the House of Lords. On one such occasion, on 29 March, he heard Lord Moira debate the civil list, and commented afterwards that among all the reams of figures for posts and sinecures he had noticed Davison's half-pay from the commissariat: 'the *enormous* sum of £152 18*s* 10*d*!'

When in town Nelson would occasionally visit the Royal Hospital in Chelsea to consult Dr Benjamin Moseley, a physician he had known since their days together in the West Indies twenty-five years earlier, about the failing sight in his remaining good eye. On these occasions he must have met, or at least seen,

Robert Mathews, his old acquaintance from Quebec and rival for Mary Simpson's heart, who had recently been appointed major of the hospital. Having achieved his goal of securing Mary's hand, Robert had left the army in 1798, taking with him a pension and a sinecure as the lieutenant governor of Antigua, a position worth 10s a day and the legacy, no doubt, of his former employer Frederick Haldimand. From time to time the Davisons dined *en famille* with Mary and Robert at their small house on Clapham Terrace. Mary and Robert now had a small son, Frederick, named after his father's patron. As Robert was kinsman to an Irish earldom, Mary held out high hopes that her son might inherit a title one day. Davison may have helped Robert to the post of inspector of army clothing at the barrack office – a place worth 20s a day to Robert and of untold value to Davison. In October 1801 Robert was appointed to the Royal Hospital, moving with Mary to elegant new apartments in Christopher Wren's great building on the bank of the Thames.

Nelson may have met Robert and Mary Mathews in town but he made sure to avoid his own wife, though she unashamedly attended the queen's birthday drawing room in January. Such brazen appearances by 'that *vile* Tom Tit', designed as they were to humiliate her, drove Emma into paroxysms of fury. By now Emma had swung most of Nelson's family behind her, but one apparently indestructible and formidable obstacle remained before she could claim complete victory over her rival: Edmund Nelson. Nelson could never be totally free of his former life while his father lived.

Then, that spring of 1802, the old man fell dangerously ill. Fanny rushed to Bath as soon as she heard. 'Of this rest assured,' the old man told her in his last letter, 'that in all places I wish for your happiness.' Nelson stayed bunkered down at Merton Place with Emma, weakly claiming he was ill himself and waiting for his father to call him. Anyway, he reassured himself, his father would probably be dead by the time he got to Bath. There was time, but not much. Edmund died on 26 April, with Fanny by his side. It was

Emma's birthday and at Merton there was a colourful and happy parade to church in the warm spring sunshine.

The news arrived the next day. Nelson reached for his pen:

My Dear Davison
        My Poor Dear Father
    is no more, God Bless you
                Nelson & Bronte

There was nothing left to say; there was nothing else he could say. Does a touch of regret, guilt even, linger in these few words found among Davison's papers so many years later? Emma made no comment herself, except to lean over Nelson and to augment the note with a request for help in securing Edmund's vacant livings for a favourite.

Davison, who called at Merton to commiserate on 2 May, was given the task of sorting out Edmund's meagre estate: a grim repetition of his role after Maurice's death almost exactly a year before. By now William Nelson was openly and vociferously expressing his distrust of his brother's agent, remarking on Davison's 'sharpness' in the business. 'I don't half like his cunning,' he muttered. Once again the fast-diminishing Nelson family gathered for a funeral in Norfolk. This time William wore deep mourning. Fanny did not attend, fearing perhaps that she would be unwelcome or that she would meet her husband. She need not have worried. Nelson did not go either.

By May word started filtering back to London that something odd was happening in Somerset. Sir William Manners' complacency in the face of the warning about a possible contest for the seats in his expensive new borough came back to haunt him. Thomas Hopping let slip to Tom Oldfield that 'he had secured the voters' for Davison. In Ilchester itself there was overwhelming physical evidence that something new was happening: for half a mile outside town, surrounded by flower-strewn meadows, a terrace of new houses was rising from White Parsons' land.

The Times soon picked up the scent. 'Sir William Manners', it reported on 12 June,

> who purchased the borough of Ilchester, is said to have found his bargain not quite so certain as most purchasers of that description expect. On his going down to nominate who should be returned to the next parliament, the worthy electors not only revolted at the peremptory demand, but enlisted under the banner of Mr. Davison, and have determined to oppose whoever Sir William shall propose.

Incensed, Sir William stormed over to St James's Square for 'interviews' with Davison. He left assured, he told his election agent George Tewson, 'that Mr Davison had given up all thoughts of the borough'. Nevertheless, Manners took the precaution of addressing the Ilchester voters through the columns of *The Times* in an extraordinary appeal which had a distinctly menacing flavour.

> A report has been circulated (although no opponent has yet made his appearance) that I am to expect an opposition, but I cannot think that you will ever suffer yourselves to be misled by designing borough agents; nor can I conceive . . . that any gentleman will be so illiberal as to create discord between a landlord and his tenants . . . or so unwise as to hope for success in a borough where the right of election is vested in the inhabitant householders of the entire parish, and where the whole of that parish . . . is, with a very small exception, . . . my property.

The election in Ilchester was called for Monday 5 July. Canvassing began in earnest a week before the poll, when Sir William and his fellow 'blue party' candidate, a lawyer called James Graham, set up their headquarters at the Ark inn. Because the blue party also controlled the George and the White Hart taverns, the opposition 'yellow party', sponsored by Davison, was forced to retreat to a public house at Pill Bridge, a mile out of town.

A few days before the poll one of the yellow party candidates, John Hudleston, a former employee of the East India Company, unexpectedly withdrew, leaving Richard Wilson, Davison's lawyer, frantically searching for a replacement. John Welsh, the yellow party's agent, strongly suspected that Hudleston had been paid off by Sir William. The other yellow party candidate, Thomas Plummer, the wealthy partner of a large West Indian merchant firm, remained at Salisbury suffering from ill-health, sending his son to Ilchester to canvass on his behalf and to gauge the state of play. The boy's report, which had to be smuggled out of town because the post office was in blue party hands, was encouraging. 'We reached this place about 10 last night', he wrote, '& found the whole town on the *qui vive* looking out for candidates. Our reception has been most highly flattering & this morning has been occupied in a most successful canvas. Sir Wm M— is universally disliked & we have no doubt of 2/3 of the votes being in our favour.' Then, in the nick of time, the replacement yellow party candidate arrived post haste from London. He was William Hunter, the 33-year-old son of Robert Hunter, the eminent North American merchant and Davison's first business mentor.

No-one knows when Davison himself arrived, though 'the gentleman who came to put up for the borough of Ilchester' was glimpsed entering a house where the yellow supporters were drinking on 2 July. On Saturday morning, first Thomas Hopping and then Thomas Plummer joined the fray. As soon as Hopping was spotted, yellow party supporters dragged him out of his chaise and four, put a hat bedecked with yellow ribbons on his head and, cheering, hoisted him onto their shoulders. A cask of cider was produced and pulled around the town 'with Mr Hopping sometimes & sometimes another sitting as a Bacchus upon the barrel'. Drunken abuse was hurled at the blue party. Buckets of cider were even taken up to the bell-ringers in the church belfry. The blue party retaliated in kind, opening a butt of beer in the market square and giving away joints from a roasted ox.

This almost festive air darkened as polling day approached. Plummer's son made sure 'never to stir out alone'. Special constables were sworn in to prevent trouble. Some of the voters stayed up drinking all night, enjoying the lavish attention, before they arrived at the town hall for the ballot on Monday morning. A rowdy crowd of opposing supporters had gathered outside to, by turn, jeer or cheer them. Somebody noticed a stranger, a 'smart looking man' in an elegant coat, handing out drink to yellow party supporters.

In the hall some of the voters were asked to swear the bribery oath. The surgeon Clement Pool, who was helping the returning officer, said that the bribery was so widespread that there would have been no election at all had every one of the voters been made to swear the oath, though his comments might have been coloured by his well-known support for Sir William. Old Bill Cheney refused the oath, so was sent away. The poll closed at four o'clock that afternoon. By then 150 men had cast a total of 300 votes for the two seats in the borough. The vote split along party lines. Only one man sat on the fence and shared his votes between the yellows and blues. The result was in doubt until the very end and was far from the 'walk over the course' many had forecast for the yellow party. The blue party received 129 votes: 65 for Sir William and 64 for James Graham. But with a majority of just 42 votes the yellow party triumphed, with William Hunter receiving 86 and Thomas Plummer 85 votes.

Sir William took his defeat very badly indeed, thundering back to Lincolnshire to lick his wounds and leaving his bedraggled supporters to drown their sorrows at a wake which quickly turned into quite a party, with 'no inconsiderable quantity of kissing' according to one happy witness. The jubilant victors, still barred from the public houses in town, paraded to West Camel wearing yellow ribbons and waving yellow flags. Here a grand dinner was held on the fields in front of White Parsons' house, with frequent huzzas and toasts to Plummer and Hunter; maybe Davison even had his promised dance with Fanny White Parsons. The celebrations continued into the next day with a feast at the public house in Pill Bridge. The yellow party voters awoke to hangovers and the news that, as White Parsons had predicted back in February, they were being evicted from their homes. Even George Tewson, Sir William's hapless election agent, was thrown out. The lucky ones moved to the terrace of houses outside the town which had been specifically built for this contingency.

The expenses for the yellow party – the cost of all the liquor, cider, bread and bacon so liberally given away to the supporters before and after the election – were settled in person by Davison's lawyer, Richard 'Morpeth Dick' Wilson. The 'jollification' at Pill Bridge alone cost over £150. Wilson asked for all the accounts to be post-dated to the day after polling day, 6 July. Davison returned to London, quietly triumphant, his goal accomplished. He had secured interest in two seats in parliament for a price far less than that attached to buying a borough outright.

Two weeks after the election, Nelson and Sir William Hamilton breakfasted at St James's Square before departing with Emma for a tour of Wales and the midlands while Davison retreated to Swarland for his summer holiday, all the anxiety before the election having aggravated his gout. He left happy and contented – unaware of a potentially devastating letter that had been received by the Treasury.

The letter was from Robert Edington, the disaffected clerk who had blown the whistle on George Walker's coal frauds back in 1799. Exasperated by Edington's subsequent, and ceaseless, pestering for preferment, laced eventually with threats to reveal various 'peculations and frauds' within the Millbank coal business unless he were rewarded, in June 1802 Davison called the clerk's bluff and sacked him – thereby inadvertently triggering a sequence of events that would end at Newgate prison.

Edington levelled a list of accusations at Davison and

Walker: overcharging the barracks by using forged certificates as evidence of the local market price; supplying poor-quality coals at high-quality prices; illegitimately surcharging cartage expenses; and failing to pass on the discounts Millbank received from the custom house for the bulk deliveries of coal through the port of London. 'I also accuse', Edington continued, 'General De Lancey of conniving at and attempting to suppress inquiry into the frauds, and endeavouring to procure from me my papers, and of depriving me of other papers by putting them into the hands of Mr Davison.'

'I wrote Mr Davison and cautioned him in his proceedings,' he finished; 'I did no more than what I conceived the duty of every faithful servant, that instead of thanking me for my advice, he discharged me of the service, whereas, had I continued silent, and winked at his frauds, I would [have] been in my situation, and he still enjoying his.'

Edington's exposé carried a price, despite his avowed sense of moral duty. He expected a substantial reward for disclosing frauds which, he calculated, had cost the government over £150,000. He was, after all, 'a man far from opulent . . . [with] a wife and small family depending on my support'. The Treasury passed the letter to Charles Yorke, the secretary for war, who calmly asked De Lancey to respond. In the meantime Davison's exclusive contract to supply coal to the barracks was suspended.

Nelson found London 'absolutely deserted' when he returned in September after what Emma described as 'a most charming tour'. 'You are right about the country,' he complained to Davison, 'London [is] so hot and stinking that it is truly detestable.' Merton Place was not ready to receive the party because the ever-resourceful Dodds, whom Davison had placed in charge of the improvements to the house as a way of keeping control over their cost, was seriously ill – so seriously that he would be dead before the end of the month. To escape the scaffolding at Merton and the dust of London, Sir William took Emma to Margate for the bathing, one of her favourite pursuits. Nelson stayed behind, forlornly tramping the dusty streets of London, calling at Davison's house on 11 September only to find it deserted. 'I own myself', he wrote despondently that evening, 'selfish enough to wish you in St James's Square, for at your breakfast I heard all that was going on in the great world, and it was a central place where any one could meet me.'

'But for your breakfasting in St James's Square I feel no very great desire of being there,' came the reply from Northumberland, 'feeling myself here much relieved of a considerable load of business and also reaping the benefit and tranquillity of my native county.' If Davison was aware of Edington's whistle-blowing, it did not seem to be troubling him. He proposed a solution to his friend's discontent. 'As there is yet near two months to the meeting of Parliament, why not take a flight to this part of the world? You have many, very many *real* friends in this quarter and how gratifying would it be to the county to view the man to whom the nation owes so much.'

Nelson passed up the invitation. He never did visit Swarland to see the Battle Park and Harriett's hothouses, or to enjoy the contents of the grand cellar beneath the hall stairs. He preferred to kick his heels in London, seeking out Addington, meeting the first lord, Earl St Vincent, to discuss naval matters (while avoiding discussion of their continuing dispute) and dining with Davison's brother-in-law William Gosling, the banker. With nothing else to do, Nelson started interfering in the Copenhagen prize business. He pressed the earl to compensate the captors for the prizes destroyed by Sir Hyde Parker, calling at Davison's office at the St James's Square house to check on the progress of his own sorely needed prize money. 'But Mr. Bowring was out, and the other clerk told me he supposed Mr. Cutler managed all the prize business.' To speed things along, Nelson brokered the sale to the ordnance office of about thirty small brass guns captured from the Danes, keeping four of them back as a gift for Davison. Two of these were eventually mounted on either side of the portico on the south front to Swarland House, where they were fired with great excitement on high days and holidays.

This prolonged lull, painful for a man of action like Nelson, ended abruptly in November, when the great mansions in the West End came alive again after the long summer recess. On 16 November a new parliament was opened by the king. Davison, who now had a vested interest, described it as 'a most curious one and [one that] will puzzle the ministers'. A week later Nelson lost his case against Earl St Vincent for the right to *Alcmene*'s share of the prize money from the Spanish treasure ships captured in the Mediterranean three years before. The judges in the court of common pleas were initially divided in their opinion, finding good arguments on both sides and preferring to withhold judgment, allowing the case to be referred to another court. Only when Nelson pressed for a decision did they find in favour of the earl, agreeing with Mr Justice Rooke 'that a flag officer returning home on account of his health ought not to be considered as having abdicated his command'. It was a severe blow. Nelson, who had gambled his career and future financial security on the case, instantly appealed.

Davison had barely time to sympathize before he was hit by a crisis of his own. Two weeks into the new parliament, Sir William Manners lodged a petition complaining that Thomas Plummer, William Hunter 'and their agents, were guilty of many gross and notorious acts of bribery and corruption'. Manners was also suing Davison for the cost of the now useless borough.

Clenching his teeth and thinking of his future, Nelson spoke in support of the earl during the debate on the naval commissioners' bill in the Lords on 20 December. The bill, the brainchild of the first lord, proposed establishing an inquiry into the 'flagrant abuses and mismanagement' in the Navy Office and shipyards. The prize money system, in particular, would come under close examination. Nelson vigorously supported the bill; it would be foolish not to. 'Great abuses', he declared, 'existed in the navy; and most especially were they practised by the prize agents.' It was often difficult, he said, even impossible, to prise money from the agents.

Every seaman, down to the 'poorest cabin-boy', should feel protected by the law. But he had one caveat to state, which bore all the hallmarks of St James's Square. 'The credit of the British Merchant', Nelson proclaimed,

> is the support of the commerce of the world; his books are not lightly, nor for any ordinary purpose, to be taken out of his own hands; the secrets of his business are not to be too curiously pried into. The books of a single merchant may betray the secrets, not only of his own affairs, but of those with whom he is principally connected in business, and the reciprocal confidence of the whole commercial world may, by the authoritative inquiry of these Commissioners, be shaken.

The bill was passed, and in February 1803 the commission of naval inquiry began its work. By then, Britain was on the verge of renewed war with France. In April Nelson was invited to give his views on prize agency to the commissioners, under oath. He was not examined but instead presented a short statement of his views on the subject, which must have echoed Davison's. In his statement Nelson suggested setting up a formal prize office to regulate the business, restricting a prize agent's commission to the net proceeds after deducting costs. Agents should be penalized for delaying the distribution, which was a widespread grievance.

The commissioners then closely examined a number of agents, though Davison was not called. They quickly identified a number of problems in the prize business. These included agents enjoying the benefits of the prize money before distribution, which they considered 'an interest at variance with [their] duty', advancing prize money before it was due (as Davison offered to do after the Nile) and failing to advertise their distributions properly in the *London Gazette*, leaving Greenwich Hospital, which received unpaid proceeds, in the dark. The agents, for their part, revealed how they were often forced to share their commission with other people, such as the admiral's secretary, his family or friends, none of whom did anything to help the business but who were merely named as a favour by the captors.

In their report, published in July 1803, the commissioners reserved their harshest criticism for recall agents, the men who managed unclaimed shares before passing them to Greenwich, and navy agents, who managed the affairs of officers and ratings, frequently lending them money against the prospect of future prizes. More often than not, the commissioners observed, navy agents were no better than 'slopsellers, publicans, and other people of the lowest and worst condition'. They plagued the ports, hoping to 'take advantage of the unsuspicious character, of the indiscretion and extravagance which prevail among seamen'. Otherwise – to everyone's surprise, and in some quarters disappointment – the commissioners concluded that 'our enquiry has not led to a copious disclosure of gross and abominable frauds practiced upon sailors with respect to their prize money'.

Nelson's cherished prize office never materialized. The 1805 Prize Act did incorporate some of his suggestions – it changed the rules on agency commission, and stipulated distribution times – but otherwise the system stumbled on largely unregulated until the end of the war. The effects of the act would occupy Davison for some years to come; but they would come too late for Nelson.

MINOTAUR

74 GUNS,
CAPTAIN CHARLES MANSFIELD

D URING THE FRAGILE peace Bonaparte allowed English visitors back into France. They needed little encouragement. Aristocrats, socialites, artists, bankers, businessmen, politicians and the downright curious descended on Paris. Ten thousand made the journey within a year. They went for many reasons: some to eat, drink and see the sights; others to make love, paint or do business. Everyone wanted to visit the grisly sites of the revolution, places with names that had enthralled them for so long. They felt the ghostly presence of the Bastille, gazed at the Tuileries and thrilled at the bloody remains of the guillotine scaffolds on Place de la Concorde. Some drove out of the city to gawp at the empty splendour of Versailles. Above all, the English tourists wanted to glimpse Bonaparte, the little Corsican devil who had terrorized them for so long. This was surprisingly easy. Bonaparte, as intrigued by his former enemies as they were by him, held regular receptions for English dignitaries in the opulent surroundings of the Salle des Ambassadeurs in the Tuileries. Lesser mortals could frequently catch sight of the first consul riding in the Champs de Mars.

At Christmas 1802, with the clouds of war already massing on the horizon again, Davison, Harriett and the twins followed the well-trodden path to Dover. Both boys were no doubt delighted to be released from sitting for their portraits at John Hoppner's studio off St James's Square. French law preventing Davison from bringing his own carriage and horses to France, the family's eight-hour crossing to Calais had to be followed by an uncomfortable two-day journey to Paris by public coach. The French capital was smaller than London. Narrow, loathsome-smelling alleyways pressed against elegant gardens and palaces. Many English tourists, fed for years on stories of the depravity of the new republic, remarked with surprise on the prosperity of the city and the elegance and ease of its inhabitants.

On 5 January 1803, within days of the Davisons' arrival, a grand parade was staged in the Place du Carrousel. Alick left no record that his family watched the spectacle, though with two fourteen-year-old boys in tow it is inconceivable that they did not. The 'full pomp and splendour of Royalty' was on display. The city rang with the sound of beating drums, trumpets and thousands of marching men. The renowned Artillerie Légère gave a thrilling display, their gun carriages clattering past the spectators at full tilt. There was a procession of Arabian horses, led by one 'caparisoned entirely in gold'. At midday a small figure, simply dressed in a plain blue uniform without decoration, rode out of the Tuileries on a magnificent grey horse which, it was said, had belonged to the late king. Bonaparte reviewed the lines of blue-coated troops from his feared Grande Armée, raising his hat whenever he passed their colours. He then passed through the ornate gates on the Place du Carrousel, which were mounted with four splendid bronze horses looted from Venice, to take petitions from the small crowd allowed to gather there. Away from his troops, one onlooker commented, Bonaparte was received in surly silence by his people, who seemed to hold him in dread.

When the parade was over, some of the English spectators were invited into the Tuileries for coffee, chocolate and wine. After a while Bonaparte, now attired in his scarlet consular coat, joined them. The doors of the audience room were locked behind him. 'His hair was unpowdered and neglected,' recalled one Englishman in the room,

his countenance cheerful, fatter and not so sallow as I expected,
his eyes I thought light, and not so large, nor so melancholy, nor
so sunk as I expected: the whole face not so picturesque. His voice
is musical and deep, he leans forward: his person is not only
little but, I think, mean . . . the armies of Europe are too great
[he said] it would be well if each Sovereign diminished his to a
fourth . . . He spoke much of hunting and asked which was the
best country for it.

From Paris, Davison had intended going to Brussels and
Antwerp, presumably to attend to some business. But William fell
dangerously ill at Lisle, forcing the family to retreat with great difficulty to the coast in an attempt to get the boy home as quickly
as possible. By Calais William was in a 'delirium', too weak to
withstand the crossing. His father was in a dreadful 'state of misery'.
The jaunt to the continent was turning to disaster. There was a
real fear that William might die. For two weeks the Davisons lingered helplessly in Calais, praying for William to recover while
anxiously watching the political situation deteriorate around
them. Davison felt as if he were in prison. Had the family been
forced to stay much longer, they all, in effect, would have been.
    Even *in extremis* Davison did not neglect his friend's needs.
'If my absence occasions you any pecuniary inconvenience,' he
wrote to Nelson from Calais on 3 February, 'apply to my bankers
and show to them this side of my letter, and I authorize them to
pay to your order five thousand pounds sterling . . . this possibly
may supply your present wants, [if not] command the purse of
your ever unalterably affectionate friend Alex Davison.' Davison's
generous offer of a sum equivalent to perhaps a quarter of a million pounds today, was timely. Nelson, who had heard of the
family emergency in France from one of Davison's daughters left
behind at St James's Square, was recovering from another riotous,
and ruinous, Christmas with Emma at Merton Place. He was also
trying to buy another £4,000 worth of land from a neighbour,
harbouring dreams of one day transforming himself into a

gentleman farmer. 'No-one', he replied, 'can have more felt for the distress you must have suffered than us of this house.' Yet he preferred to borrow the sum from George Matcham, his wealthy brother-in-law, than from his agent, uncomfortable perhaps at the thought of sinking further into Davison's debt.

As soon as William was well enough to travel, the Davisons fled France, reaching London by 10 February. They found a city gripped by war fever. Bonaparte stood indicted of contravening the spirit of the treaty of Amiens by using the peace slyly to strengthen his hold on the continent. As Nelson patriotically observed in the House of Lords: 'unsuccessful . . . in the war of valour, of martial force, of military talent, France may perhaps hope to gain more by that of artifice, of circumvention, of equivocal faith'. While Addington prevaricated, his political enemies poured scorn on his weakness. On 9 March 1803, with Nelson by his side, Lord Moira 'delivered a very animated speech' in the house in which he accused the government of appeasing the French. Raising himself to his not inconsiderable height, Moira summoned the words of 'our immortal bard', quoting the Bastard from *King John*:

> Be stirring as the time, be fire with fire;
> Threaten the threatener, and out-face the brow
> Of bragging horror!

The rising international tension did not prevent parliament responding to Sir William Manners' complaint about the Ilchester election. On 17 March a committee was appointed to examine the matter. Davison watched the proceedings, but was not called to give evidence and stayed silent throughout, listening as a succession of bewildered witnesses passed before the distinguished group of MPs. They included young John Oldfield, who was now with a firm of Spanish merchants in the City; Tom Lye, the plasterer who made up the list of voters; and Clement Pool, the town's surgeon. Fanny White Parsons, with whom Davison had promised to dance at the election ball, attended, though her father had since gone missing. The most devastating evidence came from Tom Oldfield, the disaffected election agent whom Davison had dismissed before the poll. Oldfield described his meetings with Davison in London and how the plot to bribe the voters had been hatched at White Parsons' farmhouse in West Camel. Under cross-examination, Oldfield conceded that Davison had told him the plan had been abandoned long before the election; but the evidence of malpractice was overwhelming.

Twenty, even ten years before, Sir William's complaint could have been ignored. But in the reforming spirit of the new century, which demanded increasingly high standards in public life, leaving men like Davison exposed, the MPs had to act. On 29 March 1803 the committee presented its report to parliament. The MPs found that Davison, John White Parsons and Thomas Hopping had been engaged in corruption. After scrutinizing the poll book, the MPs disallowed the votes of thirty-two bribed voters. Although this left the result unchanged, the 1802 election was declared void. The report closed by recommending 'that further proceedings should be instituted thereon'. Nelson went to St James's Square as soon as he heard. 'Cheer up,' he wrote that evening, 'you cannot be more vexed than your affectionate friend.' While Davison waited on tenterhooks for parliament to debate the Ilchester report, Sir William Hamilton became 'rather delirious'. On 6 April he died, politely, at his house on Piccadilly, 'in Lady Hamilton's and my arms', Nelson reported sadly, 'without a Sigh or a Struggle'. Sir William left Emma an annuity of £800 with an equal sum as a lump payment. Her outstanding debts, which were already substantial, were also settled by his estate. Nelson received a favourite enamel miniature of Emma; and, as the *Morning Herald* commented, 'another beautiful piece is also said to have devolved on his Lordship, in consequence of the demise of that friendly Connoisseur!'

Several MPs spoke up for Davison in the debate on the Ilchester election on 22 April. They pointed out that Oldfield admitted hearing Davison disown the plan to bribe the voters. In a typically powerful address, one of Davison's more glamorous friends, the dramatist Richard Brinsley Sheridan, challenged parliament to provide firm evidence that Davison was involved. 'It surely was not the spirit of British law to punish men for mere intentions, however criminal,' he declared; 'a man might charge a gun with intent to murder a man; but surely the law would not condemn him for murder, on a bare intention never fulfilled.' Sheridan's view was opposed so strongly by Nicholas Vansittart and Charles Bragge, both of whom were close to Addington, that they drew a rebuke from the master of the rolls, who reminded them not to prejudice a possible trial. A vote on the findings of the report was adjourned until May: time enough, Davison might have hoped, for the scrutiny of the dubious goings-on in a provincial borough to be overtaken by events. For war now seemed so imminent that Nelson, who was champing at the bit to tackle the French once and for all, was ordered to raise his flag on a new ship waiting for him at Portsmouth.

There was much to arrange in the short time left before he had to leave Merton Place and Emma. Sir William Hamilton's death had not only clarified Emma's financial position, which, though not one of boundless wealth, was more than comfortable; it had also made her relationship with Nelson less ambiguous, allowing him to make provision for her in a new will. Nelson knew, however, that almost no amount of money could satisfy her needs, so it was now, with Sir William gone, that his campaign to secure Emma a government pension began in earnest. The will was prepared at William Haslewood's offices in Craven Street on 10 May. Davison may have been present, but he was not named executor to the will; this task was given to Haslewood and William Nelson. He would, however, benefit by it, as Nelson left him three of the trophies brought back from Naples after the battle of the Nile. These were a gun, a water canteen and a sword. They were not great treasures – Davison had enough of those already – but were of inestimable value to Nelson and thus of great significance as a bequest.

Nelson's orders would force him to miss his installation as a Knight of the Order of the Bath at Westminster Abbey on 19 May – an honour conferred upon him as long ago as 1797 following the battle of Cape St Vincent. He could send a proxy to the ceremony in his place, though the proxy would have to be knighted himself before he could perform the role if he was not already of this rank or above. Nelson nominated Davison without hesitation. 'I shall', he wrote on 11 May, 'appoint no other proxy but yourself being ever my dear Davison most faithfully and affectionately yours.' But the king would not have it. The Ilchester affair was casting a shadow over Davison's reputation. Clearly embarrassed, Lord Pelham, the king's private secretary, stalled at first, telling Nelson there was no chance of knighting Davison before the ceremony. The real reason emerged in a letter the king wrote to William Marsden, the secretary to the Admiralty, just two days before the ceremony. 'The question before the House of Commons on the Ilchester election would make it highly improper that the honour of knighthood should be conferred on Mr Davison,' the king impatiently scrawled; 'probably some officer of the Navy may easily be found to represent Lord Nelson on this occasion.'

It seems Nelson broke this bitterly disappointing news as soon as he could, dashing off a note to Davison from the Admiralty at five o'clock the same afternoon, probably from Marsden's office. 'A very unpleasant thing has happened,' he wrote, his anger at yet another royal slight palpable: 'you cannot be my proxy. Do not say a word but go to Nepean. The King insists on my having a *naval officer.*' But with the king's mind made up, not even Evan Nepean's famed influence in high circles could help. The disastrous timing of the Ilchester report had undoubtedly cost Davison a title. He would never get so close to one again. The proxy was hastily given instead to a young naval captain called William Bolton, who happened to be in town to marry one of Nelson's nieces. The £70 bill for the cost of the ceremony remained unpaid at Nelson's death.

The next evening, Wednesday 18 May, 1803, the House of

Commons voted by 60 to 39 to prosecute Davison for corruption. Unsurprisingly, the house was sparsely attended, for Britain had declared war on France mere hours earlier; but the vote did not go unnoticed. Lord Moira shared his horror at the verdict with Nelson:

> *The decision against our friend Davison frets me more than I can express. Not so much from apprehension of any inconvenient consequence to him, as from the knowledge that it will wound him, do not however, let him be cast down at it, because there is nothing discreditable in the imputation of that which every member of the House of Commons is known to have done.*

Moira's letter missed Nelson. At four o'clock on the morning of 19 May, the last day of peace to dawn in the country for twelve years, Nelson met Davison at the White Hart tavern on Piccadilly to catch the first coach for Portsmouth.

Two hours later, while the coach changed horses at Kingston, they breakfasted and stretched their legs. There was just time enough for Nelson to fire off a note to Emma. They then pressed on, rattling through the deep, warm lanes of Hampshire to reach the bustle of Portsmouth around noon. Waiting patiently there for Nelson were his flag captain Thomas Hardy and his Sicilian valet Gaetano Spedillo, a short, dark-skinned man with tattoos on his arms who had been with the Hamiltons since childhood. He had driven down earlier from Merton with the admiral's belongings. This was his first voyage as Nelson's servant, and he hoped it might offer him an escape back to his sorely missed family and children in Naples.

Beside Hardy and Spedillo were two unfamiliar faces. One belonged to William Chevailler, a middle-aged, neat-looking man who had been personally recommended by Davison to replace James Bell as Nelson's steward. Chevailler's background is not known, though his surname was very familiar among the *habitants* in the Three Rivers region of Quebec where Davison had such substantial interests. It is usually spelled Chevalier, sometimes Chevallier, though never in the letters he wrote himself to Davison, which are those of an unusually well-educated steward. Perhaps he came to England to join John Bowering, Henry Cutler and Dodds among the small handful of most trusted minions surrounding Davison. He describes himself in his letters to Davison as 'your gratefull old servant', though they display an intimacy beyond that relationship. 'I have had proofs of his integrity and honesty,' vouchsafed Davison, casting Chevailler as Nelson's minder and his own informant: 'he will take care that no one else shall be dishonest about you.' Chevailler had instructions to report any prizes *Victory* sent in. It was Chevailler's first voyage too.

Another recruit to Nelson's entourage was his new secretary, John Scott. Scott was thirty-five years old and came from the *Royal Sovereign*, in which he had been purser. Scott owed his new position to Nelson's banker William Marsh who, wary of Davison's influence, was no doubt keen to ensure he had an ally close to his unreliable client in the lucrative waters of the Mediterranean. Scott had a young family and was anxious about money. His post paid £300 a year – barely enough to support his family to a respectable standard of living, let alone properly educate his children – but Scott knew that as Nelson's secretary he had the chance of managing the prize business of the most successful commander in the navy. 'Don't my Charlotte', Scott wrote to his wife the day before Nelson and Davison reached Portsmouth, 'say a word of Lord Nelson's kindness to me or ever mention my probable good fortune, the pleasure of thinking of it yourself will, I am sure, be sufficient and that by and by we may live with that comfort which we have long desired, pray kiss our dear boys for me and tell the rogues to be good.' Scott intended this to be his last voyage.

Five very different men meeting in Portsmouth and thinking of very different things: Nelson of glory, Hardy about his ship, Chevailler about his duty, Spedillo about his family, Scott about money. The fates of all five were now inextricably linked to the magnificent warship that lay peacefully at anchor outside the harbour – *Victory*.

At three o'clock that afternoon Davison and Nelson were pulled out to the ship, which they soon discovered was 'in a pretty state of confusion'. After hoisting his flag, Nelson ordered a thirteen-gun salute to Admiral Gardner, the shore-based commander-in-chief at Portsmouth. With Davison refusing to leave Nelson 'until the *Victory* is under sail', they returned to lodgings at the George inn and dinner with Gardner and Lord Minto, a suave Scottish aristocrat and old friend of Nelson's. Early the following morning, Friday 20 May, they breakfasted together, perhaps with hangovers as Gardner had a fearsome reputation for heavy drinking. Then Nelson walked down to his barge, shook hands with Davison and was gone. It was the last time the friends saw each other. Hours later *Victory* sailed.

Davison lingered on the coast a few more days, seeing to business, though perhaps also reluctant to face the consequences of the vote in London. Eventually he returned to town with Lord Minto. As usual he carried bundles of letters for Emma, together with instructions to pay her an allowance of £100 a month. There was also a letter for John Scott's wife Charlotte, written on the morning *Victory* sailed. In Portsmouth Davison had taken a close interest in Nelson's new secretary, instantly identifying a threat to his business, though all the attention flattered the still guileless Scott. In his letter he revealed how Davison

> desired me to say that he will forward all your letters &c to me, and do anything in the world you can require of him, he will write Lord Nelson weekly and will send my letters with his Lordship's so that you have only to enclose your letters my dear love for me to Mr D and he will send them on with great safety. Lady Hamilton of course will be civil to my Charly, and I trust my old girl will spend some happy days with her Ladyship. Mr Davison desires me to say that he will forward any parcel or package, he communicates twice a week with the Lord Nelson.

Davison went straight to Clarges Street when he reached town, to the house Emma had taken after Sir William's death. The brilliant Lady Hamilton was downcast, her normal ebullience gone. She had briefly glimpsed a new life, settled contentedly and peacefully with Nelson at Merton, enjoying his fame and rewards, only for it all to be snatched away. Davison, who had every reason to feel miserable himself, did his best to cheer her up. He stuck his arm in his coat, covered one eye and 'drew a laugh from her to fancy only for half an hour that "I was her lord"'. Davison's clumsy flirting seems to have had some effect, for only a few days later, on 2 June, Emma was 'wonderfully well and her spirits beginning to mend'. Unsurprisingly, Davison did not go to the lavish ball that followed the ceremony at Westminster Abbey to install knights to the Order of the Bath. The memory of the royal insult was still too painful. Yet he did become enmeshed in some unspecified row surrounding it which, he wearily sighed, 'occasioned us all a good deal of plague'. A hint, perhaps, that both Emma and Fanny wanted to attend this high-profile event?

If Fanny did go to the ball – and she must have been at the installation itself – she fled to Tunbridge Wells afterwards 'in search of health'. She now rarely stayed in London, preferring the genteel surroundings of Bath to the cruel innuendo of London society. She was again 'on the lookout' for a house, reconciled at last to living alone now that Nelson had deserted her and Edmund had died. In June, on her way to Exmouth (where she would eventually settle), she paused to look at a house near Newbury, though, like so many others, it failed to meet her exacting standards. Her once close relationship with Davison inevitably became more distant after his endorsement of her letter in Nelson's final, brutal rejection of December 1802. She must have felt betrayed and cruelly misled. Her letters dwindled and their tone became distinctly cool as she turned instead to Davison's rival, William Marsh, for support. Unhappily she was bound to Davison by the terms of her annuity, though she now began pressing him to appoint Marsh as her other trustee in place of Maurice Nelson,

who had now been dead for two years. Davison's inexplicable prevarication over the matter dogged their correspondence, and
fuelled Fanny's anger, for years to come.

London was again very edgy that summer. 'It would appear
as if we were soon to be at war with all the world,' Davison
remarked. Not only was Spain making belligerent noises, but
'doubts are entertained of the sincerity of the Russian Court'.
Henry Addington had come to power to make peace, and now that
war had returned his failings were exposed. The uneasy political
truce in parliament broke down with the treaty of Amiens.
Davison despaired: everything was in a 'state of uncertainty, one
day a change, the next day a partial movement, God knows what
it comes to.' Confusion reigned. While the prince of Wales, who
had always deplored Addington's weakness, began haphazardly
trying to unite the Whigs against the prime minister, two of his
own leading supporters, Moira and Sheridan, were actively courting Addington with the aim of convincing him that their presence
in the administration would strengthen his increasingly shaky
hand. Their strategy of co-operation seemed to work better than
the prince's hostility. When George Tierney, Addington's corpu-
lent, red-faced secretary, called to see Davison on 3 June he
revealed that Moira was on the verge of being appointed to the
cabinet. 'Little doubt remains', Davison hinted to Nelson, 'of our
friend in St. James's Place having a chief share in the
Administration, but whether the admiralty or ordnance is not certain. I hope the former.' But Tierney was pre-emptive and Davison
disappointed. Addington ploughed on 'without adding strength to
the administration', an appalled Davison wrote later in the
month; 'it is beyond conjecture and staggers everyone'. Moira
suspected that the duke of York was keeping him out of the
administration to spite the prince of Wales. York blamed
Addington, which Tierney thought 'a d—d lie'.

Nelson's appeal against the ruling in favour of Earl St
Vincent over the disputed Mediterranean prize money was heard
in the court of King's Bench on 28 June. Judgment was deferred

until the court reconvened after the summer break, but both Davison and William Haslewood were confident Nelson would triumph, although 'the Earl keeps fast and will not yield till he be compelled to it'. While they all impatiently waited for the decision, another ugly spat developed over the *Orion*, a Dutch prize sent into Plymouth by *Victory* within days of leaving Portsmouth. Captain Hardy's agent, a man called Edward Lyne, took charge of the prize, claiming authority to do so. This prompted Davison furiously to remind Lyne, who to make matters worse was Benjamin Tucker's brother-in-law, that he was Nelson's agent 'upon all occasions'. Hardy himself was embarrassed, claiming a misunderstanding. 'Had I been cruising in the Channel *alone*,' he wrote to Davison, 'it was my intention to have appointed him but it is not likely I should have given him the preference to my Admiral's recommendation.' To put an end to the affair, Nelson sent Davison power of attorney for the *Orion* 'whole and sole' – though, in a sign that power was shifting, he meekly asked him to remember John Scott in the business, who sailed in high expectation of being named the fleet's sole agent. 'Particularly', Scott reminded his wife, 'when it's to be remembered that the future welfare of My dear Girl and children depends in some measure on that circumstance.' Many of the captains in Nelson's squadron had already nominated him as their agent in deference to their commander-in-chief. Scott himself still saw Davison as a partner rather than rival in the business, naming his third son, born that October, Charles Davison Scott after him. The seeds had been sown, however, for a bitter struggle that would continue to the death.

By July Nelson was off Toulon, trying to lure the French fleet out to face him. William Chevailler had adapted quickly to life in a warship and Nelson was impressed with his new steward. 'I find Mr Chevalier everything which you recommend,' he wrote to Davison, 'and I wonder he has not set up some hotel.' The steward's day began well before dawn, for Nelson, his senior officers and staff expected breakfast at seven o'clock when at sea and as early as five o'clock when in port. Breakfast generally consisted of ham, tongue, hot rolls and toast. Tea and coffee were served in the handsome silver pots paid for by Lloyd's. Another octagonal silver coffee-pot, a birthday gift from 1801 and made appropriately in Newcastle, was engraved: 'To Lord Nelson from A.D.' After breakfast the officers went to their stations, the men started the endless round of cleaning, polishing and sail-mending, and Chevailler turned to the laundry. Nelson disappeared into his cabin to concentrate on correspondence with his captivated secretary, who wrote that 'there is more business transacted before twelve o'clock than with many Admirals during the day'. Some days Nelson barely ventured out of his cabin, and occasionally did not emerge at all, remaining to his men an invisible, brooding presence in their lives.

Dinner at four o'clock was preceded by a lively rendition from the ship's band. This was the most sociable meal of the day, when the officers were often joined by friends in the fleet. The table rarely sat fewer than twelve. Close to shore, the officers ate very well, their cosmopolitan diet enhanced by deliveries from St James's Square of Yorkshire hams, Gloucester cheeses, piccalillis, sauerkraut and 'Hamburger beef'. John Scott sat at the end of the table, opposite Nelson, carving 'all the legs of sheep, pigs etc'. Dinner was washed down with champagne and claret, though Nelson once asked Davison to send him 'fifty dozen of Browns Stout'. Nelson was a generous and affable host. Scott thought there was 'something peculiar to himself in making every one happy'.

After dessert (usually of fruit), coffee and liqueurs, dinner finished around six o'clock. This allowed everyone to take 'a little walk or other recreation' on the deck while Chevailler prepared tea. This was a relaxed affair with light-hearted conversation, ending around eight o'clock with cake and a glass of punch. Except for the watch, most of the men were already in their hammocks by this time, although the officers were allowed to use candles until ten o'clock. John Scott, 'a restless animal', used this precious time to write to Charlotte. Nelson slept badly and little, sometimes pacing the deck all night.

News of Davison's 'damned electioneering scrape' caused Nelson 'real sorrow' when it reached him in *Victory*, proof that Davison had not mentioned the matter before they parted.

> *I am sure that no action of your life, much less this which has been absolutely honourable to you, will ever hurt you in the opinion of our real friends, yet it is that very circumstance that makes me, and I hope others, of your friends so distressed on your account for your envious enemies rejoice – may God eternally damn them.*

As the weeks passed, Davison began to hope vainly that the vote in parliament was the end of the affair, rashly declaring at the end of June that it was 'as much forgotten as if nothing had ever occurred to give me a moment's uneasiness'. He spoke too soon. In August he was called before Spencer Perceval, the attorney-general, to explain himself. He emerged triumphant, believing his reputation, his most valuable asset, intact and the painful episode over. 'I am perfectly secure,' he declared to Nelson:

> *nothing can occur to give me one moments concern. I came off with flying colours and as my best friends all say, I stand higher in the opinion of the public than I ever did in my life. It proves however one thing, that no man in this country can do either a great or generous act without bringing upon himself all the venom, spite and jealousy of others, which their own pitiful souls ever shrink from and carefully avoid. I am myself again and over head and ears in business. I need not tell you why but the different departments have condescended to call forth again, or rather to solicit my aid, for my spirit would neither allow me to ask, much less to court favour.*

Sir Joseph Banks, president of the Royal Society, told Davison his conduct during the investigation had earned him 'Immortal honor'.

Everything was on the up, it seemed. The renewal of the war brought a dramatic boost to Davison's business, damaged not at all by the simmering controversy over the supply of coal. In the closing months of 1803 Davison supplied goods worth almost £200,000 to the barrack office – £10 million in today's prices – compared to just £44,000 worth throughout the whole of 1802. In just six weeks he provided supplies for 45,000 men. Half of this huge sum was spent on bedding made at Davison's own factory, though he was careful, after Bowering's warning in early 1802, not to add his agency fee to these goods. There is no doubt that he was now neglecting his role as agent, preferring to supply the barrack office directly, because the increase in profit margins thus gained outweighed the loss of his commission. General De Lancey, the barrackmaster-general, was happy, though the shift brought howls of protest from Davison's old suppliers, who saw their barrack-office business sharply fall off. In December 1803 Davison calculated his wealth at £307,940, not including his personal loans which had reached a staggering £273,776. The few thousand pounds Nelson owed him amounted to only a negligible drop in the ocean.

This huge fortune did not go unnoticed. In August 1803, Davison was invited to join a prestigious firm of West End bankers, 'upon *equal* terms with the present partners', he revealed in a gushing letter to Nelson; 'nay, they have actually agreed, that if I will come in a partner, that my name shall be the *first* in the firm'.

Messrs Edwards, Noel, Templer, Johnson & Wedgwood stood proudly at 18 Stratford Place, a fashionable address near Bond Street. Founded in 1792, the firm was one of many new banks that sprang up at the end of the century to cater for the growing number of affluent private customers in London. This partnership in a West End bank was an excellent investment opportunity for Davison, as well as giving him a stake in the interests of many influential, often aristocratic, clients. Moreover, a partnership in a bank was that rare thing, in those days at least: an acceptable business pursuit for a gentleman and a fitting legacy for a son. By becoming a banker, Davison was enhancing his status and reputation, drawing away from his mercantile origins and thereby easing any social insecurity he felt alongside his in-laws, the Goslings. Despite being confined to bed by another attack of gout – and they were becoming more frequent now – Davison signed the articles of agreement on 23 September. Two days later, notices appeared in all the London newspapers announcing the formation of the new banking firm of Alexander Davison, Noel, Templer & Co.

Like him, Davison's new partners had been attracted to banking by the prospect of extending already substantial fortunes. Richard Johnson had made his in India, where he had enjoyed the patronage of Warren Hastings, the governor-general. Hastings, having survived his dramatic impeachment for corruption, was now living in quiet retirement. On his return to England, Johnson was briefly MP for Milbourne Port, that other borough in Somerset that had interested Davison, though he had spent most of his time and money building up an impressive collection of oriental manuscripts and paintings. What was left of his fortune had been absorbed by the bank, leaving his original business in crisis and Johnson facing ruin. The inability of Johnson to meet his liabilities was the spur for the other partners to approach Davison for a life-saving cash boost, though the bank's problems went deeper than the failure of one partner. Johnson resigned when Davison joined, leaving debts in his wake that the firm would never shake off. The banking house in Stratford Place, which belonged to Johnson, was sold and the bank moved, surely at Davison's insistence, to prestigious new premises on Pall Mall opposite Carlton House.

George Templer was an associate of Johnson's in India, where he had been deputy commissary-general and contractor for elephants. Returning to England in 1785, Templer, like Johnson, had found a parliamentary seat in the west country, in his case at Honiton. Templer was the most active partner in the bank, responsible for the daily management of the business. The third partner, Sir Gerard Noel, owned large estates in Northamptonshire and Lincolnshire. Noel, a kinsman to the earl of Gainsborough and MP for Rutland, was the most forceful and aristocratic of the partners. He had to swallow his pride when Davison superseded him as the senior partner.

The fourth partner, Nathaniel Middleton, was another nabob who, it was rumoured, had made a million pounds as a director of the East India Company. In India, Middleton had sired three children with a native woman and then ten more with his wife. His eldest son was named after Warren Hastings. Middleton was a neighbour of Davison's in St James's Square and related through marriage with Noel.

The fifth and final partner carried the most famous name, if not the greatest fortune. John Wedgwood was the eldest son and heir to the potter Josiah Wedgwood, a position he found burdensome and a source of anxiety. Rather than concentrating on the family business in Staffordshire as he should have done, John had become involved in a series of ill-starred ventures. He was a gentle, quiet man and his failure to manage his affairs properly, exacerbated by an extravagant and wilful wife, had preyed on his nerves. Like his younger brother Josiah Wedgwood II, John felt that his family had crossed over from trade to gentry, and this perception prompted the brothers to open an extravagant new showroom for the Wedgwood factory in St James's Square – a highly fashionable location but a commercial backwater. It was a mistake their father would never have made. By 1803 John had sunk most of his inheritance into the bank.

The best years of the old firm, which had never particularly flourished, were already well behind it when Davison joined. Apart from competition from well-established names such as Thomas Coutts, William Drummond and Davison's brother-in-law William Gosling, the rash of new, often short-lived partnerships made it difficult for the bank to build up a profitable list of customers. Edwards & Co. was also badly undercapitalized, lurching from crisis to crisis and almost failing completely early in 1800. Only regular cash injections from the partners had kept it going. On the face of it, the books looked sound enough. The bank assets, including customer debts and bills becoming due, were calculated at over £700,000. The debts, including customer balances and outstanding notes, were £670,000. The profits of the bank were said to be about £25,000 a year. Its cash reserves were low, however, only £40,000. It was solely for this reason, Davison was told, that the partners were looking for new funds.

Davison agreed to buy £100,000 worth of newly issued bank stock called Omnium. But he was shrewd enough not to trust the rosy picture presented by the partners, insisting on a two-year indemnity against any outstanding or unforeseen debts owed by the old firm. He also appointed his own people, his solicitor William Leake and the manager of the prize agency Henry Cutler, as the bank's trustees. The other partners, facing ruin if the deal failed and so in no position to argue, conceded to all his demands. The papers signed, Davison looked forward to his new career with an ambition undimmed by gout or some thirty-five years in business. 'The situation that I shall in the firm be placed', he wrote to Nelson in an expansive frame of mind,

> is the most flattering and at once will declare to the world the estimation in which I am held by the community. Indeed, my friend, I have reason to be vain . . . I am a D—d lucky fellow. What also will those people think whose spite envy and malice have been so conspicuous of my situation now feel on seeing my name at the Head of one of the leading banking houses in London – they will be silent . . . I am now told that my character and good name will do anything and that there is nothing that I might not achieve.

Unlike the rest of the nation, Davison was again unconcerned by the threat of invasion. He thought Bonaparte was looking east. Besides, 'while Lord Nelson keeps the command of

the British fleet,' he assured Lord Minto, 'we have nothing seriously to apprehend, unless he should unhappily be overpowered
by numbers'. Nevertheless, buoyed up and brimful with the infectious patriotic fervour which was sweeping the country, Davison
responded with typical enthusiasm to the government's urgent
call to arms. Like almost half a million other men that year he
would join a volunteer corps, though unlike them he had the
resources to make it his own. This gave him some sarcastic satisfaction: 'though the King would not allow me the gratification
of representing my Baron friend on the 19th May last,' he wrote
to Nelson, revealing his plan in August, 'yet His Majesty has
graciously condescended to place me at the Head of a Volunteer Corps!'

'The King, I hope, will make you a Baronet, or a Peer, in the
stead of a simple Knight,' came the reply from off Toulon. 'You
know my answer to such dirty dogs as wanted to pull you down.
They be d—d.'

Davison celebrated his new lease of life by getting 'half seas
over' on Nelson's birthday, 29 September. He then devised the
rules for his regiment, which he hoped might rival the duke of
Northumberland's Percy Tenantry, in size if not in grandeur. In his
application, which he sent to the lord lieutenant of Middlesex, the
marquis of Titchfield, Davison anticipated recruiting as many as
two thousand men. This highly ambitious goal would be achieved
by aiming the regiment at 'the very numerous class of inferior
tradesmen, journeymen, artificers, &c' who were wealthy enough
to dodge the ballots for the militias but who could not afford to
join the other volunteer corps in Westminster, which were often
run more like exclusive private clubs than army regiments, with
ludicrously expensive uniforms and subscriptions as high as £20 a
year.

Davison's corps, which he named 'The Loyal Britons',
would be different – though his egalitarian principles did not
stretch to commissions, which would be restricted to gentlemen.
The subscription would be just one guinea and the uniforms (all

made at Davison's factory, of course) would cost no more than £3. The government would pay for arms and ammunition. Davison would invest £1,000 in the corps in the first year and £500 a year after that. There would be no 'unnecessary or useless parade', he assured Titchfield in a reference to the main charge levelled against the other corps, for his men would be 'trained entirely for service':

> we will be in readiness to assist the civil magistrates in suppress-
> ing all tumults and riots [and] be ready to act with other
> Volunteer Corps within the metropolis as occasion may require,
> and in case of the actual invasion of Great Britain by a foreign
> foe, hold ourselves ready to march to any part thereof as His
> Majesty shall be pleased to direct.

Titchfield gave Davison permission to raise a corps of at least three hundred volunteers, a far more sensible target considering the competition for men in Westminster. To attract recruits, a sample uniform was hastily put on display at regimental headquarters in St James's Square, run by Davison's private secretary Henry Hill. Davison hesitated at first over whom he should invite to lead the corps: whether 'a very popular character' like Lieutenant-Colonel Richard Brinsley Sheridan of the St James's Volunteers, 'or else a gentleman of military knowledge' such as Lord Hobart of the Queen's Royal Regiment. For the sake of appearances a number of candidates were considered, including a certain Lieutenant-Colonel Davison of the Northumberland Militia, a suggestion hastily rejected as far too confusing. Inevitably Davison chose himself in the end, irritating Titchfield by presumptuously asking to be made a lieutenant-colonel right away. He was told to settle for a majority, like everyone else, until the corps reached a strength of 260 men, a number eventually passed by 18 October, when his commission was gazetted. Ten days later the king reviewed the Loyal Britons in Hyde Park, although only 127 volunteers turned up.

Nelson was amused and impressed. 'I wish you would get

rid of the gout,' he remarked, 'you will never be able to run after Buonaparte. Are Colonels allowed to ride?'

The Loyal Britons might have been nobly intended for 'inferior tradesmen', but Davison ran the corps like a pocket army, giving out commissions to friends like William Leake, Nathaniel Middleton and Henry Cutler. Such brazen bias caused problems among men who were not subject to the normal rigours, or penalties, of army life and who had joined the corps out of choice. And it led directly to a very unpleasant scene on Putney Common in January 1804.

The day began with the corps parading as usual at Smith's riding school in Shepherd Market off Piccadilly, before heading to the common for manoeuvres at around ten o'clock. After pausing for refreshments at a public house the men continued marching with such a noise that when they eventually lined up by the telegraph on the common, Captain Leake, his patience exhausted, strode angrily up to reprimand their corporal, Benjamin Wood:

'Sir, I have observed you talking several times today, I must beg you will be silent otherwise it will be impossible for me to attend to my duty.'

'Sir,' replied Wood insolently, 'it is impossible you could have heard me talking before today for I have not been within thirty yards of you.'

'Sir,' continued Leake, his face reddening, 'it is not material whether I have or have not heard you talking *before*, I hear you talking now and desire you will be silent.'

'Sir,' Wood retorted, in similar vein, 'I do not belong to your company and you have no right to order me to be silent.'

With this Leake drew his sword. 'I have a right to order you to be silent,' he cried, 'and if you do not choose to obey my orders, I desire you will leave the ranks.'

'I will not leave the ranks! You have no right to order me to do so!'

Leake seized Wood's musket, throwing it to the ground. Then, grabbing his obstinate corporal by the collar, he pushed him away from the column. Attracted by all the commotion, Lieutenant-Colonel Davison rode up. Commending Leake for his action, he turned on Wood:

'Sir, I have observed your conduct and never desire to see you in the corps again.'

Wood trudged off, but this was not the end of the matter. At the next parade he brazenly appeared in full uniform, 'but without arms or accoutrements', demanding an apology from Leake. He then sent a fearless letter to his commanding officer. 'I am desired by the several privates in my company to acquaint you that it is their determination to withdraw themselves unless you order Leake to resign. He may bless his stars I did not bayonet him but *damn* him I have done with him.'

As Edington had already discovered over the frauds in the coal business, Davison did not respond well to the threat of blackmail. So far from expelling Leake, Davison promoted him, causing another captain, one John Stockdale, to complain to the marquis of Titchfield about favouritism in the corps. It did him no good. Davison briskly forwarded Titchfield a copy of the 'Rules and regulations of the volunteer corps of Loyal Britons' underlining, in his own hand, the fifth resolution stating that 'all Field Officers be recommended for his Majesty's appointment by the Colonel'. Titchfield dismissed Stockdale's complaint, Davison dismissed Wood, and Leake was gazetted major.

On 14 November 1803 Davison went to the court of King's Bench in Westminster Hall to hear the result of Nelson's appeal against the earlier ruling giving the *Alcmeme*'s flag share of the Spanish prizes to Earl St Vincent. It was 'a glorious day!!!': 'Your great cause is decided in your favour,' he breathlessly reported as soon as he reached his desk, 'and that too *unanimously* . . . I really feel so rejoiced that I hardly know whither my head or my heels are uppermost'. In his judgment Lord Ellenborough, whom Davison would one day meet again in less happy circumstances, ruled that command of the Mediterranean station in 1799 had automatically devolved to Nelson during Earl St Vincent's absence due to ill-health. Benjamin Tucker, the earl's agent and henchman, was ordered to hand over the £14,000. The earl said nothing, though a jubilant Davison uncharitably thought the decision would 'go far to *place* him in the other world'. An ecstatic Emma celebrated the victory with a 'leg of pork and pea pudding dinner' at Merton Place. 'She is always so happy to see me,' sighed Davison. The money was soon spent. After clearing his mortgage and George Matcham's loan, Nelson was left with only £1,000, which he deposited with Davison & Co. in a valuable celebrity endorsement. Davison himself was still owed over £3,800 though this scarcely troubled him; he told Nelson not to give the debt a second thought.

It had been an eventful year, which at one moment had seemed to bring Davison close to personal catastrophe. With its close he felt 'beyond the reach of malice and envy'. The bank was 'going on swimmingly' and he was 'tied hand and foot to town for public business', boasting that Nicholas Vansittart, the joint secretary to the Treasury who had voted for his prosecution after the Ilchester inquiry, had 'discovered that I can do more for Government than those he has been in the habit of employing'. Vansittart asked him to supply goods for 'all secret service business', while his old friend William Huskisson, whom Davison had nurtured for years, gave him the task of organizing six million coins for Ceylon, reuniting Davison with Matthew Boulton. He even sustained a 'secret correspondence' with the prime minister, forwarding Nelson's letters to Downing Street because Henry Addington 'wished to know everything regarding you'. Nelson was happy to play this game if it would bring Emma a pension. Addington hinted that he would view her claim favourably, but the issue drifted and Christmas came and went with no sign of the government loosening the purse strings. 'I wish', Davison chafed, 'we could but bring the minister to settle the pension, why it is put off from him is most extraordinary.'

His access to the prime minister gave Davison a valuable insight into the intrigues at the heart of government. So when he picked up intimations that Addington was pressing the king to appoint Lord Moira to the cabinet, he put this privileged information to good effect. For some time Moira had been using Davison's influence to try to secure Nelson's proxy vote, a priceless PR tool, in the House of Lords. Now persuaded by Davison that Moira was close to power and thus the key to breaking the deadlock over Emma's pension, Nelson finally surrendered it, albeit reluctantly.

> *I have broke through a resolution I made, never to give a Proxy; nor could anything have induced me to swerve from it, but to such a man as Lord Moira. Whether he is in or out of Office, my opinion of him is formed for ability, honour, and strict integrity, which nothing can shake, even should ever we differ on any particular point.*

Moira, who had been appointed commander-in-chief of armed forces in Scotland, was familiar with Nelson's sensitivity to criticism and promised to use the proxy to defend Nelson against the 'envy' of parliament. 'I will give myself the pride of being ostensibly confided in by him,' Moira assured Davison, 'and in political questions I shall hold myself bound to give his vote as his relation to the Ministry requires, though it may be in contradiction to my own.' Nelson wavered until the very moment of sending the signed proxy for Davison to pass to Moira. He knew the risks of relinquishing control of his voice in parliament, and Moira's could hardly be construed as the most reliable, or loyal, pair of hands. 'I have entrusted him with what I did not believe I would entrust any man,' he quivered; 'I hope he will be a firm supporter of Mr. Addington's Administration.'

Davison, who would be rewarded for brokering this sensitive pact, was supremely reassuring. 'I delivered your proxy to Lord Moira who values the confidence as he ought,' he wrote on 17 March 1804, *and never will use it but upon very extraordinary occasions and then only in the way he is sure you would vote yourself were you present. He is now gone to Mr Addington in consequence of a note he received this morning from Downing Street requesting to see him. If Mr Addington acts properly he will at once act openly and declare his wish of Lord Moira uniting with him.*

With Nelson's squadron held up off Toulon, waiting tensely for the expected showdown with the French, 'a glorious one . . . that shall never bring a blush on the cheeks of my friend when my name is mentioned', the jockeying for the prize agency intensified. Impatient for news, William Marsh sent letters on the subject to both Nelson and his secretary John Scott. Ten months at sea alongside Nelson had turned Scott wholly against Davison, whose influence over his chief he profoundly distrusted. He revealed to Marsh that Nelson was being assailed by 'repeated requests from a certain quarter' on the matter of the agency, though Davison's surviving correspondence shows no evidence of this. Scott was convinced that Nelson, 'against his inclination', was going to give the agency to Davison again. 'It will pain him to the heart to act as it appears he must,' he wrote, adding urgently, 'the circumstances of this subject will of course be buried in oblivion.'

Nelson's reply to Marsh's letter, which echoes his earlier denial to his brother Maurice after the Nile, seemed to confirm his, and Scott's, worst fears.

I am truly sensible of the uniform kindness of your House and of yourself in particular . . . could I see you for five minutes you would be satisfied why the Nile prizes could not be put into your hands . . . I care not for money myself but as it may be useful to my friends and it is this alone which drains my pocket.

Nelson felt torn. This clash of interests caused him real anguish. The sticking point was Davison's point-blank refusal to share the agency with anyone else. He poured out his torment in a letter to Emma which reveals an extraordinary, even craven dependence on his friend which goes way beyond mere financial indebtedness. What form of unbreakable loyalty bound them together? 'To say the truth I am so situated between Davison and Mr Marsh that I do not think I ever can name an agent again,' Nelson wrote.

> *I have had many and great obligations to both of them and I never put a sixpence in Mr Marsh's pocket − to Davison it has been twice in my power. Say he has touched (besides the use of the money, which you may lay at £10,000) full £15,000, and when I told Davison how I was situated with Mr. Marsh and that I wish to name them together, Mr Davison declined it, and said, 'Whatever you do, let me stand alone.' I may never have the power of naming one alone, for secretaries and other admirals will naturally look to the compliment being also paid them of joining together. Therefore if Davison will never be joined, I see but little chance of my being able to name him alone . . . I have wrote Davison pretty near as much some time ago . . . I am sure he is too much my friend to wish to place me in difficulties, but keep this to yourself. I will for a moment suppose a case which may happen: we take the French fleet, the Captains name the three secretaries, and pay me, perhaps, the compliment of asking me to name a person in England to do the business. I should, of course, wish to join Mr. Davison and Mr. Marsh; it would hurt me for him to refuse to be joined to Mr. Marsh and the secretaries here, and yet he would do it. I know he would not give up the proportion, and only ask to have his name stand alone, but neither the captors not the other parties would agree to it.*

With everyone pressing for an answer, Nelson brooded on his self-imposed quandary, his health suffering beneath the stress. Eventually, he tentatively proposed a compromise. He suggested that Davison share the 5 per cent agency commission with Scott. Two per cent would go to Scott 'for his trouble' and 3 per cent to

Davison 'for making the distribution'. It was a deal to which Davison would never agree, as Nelson must have known.

Nelson's inability to tackle this problem properly, or to be honest with any of the people involved, came from the same fear of personal confrontation that he showed during the breakdown of his marriage. Frequently bitchy behind people's backs, Nelson could never disappoint face to face. Davison exploited this weakness, using it to tighten his hold. In private Nelson wriggled desperately, but he would never climb off the hook. There was no-one else who would help him as Davison had helped him to desert Fanny. So he bottled up his anxiety, releasing it only in his letters to Emma, which could veer wildly between miserable self-pity and great tenderness. Nelson could play many roles, depending on the audience; but it was as a drama queen that he revealed the only certain solution to the agency dispute, for the want of the ability to resolve it himself. 'I know of no other way but not taking the French fleet,' he wrote miserably to Emma, 'and that would be very hard upon me.'

XI
SPARTIATE

74 GUNS,
CAPTAIN SIR FRANCIS LAFOREY

EMMA WAS ANXIOUS, ill and restless. Late in 1803 she even threatened, as Fanny had before her under different circumstances, to join Nelson in the Mediterranean. He rebuffed her suggestion, although more gently this time. The crisis past, Emma threw herself into the improvements at Merton Place. The cure worked. After Davison saw her in December he reported that 'every day, she looks better and better *and better*'. Never happier than when she was the centre of attention, Emma surrounded herself over Christmas with a noisy assortment of children, friends and members of Nelson's family. The Davisons took two-year-old Horatia and three-year-old Alexander Horatio to the theatre for a treat, presumably to see a pantomime. Over the holiday no-one noticed, or at least no-one commented, that Emma was heavily pregnant. She was in any case so plump by now that the bump hardly showed. She blamed a sore throat when she briefly retired to her bedroom before the New Year, brushing aside everyone's concern. With her mother by her side, Emma gave birth to Nelson's second child, a girl: but the baby, if not stillborn, died soon afterwards. Heroically, Emma dined with Davison on 5 January as if nothing had happened. Davison, in a letter he wrote to Nelson afterwards, gave no sign of having spotted anything unusual: he discussed instead the widespread invasion panic that

Dido in Despair: *James Gillray mocks Emma Hamilton's anguish as Nelson sails for the Baltic and Sir William Hamilton sleeps on, blissfully unaware. Among the many allusions, note the horned figure of a cuckold among the collection of antiquities on the floor and the artfully drawn fragment referring ironically to Sir William's fascination with Priapus, an ancient fertility god.*

was again sweeping the country, talk he held 'in contempt'. Bonaparte would not, he declared, be 'mad' enough to attempt a landing in England.

Sir William Manners finally caught up with his quarry in April 1804. Just when he must have hoped the scandal was blowing over, out of the blue Davison was charged with seven counts of corruption and conspiracy to corrupt thirty-six people by gifts of money before the Ilchester election. The news must have shaken him to the core. The case was listed to be heard during the Lent assizes in Taunton. This was a major local event, almost a festival, and the town was crowded with people when Davison arrived, ignominiously escorted by a guard from the Marshalsea prison in London. Apart from the assizes balls, everyone came hoping to enjoy some hangings, and Sir Robert Graham, the presiding judge, did not disappoint. Six men were condemned to death before Davison's case was heard: two for stealing sheep, two for burglary and two for stealing $5\frac{1}{2}$ guineas, though only this last unfortunate pair, Bill Dowder and Bill Meeds, were hanged, the others being reprieved. Two unmarried women, Elizabeth Winter and Jane Chaplin, were acquitted of murdering their 'bastard children' but were imprisoned for six months for concealing their pregnancies. More criminals faced transportation to the convict colony at New South Wales for stealing, variously, breeches, bridles, wool and a watch. Few, if any, realized that the colony had been built to a large extent by their celebrated co-defendant.

At nine o'clock on 3 April Davison followed this motley collection of criminals into a courtroom overflowing with excited spectators. Alongside Davison in the dock were John White Parsons and Thomas Hopping.

The prosecution was led by Robert Dallas, a lawyer who specialized in contested elections. Dallas outlined the crown's case, describing Davison as 'a gentleman of reputed and I have no doubt of real opulence . . . who has long been in the possession of . . . the execution of very lucrative government contracts'. Among the prosecution's witnesses was the post-boy from the

Greyhound inn at Wincanton, who remembered a smartly dressed gentleman staying at the inn the night before the plot was hatched at West Camel, and Phyllis Appleby, one of White Parsons' servants, who had served the gentlemen breakfast. Evidence even more damning was given by Bill Jones, a clerk at Stricky & Bagit, a company of brickmakers in Langport, who recalled Davison buying ten thousand bricks for the new houses outside Ilchester. Several voters from the town, enjoying their moment of fame, were asked to describe how the stranger slipped them their £30. The prosecution's star witness was Tom Oldfield, the disaffected election agent dumped by Davison before the poll. Oldfield described his meetings at St James's Square and West Camel with all the drama he could muster, though he was forced to concede that Davison had personally told him he had 'given up Ilchester' well before the election, as he was 'a great deal alarmed at the bribery'.

Davison was defended by the celebrated Thomas Erskine, a freemason and the favourite lawyer of prominent Whigs, who was close to both Lord Moira and the prince of Wales. Like Dallas, Erskine was, in Davison's words, a member of the 'cursed wigg'd gentry' who had lived alongside him at Lincoln's Inn in the 1780s. Erskine was on his feet for an hour, basing Davison's defence almost entirely on the discrediting of Oldfield. Witnesses spoke of the boroughmonger's 'rank' atheism and his republican tendencies. Turning to the jury, Erskine asked them whether they could seriously believe that Davison, 'a man of the world [who] has made wealth for himself by the exercise of his own facilities', would get involved with such a man. Erskine asserted that the houses outside the town had been built by White Parsons, with Davison's help, as an act of benevolence to the local community. There was no evidence of a systematic attempt to bribe the voters or of a connection between Davison and the stranger seen in the town handing out the money. Unaware of, or concealing, Davison's relationship with William Hunter's father, Erskine said there was no link between his client and the yellow party candidates.

No-one doubted that Oldfield and Davison had met, but had not Oldfield himself just said that Davison had abandoned Ilchester before the election?

Dallas cleverly tackled Erskine's defence by pointing out that the contact between the 'pure and immaculate Mr Davison' and Oldfield confirmed Davison's guilt. 'Does not the instrument prove the intention?' Dallas asked the jury;

> Does not the workman employed show the work and prove the sort of building to be raised? . . . Upon what ground . . . was this gentleman . . . received into the house of Alexander Davison in St James's Square and why Mr Davison afterwards took the trouble to meet this bad man and spend a day with him in the house of Mr Parsons except that he was an electioneering agent and a borough monger that he was fitted for this work and therefore he made choice of him for this reason.

Why had Davison not defended himself before the House of Commons committee? Dallas asked, or discredited Oldfield before today? The suggestion that, out of the blue, Davison lent money to White Parsons to build the houses outside Ilchester was simply preposterous.

In his summing-up, the judge drew the jurors' attention to Davison's interest in the other boroughs before the election, reminding them that a conspiracy to bribe was criminal even if there were doubts about the bribery itself. After a trial lasting eight hours, the jury adjourned for only five minutes, 'after a pause of that space finding *all the defendants guilty*' – a judgment which was, noted one of the court clerks writing from his lodgings that evening, 'the universal opinion of the audience'. When the hubbub died down, Sir Robert sent all three men to the Marshalsea prison for a year.

While his lawyers lodged an appeal, Davison returned to London on bail, fearing that his reputation, the one thing his money couldn't buy, was shattered. 'Davison's folly', the terrace of houses he had had built outside Ilchester, was left behind in Somerset, where they still stand at a distance from a town that is little changed, a lasting tribute to Davison's ill-judged venture into politics. But he still had influential friends, and few of them saw any dishonour in his crime. Lord Moira, in Edinburgh, was horrified when he heard the verdict. There was little he could do to reverse the judgment, but as Sir Robert Graham was the prince of Wales's principal lawyer, he could use his influence at Carlton House to try to ease Davison's sentence.

'Cannot you get somebody to hint to Baron Graham how earnestly I am interested about Davison?' Moira asked Colonel John McMahon, the prince of Wales's secretary. 'Graham's report must decide much; old Graham is partial to me.' Moira's efforts were in vain. For a while it seemed Davison might escape imprisonment by paying a fine, but even these hopes were scuppered when the attorney-general observed that any fine, however large, would be no punishment to a man of Davison's means. The sentence would stand.

The Marshalsea in Southwark lay within the jurisdiction of the much larger King's Bench prison, and it was in the King's Bench that Davison was confined. The prison, which stood on Borough High Street, consisted of a rambling collection of buildings surrounded by a 30-foot wall. Looming over everything else was the statehouse, an imposing modern building about 120 yards long with a high pedimented front. It replaced an earlier structure burnt down during the Gordon riots in 1780. Designed to accommodate four hundred prisoners, by 1804 the statehouse may have held as many as eight hundred, though no-one was sure of the exact number. Each prisoner paid one shilling a week to share a room no bigger than 16 feet by 13 feet with up to ten other 'chums'. The wealthier prisoners often bought out their poorer chums, creating pockets of overcrowding so severe that many prisoners resorted to sleeping in the chapel. Around the statehouse sprawled shops and stalls selling meat, vegetables and goods of every description. There was also a prison coffee house and a

*King's Bench prison in Southwark. During his incarceration Davison
rented an apartment in the Terrace, a separate building reserved for
wealthy prisoners shown to the left of the Statehouse, beside the wall.*

public house known as the tap, where beer was fivepence a pot. Inmates spent their days largely in idleness, although racquets, tennis and skittles were available for a fee. Gambling and drinking were rife. For those with artistic talent, such as Arthur William Devis, who was in the prison at the same time as Davison, the hours could be used productively.

Many of the prisoners confined for debt sought refuge in the 'rules' – a system which allowed them to live, for a fee, on parole in 'sponging houses' outside the statehouse. Officially the rules covered an area of about a square mile to the west of the prison, though they were so universally abused that Lord Ellenborough, the chief justice of the King's Bench, commented wryly that they seemed to stretch as far as the East Indies. At the heart of the rules, close to the Freemasons' School for Girls, was a great obelisk that had been raised in 1771 by the lord mayor of London as the centrepiece for the newly created St George's Circus. An inscription on it states that it is exactly one mile from London Bridge and one mile from the Palace of Westminster. Recently restored, it still stands in the same position (unlike the Freemasons' School for Girls, which is now in Rickmansworth).

Perhaps because he was a felon and not a debtor, Davison remained lodged within the prison walls, where the stink of urine and excrement from the statehouse still hung over him like a soiled blanket. He moved, however, to rooms in the King's Bench Terrace, a small separate building alongside the statehouse reserved for the richest prisoners. It was here that Davison spent the next year, glumly surrounded by his books, a few prized pieces of furniture and some family portraits from St James's Square. To cheer things up a little he arranged for the rooms to be redecorated.

Nelson did not even hear about Davison's prosecution until it was over. 'I am quite hurt about his getting into such a scrape,' he commented when Emma passed the dramatic news on. His shock and upset were genuine, though he failed to disguise a certain smug satisfaction: 'he always told me: "Oh! I know my ground

– leave me alone – I cannot be deceived". It often turns out that these very clever men are oftener deceived than other people.' Not knowing the trial verdict, Nelson none the less judged its likely outcome when he wrote to Davison to commiserate: 'I expect this will find you in prison. I am sure it will be a lesson never to touch an election for any friend however dear. Your generous way of thinking will not do for the gamesters of Boroughs.'

Davison's fall from grace coincided with the prime minister's fall from power. Early in the year the king suffered a bout of madness, renewing talk of a regency. The speculation isolated Henry Addington, because a regency would inevitably bring in an administration packed with the prince's favourites. Lord Moira, for one, no longer had the least desire, or need, to be associated with Addington. He moved into direct opposition to the government, taking Nelson's proxy vote with him. The king recovered – this time – and a regency was, for the present, avoided; but Addington, whom the duke of Northumberland always thought an 'arrogant & insolent man', was so weakened that he resigned on 29 April 1804, heralding the return of William Pitt.

Emma, who had pinned her hopes on Addington's awarding her the sorely needed pension, bitterly accused Nelson of hastening the prime minister's destruction by giving away his vote to Moira, one of Addington's assassins. Nelson, who had confided to Davison as early as March that he thought Emma's cause was lost, vehemently defended himself. 'I am no party man as a tool,' he cried. Even if the proxy had reached London before Addington fell, which he doubted, it had been given on condition that Lord Moira would support the prime minister. If anyone was to blame for the unfortunate impression that he had stabbed the prime minister in the back it was the messenger. Davison, Nelson claimed, was 'the innocent cause of any one having my proxy, for I never liked giving it'. At any rate, all was not lost. With Pitt's resurrection, the sympathetic figure of Henry Dundas, now Viscount Melville, returned to power, replacing Earl St Vincent as first lord of the Admiralty.

Confirmation of Davison's sentence in the King's Bench reached *Victory* in June. 'I am not surprised at the time poor Davison is to be confined after what passed in Parliament,' Nelson wrote to Emma:

He would only consult Lord Moira and such clever folks, but an ignoramus like me could only warn him not to touch Boroughs. He has, poor fellow, been completely duped, and who cares? Not one of those great folks. I am most sincerely sorry for him, but a year will soon pass away. Have I not been shut up in a ship without any one comfort? He is ashore with his friends round him, and even you to go to see him. I would change with him with much pleasure. I shall write him a line, he must not kill himself, that his enemies would rejoice at, and I hope he will live to plague them.

As promised, he wrote to Davison the same day.

By dear Lady H's letter of May 13ʰ received last night, I received the distressing intelligence of your sentence, at least the confinement but I fear you have likewise a fine to pay however, my dear friend, hurt as I feel upon your health's account (for in no other way do I feel that my friend can suffer) yet there is a comfort in all things. It has been long hanging over you and the day was sure to arrive. Now the time is passing away and before you receive this letter one quarter of a year will be over, and by the kind attention of your friends time will not hang heavy, and even I intend to dine with you in the Xmas holidays . . . Now my dear Davison, if I had not gained my cause against the Earl, I should most certainly have been liable to be in your apartments for debt, therefore you see how near you have been having my company. But joking apart I curse from my heart those who did you such an ill natured turn but never mind, it arose from envy. Better to be envied than pitied. Never, never, my dear friend, have anything more to say to electors or elections. They will not be

Davison's version from Lemuel Abbott's series of portraits of Nelson. Nelson sat to the artist during the autumn of 1797 while recovering from the loss of his arm. Davison received one of the first finished paintings, which hung first at Harpur Street and then in St James's Square.

Below: *The Prize Agent Refusing to Give Money* by Thomas Rowlandson. This was no doubt a familiar scene illustrating the low regard in which agents were held.

Opposite page, top: A note prepared by Davison for Nelson 'to shew how little Prize Money he received in proportion to Other Admirals'.

Opposite page, centre right: John Jervis, Earl St Vincent. Nelson's pugnacious chief was also his bitter rival for the Spanish treasure prize money.

Opposite page, bottom: The gold medal struck by Matthew Boulton to a design by John Flaxman which Earl St Vincent presented to Davison in 1801. Is this a masonic handshake?

Lord Nelson –

To shew how little prize money he received in proportion
    to other Admirals.

For the Battle off St Vincent 14.th Feb.^{ry} 1797

    Lord St Vincent shared . . . . – 10,730..2..1

    Lord Nelson . . . – shared – –––––––– 2146..0..4

For the Battle of the Nile 1.&2 Augt 1798

    Lord St Vincent . . . shared ––––––– 14,149..13..0

    Lord Nelson - for fought & conquered shared only 2358..4..6

    Sir John Orde, who was not in the action shared 2358..4..6

For the Battle of Copenhagen 2.^d April 1801

    Sir Hyd.^e Parker . . . shared

    Lord Nelson who fought & conquered shared not

The Death of Lord Nelson, painted by Benjamin West in 1806. West, rooted in the heroic tradition, was happy to paint 'what might have been, not of the circumstances as they happened'. Nelson's secretary John Scott is shown mortally wounded to the middle left of the picture.

The Death of Nelson painted by Arthur William Devis (1807): 'the Steward, with silent eagerness, explores and interrogates the Doctor's eye, to catch, if possible, a glimmering of hope'. This was the moment Nelson's purse (*above*) began its journey.

Nelson's burial in the crypt of St Paul's Cathedral, directly beneath the dome, 9 January 1806. Davison stood alongside Haslewood and Marsh within the specially built hexagonal enclosure.

considered by me or your friends who ever ask you. Probably this
event will be useful in making your friends damn your enemies.
Amen amen. I have done and we shall laugh at all this one of
these happy days to come.

'I certainly would have thought less in paying a fine of five
or ten thousand pounds than being sentenced to the rules of the
King's Bench,' Davison replied;

envy has done its worst, and the very persons that were the chief
instruments of resentment now say how hard, how cruel and how
unjust is my case – so much for my attempts to be of use to
Government! . . . I have a very comfortable house and live just as
I like and go out where I like so that it really is more the idea
than the thing itself creates punishment.

He further reported cheerily that, far from his imprisonment
harming his business, he was able to achieve more within the quiet
confines of the King's Bench than in the bustle of St James's
Square. And he made a resolution:

after this year is over I shall cut all my public concerns and stick
to others more pleasant . . . My banking House . . . will be a
good friend to my boys when I am no more, and as to my ever having any thing again to do in Electioneering matters I ought to be
burnt for a fool, if I muddle in any shape, tho' I shall most certainly buy myself a seat the moment I am a free man.

Unsurprisingly, Davison was putting on a brave face to his
friend. He complained to John Maitland, the army clothier whom
he had embroiled in his ill-fated brandy smuggling scheme during
the American war, that the 'particular inconvenience' of his deten-
tion had forced him virtually to suspend his work. He spent his
time instead brooding over his predicament, anticipating the day
when he could look 'face to face at those vertuous characters who

(as Mr Pitt says) would not – nor never did do any thing in the shape of a Bribe at an Election!!! My line is to support my friends and bid defiance to my enemies.'

Those friends visited when they could. Evan Nepean, who had incontrovertibly won a seat in parliament at the same election, spent a whole day in the prison with Davison in August. After a disastrous spell as chief secretary to the lord lieutenant in Ireland, where his political skills were found to be badly wanting, Nepean (now Sir Evan) had returned as Melville's 'labouring oar' at the Admiralty. William Huskisson was also back in favour, and office, becoming joint secretary to the Treasury. Lord Moira was another loyal supporter, dining with Davison and a 'select party of friends' in King's Bench Terrace on 28 June. There was cause for a small celebration on this occasion, for Moira, who was almost fifty, had finally found himself a wife. According to Davison, Flora Campbell, countess of Loudon in her own right, was 'an uncommonly clever, accomplished woman'. Apart from another title, the countess brought Moira a 'clear estate of eight thousand pounds a year'. Nelson sent his congratulations.

Davison's most indulgent ally was Emma, who tried to rush to his side as soon as the sentence was passed. 'I waited all day yesterday my dear sir for permission to come to you as I was told it would be inconvenient to you having paperers and carpenters with you tell me are you comfortable and when can I see you . . . that villain Oldfield he ought to be hanged.' Unable to visit in person, she sent cases of honey and maraschino cherries to lift Davison's spirits. 'You will only shine the more after this oppressive and unjust cloud has passed,' she assured him.

After the birth and death of her child, Emma launched herself into a giddy round of balls, routs and concerts, as if trying to purge the pain of her hidden bereavement. Her exhausting routine was also a means of spiting Fanny, as she explained to William Nelson. 'I thought it right to show myself in some respectable houses,' she wrote, 'as *Tom Tit* said she would shut me out.' Emma's victory over Fanny – for Nelson's heart and his family's affection – was now total. Yet while her rival lived, Emma could never have the one thing she wanted more than anything: the chance to be Nelson's wife. In her letters to Davison, Emma vented her fury at the injustice of Fanny, a woman 'without youth, beauty, riches, talents or any thing to recommend her', enjoying Nelson's titles and position at her expense; the eternal cry of a thwarted mistress. In July Emma's hatred of Fanny scaled new heights. 'The apothecary's widow, the Creole with her heart black as her fiendlike looking face, was never destined for a Nelson, for so noble minded a creature. She never loved him for himself,' she raged in a letter to a bewildered Davison;

> when he came home, maimed, lame and covered with glory, she put in derision his honourable wounds. She raised a clamour against him, because he had seen a more lovely, a more virtuous woman who had served with him in a foreign country and who had her heart and senses open to his glory, to his greatness and his virtues. If he had lived with this demon, the blaster of his fame and reputation, he must have fallen under it and his country would have lost their greatest ornament.

Emma was writing from Ramsgate, whither she had gone to avoid the builders, and their bills, at Merton Place. With Nelson away and Sir William dead, she had become, if not intimate with Davison, certainly closely attached to him, leaning heavily on him for emotional support. 'Nelson loves you and therefore I do the same,' she assured him. Her letters begin to end simply with 'Emma', a familiarity Fanny would never have contemplated for an instant. Davison returned Emma's affection, counting the days to her visits and making no attempt to disguise his upset when they were prevented. 'I was greatly disappointed in not seeing you on Friday,' he wrote in October, 'and was fearful some accident had happened; but your letter on Saturday explained . . . when you are well enough to take an airing, a ride even to a prison will do you no harm and me much good.'

There were sound practical reasons for Emma to remain close to Davison. Apart from his usefulness in buying her lottery tickets and sending her champagne when she was out of town, Davison was a dependable, and discreet, source of money beyond her income from Sir William's estate and her £100 monthly allowance from Nelson. Her extravagant lifestyle and the escalating works at Merton Place ensured that his goodwill was frequently called upon. Perhaps inevitably, even so close a friendship as they had established did not protect them from the occasional clash; and the ceaseless building and embellishments at Merton became a significant bone of contention. After James Dodds died, Nelson had placed the works in the hands of 'Mr Davison's architect', a Mr Chawner. Like Dodds before him, Chawner worked under Davison's supervision because Davison was paying the bills. Emma was left in charge of Thomas Cribb, the head gardener at Merton Place, who was making improvements to the grounds.

This division of responsibility inevitably led to conflict. Within weeks of Nelson's leaving England, Emma was interfering in all aspects of the project – so much so that Davison, after hearing that the projected costs of the works had risen to over £4,000 against a budget of a few hundred, was forced to order Chawner to intervene and forestall one of Emma's more ambitious schemes. His rebuke for this apparent impertinence was swift.

'I wish to God you had explained to me about the moat instead of Mr Cribb,' Emma wrote from bed on 13 June;

> we had better stop everything till my Lord writes to you or comes . . . I am myself the surveyor of the alterations of the grounds as my Lord wishes it should be my taste therefore the builder can have nothing to do with my department as I shall have nothing to do with his . . . if you think it proper that these improvements should go on and Cribb be accountable to you only we will be happy so to do . . . we do not want a Capability Brown . . . we have spent little money considering what has been done and this I can assure you, not to be all ways asking.

'I ever have most studiously avoided meddling with your exclusive prerogative in your schemes and plans,' Davison replied, stung by the insinuation that he was overstepping the mark;

no such thought could possibly have entered my head, or could ever be, in contemplation of either Mr Chawner or myself to interfere in any shape whatever with Mr Cribb who appears an intelligent, plain, fair, correct well meaning man . . . Let me ask you if you really seriously believe it to be our Dearest Lord's intention to spend this sum upon the premises?

'I can only say,' Emma churlishly retorted,

I have not acted for myself in any way. What I have done has been to make comfortable the man that my soul dotes on, that I would think it little to sacrifice my life to make him happy. Nelson and Emma can have but one mind, one heart, one soul, one interest, and I can assure you that if the nation was to give my beloved Nelson a Blenheim, Merton would be the place he would live in. Therefore as I know all his thoughts on this point, I need not say how anxious I was to go on with what he so ardently desired. I daresay your prudence is right, that I cannot say anything about.

'My prudence (as you call it)', came the swift reply,

can only be connected with that Duty, Regard, and affection I owe to our dearest Nelson . . . if by my giving my opinion in such manner it should unluckily disoblige — it is my misfortune, not my intention to offend. I feel, and must ever feel, the most lively solicitude in Everything in which our dearest Nelson's interest, wish, gratification, happiness or by whatever term it may be called is concerned — I trust we shall see him in England before the year is out, and in that good state of health and spirits as to afford joy, transmitting bliss to His Emma — and not a little pleasure to myself.

An uneasy truce was reached. Davison sent Chawner's drawings to Emma, promising her that Davison & Co. would meet Cribb's bills. He took the precaution, however, of relaying his side of the story to Nelson as soon as he could, knowing another version would reach *Victory* from Merton Place. The casual friendliness of Davison's letter – 'with *women*', he wrote, 'it is right to state matters explicitly' – betrays unease at the damage that incurring Emma's wrath might do to his position. Davison's fears were justified, because Nelson instinctively took the side of his mistress, his reply to what had obviously been a complaining missive from her revealing the full extent of the spin she put on the affair.

'As to ——, I know the full extent of the obligation I owe him,' he wrote;

> *he may be useful to me again; but I can never forget his unkindness to you. But, I guess, many reasons influenced his conduct, in bragging of his riches, and my honourable poverty; but as I have often said, and with honest pride, what I have is my own; it never cost the widow a tear, or the Nation a farthing. I got what I have with my pure blood, from the Enemies of my Country. Our house, my own Emma, is built upon a solid foundation; and will last to us, when his house and lands may belong to others than his children. I would not have believed it, from any one but you! But, if ever I go abroad again, matters shall be settled differently.*

Davison told Emma that many factors were forcing him to rein in the spiralling costs of Merton. He did not tell her that one of them was a crisis at the bank. On 19 June two of his partners, George Templer and Nathaniel Middleton, visited the King's Bench accompanied by the bank's solicitor, William Leake. They brought bad news. The precarious political and military situation was causing jitters among their customers, who were draining the bank of up to £6,000 a day. As daily cash receipts and bills owed averaged only £4,000, this meant the partners were losing £2,000 of their own money every day the bank was open. Already badly undercapitalized, the bank could ill afford such a loss of funds. This critical situation was exacerbated by Lord Moira's reluctance to settle debts with the bank for over £30,000, despite having sold his Irish estates for £100,000 and acquiring a rich wife. It also seems that Davison either had not paid for his Omnium stock or had already sold it, possibly to meet Sir William Manners' claim for compensation and his legal fees.

At a highly charged meeting on 21 July, which Davison was unable to attend, the partners discussed their options. All of them felt 'soured' after the euphoria of the previous year, when it had seemed the promise of Davison's money would save them from ruin. Once again they were staring into the financial abyss. Various temporary solutions were considered, including the 'unbecoming' practice of discounting bills to customers 'when the accounts do not require it'. Rising wearily to his feet, George Templer then addressed the issue they had been skirting around. 'The question is a short one,' he said:

> ought the House to continue or not. We must all agree in the answer . . . if the House can be supported it will amply pay and remunerate the cares and vexations it has . . . if on the contrary the means do not exist, dreadful as the alternative is, let it close. But in that word is a general wreck of all things, before commissions, all must be brought forward . . . little sums I repeat will only add to the difficulty.

The partners knew they would all have to sell their own property and estates to settle the bank's debts – all, that is, except Davison, who was still indemnified against any losses under the terms of his partnership. John Wedgwood was already selling up. Such drastic action could, however, damage the confidence of their customers and might even hasten the bank's demise. Templer ended the meeting with a plea to the bank's senior partner, who was currently languishing in prison. They had, he said, to beg Davison to restore to the bank

those aids and that confidence . . . by that means we may again
try to regain our credit with our customers, which must lessen as
our means lessens, . . . If Mr Davison has only withdrawn his
funds as having actually used them and does not possess the
means and candidly declares we have not full his confidence
then I repeat I submit with all humility to that alternative of
doing in time what cannot under such aid only be put off a week
or a fortnight . . . I ought not to hint at such a thing, since I am
sure all my colleagues will spurn such an idea but who can say
to what a moment of necessity may lead.

Calling for biscuits and a pitcher of water, a clearly distressed
Templer then sat down.

One celebrated customer, at least, knew about the problems
facing the bank, privileged inside knowledge gleaned either from
Merton Place or from Davison himself. 'I think it impossible that
my friend the banker', Nelson wrote to Emma in August,

would allow me to be distressed by loss of money in his banking
house. I cannot believe it . . . but I hope poor as I am, if the
money I have in the house would save my friend, he should be
welcome to it, but why should my all go to save a parcel of peo-
ple that I never saw or care one farthing about?

On 29 September Davison held a lonely little party in the
King's Bench to celebrate Nelson's birthday. 'I did not fail to drink
your health *here* in bumpers of three times three, tho' I had noone
that could give me a song afterwards.' The row over the improvements at Merton Place was long forgotten, with 'all parties . . . in
harmony' and the bills paid, despite, as Nelson described it, a
'want of the needful'.

Davison was now preoccupied with far more exciting matters than Emma's new dining room. One of the 'confidential' tasks
the government had given him during his imprisonment was to
help a maverick American inventor called Robert Fulton build his

'infernals', an eccentric assortment of torpedoes and mines with clockwork fuses. On the face of it Davison and Fulton were unlikely bedfellows, except for a shared love of money. Fulton was a friend of Thomas Paine, Davison's *bête noire*, and had already offered to build a submarine for Bonaparte to use against the British navy. But by the time the emperor agreed to back him, Fulton had been lured to Britain, Pitt's pounds proving more persuasive than Paine's politics. Fulton's plans were assessed in London by a top secret committee chaired by Sir Joseph Banks and including William Congreve, the inventor of the artillery rocket, and an ambitious naval officer called Sir Home Popham, who had a reputation for sailing close to the wind. The committee was sceptical about the viability of Fulton's submarine but persuaded that his 'infernals' had military merit. Over breakfast in Downing Street in July 1804, William Pitt and Viscount Melville, Fulton's most enthusiastic supporter, agreed to fund the development of the 'infernals' in conditions of the utmost secrecy at Portsmouth dockyard. Popham was put in charge of the project and £7,000 given to Davison to supply all the necessary materials.

On 4 October the first 'infernals' were tested in a raid on Boulogne, watched in person by Melville from the deck of the frigate *L'Aimable*. The minister was treated to a spectacular fireworks display as most of the 'infernals' detonated – but they destroyed only one small French boat, sent out to investigate the strange contraptions drifting towards the town. Davison, still confined to prison, bitterly regretted missing the action. 'Had I not been here I would have now been afloat to have taken a share in the execution,' he wrote to Nelson on the evening of the attack; 'my head for near three months has been much occupied with this Grand Object. The whole of the machinery has been provided for under *my* orders.'

Despite the raid's apparent failure, Melville was sufficiently impressed by the pyrotechnic hullabaloo to allow Popham and Fulton to persevere. Only after the 'infernals' failed again in December did the government's enthusiasm for these expensive toys start to wane. Fulton was outraged when his salary was stopped, appealing directly to Davison for help. Despite its intemperate and boastful tone, the letter reveals the attraction felt by Davison for mavericks like Fulton, Popham – and Nelson.

Should you mistake the Nation's interest, the Sin will lie at your own door, this you will perhaps think odd Language, but let any man place himself in my situation and then ask himself if he has not a right to convert his labours into fame and emolument, for what other objects do men labour? . . . I have now to confess to you as a Friend that I have for sometime felt myself awkward in this Country. I see a kind of suspicion attached to my character which I detest, and I am kept amused dancing after publick affairs though I were asking favours, whereas I know my strength and resources came here by invitation to grant Favours and not to ask them.

Nelson was in another sort of prison. Through the summer and into the autumn of 1804 he continued to pin down the French fleet at Toulon, desperately hoping it would leave its 'nest' and face him. This 'dreadful wearisome time', as Davison described it, was damaging Nelson's health. He suffered bouts of sweating, heart palpitations and dizziness. The sight in his remaining good eye was fading, and a swelling the size of his fist appeared on his side where he had been wounded years before at the battle of St Vincent. 'I am afraid he will not mend *here*,' observed his ever-solicitous steward William Chevailler, 'for he is deprived of the common necessaries of life.'

Their stressful existence affected all the men around Nelson, straining the ties of loyalty that bound them together. First it seemed Gaetano Spedillo, Nelson's Sicilian valet, would abandon the ship to return to his family; then, in March 1804, Chevailler asked to speak with Nelson. 'I beg pardon,' William said, 'but I find myself so disagreeably situated in the ship, that I beg of your Lordship to send me to England by the first opportunity.'

Nelson agreed to his steward's startling request, blaming 'some *vagary* or *other*'. 'I never said a harsh word to him, nor any one else I am sure,' he told Davison; 'he is very much respected, and an excellent servant.' This news 'astonished' Davison. In his letters Chevailler had seemed perfectly happy and content. Like Nelson, Davison put his man's behaviour down to 'some sudden frick'. Whatever the cause, the crisis passed, the matter was dropped and Chevailler stayed in *Victory* until Trafalgar.

Six months later, Chevailler himself hinted at the cause of his unhappiness in a letter he wrote to Davison.

> *I have met with many disagreeable treatments here, tho' never once from His Lordship, but from an other quarter so much that I begg'd to be sent home, however I am in hope that you will believe me when I assure you that for Lord Nelson I have done all you could wish; as for others I never will consider them as my masters. If ever I return to England I have no doubt of justifying my conduct before you, I mean for having asked to leave my place, for I am sure no complaints [could] have been made to you of my behaviour here.*

Chevailler's letter, found among Davison's papers, is evidence of bullying in *Victory*. Were there accusations of favouritism? Was Chevailler abused because he was seen by the others as Davison's stooge? Or because he had a French accent? Was the '*other quarter*' John Scott, Davison's bitter rival in the ship?

So far as his principal aim was concerned, Scott was playing a close game. Satisfied he had endeared himself to his chief, he was resigned to waiting patiently for his reward. Writing in November 1804, he asked his wife Charlotte to do the same, 'particularly when it may bring with it what will make us and our dear boys happy and independent for life, certainly prevent us from ever parting again. Should a Spanish war take place, certainly something good must come our way.'

In August 1804, ill and missing Emma and his daughter

Horatia, Nelson took the highly unusual step of writing to Nepean at the Admiralty asking for leave. He told Davison that he thought a few months' rest would set him up for another year's campaign in the Mediterranean. Davison predicted, wrongly, that Melville would refuse Nelson's request – which Nelson regretted almost as soon as he had made it. War with Spain, now thought inevitable, would make the Spanish treasure ships plying the Atlantic fair game again. Having just set legal precedent for a commander-in-chief conceding his prizes to his temporary substitute, Nelson was suddenly anxious to know who that would be, or even whether he would be allowed to return to his station at all. His own choice of locum was Sir Richard Bickerton, a safe and loyal pair of hands who was already cruising in the Mediterranean. The Admiralty's decision, forced upon it by Nelson's request, was both surprising and alarming. Bickerton would take Nelson's place, but only to the east of Gibraltar. The rest of the station, covering the potential jackpot of Cadiz, was given to Sir John Orde, a longstanding rival of Nelson's. At a stroke Nelson faced not only losing out on the lion's share of the prize money but of returning to a diminished command.

Such gloomy thoughts were far from the minds of those people in London who were desperate to see Nelson come home. The anticipation was so great that by October, as she gazed out at Cribb's men planting her new borders in the steady autumnal rain at Merton, Emma's heart leaped every time she heard the doorbell. 'He is *very very* anxious to come,' she wrote to Davison,

> *and I am anxious and agitated to see him. The disappointment would kill me. I love him, I adore him, my mind and soul is now transported with the thoughts of that blessed ecstatic moment when I shall see him, embrace him. My love is no common love. It may be a sin to love I say it might have been a sin when I was* anothers *but I had then more merit in trying to suppress it. I am now* free *and I must sin on and love him more than ever. It is a crime worth going to Hell for.*

Davison urged patience. He was suffering from gout – 'I cannot set a foot to the ground,' he moaned – but his reply shows an intimacy otherwise rare in his letters. His mention of the 'All Ruling Power', a masonic allusion to God, is notable.

> *We cannot command the winds, and am afraid neither you nor I have influence sufficient with that All Ruling Power to deviate from that which is best for us, tho' however much we at the present moment consider it otherwise . . . I most firmly believe our friend is, and will be, protected, amidst all dangers and difficulties; reserved for* FUTURE *comforts,* domestic pleasure, *and* TRANSPORTING HAPPINESS *. . . Tomorrow, I trust, and depend and pray, will afford us the most joyful tidings. I shall otherwise give up thinking at all. Yours, yours, yours.*

But the next day passed with no sign of Nelson, as did the next and the one after that. As the weeks slipped past, letters began arriving from the Mediterranean talking of delay. A flag officer had fallen ill, forcing Nelson to wait impatiently for a replacement from England before he could leave the station himself. Events overtook him. In December, Spain declared war on Britain. Then, on 17 January 1805, under cover of darkness, the French fleet slipped his knot and broke out of Toulon.

XII

DEFIANCE

74 GUNS,
CAPTAIN PHILLIP DURHAM

Early one Sunday morning in January 1805, ten days before the French eluded Nelson at Toulon, Davison left his rooms in King's Bench Terrace with a ticket in his pocket allowing him out of prison for the day. Huddled against the cold on the worn leather seat of his carriage, he gazed out as the villages of Kennington, Battersea and Wandsworth passed his window. He was on his way, not to Merton as so often before, but to the neighbouring village of Wimbledon. Here his carriage stopped before 'Cannizaro', a handsome villa on the west side of the common, one of many that lined the road to London. He interrupted Viscount Melville's breakfast. Davison could, and did, boast that the first lord 'has taken me *strongly up* as a man of business, as a friend, and as a person he can depend on'.

The two men passed the morning discussing politics and the war. Melville said that William Pitt was keen to have Lord Moira in his cabinet, as a unifying presence. But this would never happen while the prince opposed the idea, for Moira would never act against the prince's wishes. Davison marvelled that Moira was now a favourite not only apparently of both the king and the prince, but to Pitt and Melville as well. As to the war, Davison hoped that the intervention of Spain on the side of Bonaparte, news which was still being kept secret from the rest of the country,

278

would enable Britain to act with 'more vigour'. Davison and Melville agreed that the war would cost Spain its possessions in South America. Sir Home Popham, who had returned to the Channel fleet after abandoning Fulton's 'infernals', was urging the government to allow him to lead an expedition against Venezuela. Pitt and Melville were being charmed into this adventurous scheme by a colourful Venezuelan patriot called General 'Count' Francisco de Miranda. Miranda spoke extravagantly of delivering the whole of South America to Britain.

Nelson scorned such fanciful ideas. 'I hope we shall have no buccaneering expeditions,' he wrote to Moira; 'such services fritter away our troops and ships, when they are so much wanted for more important occasions, and are of no use beyond enriching a few individuals.' The government, having wavered, decided that it agreed with him. In February Popham was ordered, not to South America as he wanted, but to the Cape, to take the colony back from the Dutch. Nelson, who was still impatiently waiting to take his leave, was back on blockade duty, for the French fleet had returned to Toulon, defeated not by the British navy but by the terrible storms that were sweeping the Mediterranean. The British fleet was equally battered, but had nowhere to hide. Nelson was magnificent throughout the ordeal; had it not been for his 'astonishing care', thought Chevailler, 'not half of the fleet would have had a standing start'. 'Maimed as he is', Nelson stayed on deck, stripped to the waist against the howling gales and 'such heavy rains as are never seen in England'. When a fire broke out in *Victory*'s powder magazine he remained 'as cool and as composed as ever I saw him', while all the panic-stricken men around him 'rund up the riggin'. Nelson was in his element against the elements.

And it was towards Nelson that the conversation at Wimbledon that morning soon turned. Melville read out a letter from *Victory* dated 4 December, a more recent one than either Emma or Davison had seen. The first lord asked Davison whether he thought Nelson would reconsider his leave and stay out on his command. Spain's intervention in the war changed everything. Davison told Melville he hoped Nelson would remain in the Mediterranean to return in six months 'rich in pocket' and covered in glory. Then, in the convivial surroundings of Melville's dining room, Davison took the opportunity of raising the sensitive issue of Emma's pension – having, no doubt, been primed to do so. Melville revealed he had discussed the matter personally with Pitt. A figure of £500 a year was mooted. Melville was confident of success, telling Davison to reassure Emma that he would continue to press the prime minister for a decision.

None of these subjects, however, was the primary reason Davison was taking coffee with Melville. That arrived with Major-General Sir John Moore, who came to Wimbledon during the morning directly from Lisbon. Davison knew Jack Moore from Lord Moira's camp at Lyndhurst ten years before. Since then Moore had carved out, in actions around the world, a reputation as the army's brightest star. There was much for Davison to admire in this resourceful, highly capable man from a similar background to his own. But Moore was no fan of Nelson's. Having met the jewel-bedecked admiral on his way back to England in 1800, he described him as 'more like the prince of an opera than the conqueror of the Nile' – a view undoubtedly shared by many in Moore's army circles.

These three men were meeting to discuss a pre-emptive strike on Spain. Pitt was determined to take the war to Britain's growing number of enemies, and the general had just returned from a clandestine reconnaissance trip of the country's coast near Ferrol as part of the planning for a major amphibious landing. Davison had been 'a great deal' involved in the preparations for this top secret expedition for weeks, long before Spain declared war. But Moore's report was disappointing. The terrain around Ferrol was too hostile for a mass landing. Pitt would have to look elsewhere for his 'great event'.

There was one piece of good news for Davison to take back with him to prison. A Spanish treasure ship laden with 'many chests of silver plate etc', provisionally valued at over £220,000, had been sent into Plymouth. The captor was *Naiad*, one of the frigates involved in the seizure of *Santa Brigida* and *El Thetis* in 1799 that had prompted Nelson so controversially to sue Earl St Vincent. *Naiad* was captained by George Dundas, a kinsman of Melville's and one of Davison's prize agency clients. 'This is not an unfavourable beginning for me,' Davison wrote excitedly to Nelson: 'a prize agent this war.' The news, however, confirmed Nelson's worst fears following the division of his station. As *Naiad* was cruising in Sir John Orde's sector of the Mediterranean at the time of the capture, the flag share of her prize would go to his rival. Davison tactlessly pointed out that 'in one month Sir John Orde will have acquired more riches (*not honour*) than you (I will say ten times) have done all your life! What a shame . . .' The prickle of spite in Davison's comment may have been caused by his deep-rooted resentment at Orde's apparently effortless success, for the two men had both been born in Northumberland, within a few months and few miles of each other. The Ordes, who appear intermittently in the Davison family letters from the 1760s, were substantial landowners who might have lorded it over their humbler neighbours.

The injustice of the Mediterranean prizes was made worse by Nelson's paltry share in the Copenhagen prize money. This was paid out by Davison in January, putting an end to renewed 'insinuations' circulating in the fleet – no doubt fuelled by his imprisonment – about his management of the business. Even after the Admiralty boosted the Copenhagen prize money by £65,000, Nelson's share was only £700. Sir Hyde Parker, the commander-in-chief of the Channel fleet at the time of the action, reaped over £3,000. This inequality caused even Davison 'much vexation'. In vain he tried to resurrect the idea of a Copenhagen medal when he saw Melville.

Davison used *Naiad*'s capture to remind Nelson to send his prizes home to England and not into Gibraltar, 'as London is the only market that any ship or cargo can be disposed of to advantage'.

The real reason for this apparently friendly advice was probably Davison's rising concern about John Scott's influence on Nelson and the secretary's apparent attempts to seize the Mediterranean agency. Rumours had reached Davison that William Marsh, his rival since the Nile agency, was colluding with Scott. Emma tried to reassure him. As far as she was concerned, Nelson still saw Davison as his agent. There must have been 'some dreadful mistake about his agency'. Emma was not going to support William Marsh, a known intimate of Fanny's and a relic of Nelson's dreary pre-Neapolitan life. 'I detest Marsh and Creed,' she wrote to Davison, 'for they are false.'

Davison would not sit idly by while Scott stole the agency. Together, the troubling rumours, the silence from the Mediterranean and the knowledge that Scott enjoyed unhindered daily access to Nelson spurred him into drastic action. In February 1805 Davison sent a circular, from prison, 'to all my naval acquaintances and generally to others (I do not know) with offers of my services as prize agent finding it a business I can carry on so easily and so beneficially without its interfering in the least with my other concerns'. Davison told Nelson he hoped to 'make up my *losses I have sustained by a wish I had of being useful to government*'. Davison brazenly used Nelson in his advertisement, naming him as a reference to his own 'Birth Character and Education &c &c'. 'It is possible', he cheerily warned his friend, that 'you may be asked if you know such a person as Alex Davison of St James's Sq.'

From their long conversations night after night in the great cabin of *Victory*, Scott thought he had Nelson's agency in the bag. He did a deal to share the work with James Cutforth and Patrick Wilkie, both of whom were agent victuallers in the Mediterranean. William Marsh was made ready to steer the business through the courts in London and to handle the distribution from his offices in Soho. It was agreed the men would share the 5 per cent agency commission. Scott, who clearly distrusted Wilkie, asked Cutforth to put the pact in writing 'in case of anything happening to me, that my family may derive the advantages of my *hard* labour'.

On 26 March 1805 a flag officer at last arrived to fill the vacancy in Nelson's squadron. Unless the enemy stirred again, it seemed that Nelson and Scott would finally be going home, though most probably in *Superb* not *Victory*. For Scott, the joyful prospect of seeing Charlotte and his boys was overshadowed by the fear that Davison would regain the ascendancy once Nelson was back in London. He knew that Davison's influence, secured by the admiral's debts, would be as quickly restored as his own faded. 'But', vowed Scott, writing to his collaborator Patrick Wilkie on 27 March, 'I shall be able to *frustrate* his intentions.' Confident he had secured the agency of the captains already in the Mediterranean, Scott turned his attention to those ships coming out from England to join the fleet. What he needed was a strategy to counteract the attempt by Davison (that 'little dirty undermining person') to use his '*interest* and *influence*' to win over the captains to his side.

Scott's plan was simple. He gave Cutforth twelve copies of a letter to distribute to the captains as they anchored and victualled at Gibraltar before going further up the Mediterranean. In his letter Scott invited the captains to join his agency, 'if it is not interfering with your other engagements'. There was one problem. As Scott's agency had not been formally announced, least of all to Davison, it would be very embarrassing if Nelson accidentally saw a letter which 'prematurely exposed a circumstance which no one here knows but myself'. The partners agreed that Cutforth would not hand out the letters to the captains until either he heard from Scott that Nelson was leaving the Mediterranean or he saw for himself *Superb* passing the rock of Gibraltar showing the commander-in-chief's flag. If Nelson and Scott lingered in the Mediterranean or he missed the signal, Cutforth would recruit the captains by talking to them in person. This avoided the risk of Scott's incriminating letter circulating while Nelson was in the vicinity. In this event, Scott would send out the letters himself once he reached London, using his contacts at the Admiralty. This would give him the chance of soliciting the

captains before they even sailed for the Mediterranean, something
Davison was trying to do. But 'should one *escape*', Scott ordered
Cutforth in a 'Secret and Confidential' letter dated 24 March,
'your vigilance will *arrest* him before he gets higher up the
Mediterranean . . . Be assured everything I can do to secure you
and myself the agency shall be most strictly attended to.'

Scott and Davison alike faced another unforeseen obstacle in
their struggle for supremacy. By splitting Nelson's command, the
Admiralty had created another claimant for the valuable
Mediterranean agency: George Hulbert, Sir John Orde's secretary. Hulbert was already a widely respected prize agent who
would not be satisfied simply with managing Orde's flag share: he
too would go after the ultimate prize of the fleet agency. Hulbert
upset Scott as much as Orde irritated Nelson.

Then, on 30 March, just as Nelson and Scott were preparing to sail home, the French fleet escaped again. Returning to
England was inconceivable. Nelson prepared for battle.

Apart from the disappointment of having his reunion with
Charlotte and the children postponed, this dramatic turn of
events appeared to benefit Scott. His carefully laid plan to nab
the captains from Davison before they even reached the
Mediterranean was in tatters, but pursuing the French kept
Nelson away from the malign influence of St James's Square,
hopefully until after the inevitable battle. Scott was further
buoyed up to hear that, following a quarrel between Orde and
Nelson over a prize captured near Gibraltar, the Admiralty had
not only ruled in favour of Nelson but had also confirmed his
precedence over Orde in the appointment of the fleet's agent.
Hulbert's ambitions were crushed.

Davison still had to be overcome. But here too there was
good news. Davison's advertising campaign had badly backfired.
Most of the recipients of his presumptuous letter were unimpressed. Admiral Collingwood's response was typical. 'I am sorry
to say that I have little to do in that way,' he loftily wrote from
Dreadnought, 'and the gentleman who manages that little for the

flag officers of the fleet does it so correctly that we have every reason to be satisfied with his conduct.' Davison might have expected more from a fellow Northumbrian. More damaging still, as Scott gleefully reported to Cutforth, Davison's 'unreasonable demand did not please' Nelson. 'Self is outwitted,' the secretary rejoiced, 'and we have profited by his fair and honourable intentions. I mention these circumstances to you in confidence and you may as well tear this when read and leave the purport in mind, least by accident it should fall into improper hands.'

Davison's ill-judged appeal to the captains seems to have given the balance a final and decisive tilt towards Scott. Until then Nelson had ducked the issue in his letters to Davison, but afterwards, his patience exhausted, he awkwardly confirmed Scott's appointment as agent, at least for the valuable fleet flag share. Unexpectedly, Scott and Cutforth were soon able to meet in person. Nelson heard that the French fleet, after 'leading me a dance', as he put it in a letter to Haslewood, was sailing west, not east as he had first thought: out of the Mediterranean and into the Atlantic. The West Indies had to be the enemy's goal. Any thought of going home forgotten, Nelson raced after them, suddenly energized and fully focused on the task in hand. 'Salt beef and the French fleet', he told Davison, 'is far preferable to roast beef and champagne.'

Victory entered the Straits of Gibraltar in hot pursuit on 6 May. At two o'clock that afternoon the ship anchored for a few hours in Gibraltar Bay, long enough for John Scott, but not Nelson, to be pulled ashore with the post; the secretary found time for a short walk with Cutforth as well, during which the agency must have been discussed. By six o'clock that evening *Victory* was gone. Before leaving sight of land, Scott scrawled a last letter to William Marsh asking him to manage the prize business in his absence and to be executor to his will, 'not that I mean to give you the trouble *if possible*'.

'Observe some *little* respect to *Mr Davison*,' Scott closed, *but in the event of my death claim and demand everything that justice and the law entitle me to expect, for I owe no favour in that quarter and when I tell you that he has most unhandsomely requested the agency of every ship on the station, and of those who were intended, but never came out you will agree with me. But in this he has failed and hurt his interest much but perhaps by and bye he may have other fish to fry, to him therefore adieu.*

Emma was suffering the anxieties that had once been so familiar to Fanny. News from *Victory* was patchy, and knowing that the French fleet had escaped made her apprehensive and ill-at-ease. In July 1799 Fanny had asked Davison: 'I have not had a line from him this age – I am sure he writes, who can be so wicked as to take my letters?' Now Emma demanded of him: '*Where can our letters be for letters there are?*' She tried to concentrate on the improvements to Merton Place, just as Fanny had immersed herself at Roundwood. She even made an effort to 'clear away our many little debts', although this only involved asking Davison for £530, which he promptly paid. Then she fell ill, purging herself with calomel before retiring to bed at Clarges Street, where she whiled away the time composing 'some bad verses'. These she inflicted on Davison:

Emma to Nelson

I think I have lost my heart,
Since I with truth can swear;
At every moment of my life,
I feel my Nelson there!

If from thine Emma's breast, her heart
Were stolen, or flown away,
Where, where, should she my Nelson's love
Record, each happy day?

If from thine Emma's breast, her heart
Were stolen, or flown away,
Where, where, should she engrave, my love!
Each tender word you say?

Where, where, should Emma treasure up
Her Nelson's smiles and sighs?
Where, mark with joy, each secret look
Of love from Nelson's eyes?

Then do not rob me of my heart,
Unless you first forsake it;
And then so wretched it would be,
Despair alone will take it.

There were still occasional glimpses of Fanny. In January, out of the blue, Davison received a terse demand from her to deal with the transfer of Maurice Nelson's trusteeship of her uncle's legacy to William Marsh, 'the only earthly business I have to do'. 'God knows which of us are to go first,' she wrote, 'and your executing your part of the Deed of Trust would very much oblige me and relieve me of great uneasiness.' Fanny was in Bath, where she now spent most of her time. Her health was so poor that for a time that summer her physician thought she might die. There was no possibility of the two women ever making contact, but they kept a close eye on each other. Fanny relied on information from William Marsh, on Bath gossip and on the often salacious reports in the newspapers for information on her usurper. Emma, meanwhile, had built up an efficient network of family informers led by Nelson's sisters, Kate Matcham, who said she wished Fanny was dead, and Susannah Bolton. In February Susannah spotted Fanny in Bath. 'I have seen Tom Tit,' she wrote to Emma with evident relish; 'she called at Lady Charlotte Drummond's who lives next door. The Lady was not at home, but she got out of her carriage, walked as stiff as a poker about half-a-dozen steps, turned round, got in again. What this manoeuvre was for I cannot tell, unless to show herself.' By July even Susannah was taken aback by Fanny's decline, reporting that she looked 'shockingly really and very old'.

In the spring Davison was restored to St James's Square and Emma to health. Both were in buoyant mood. On 'the glorious' 2 April, Davison celebrated the fourth anniversary of the battle of Copenhagen and his own fifty-fifth birthday. 'I shall drink a bumper to your health with Hip! Hip, Hip, three times three,' he wrote to Nelson. The only clouds on an otherwise sunny horizon were more reports that Sir John Orde, and his 'horrid detachment off Cadiz', were stealing Nelson's prize money. 'Already about £200,000!!! Oh my dear Nelson, my heart bleeds for you.' As the London season got under way Emma, looking 'as hearty and as well as you could wish her', plunged into an endless round of parties and concerts. There was no sign of the social isolation she had feared and Fanny's friends predicted. Instead, Emma was welcomed to, among many others, the drawing rooms of Lady Cholmondeley, Lady Cawdor and Lady Abercorn, where, despite her now enormous size, she reprised her 'Attitudes', the erotic classical posturings that had captivated Nelson in Naples. To many in the room they must have seemed quite ludicrous, even humiliating. Davison called it 'the *Mad* season of the year when every female is occupied by Routs, Balls and Squeezes'.

Conversation within those elegant drawing rooms must have revolved around the fate of Lord Melville, Pitt's close friend and his oldest political ally, who had just been forced out of office. The cause of Melville's downfall was the commission of naval inquiry which, after examining the business of prize agency, had moved on to probing the office of the treasurer of the navy, a position he had held, as Henry Dundas, between 1783 and 1801. The commissioners soon discovered serious discrepancies in the treasurer's accounts. Most attention was focused on the activities of Melville's subordinate, Alexander Trotter, the paymaster of the navy. Trotter was found to have put the public money with which he was entrusted through private accounts at Coutts' bank, not the Bank of England as he should have done. There was no evidence that any public money had actually been stolen, but Trotter, with Melville's knowledge, had certainly made good use of the funds under his management. Over £6 million had passed through his hands over the years – £300 million in today's terms. This Trotter invested, to his own advantage, in shares and consols, while insisting that using Coutts made it easier to handle the treasurer's complicated transactions. It was a practice, he claimed with justification, which was not unusual within other large government departments. It was not, however, a routine that stood up to close scrutiny in the early years of the nineteenth century.

The inquiry published its report, its tenth, on 10 February 1805. Melville was not accused of any crime, but he was heavily criticized for knowingly putting public money at risk. The report left Pitt dithering and Melville's many enemies scenting blood. Davison reported 'great bickerings in cabinet'. Melville gamely hung on as first lord until 9 April, when he was given no choice but to resign after losing a dramatic vote of censure in the House of Commons on the casting vote of the speaker. The vote left Pitt bereft, Davison without a valuable source of patronage and Emma's hopes of a pension in ruins. 'I believe Lord Melville would have been a good friend to the Navy,' observed Nelson equably when he heard the news, 'and, therefore, am sorry he is out. I have no idea of his pocketing the Public money.'

The tenth report of the commission of naval inquiry, with its revelations of corruption and malfeasance, brought to a pitch the clamour for reform of the public departments. It was commented that parliament had at last found a 'touchstone' with the people. Once discovered, the government was not slow to exploit it, turning Melville's personal catastrophe to political advantage. While parliament debated whether to prosecute Melville, a commission of military inquiry was hastily assembled to examine the activities of the barrack office under General Oliver De Lancey. De Lancey had retired as barrackmaster-general in November 1804, dogged by questions about his probity, and his departure had ended Davison's lucrative engagement as agent of supply to the barrack office. Responsibility for supplying the barracks shifted to the commissary-general, a position currently held by Brook Watson, Davison's old one-legged rival from Quebec. Nelson expressed doubts that must have begun to nag Davison: 'I sincerely hope these inquisitors will not find fault with your numerous Public accounts but I believe you are regular, and therefore, I hope, from my heart, may defy them.'

The British fleet crossed the Atlantic in under a month, reaching Barbados on 4 June. The French were certainly in the West Indies – somewhere. Ten days later, after scouring the islands in vain for them, pulled this way and that by vague sightings, Nelson gambled that they were already heading back to Europe. Once again he set off in hot pursuit, and by 20 July the British fleet was again off Gibraltar. Nelson's instinct was right: the French had returned to Europe, although they were heading northwards away from him. Pausing to victual at Gibraltar, Nelson went ashore for the first time in almost two years, furious that faulty intelligence had allowed his enemy to elude him. Reports that the French had limped into Ferrol after an inconclusive encounter with Sir Robert Calder's squadron off Finisterre gave Nelson the chance at last to head home for his long overdue leave.

In England, while the fleets criss-crossed the Atlantic, Emma kept up her frantic socializing, accompanied for much of the time by Nelson's nieces Charlotte Nelson and Eliza Bolton. On 4 June, the king's birthday, they visited Eton College to see Charlotte's brother Horatio perform in the festival of boats on the Thames. Percy and William Davison, contemporaries of Horatio at the college, joined the girls to watch the pageant. Horatio's boat was first. 'He was in a beautiful Gold and White dress,' Charlotte trilled, 'his pullers were Gallic Slaves. We were all delighted with the sight.' Three days later the rest of the Davisons joined this happy party to watch all three boys take part in *Ad Montem*, an arcane Etonian ritual which involved the boys marching in fancy dress to Salt Hill in nearby Slough. The aim was to raise enough money to see the 'Captain of Montem' through Cambridge University, although the event generally descended into a drunken shambles, with the boys fighting lads from the town. Marching alongside the Davison twins and young Horatio Nelson that year were Sir Evan Nepean's two sons and a slovenly-looking boy called Percy Bysshe Shelley. Davison kept the programme as a souvenir. It is a cast list for the British Empire.

Emma was falling deeper and deeper into debt, her demands for money becoming more frequent and more urgent. The bills at Merton were again mounting up. Davison had to forward her £30 simply to cover her trip to Windsor, followed by a further £100 a month later. In August he escaped London for Swarland, visiting his country house for the first time in nearly two years. His affairs in Northumberland had fallen into some 'confusion' because of 'the peculiar situation I have individually been in', calling 'most loudly for my presence'. Thus he missed a hastily scrawled note which reached St James's Square days after he left. 'The Victory is at Spithead,' it read; 'I shall see you very soon.'

Emma received this sudden and unexpected news by express at Southend, where she had gone to bathe and recover from 'nettle rash'. She rushed back to Merton and began filling the house with friends and family. After a day in quarantine at Portsmouth, Nelson and John Scott parted for the first time in over two years. Scott drove 'like *lightening*' to his family, carrying a note from his chief in his pocket: 'I believe your superior is not to be met with; and as a gentleman, that your whole conduct has been most exemplary.' Nelson, trailing huzza-ing crowds, arrived at Merton at dawn on 20 August. He looked thin and tired, his features gaunt and burned by the Mediterranean sun. But he was not idle, and his short leave was hardly restful. Unsure how long the French would lie low and with *Victory* waiting patiently at Spithead, Nelson threw himself into a frantic round of meetings. He saw William Marsh and William Haslewood to catch up on his private business, Lord Barham, the new first lord, to discuss strategy, and the foreign secretary, Lord Castlereagh, to ponder matters of state. The prince of Wales insisted he visit Carlton House. At the Colonial Office he even bumped into Sir Arthur Wellesley, the future duke of Wellington. One day he was spotted entering John Salter's shop on the Strand to inspect his Nile jewels. Only the presentation swords, some of his boxes, the diamond star and the *chelengk* were left over from Davison's sales in 1801. As usual, a large crowd gathered on the pavement to gawk at their hero, clad in dark green breeches and plain blue coat with a yellow waistcoat. On his head was a square cocked hat with a shade for his failing left eye. He was carrying a gold topped sword cane. Someone recalled he looked preoccupied, perhaps a little irritable, as he pushed his way out of the shop.

Merton was no quieter. Apart from the noisy invasion of relatives, a stream of distinguished visitors called at the house which, now that Emma's improvements were finally finished, was looking splendid. Sir Peter Parker, the duke of Clarence and William Beckford, all freemasons, enjoyed the comforts of Nelson's elegant new dining room. Perhaps Davison's wine-coolers were on the sideboard. There were trips to Richmond Park to meet Henry Addington and to Morden to visit his friend the Jewish financier Abraham Goldsmid, who was enmeshed as a witness in the naval inquiry that had destroyed Melville. There were letters from Swarland. 'Your not meeting with the combined fleet is a national misfortune,' Davison wrote; 'my idea is that a war is now only commencing seriously and that next year all the world will be in arms . . . God Almighty bless you and with love to *Emma*.' Davison reminded Nelson that his purse remained open 'and at your disposal'.

Before dawn on 2 September, a post-chaise carrying Henry Blackwood of the *Euryalus* clattered up the gravel drive at Merton Place. The French fleet had left Ferrol, joined the Spanish fleet, and taken refuge at Cadiz. Admiral Collingwood was watching them, but Nelson's days in England were numbered. The Admiralty gave him *carte blanche* to plan the destruction of the combined fleets. Preparations began immediately for the final confrontation. Merton Place was awhirl with activity. On 5 September, Chevailler and Spedillo loaded Nelson's trunks onto a wagon and left for Portsmouth.

Before meeting the prime minister on 11 September, Nelson met Haslewood to discuss the matter of his proxy vote in the Lords, something that had been troubling him ever since he had given it to Lord Moira. It had been given in the mistaken belief, encouraged by Davison, not only that Moira would support Addington's government but that he might even join the cabinet. To Nelson's dismay, Moira had then used the vote against Addington. When William Pitt succeeded Addington as prime minister, Nelson reluctantly allowed the proxy to continue, again trusting Davison's reports that Pitt wanted Moira in the cabinet. He was wrong to do so. After so many years of hostility, any reconciliation between Moira and Pitt was impossible. This left Nelson's voice in parliament in open opposition to the government during his absence at sea.

Nelson told Haslewood that he did not think Moira was exploiting his proxy. After all, he was 'a distinguished officer, an enlightened statesman and a man of too much honour to abuse so sacred a confidence'. But he feared 'that partiality might cloud the judgement and that Lord Moira might become attached to a party'. Nelson, like Davison, valued his independence, telling Pitt later the same day 'that England's welfare was the sole object of my pursuit' and that he would never attach himself to any party or man 'in or out of place'. Moira was, in fact, already the linchpin of the Carlton House party in parliament, as was well known. The prince of Wales's power was growing as fast as the king's health failed; and Nelson could not support a man he once described as 'an unprincipled liar' for coveting Emma. There were other, more personal reasons for recalling the proxy. With Melville out of office, Nelson needed to get on good terms with Pitt if he were to be in a position to reopen negotiations for Emma's pension. And, with an eye to the future, the elderly Lord Barham, who had replaced Melville at the Admiralty, could not last for ever. Surely a new first lord would be needed soon?

His mind settled and without Davison around to dissuade him, Nelson composed a letter to Lord Moira as soon as he reached Merton Place that evening – though he resented having to write it, believing that Davison, who had brokered the arrangement in the first place, should have retrieved the proxy. 'I find that having entrusted my conscience to you (even under the greatest restrictions)', he began,

> has, both by the last and present Ministry, been perfectly misunderstood. Therefore I am under the painful necessity of withdrawing this precious deposit, but I shall trust at present no other person with it. I must therefore . . . beg you to consider my proxy as no longer in force. I am an officer serving [and] I ought not to be considered as taking any party, except that of my King and country.

Davison stayed away throughout Nelson's short last leave – but not, it seems, intentionally. In a letter written on 31 August, two days before Blackwood arrived hot-foot from Portsmouth with news from Cadiz, Nelson assured Davison that 'My time and movements must depend on Buonaparte . . . we are ignorant of his intentions.' No doubt reassured that Nelson would be in England for some time, on 5 September Davison travelled further north, spending two weeks in Scotland visiting his sister Katty Home and meeting Moira in Edinburgh.

It seems his post was not forwarded during his trip, perhaps because he was on the road much of the time; so when he returned to Swarland he found two pieces of bad news waiting for him. One was contained in a letter from William Leake, his – and the bank's – solicitor. The bank was again facing disaster. A competitor in the West End had failed, causing panic and leaving Davison & Co. with hundreds of worthless bills and a £30,000 hole in its accounts. 'This', wrote Leake, his letter revealing that Davison had still not invested in the bank as he had promised,

> *I solemnly consider as the last call which will be made upon your liberality . . . and you will ever have the satisfaction of reflecting on having been the means of saving five worthy families from destitution . . . I feel it my duty to say that unless you place your whole confidence in your partners all will be of no avail.*

Davison stayed calm. He ordered Leake to 'keep the drawer up for a few days till the alarm has subsided'. The bank still held some 'very respectable bills'.

The other unpleasant surprise was contained in a letter from Nelson dated 6 September that must have sat unopened at Swarland throughout Davison's trip to Scotland. Nelson now knew he would be leaving England soon to face the combined fleets, and he feared that they would not meet before he did. He thanked Davison for his help, apologized for his debt and hoped he would be gone only a short time. 'I go because it is right, and I will serve the country faithfully.'

Davison left Swarland immediately, but it was 25 September by the time he reached London, 'after travelling night and day to reach town in hopes of catching you'. He was too late. Waiting at St James's Square was another note from Nelson, written 'beating down Channel with a foul wind' the week before. 'My fate', he wrote, 'is fixed, and I am gone.' At this critical moment, Davison's famed ability to keep on top of events seemed to have deserted him. 'Vexed beyond all belief', he rushed to Clarges Street, only to find an inconsolable Emma. After a no doubt tense meeting with his banking partners, he trudged back north 'to lament my ill fate'.

'I am vexed you should have had such a fag upon my account,' Nelson replied on 13 October, poised over the horizon from Cadiz waiting for the French to move; 'some happy day I hope to get at their Fleet, and nothing shall be wanting on my part to give a good account of them. My dear Lady Hamilton has told me of your kindness.' Nelson had left England, as his accounts reveal, having paid back his debt of £3,370 to Davison. Was he, in the weeks before his death, loosening the bonds of loyalty which had bound the men together for so long?

The nature of Davison's kindness to Emma, to which Nelson refers in this letter, is lost. Had Emma definitively revealed the name of Horatia's father? The child, now four, having in her infancy been left to the discreet care of a wet nurse in London, had since Sir William Hamilton's death been increasingly seen at Merton Place. There was no need for Davison to take notice of the child, if she was ever there when he visited. Various children were often to be found among the visitors at Merton Place, and if she were asked about the little girl Emma would claim Horatia as a ward. Whatever Emma said to Davison, Nelson was not happy about it, his words betraying, in the last days of his life, a sudden and marked distrust of his friend. 'I don't think Davison a good hand to keep such a secret as you told him. I fear I cannot even write him a line.' On 7 October, John Scott found time to write home. With the battle imminent, he clung to the thought of spending Christmas with 'my dear Charlotte and dearest boys', vowing that 'no advantage or interest' would ever separate them again. 'I am still hopeful', he finished, 'this said month may close my naval career and put us in possession of something independent.'

Two weeks later, on the morning of the 21st, Scott finished his wine and waited for Nelson. He checked his gold pocket watch, a present from Charlotte, fumbling with the button to open its cover. It was a little past eleven. At a quarter past, the admiral appeared from the great cabin. Scott followed him onto the deck, remembering to take his paper and pen. The enemy were straight ahead, about two or three miles distant, stretched like a great hurdle across the horizon. Carried along by the gentle breeze and a heavy swell, *Victory* was taking her crew to their fates at no more than easy walking pace. To his right Scott saw the second British division, tagging behind Collingwood in *Royal Sovereign*. The deck was crowded with officers, tars and marines. Everything was ready. The band was playing. Scott looked up to the mastheads as the signal began. During the long sequence of flags, he saw, with a violent surge of resentment, Chevailler going below to safety.

Towards noon, Scott heard the first distant cracks and watched as *Royal Sovereign* was wrapped in smoke. He stayed close to Nelson. The first shots splashed harmlessly short. The next volley was lethal, tearing through the sails, ripping off yardarms and biting into the masts. The deck shook as shot thudded into the ship, followed by the patter of the splinters. Men started to fall. Nelson moved off a short distance, leaving Scott transfixed as he was showered by tiny fragments of wood. Clutching his papers to his chest, he watched in wonderment as the balls left the muzzles of the enemy guns, punched through the smoke and arced gracefully towards his ship. Suddenly one gun flashed more brightly than the others, catching his eye. The shot came slowly and silently towards him, growing darker and larger. He closed his eyes and saw Charlotte. Then nothing.

Nelson turned. 'Is that poor Scott?' he asked, horrified, as two marines struggled to tip the shredded remains into the sea. His secretary's blood was left soaking into the planking of the deck. Every last drop. An hour later, the battle in full spate, Nelson fell where Scott had fallen, the secretary's guts smearing his coat, his breeches and his purse.

XIII
PRINCE

98 GUNS,
CAPTAIN RICHARD GRINDALL

Today will exceed everything that has ever occurred in this Isle before, or perhaps ever will again. Such a scene would be too much for my feelings who mourned this Immortal character not only an irreparable national loss, but as a friend of my early life, which renders it the more affecting to Mathews (who was also well acquainted with him) & neither of us had fortitude enough to witness the melancholy sight! The most awful & dismal that ever caused the British Heart to ache, or tears to flow! & torrents I am sure are shedding at this instant — Human Invention has been on the rack ever since Our Country's Pride & Favorite fell to suggest suitable Honors & Homage for this solemn occasion, The Pomp & magnificence of the preparations can hardly be described & will be a grand sight to those who can bear to look at it.

MARY PUT DOWN HER pen and gazed out across the rooftops of Chelsea to the river. After the storms the day before, the sky was now a sharp clear blue and the water sparkled beneath the low wintry sun. Did she remember a similar crisp autumn morning in Quebec, where she met Nelson all those years ago?

Davison was ready before six o'clock. He was dressed from head to toe in black. On his head was a cumbersome, heavily powdered bag wig. It itched, badly. Haslewood and Marsh arrived for

298

breakfast at seven. Little was said. Each of them held a long, thin, stave of office carved from ivory. Anticipation filled the silence. Towards eight the mourning coach arrived in the square, the heads of the horses tossing plumes of black ostrich feathers. The coachman and postilions were wearing mourning cloaks along with high hats wrapped in black crepe. Another servant walked beside the coach. A small, excited crowd gathered to watch as the three officers of Nelson's household – Davison as treasurer, Haslewood as comptroller and Marsh as steward – climbed, sombre-faced, into the coach. Davison checked that the coachman had remembered the wine and sandwiches.

On the short drive to Hyde Park, Davison noticed that the streets had been spread with gravel during the night. A vast tide of people was moving east towards the City. The scene within the park was one of confusion. Dozens of carriages were already there, parked between huddles of freezing dukes, earls and baronets. Naval officers stood shivering in full dress uniform. Clouds of vapour enveloped the horses as they impatiently stamped the hard ground. Only with the greatest effort, and a great deal of shouting, were the marshals able to arrange the carriages into some order before leading them across Piccadilly into St James's Park. There were thousands of red-coated troops on Horse Guards Parade; the sun glinted off the guns and the sound of the bands drifted over the park. There was another long wait while the troops formed up under the command of General Sir David Dundas, the governor of Chelsea Hospital. Most of the dignitaries left their carriages to greet one another. Davison saw Chevailler and Spedillo standing awkwardly apart, uncomfortable in their cloaks. Charles Fox and Evan Nepean were there, but not Earl St Vincent, nor the duke of Northumberland – nor William Pitt, who was gravely ill. Lord Moira chatted with the prince and the duke of Clarence.

Towards midday the troops moved off, led by the Light Dragoons. The procession fell in behind them, but only with great difficulty and not strictly in the prescribed order. Davison saw a group of tars file in among the troops, a patch of blue in a sea of

The order of procession from the Admiralty to St Paul's Cathedral on 9 January 1806. The three members of Nelson's household — Davison, Marsh and Haslewood — were driven in front of the funeral car, between the barons and baronets.

THE FUNERAL PROCESSION of LORD VISCOUNT NELSON, Jan.ʸ 9ᵗʰ 1806.

Nelson's coffin was carried to St Paul's Cathedral on an ornate funeral car designed to look like Victory *and hung with trophies and heraldic devices.*

red. They carried *Victory*'s Union Jack, which was clearly shot with holes. Davison's coach was ushered in behind the Knights of the Bath and the baronets. As they passed the Admiralty, Davison caught a sight of the funeral car. This was a prodigious 18-foot-high construction, a homage to *Victory*, with a gilded prow and stern. The coffin sat on the car beneath a canopy of black velvet decorated with black ostrich plumes, branches of laurel and palm leaves.

It took three hours to reach St Paul's Cathedral. The crowds of people along the Strand were immense, all silently packed in behind ranks of volunteers from the London regiments. Every window was occupied, every vantage point taken. Inside his coach, Davison could clearly hear the sound of the muffled drums and fifes and, further off, the tolling of a great bell. He entered the cathedral through the west door. On either side, clustered on the steps, were tars from *Victory*. The aisle was lined by Grenadiers resting on reversed arms. Walking slowly to the choir, Davison passed between the steep wooden grandstands built beneath the dome. Nine thousand spectators were already in the cathedral, many of them there since dawn. The huge, torn flags of Nelson's enemies, each as high as a house, hung from the balconies. The coffin reached the cathedral at four o'clock, covered by a pall decorated with escutcheons. Six tars, surrounded by naval officers and heralds, bore it up the aisle to the choir. Admiral of the fleet and deputy grand master Sir Peter Parker walked behind the coffin as the chief mourner. Sir John Orde was one of the pall-bearers. As the pale light faded during Evensong, servants lit a great octagonal lantern holding over a hundred large candles which had been specially made to hang from the dome.

When the service in the choir was over, the body was carried to a bier directly beneath the dome and above the grave. With the pall removed, the spectators could see the devices upon the black velvet-covered coffin. They included a sphinx, a crocodile and a weeping, draped female figure. The bier was in a wooden enclosure, draped with banners, beneath the great lantern. Only official mourners, heralds and the highest dignitaries were allowed within. The emblems for a Knight of the Bath hung at each corner: a surcoat, a plumed helmet, a pair of gauntlets and a sword. Davison, Marsh and Haslewood stood together opposite the prince, the duke of Clarence and Earl Nelson. Sir Peter Parker, old and weary, sat at the head of the grave.

When the Dean of St Paul's had finished the words of committal and the choir had sung an anthem by Handel, secret machinery lowered the coffin slowly into the grave 16 feet below. As it descended, the solemn voice of Sir Isaac Heard, the Garter King of Arms, echoed around the cathedral:

> *Thus it hath pleased Almighty God to take out of this transitory life, unto his divine mercy, the Most Noble Lord Horatio Nelson, Viscount and Baron Nelson of the Nile, and of Burnham Thorpe, in the County of Norfolk, Baron Nelson of the Nile, and of Hilborough, in the same County; Knight of the Most Honourable Order of the Bath; Vice-Admiral of the White Squadron of the Fleet, and Commander in Chief of His Majesty's Ships and Vessels in the Mediterranean; also Duke of Bronte in Sicily; Knight Grand Cross of the Sicilian Order of St. Ferdinand and of Merit; Member of the Ottoman Order of the Crescent; Knight Grand Commander of the Order of St Joachim; and the Hero who, in the moment of victory, fell covered with immortal glory! Let us humbly trust, that he is now raised to bliss ineffable, and to a glorious immortality!*

When he had finished, Heard turned to Davison, Marsh and Haslewood. Each, in turn, broke his stave of office. The pieces were thrown after the coffin into the gaping grave.

Throughout the long service Davison had been aware of little more than the presence of the thousands of people sitting in the gloom around him. But now, at the end, the background noise of coughing, sneezing and the rustling of the women's gowns was joined by a new, unfamiliar sound. Turning to discover what it was, he saw the tars tearing up *Victory*'s flag, stuffing small portions of it into their coats.

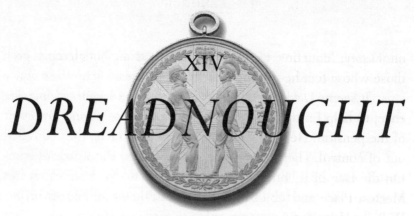

XIV

DREADNOUGHT

98 GUNS,
CAPTAIN JOHN CONN

ONCE THE SUN HAD gone, the stars dimmed or, in Emma's case, exploded spectacularly. Her decline after Nelson's death, imperceptible at first, precipitous at the end, is infamous. Tracing the vapour trail two hundred years later is still very affecting. Of the many letters she wrote Davison that survive, the first I ever saw remains for me the most poignant. There are few better expressions of the essence of that extraordinary woman, or of her love for Nelson, than her words to Davison in November 1805:

> How are you to night my Dear Sir — I have been very ill all Day My Heart Broken & My Head Consequently weak from the agitations I suffer — I tell you Truly — I am gone nor do I wish to Live — He that I Loved more than Life He is gone Why then shou'd I Live or wish to Live I lived but for Him all now is a Dreary prospect before me.

Davison did not desert Emma. If anything, their friendship deepened as the years passed. Nor, however, did he escape the occasional lash of her tongue — as when she commented on his Damascene conversion to the merits of Lord Grenville, the new prime minister who stood noisily accused of stalling her pension. 'Look at Alexander Davison,' she wrote to Dr Scott, the chaplain on *Victory*, 'courting the man he despised and neglecting now those whose feet he used to lick. Dirty vile groveler.'

It seems Davison did his best, within the limits of his influence, to help Emma in her futile, and increasingly lonely, pursuit of the pension. He tried to stem her debts even as they spiralled out of control. There was no reason why they should have done. On the face of it, Emma was well provided for. Nelson left her Merton Place and £2,000, believing her £800 annuity from Sir William Hamilton's estate would cover her living expenses. She also had the interest on £4,000 Nelson had placed in trust for their daughter, Horatia. But however much Emma received, it was never enough. Within months of Trafalgar she was borrowing money from friends, a habit begun, as Davison well knew, long before Nelson died. Yet there was no sign of restraint and, for the time being, the lavish lifestyle at Merton Place continued unchecked.

It may have been around this time that the diamond anchor, that glittering key to the discovery of Davison's treasures, was created. Emma owned few significant jewels at the time of Nelson's death. Many were sold in 1801 to finance the Hamiltons' new life in London. At the time Nelson regretted being unable to replace them, comforting himself, and Emma, by rightly declaring that 'diamonds do not constitute happiness'. Most of Nelson's Nile jewels had also had to be sold; but two, both gifts of the sultan of Turkey, survived to be mentioned in his will. One was the *chelengk*, the diamond plume of triumph plucked from the sultan's turban; the other was a diamond star. The *chelengk*, which Lady Minto airily dismissed as 'very ugly and not valuable, being rose diamond', was left in trust to William Nelson as a family heirloom; 'as a memento', Nelson told Emma, 'that I once gained a victory'. William wrapped it in brown paper and stuffed it into a drawer. It was stolen from the National Maritime Museum in 1951.

The fate of the star, however, is not known. Nelson promised it to Emma as early as February 1801, assuring her in a letter

'How are you to night my Dear Sir — I have been very ill all Day My Heart Broken & My Head Consequently weak from the agitations I Suffer — I tell you Truly — I am gone nor do I wish to live — He that I Loved more than Life He is gone Why then shou'd I Live or wish to Live I Lived but for Him all now is a Dreary prospect before me': Emma Hamilton to Alexander Davison, November 1806.

that 'nobody would take that *memento of friendship, affection and esteem* from you'. This supports the assumption that Emma returned to London wearing the star in November 1800 because it does not appear in the inventory Fanny made of the Nile jewels before they were taken to St James's Square for safe keeping though it does in the list Nelson made when the jewels were moved to John Salter in 1804. It duly appears in his will, when it is left to Emma 'as a token of my friendship and regard'. The star makes its final appearance in a letter Emma wrote to Davison on 7 June 1806, in which she asks him to take her 'dymond Star' to Salter 'as he is to do something to it'. As Salter had already been entrusted with making the customary gold mourning rings for distribution among Nelson's circle of friends before the state funeral, did Emma order him to transform the star into her own glamorous *memento mori*?

While the 'dymond star' apparently vanishes, a 'brilliant anchor' appears for the first time among Emma's possessions. Salter mentions repairing one for 2s 6d in an account he sent Emma in 1812 – probably never paid. Was this the anchor I gazed at nearly two hundred years later? Was the old lead repair I noticed on the back Salter's work? Who else could have owned it? Certainly the use of Nelson's personal initials HN rather than those of his adopted title NB, for Nelson and Bronte, suggests an intimate history. Had Nelson owned the anchor himself, possibly as another gift from a grateful potentate, he would surely have mentioned it, for he was punctilious in recording and displaying his rewards, often to the amusement or disdain of those around him. He would be unlikely to ignore such a precious jewel. Even if he had, in the years before his death he was one of the most talked about, written about and painted people in Britain. Nowhere is there a glimpse of the anchor.

Three women could have owned the anchor: Fanny, Emma or Harriett Davison. Fanny can be ruled out, principally because by the time her husband could have afforded such an extravagant gift he no longer loved her. Moreover, she would undoubtedly have thought that such a flashy jewel was vulgar and a waste of money. Harriett is the obvious candidate. The anchor was found with her descendants, and she certainly liked jewels – or Davison liked giving them to her. In 1803 her collection was valued at over £7,000. But I think it is implausible that Harriett could have worn such a highly personalized jewel, for she was far closer in temperament to Fanny than to Emma. These two women probably remained in close contact long after Fanny's friendship with Harriett's husband turned sour. Everything points to the piece's owner being Emma: the only woman of the three who unquestionably owned a diamond anchor jewel. But if, as seems likely, she recycled the diamonds from the sultan's star into the anchor, why was it found with Davison's descendants so many years later?

The answer is money, or her lack of it. Men had paid to be with Emma since her childhood; now the only man who had not bought his way to her favour was gone. She had no female support system, for she had never cultivated one. She had always been surrounded by men. Women had always exploited her, envied her or hated her. Now she was alone; and her beauty, her most valuable asset, was spent. Lacking the emotional resources to protect herself, Emma did what she had watched men do her entire life: she drank, and tried to buy happiness. She had nothing left to offer except her money, and when that was gone she had nothing at all.

'I have no father, no brother, no Nelson. I have no one but you & God,' she wrote to Davison. And he responded. On 25 November 1808 a meeting was called to discuss how to save Emma from herself. Alongside Davison were Sir John Perring, a City banker; Abraham Goldsmid, the financier; Germain Lavie, a solicitor; and two of Davison's closest friends, his lawyer Richard Wilson and Sir Robert Barclay, who, in a colourful past, had been a secret agent and a brandy smuggler. Apart from giving legal advice, Wilson was probably drafted in because he was a commissioner for bankrupts, while Lavie sat on the committee for the patriotic fund at Lloyd's, a possible source of financial relief.

Emma herself was not present, though she sent a heartfelt note thanking 'my saviours' for their efforts.

At the meeting it was revealed that Emma's debts stood at about £18,000. As her assets, principally comprising Merton Place and its contents, were valued at £17,500, it seemed that all was not yet lost. Her self-appointed trustees resolved to sell the assets and 'to follow up the claim on government, in which all the friends of Lady Hamilton be requested to cooperate'. A sum of £3,700 was pledged immediately to pay off her most pressing debts. Davison and Goldsmid each offered £1,000. 'The death of Nelson', Emma wrote to Davison afterwards,

> has shown me how many persons had two faces. Your munificent friendship . . . has engraved on my heart an everlasting gratitude & be assured to my last breathe I shall feel a glory in having had Alexander Davison for my friend; as did Nelson, to his death, die loving & respecting you more than he did any man living. Relations not excepted.

The meeting and its results gave Emma a brief respite. Merton Place was put on the market and Clarges Street sold. She moved to Richmond, where a house was lent to her by the sympathetic duke of Queensberry, taking with her the portrait of Davison that had hung over the mantelpiece at Merton. She even tried to persuade Davison to buy Bronte, the estate on Sicily given to Nelson by King Ferdinand IV. Earl Nelson, she observed, 'does not value it'. The trustees valued all the 'statues, vases, china, pictures, and other articles of fancy' at Merton Place at only £1,500, £500 less than the wine in the cellars. The masonic wine-coolers were probably among these items; as with the anchor, given the prominent use of his coat of arms it seems unthinkable that anyone except for Nelson could have displayed these extravagant objects on his sideboard; and he would have made sure to keep them away from Fanny during the unedifying division of their marital belongings in 1801.

As Emma's life drifted, she began shedding her collection of Nelson relics. There was an auction in July 1813 (among the many books was lot 190, 'The wife and the Mistress, 4 vols.'), while the items of greatest value, including the coat Nelson had worn at Trafalgar, were sold piece by piece as she descended to living from hand to mouth. It is hard to be certain when the anchor and wine-coolers came to St James's Square, though there is a record of Davison paying Emma £200 in January 1813 for the enamel miniature left her by Sir William Hamilton. Davison muttered privately that he did so 'merely to oblige her' after failing to interest the prince of Wales in it. The jewel and china probably followed in a similarly casual deal. The singular nature of the coolers makes it hard to believe Davison would have allowed them to go to auction.

It was all too little, too late. Days after selling the miniature, Emma was arrested for debt and taken to the King's Bench. Unlike Davison, she was able to live on parole outside the prison walls. Rooms were found for Horatia and her at a sponging house in Temple Place, close to the obelisk in St George's Circus. Emma's letters show that Davison was a regular visitor to her in her hour of need, as she had been in his. He must surely have been among the 'sincere and valued friends all hearts of gold, not pinchbeck' who joined her at Temple Place in August to celebrate the fifteenth anniversary of the battle of the Nile. Six months later, while preparing a desperate final appeal to the government for a pension, Emma recalled the wintry morning many years before when Nelson's belongings arrived at Clarges Street from *Victory*. 'I was then very ill from the shock Dear Lord Nelson had given me,' she reminded Davison,

> & I begged you to send a copy of the codicil of the will to the Prince of Wales, then at Brighton, who did you the honour to make you a long letter & a message to me which you read most flattering to my wounded mind. You said after you would give me the extract which concerned my self, but since that time you have

not kept your word. I can remember much of the message to my self but as I wish to be correct I claim your promise, as his Royal Highness is goodness itself and will do all he can to assist an oppressed woman who writes her letter from this place not being here from any crime but having been too good, too noble minded & generous. For I can lay my head on my pillow with a firm conscience that I never injured man, woman or child and that, sir, is a great comfort to Emma Hamilton.

Davison was confined to bed with gout. He remembered the meeting at Clarges Street, but not his promise to give Emma a copy of the prince's reply, though he would send it as soon as he could reach his desk. 'I sincerely pray', he wrote,

that you may speedily be extricated from every embarrassment and difficulty and that the Nation will ultimately do justice to you by granting you the pension which you so many years have been led to expect – and which in my humble opinion your claims so fully entitle you to – I feel for your situation, as much as any one – but who is there, on Earth, that has suffered equally with myself? Could my wishes avail, you would soon very quickly be relieved from every unpleasant sensation – remember me to Horatia, and am, as I have ever been, your faithful servant Alex Davison.

Emma's desolate plea to the royal heir fell on deaf ears. The prince of Wales was now the prince regent, and Emma no longer had anything that could interest him. It was an age for heroes, not for the mistresses they left behind. Emma was from another age.

On 2 July 1814, she eluded her creditors a last time. Taking advantage of a lull in the war, she slipped across to France with Horatia and her sole remaining servant, a woman named Mary Cornish. From Calais, her spirits revived, she wrote excitedly to Davison:

*the air & exercise & liberty has done me more good than all the
calomel in the world . . . who would vegetate in fog and vapour
when they can live cheaper & better & breathe pure air in another
country. England has never done anything for me . . . Horatia is
at her lessons but begs her love to you she is charming & grown
since you saw her in vile* Banco thesio *[she] speaks such good
French she was taken for a French girl.*

This is Emma's last surviving letter to Davison. On 15
January 1815, still in Calais, this extraordinary, vital woman died
– in a narrow, shabby house on rue Française, in conditions close
to those in which she had begun life fifty years before. As the light
faded in that cold room and the faces of the women by her bed
grew dim, did Emma grasp the memory of her fame? 'I was', she
once told Davison, 'Queen of Naples for *seven years.*'

The one man who could have helped Emma, and should
have helped her, did not. Instead, William Nelson thought only of
himself and of his family name. After Trafalgar and the death of his
brother, a grateful nation gave Nelson's thoroughly undeserving
brother an earldom, a £5,000 annuity, £90,000 to buy an appropriate estate and £10,000 to furnish it. Kate Matcham and
Susannah Bolton each received £10,000. A draft of the earl's reply
to an appeal from Emma that he honour the 'evident intention' of
his brother's last codicil is revealing. 'No one is more ready & willing to comply with every wish of my Late Dear and Lamented
Brother than myself,' he wrote; 'if you will point out to me what
it is you want me to do, either for yourself or the child, I shall be
ready to give you every assistance in my power.' The earl did not
obstruct the codicil in the months following Trafalgar, but he did
little to promote it either. Contact with Emma, who was becoming an embarrassment to the 'immortal memory', dwindled to
nothing. The earl remained sensitive, however, to suggestions of
unkindness. As late as February 1813, with Emma approaching
nadir, the earl complained to Davison that 'secret insinuations'
were circulating regarding his cruelty towards his brother's

mistress. Sarah Nelson, the new countess, suffered no such qualms, dropping Emma like a stone.

Davison was never close to the earl. Before she died, Emma recalled how, when Nelson had been alive, Davison had 'detested the present Earl Nelson nor would you let him come within your house'. Yet for a time Davison dutifully managed the earl's affairs, much as he had done for Nelson. He was made trustee of the earl's enormous grant, suffering the indignity of having to chase the government for every penny of interest earned on the money before it was eventually paid in October 1806, a year after the battle. The interest alone exceeded £6,000 and 'if the 21st is included', the earl shamelessly prompted, 'it will be a day's more interest & pensions – making more than £20 difference I think'. Davison was also instructed to find the earl a suitable country seat. 'The house & estate to be in Norfolk & to be called Trafalgar . . . Houghton [the magnificent seat of the Walpoles] recommended if possible – will be cheaper than building a new one, although it is a large house.' In fact it took until 1814 for the earl to spend his windfall on Stanlynch Park in Wiltshire – by which time his heir Horatio, the Davison twins' friend from Eton and the vessel of his father's dynastic hopes, was dead, of typhoid contracted during vacation from Cambridge University. Davison attended the funeral on 25 January 1808, watching the boy join his uncle in the crypt of St Paul's Cathedral. When Sarah Nelson died in 1828, the earl, by now over seventy years old, married a woman half his age in a frantic effort to replace his heir. He failed. To the day he died in 1835 the earl did nothing to contradict the comment Fanny made about him after Maurice Nelson's death: 'gain gain is his *motto*'.

Fanny's reaction to her husband's death was typically dignified. She could still, however, veer into the haughtiness which had so fatally alienated her husband and his family, reprimanding Davison when he visited her with his sons on 13 December 1805. 'Recollect', she wrote the next morning, 'I have refused to see some of my Lord's old acquaintances and even my female friends, therefore never bring any person with you, without previously acquainting me, and I will then say what I think right.' Protocol prevented Fanny from attending the state funeral in an official capacity. But in a poignant gesture she arranged, with Davison's help, for her carriage to join the procession, with the blinds up to show it was empty.

Fanny's remaining correspondence with her former confidant was almost exclusively concerned with the long-running saga over her uncle's legacy. By the time of Nelson's death, Davison had still failed to complete the paperwork necessary to replace Maurice Nelson with William Marsh as his co-trustee of the legacy with its annuity. Now that Nelson, and his influence, were gone, Fanny, with the help of William Marsh, pressed Davison to relinquish his role as her trustee. The matter dragged on for years, caught up in the machinations of lawyers on both sides. When it was eventually settled in May 1814, Fanny gained financial independence for the first time in her life. She had no further need for Davison, and there is no record whether they met when they both visited Hyde Park in August to watch a splendid *naumachia* on the Serpentine re-enacting the battle of the Nile.

Fanny remained close to William Marsh, telling the banker he 'had proved a friend in need when little known, living in obscurity and forgot by one or two who had *promised* and given *hopes of Notice*'. She gave him her only relic of her husband, a lock of Nelson's hair cut off in 1797. Marsh would outlive everyone else in this tale, dying in 1846 aged ninety-one.

Fanny settled in Devon, buying a house overlooking the sea at Exmouth. As time passed, some of the wounds healed. A reconciliation of sorts was made with Nelson's family after Emma died. Josiah, of whom his stepfather had once despaired, proved a better businessman than naval officer, building a fortune dealing in stocks in Paris. During the 1820s his mother was a frequent visitor to his handsome house on the quai Voltaire. On one of her visits to the continent Fanny went boating with Lord Byron on Lake Geneva. Josiah died of pleurisy aged fifty in July 1830. By then Paris was again in the grip of revolution, forcing Josiah's wife and children to flee the city dressed as peasants. Fanny died in London less than a year later, on 6 May 1831. She was seventy. Her body was taken to Devon and buried alongside Josiah's in the small churchyard at Littleham outside Exmouth. Earl Nelson and Thomas Hardy, Nelson's old flag captain who had always strongly disapproved of his friend's affair with Lady Hamilton, were both at her funeral.

Thirty years before, in March 1801, at the height of the turmoil surrounding the breakdown of her marriage, Fanny vowed that 'no one shall know of these harsh and cruel letters'. It seems she was as good as her word. Almost two hundred and fifty letters survive from Nelson to his wife, but only nine can be traced to the critical period after his return to London with the Hamiltons in November 1800. Fanny's 'letter of dismissal' from 4 March 1801 has been defaced with a section chopped out, while another in which Nelson demands to be left alone ('I only wish people would never mention My name to you') exists only as an extract in a letter Fanny wrote to Davison. It seems she remained loyal and discreet to the end. Her reward was to be cast as cold and insensitive, almost as if she had deserved her husband's cruelty. Until the discovery of her letters to Davison, Fanny had been judged on scant evidence and she had generally been judged harshly.

Mary Mathews outlived Fanny by eight years, dying aged eighty on 26 October 1840. For the last years of her life she lived quietly in Sloane Street, worrying about her son's career and his health. The 'noble and majestic' Mary Simpson, who captured Nelson's heart so long ago, lies beside her husband in the graveyard of the Royal Hospital at Chelsea, a hundred yards away from the modern-day traffic and bustle of the King's Road.

Davison never got the Trafalgar agency. Had John Scott survived the battle, the captains would have appointed him their agent and he would have shared the role with William Marsh, Cutforth and Wilkie. 'God bless you all,' Scott wrote in his last letter to Charlotte, which she received with the news of his death, 'if my endeavours . . . make you happy, whatever sacrifice I may be obliged to submit to, the gratification of having done so will make me a most *ample* recompense.' Charlotte was left to look after three boys under eleven on £400 a year, 'very inadequate means for their Maintenance and Education'. The duchess of Gordon, affected by 'the sufferings of a lovely young woman', took Charlotte beneath her wing, appealing to the Patriotic Fund at Lloyd's for help. William Marsh supported the petition, mourning the fact that Scott's death had deprived his family of the 'independent property' he would have received as Nelson's prize agent. Marsh also observed that Scott was the first secretary to be '*slain in fight*' for more than a century. Charlotte Scott sent her own memorial to the king, enclosing the note praising her husband that Nelson wrote while both men were languishing in quarantine on their brief return to England before Trafalgar. The Patriotic Fund awarded Charlotte a £50 annuity. She died in 1835.

With Nelson gone, the captains delayed appointing their agent until they reached Gibraltar. Their main concern was saving themselves and a remarkable nineteen prizes from the ferocious storm that fell on them after the battle. When the fleet eventually limped into port a week later, only four prizes survived. At a meeting that followed, several agents were proposed. Captain Durham of *Defiance* and Captain Digby of *Africa* both spoke for Davison. But no agreement could be reached and so, by 'general opinion', the captains left the matter to the decision of their new commander-in-chief, Cuthbert Collingwood. Like Nelson before him, Collingwood affected modesty, saying he could not involve himself in the captains' business, though he was flattered when the agency was given to his secretary William Cosway, who farmed it out to the firm of Cooke & Halford.

Davison was furious when he heard the decision from Captain Blackwood in late November. He had feared Scott's influence, but he had never dreamed that, with his rival out of the way, he would be betrayed by captains he had been so diligently nurturing all these years. He hastily wrote a letter for Collingwood, sending it out by way of Sir Evan Nepean for added emphasis. Davison annotated his retained draft with Nelson's words from March: 'We all back you as our agent.'

My Lord

When my late valuable friend Lord Nelson left England he gave me the most positive assurances that he should not only appoint me his sole agent, but that he would recommend me to the rest of the Officers of the Fleet to be employed by them, to this promise on the part of His Lordship, there are other people that can bear ample testimony — This being the case, you may readily imagine that it was a matter of no small degree of mortification to me when I learnt on my speaking to Captain Blackwood that a different arrangement had been made to my entire exclusion — I am aware that if the Power of Agency has been granted, that it is impossible for me to participate in the advantages to be derived by the agents on the late captures, but I am willing to hope that you will, if any further occasion should occur allow the circumstances I have now taken the liberty of stating to your Lordship, to have some weight on consideration in the choice of future agents — what could have induced Lord Nelson to omit the making a communication of his sentiments on this subject to you before his death, I can by no means account for, as from his letters I have received from him by every opportunity which offered before that unfortunate event took place, it is evident that there could not be the smallest diminution of the regard he bore towards me, or for the anxiety he had to promote my interest to the utmost of his power.

PS

I think it right to add a postscript to my letter, for the purpose of mentioning to your Lordship, that when I discussed the subject of agency with Lord Nelson, I told his Lordship, that though he had not then proposed any stipulation in favour of his secretary, I thought it becoming in me not to be inattentive to the situation

*he held, and that with his Lordships concurrence I should be
accounted to him for one third part of the agency. This offer His
Lordship approved, and had I been appointed I should have fulfilled scrupulously my engagement.*

Collingwood's reply was crushing. Despite a mutual
Northumbrian upbringing, he would show Davison no favours.
The decision was the captains'. 'What makes it more extraordinary', he wrote, 'is that although I saw Lord Nelson almost every
day . . . both before and after Mr Scott was appointed the agent,
I never heard his Lordship name you, as either considered or
intended to be concerned in the agency – Indeed our conversations did not turn much either on prizes or agents.' Emma
commiserated when Davison quizzed her about Nelson's intentions before Trafalgar, assuring him that Nelson told her he
wanted Davison to be the agent as late as September, 'as you had
been for the Nile and Copenhagen'. There is no reason to doubt
Emma; as so often before, Nelson probably avoided discussing
such an uncomfortable subject candidly, telling her instead what
he thought she wanted to hear. She even wrote to Collingwood
herself, questioning the captains' appointment. Collingwood
responded by explaining the background to the decision. 'I am
very much hurt', he wrote, 'that there should have been any cause
of disappointment to Mr Davison.'

With so many prizes lost in the storm after the battle,
Trafalgar might have been far less rewarding than the battle of the
Nile. Captain Hardy was owed less than £1,000 in prize money,
compared to more than £2,000 in 1798. A tar's share was a little
over £1. Parliament, however, recognizing the unique character of
the victory, added £300,000 to the prize money. This increased a
captain's share by over £2,300. One unfortunate consequence of
parliament's largesse was to raise Earl Nelson's already substantial
share as heir to the commander-in-chief by a further £18,500.

Undaunted by his humiliation over the Trafalgar agency,
Davison stayed in the prize money business until the end of the

war. He diversified into general navy agency, moving his office closer to the other agents on the Strand by taking rooms in Gray's Inn. The business, however, was in terminal decline: Trafalgar was the last great fleet action not only of the war but of the still young century. Davison's part in it was sustained by loyal clients such as the freemason Admiral Sir John Borlase Warren, the duke of Northumberland's nephew the Hon. Joceline Percy and Captain, later Admiral, Thomas Dundas. Even so, Davison continued to attract criticism to the end of his career. In 1811 the earl of Galloway complained that 'I have long been vexed at the conduct of those you employ in your naval agency'.

There was one more great prize money coup for Davison, however. Having retaken Cape Colony from the Dutch as he had been ordered, Sir Home Popham took it upon himself to pursue General de Miranda's dream of liberating South America. On 25 June 1806 Popham launched an audacious attack on Buenos Aires, fielding a hastily assembled force of about 1,600 against 3,000 crack Spanish troops and a population of 40,000. It was all over in less than a day. Three months later Popham's dispatches arrived at Plymouth in *Narcissus*, accompanied by over 27 tons of Spanish silver. There were also letters for two of Popham's closest friends, Davison and Viscount Melville. The three men had much in common, not least a shared sense of grievance at having faced public scrutiny: Melville for malfeasance, Davison for electoral corruption and Popham for conspiracy to defraud the admiralty while refitting a ship in Calcutta years before. Like Melville, Popham had fallen foul of Earl St Vincent's naval inquiry, an experience that had left him sharing Davison's extreme dislike for Benjamin Tucker, the earl's henchman. Writing to Davison after hearing about their mutual friend's outrageous exploit, Melville hoped the lords commissioners at the Admiralty would 'blush' when they recalled 'the multiplied injuries they have done to that gallant and meritorious officer'. In fact, when news of the fall of Buenos Aires reached London – on 13 September 1806, the same day Charles Fox died – the Admiralty officers were as appalled by

Popham's maverick action as the City merchants were overjoyed at the prospect of rich new American markets.

Popham's silver was loaded onto wagons decorated with captured Spanish flags and daubed with the words 'Treasure Chest'. The wagons were protected by captured Spanish guns and escorted on the long journey to the Bank of England by thirty of Popham's tars. Salutes were fired each time the procession neared a town along a route lined with cheering crowds.

When the procession was nearing London, Davison mustered the Loyal Britons as usual in Shepherd Market before marching them to Clapham. Here they fell in with the Clapham Volunteers as they waited to escort Popham's treasure into the City. The Loyal Britons marched in front of the wagons with Davison riding at their head. A band played 'God save the King' and 'Rule Britannia', cheered on by the massed crowds. After pausing outside the Admiralty in Whitehall to rub the noses of the lords commissioners in Popham's triumph, this noisy, colourful procession turned into St James's Square. Outside Davison's mansion, Elizabeth Popham, with Harriett at her side, saluted her husband's brave tars, presenting them with yet more flags embroidered with 'Victory' and 'Buenos Ayres'. From St James's Square, the procession continued up the Strand to the Bank of England where, with great ceremony, a box of jewels and 'a million of dollars' was presented to the governor. Every window on the route was crammed with excited faces, as they had been with stricken ones in January. Afterwards the tars pulled the captured guns to the Ordnance Office in the Tower of London, where they shared two butts of porter – paid for by Davison, who also gave each man a guinea.

It was a fitting end to Davison's great day, for the master-general of the Ordnance was his patron Lord Moira, who had finally reached the cabinet in the 'Ministry of All the Talents' ushered in by the death of William Pitt. Moira's first act in office had been to appoint Davison as treasurer to the Ordnance, replacing Joseph Hunt who was being investigated by the commissioners of military inquiry. The position was public recognition for years of pandering to Moira's needs, although – taking all his loans into account – it had been bought at a very high price. William Marsh had expressed his outrage to Fanny in February 1806:

> *Your Ladyship will have heard that Mr Davison's loan to Lord Moira is likely to bring him some interest at last – my friend Mr Hunt is displaced as the Treasurer of the Ordnance Office & Mr Davison appointed his successor – salary £800 per annum & computed value about £4000 from the balance always in his hands. This for a man who passed the last year in the Kings Bench for gross misconduct, & who also is a* contractor *in any office he can push himself into . . . I heard yesterday what, if* true, *ought to be taken up by the whole country – namely, that the* salary *is to be raised from £800 to £2000 per annum!!! I really cannot believe it, & yet I heard it most confidently asserted – I know a Gentleman to whom he boasted that his new appointment was worth £12,000 per annum! this is proof that his* Vanity *has completely conquered what* sense *&* judgement *he may ever have been in possession of – the same Gentleman told me he was to have the Prince, the Chancellor, Lord Erskine, Lord Moira &c &c to a* Grand Dinner *on Saturday next, but I did not hear* Judge Grose *had been invited! . . . what are we to expect from the present administration? Like the fable of the Fox & swarm of flies . . . hungry indeed & will suck us hard . . . I think to have already damped the* hopes *of the few thinking men, who augured so well of the* new broom! *Alas poor Mr Pitt! The fools in the City as well as many others will too soon know & feel his loss.*

Davison's employment was undoubtedly controversial. Nelson's victory had already prompted letters to *The Times* questioning his role as treasurer to the committee for the duke of Clarence's still unbuilt naval pillar. Two anonymous correspondents, 'Aristides' and 'Verax', wanted to know what had become of all the subscriptions and the interest accruing on them. *The*

Times published Davison's lofty reply on 22 January 1806. He objected strongly to the 'oblique reflections on the conduct of the committee', revealing that although £7,500 was pledged to building a naval pillar, he had actually received only £4050, too little to begin the project. 'Oh, that the recent and glorious fate of Nelson', he implored melodramatically,

> *whose name will ever be dear to me as that of a revered friend, would stimulate a generous people to supply what is still wanting to the means. Before I quit the subject I will just add, that the money received has been uniformly put out at interest for the benefit of the fund, a measure too obvious to have been overlooked by the Committee.*

The naval pillar would never be built as originally proposed. Davison's accounts show that he was still holding over £4,000 in subscriptions in 1809; but after that the money, like the grandiose idea itself, seems to vanish. It seems unlikely that Davison would misappropriate so public a sum, or that he could have returned it to the subscribers. More likely he passed the money to the committee of one of the numerous monuments to Nelson, many columns or pillars being built around the country in the years after Trafalgar. The best candidate would be the great Doric column erected in Yarmouth, a town full of memories for Davison. The column rises from an Egyptian temple and is crowned by a figure of Britannia holding a trident and an olive branch in a design which uncannily resembles the description of the silver centrepiece, now lost, Davison gave Nelson after the battle of the Nile. Subscriptions for the column, the largest dedicated to Nelson outside London, opened in 1806, although the project took another ten years to complete. The dedication ceremony was conducted by local freemasons. The most famous monument to Nelson, the Corinthian column in Trafalgar Square, was not begun until 1840, long after Davison died. Here too, however, there is the echo of a connection, because the column's foundation stone was laid by

The Nelson pillar in Yarmouth rises from an Egyptian temple and is surmounted by a figure of Britannia holding out an olive branch.

Charley Davison Scott, the youngest son of Nelson's tragic last secretary.

Nelson duly received his monument by John Flaxman in the 'Hall of Fame' at St Paul's Cathedral. It towers opposite the plaque to Captain Ralph Miller. Flaxman also copied a bust of Nelson for Davison. In doing so he corrected a mistake on the original 1800 bust which had irritated Nelson. 'They have put the King's medal to the button hole instead of yours,' Nelson had apologetically written to Davison at the time. Another marble memorial Davison ordered after Trafalgar 'as a tribute of respect to the immortal memory of his friend' was a 'superb statuary two-handled urn . . . richly ornamented with emblematic devices'. These included crocodiles, ships, sea-creatures, and masks of Neptune and Amphitrite. This 7-foot high urn, which once stood in the hall of St James's Square, was discovered recently beside playing fields in south London.

The most dramatic of Davison's monuments to Nelson was the 40-foot high sandstone obelisk he placed on the spot where the edge of the Battle Park at Swarland Hall touched the Great North Road. The obelisk pinnacle was broken to symbolize Nelson's death. On its east face, Davison incised a simple but suggestive dedication which hinted at the philosophy which had bound the men:

VICTORY, 21ST OCTOBER, 1805
'ENGLAND EXPECTS EVERY MAN TO DO HIS DUTY'
NOT TO COMMEMORATE THE PUBLIC VIRTUES
AND HEROIC ACHIEVEMENTS OF
NELSON,
WHICH IS THE DUTY OF ENGLAND;
BUT TO THE MEMORY OF A PRIVATE FRIENDSHIP,
THIS ERECTION IS DEDICATED BY
ALEXANDER DAVISON
SWARLAND HALL

John Flaxman's monument to Nelson stands opposite his earlier memorial to Captain Miller in the south transept of St Paul's Cathedral.

The obelisk was an unashamedly public, even ostentatious, gesture on the main arterial road linking England and Scotland. Over the years many thousands of people must have become familiar with it, although, bypassed by the rerouting of the modern-day A1, it now stands in peaceful seclusion. Davison would build another obelisk on the hill overlooking his childhood home at Lanton after his brother Jack died in 1827. Here William Davison later added his father's name to the inscription, a tribute in turn to his 'private virtues'.

There was one other, miniaturized, sepulchral monument. Shortly after his meeting with Earl Nelson and William Haslewood at St James's Square on 17 December 1805, Davison arranged for eighty-four of the ninety gold guineas found among Nelson's belongings in *Victory* to be incorporated into a unique reliquary 13 inches high. At its heart was a model, in gilded bronze, of the sarcophagus marking Nelson's grave in the crypt of St Paul's Cathedral. Inside it, like the core of a nuclear reactor, was a glass phial holding a few precious strands of Nelson's hair, presumably given to Davison by Emma. The sarcophagus was placed on a black hardstone plinth, at the corners of which four shrouded and weeping female figures supported a pyramidal canopy formed from the guineas. At the apex of the pyramid was a trident around which two snakes were entwined – a powerful masonic emblem. Davison must have ordered this 'Nelson cenotaph' before the state funeral, because originally a large wooden pyramid had been built above Nelson's grave in St Paul's, only to be removed just days before the service after the choir complained that it obstructed their view. If, as seems likely, this temporary pyramid was supported by weeping figures, figures which were also present among the devices on Nelson's coffin, Davison's 'Nelson cenotaph' would have been a remarkably good reproduction of the intended effect within the cathedral. The introduction of a rostral prow and stern on the model sarcophagus, where none are present on the original, imitates the devices on the barge that brought Nelson's body upriver from Greenwich

The 'Nelson Cenotaph' made by Davison using eighty-four of the guineas recovered from Nelson's belongings in Victory.

and may also indicate an unfulfilled plan by the organizers of Nelson's funeral.

The plinth of the 'Nelson cenotaph' was mounted with four plaques. Three commemorated Nelson's victories at Cape St Vincent, the Nile and Copenhagen. The fourth was engraved: 'These Guineas were in Lord Viscount Nelson's purse at the time he received the fatal wound off Trafalgar, Oct. 21, 1805.'

According to the tally made at St James's Square on 17 December 1805, removing eighty-four guineas to create the cenotaph would have left six guineas, nine half-guineas, three third-guineas and an unidentified number of silver coins (worth £2 0s 6d) in Nelson's purse: a total of £26 2s 0d from the original sum of £102 6s 0d. Yet when the purse was opened two hundred years later it held only £14. This was all in gold and comprised eight guineas, six half-guineas and seven third-guineas. This means that £12 2s 0d has gone missing from the purse over the years, the coins possibly being distributed as souvenirs. The discrepancies in the numbers of particular coins also indicate that, assuming that all the guineas used in the cenotaph came from the purse and that the manuscript found in it can be trusted, at least two guineas and four third-guineas were added to the contents at some point.

Only one other sighting of the purse is recorded between 1805 and its discovery in 2002. On 6 April 1866 an inventory was made by Davison's son William (by then a very elderly man) of the contents of a chest of drawers at Swarland Hall. Buried within it is the mention, in the second drawer of the chest, of 'a Bag with *Gold* and *Silver* coins (guineas, ½ guineas)'. Alongside the purse was a silver Nile medal, a 'gold snuff box made from the mast of the victory Lord Nelson's flagship at the Battle of Trafalgar on which he was killed' and, most intriguing of all, 'the *Gold* nile medal worn by the immortal Nelson when he fell 21st October 1805 at Trafalgar'. Seven years later, on William's death, these treasured relics passed to his daughter Rosalie.

If freemasonry gave Davison the urge to build monuments, patriotism defined his taste in art. The paintings on Davison's walls were already gravitating towards British artists when, after Trafalgar, he embarked on an ambitious plan to create a gallery in St James's Square devoted to heroic pictures inspired by the history of England. His aim was to encourage 'the talents of our Native Artists, and to bring them fairly in contrast with those of the Foreign Schools'. The diarist Joseph Farington claimed the idea for the gallery was given to Davison by his friend Robert Fulton, the American inventor of the 'infernals'. But it was not an entirely original one. Two other galleries, Robert Bowyer's Historic Gallery on Pall Mall and the British Institution, already existed to patronize artists painting scenes from British history, while another, John Boydell's Shakespeare Gallery, had recently closed. Nevertheless, Davison's scheme would be one of the greatest acts of private patronage in the fine arts within living memory.

The keeper of the British Institution, a 'cunning & circumventing' dealer called Valentine Green, was recruited to invite eight artists each to submit three subjects from English history. Davison would choose which of these subjects the artist would paint. When finished, the painting would be paid for and, if judged good enough, hung in Davison's gallery; if not, it would be sold. If all went well, Davison envisaged expanding the collection to sixteen paintings. He made one novel stipulation. All the artists had to incorporate self-portraits in their paintings. The list of the artists Green approached defines the peculiarly British school of history painting though only one, David Wilkie, commands widespread critical attention today. The others were James Northcote, Henry Tresham, Robert Smirke, John Singleton Copley, Richard Westall, Benjamin West and finally Davison's old friend from the King's Bench, Arthur William Devis, who was still working on his *Death of Nelson*. When it was finished, a year later, this vast canvas, 9 feet long, was engraved and published, as planned, by Josiah Boydell. The prints were accompanied by a melodramatic key describing the tragedy: 'the Steward, with silent eagerness, explores and interrogates the Doctor's eye, to catch, if possible, a glimmering of hope'. Devis's painting was then offered for sale at the British Institution for £1,000 (the diarist Joseph Farington complained that 'Green has been unconscionable enough to demand 10 per cent should the picture be sold & letters have passed on the subject'). It was bought by Lord Bexley, who gave it to the commissioners of Greenwich Hospital in 1825. It is now at the National Maritime Museum, while a smaller version by Devis is in the cockpit of *Victory* at Portsmouth.

Seven of Davison's hand-picked artists were members of the Royal Academy – West had recently retired as president – and, despite Davison's avowed intention that they should all be 'native artists', two of them, West again and Copley, were from America. West was steeped in masonic culture, had already painted the seminal *Death of Wolfe*, and had taught Fulton to paint. West told Davison he thought the bold plan was 'honourable to patronage, and to yourself', while Devis thought it could 'scarcely fail to operate as an incitement to others, and ultimately diffuse a love for the Fine Arts throughout the British Empire; at the same time it must form a lasting monument of your own taste and munificence'.

The nascent collection received an early and unexpected boost when Davison won Copley's *Death of Lord Chatham* in June 1806, having paid 100 guineas to join a lottery for it. The painting shows the earl of Chatham, William Pitt the Elder, falling ill in the chamber of the House of Lords. It was fitting that Copley's great work, a follow-up to his gripping, and highly successful, *Watson and the Shark*, should find a new home with Davison in St James's Square next door to Lord Chatham's old house.

All the paintings except Copley's planned contribution were completed by the end of March 1807. As a collection, the focus of the paintings leaned distinctly towards the middle ages, which was seen as the best backdrop against which to play out scenes of Britons resisting tyranny and defending democracy. Two

DEATH OF LORD NELSON,

PAINTED BY A. W. DEVIS, ESQ. ENGRAVED BY W. BROMLEY, ESQ.

DEDICATED TO THE BRITISH NAVY.

1... Lord Nelson.
2... Lieutenant Capt.y Yule.
3... Mr Willinger, Midshipman and Clerk.

4... Mr Scotten, Secretary to Nelson.
5... Revd W.P Scott, Chaplain.
6... Mr W. Burke, Purser.

7... Captain, Sir T.M. Hardy, Bart.
8... Mr Chevalier, steward.
9... Dr Beatty, Surgeon.

10... Secretary Capt.y Bligh.
11... Mr Smith, Assistant Surgeon.
12... Mr Bunce, Carpenter.

Published March 20.1811 by Mefs Boydell Young & Vine Cheapside London.

The key to the portraits in Josiah Boydell's print after Arthur William Devis' The Death of Nelson.

voguish Whig heroes, Alfred the Great and Mary Queen of Scots, made an appearance as did, tactfully, an ancestor of the duke of Northumberland. They were large paintings, on average 6 feet square, and must have completely covered the walls of the room set aside for the gallery in St James's Square. Davison gave very precise instructions for their arrangement:

NORTH SIDE

I   *Henry Percy, fifth Earl of Northumberland, presenting the Princess Margaret, eldest daughter of Henry the seventh, to James the fourth, King of Scotland, at Lamerton, two miles beyond Berwick, where he and his nobles were attending to receive her as his Queen by James Northcote, Esq R.A*

II   (over the door) *The wife of the neat-herd rebuking King Alfred, (who had taken refuge in their cottage, disguised as a peasant) for having suffered her cakes to burn, which she had committed to his care, by David Wilkie, Esq.*

III   *Lord John Warren, Earl of Surrey, resisting the unconstitutional attempt to question, by a quo warranto, the tenures and liberties of the ancient barons, anno 1275, by Henry Tresham, Esq. R.A*

EAST SIDE

IV   *Elizabeth, Queen Dowager of Edward the fourth, in the sanctuary at Westminster, receiving a deputation from the council of state, sent to demand her younger son the Duke of York, by Robert Smirke, Esq RA*

V   (over the fireplace) *The offer of the crown to lady Jane Gray, by the Dukes of Northumberland and Suffolk, and other lords, deputies of the Privy Council, by John Singleton Copley, Esq RA*

VI   *Mary Queen of Scots, after her defeat at the battle of Langside, finally quits her country, and embarks in a fishing boat for England, with a determination to seek the protection of Queen Elizabeth, by Richard Westall, Esq RA*

WEST SIDE

VII   *The conspiracy of Babington against Queen Elizabeth, detected by her minister, Sir Francis Walsingham by Arthur William Devis, Esq*

VIII *The death of the Earl of Chatham by John Singleton Copley, Esq RA*

IX   *Sir Philip Sidney, mortally wounded, rejecting the water offered to him, and ordering it to be first given to a wounded soldier by Benjamin West, Esq*

Westall later added to the collection by painting *Melancholy*, a subject inspired by John Milton's poem *Il Penseroso*, while Devis, with an eye on the lucrative print market, filled a depiction of the signing of the Magna Carta with portraits of Davison's aristocratic friends and patrons, including Lord Moira and the duke of Northumberland. On Saturday 4 April 1807 a dinner was held at St James's Square to celebrate the completion of the project. 'Everything sumptious,' reported the diarist Farington, who was present. All the artists, except Tresham and Smirke, attended, watched over by Valentine Green. Alongside them were two of Davison's favourite sculptors: Joseph Nollekens and John Flaxman.

Another guest was John M'Arthur, Admiral Lord Hood's former secretary. With Davison's help, M'Arthur was about to embark on writing the official biography of Nelson. Earl Nelson, who wanted a more famous writer to record his brother's life, was persuaded to support the book only when the prince of Wales lent his personal chaplain, the Revd James Clarke, to the project. Emma refused to have anything to do with it. *The Life and Services of Horatio Viscount Nelson* would be published in 1809. It was a mammoth two-volume work with a magnificent frontispiece by Benjamin West. Davison, who was interviewed for the book, commissioned a four-volume deluxe limited edition of just three copies, printed on vellum, illuminated in gold, and bound in purple and white morocco. He kept one set for himself; another

KEY TO THE PORTRAITS, IN THE ENGRAVING OF MAGNA CHARTA.

1 The Earl of Shannon.
2 The Earl of Norfolk.
3 The Earl of Buckingham.
4 The Duke of Devonshire.

5 The Marquis of Tavistock.
6 The Marquis of Hertford.
7 Late Lord Erskine.
8 The Earl of Egremont.
9 The Earl of Tankerville.

10 The Duke of Cleveland.
11 The Duke of Sutherland.
12 The Earl of Gallway.
13 The Earl of Morton.
14 The Marquis of Hastings.

15 The Duke of Gordon.
16 The Duke of Northumberland.
17 Lord Viscount Hereford.
18 Lord De Ros.
19 Stephen Langton, Archbishop of Canterbury.

The key to the contemporary portraits used by Arthur William Devis in his painting depicting the signing of the Magna Carta. Many of the figures, such as the duke of Northumberland and Earl Moira (created the marquis of Hastings in 1816) were friends of Davison; the others were flattered to be included.

went to the eccentric millionaire collector William Beckford, with whom Nelson and the Hamiltons had stayed over Christmas 1800; the third was presented to the prince. When the book was finished Clarke urged Davison to 'give your own life: it would be very interesting & important'.

In July 1806, before going 'broken hearted' into Norfolk on a maudlin tour of Nelson's surviving family, Emma left instructions for her mother to send Davison the Turkish gun and water canteen which Nelson ('our departed angel') had left him. These were both safely delivered, but when Emma returned to Merton Place in September she found a note from Davison chasing her for the last part of his legacy: Nelson's 'Scimitar'. A couple of days later, on 17 September, she duly sent up to St James's Square 'the Turkish sabre which my ever Dear Glorious ever to be Lamented Nelson left you'. In fact the weapon Davison received was a French cavalry sabre and not a Turkish scimitar, although its blade was decorated in fashionable *faux Damascus* style with pseudo-Islamic script. Davison arranged for the gun and sabre to be engraved as having been presented to Nelson by the 'Grand Signior', Sultan Selim III of Turkey, after the battle of the Nile. No record of any such presentation survives but Davison is unlikely to have invented it, even if he had never seen the awards themselves. Not only had he been very close to Nelson but there were many people around him, not least Emma, to contradict any erroneous claim – and some would have taken pleasure in doing so. Yet it seems unlikely that the French sabre Davison received was the 'Scimitar' referred to by Nelson in his will. This might not have been available to Emma in July 1806, perhaps having already been sold or lost. It might be telling that Emma failed to mention it to her mother before she left for Norfolk in July. She must have scoured the details of Nelson's will. Did she omit it because she knew it had gone? Or did she hold it back to cheat the intended recipient? Davison was certainly not popular with her at the time. His impatient request for the sabre coincided with her description of him as a 'dirty vile groveler'. When Davison pressed her, did

Emma send him the French sabre, presumably a captured weapon from Nelson's collection, as a deliberate substitute, or was she genuinely confused by the decoration on the sabre's blade? What happened to the original sultan's scimitar may never be known. Either way Davison seems to have accepted the sabre in good faith as that scimitar, or at the least to have been prepared to go along with the deception. When the Loyal Britons commissioned Arthur William Devis to paint him in 1808, Davison ensured he was prominently shown carrying Nelson's sword.

After William Davison's death in 1873, many of his father's Nelsonian treasures passed to the Royal Greenwich Hospital by his bequest. These included 'four cannons taken by the Lord Nelson at Copenhagen and the Turkish Gun, Sabre and canteen presented to him by the Sultan after the battle of the Nile and also the portrait in Oils of Lord Nelson by Abbott at Swarland'. Yet for some still elusive reason, Greenwich Hospital received only the scabbard for Nelson's sabre, not the sabre itself. Instead, the scabbard arrived with an Egyptian Club sword engraved with Davison's crest, indicating that, although he was not properly entitled to one, Davison had ordered at least one of the distinctive crocodile-hilted swords from Rundell & Bridge for himself. This misfit was displayed first in the Painted Hall at Greenwich Hospital and then, from 1936, at the National Maritime Museum.

The mistake was probably an innocent mix-up, the result perhaps of William Davison's executors assuming the far more exotic-looking Egyptian Club sabre to be the one referred to in the will, or of some long-forgotten nursery game at Swarland Hall. Whatever the reason – and the mystery resembles the puzzle of the coins in Nelson's purse – it left the scabbard on display in a national collection for a hundred and thirty years while the sabre hung forgotten on the wall of a distant castle. The two were briefly, although sadly not permanently, reunited in the basement of the museum in July 2002.

XV

AFRICA

64 GUNS,
CAPTAIN HENRY DIGBY

I N JUNE 1805 THE commission of military inquiry set up in the
wake of the Melville scandal began to delve into the business of
supplying goods to the barrack office. Questions were being asked
about the probity of General Oliver De Lancey, the barrackmaster-
general who had retired under a cloud the previous November,
ending Davison's contract as agent of supply. The commission had
a wide-ranging brief but it soon came to focus on De Lancey's
relationship with Davison. Among the first witnesses the commissioners called were John Lodge, the former packer of barrack
office supplies at Bedford Street; Henry Cutler, the ironmonger
turned manager of the prize business; and the commissary-
general Brook, now Sir Brook, Watson, who had taken over control of supply from the ill-fated barrack office. Davison appeared
before the commission on 6 December, the day after William
Chevailler arrived in London from *Victory*.

Davison was invited to describe his terms of engagement by
De Lancey as agent of supply for the barrack office, as agreed
by their exchange of letters over Christmas 1794. He confirmed
there was no other or subsequent agreement.

'During your connection with the barrack office', he was
asked, the commissioners leaning forward, 'were all the articles you
provided procured on commission, or were any of them your own?'

'There were some articles that were furnished from my army clothing warehouse,' replied Davison equably; 'upon these no commission was charged.'

'Were any persons, connected with the Barrack Department, employed by you at any time in purchasing Barrack Stores?'

'I think not.'

Without pressing any further, the commissioners turned their attention to the large amounts of public money Davison held on account from the barrack office, the issue which, in relation to the office of treasurer of the navy, had ultimately undone Melville. Specifically, the commissioners wished to know why Davison continued to request, and to receive, advances totalling more than £75,000 during the peace of 1802 when supplies to the barrack office were suspended. Davison, who would have seen where the question was leading, claimed he held the money in anticipation of future orders and that he had no obligation to pass on any interest he earned in the meantime. Moreover, he claimed that, over the years, the barrack office had usually owed him money, rather than the other way around. However, he accepted that his closing accounts still showed a surplus of over £6,000, and this he promised to pay back right away.

In May 1806 the commissioners turned their attention to the business of supplying coal to the barracks. In their hands was Robert Edington's letter to the Treasury from June 1802, in which the disaffected clerk accused Davison and George Walker, the coal dealer in the Channel Islands, of 'peculations and frauds'. The commissioners criticized De Lancey's lackadaisical response to these serious accusations: 'The required investigation was not proceeded on with much activity or in the way expected by the Secretary at War it would have been.' Davison was recalled on 30 May to explain his relationship with Walker. Walker himself could not appear as he had since been executed for forging a will. With Davison stonewalling and Edington's evidence discredited because of his involvement in Walker's forgery, the commission could not establish a clear link between Davison and the coal dealer's crimes. All the same, there were plenty of other shortcomings in the coal business for the commissioners to concentrate on. These included Davison's failure to pass on his trade discounts for his bulk orders; charging the barracks retail, not wholesale, prices; and buying the coal cheaply in the summer before delivering it to the barracks during the expensive winter months. There were also significant inconsistencies in the amounts of coal that Davison was apparently buying and those for which he was charging the barrack office. 'Our first impression', the commissioners commented, 'was that this increase must have arisen from some fraud or negligence.' 'Why', retorted Davison when he saw their report, 'should such have been the first impression?' The problem, as a number of expert witnesses confirmed, was that Davison, like other contractors, bought his coal in the north of England by bulk calculated by weight, but sold it to the barracks by bulk calculated by volume. If the coal was wet when loaded into the colliers into the north but was dry when delivered, this could cause discrepancies in the amounts of coal Davison was apparently buying and selling.

The commissioners completed their work in July 1806. They had found no evidence of serious wrongdoing, but their investigation caused enough concern for them to recommend that two special commissioners be appointed by parliament to investigate exclusively the barrack office accounts before 1805. Their recommendation landed on the desk of Nicholas Vansittart, the secretary to the Treasury. Vansittart and Davison had done plenty of business in the past, notably involving the supply of goods for 'secret service' work. But Davison would have been wary of assuming any inclination in his favour, because the minister had also sat on the inquiry into the Ilchester election, later voting for his prosecution. Vansittart gave the task to his private secretary Charles Herries and to William Bragge, a career civil servant. They were ordered to focus specifically on Davison's dealings with the barrack office. In the autumn Herries and Bragge wrote three times to Davison asking to see his final cash account with the barrack office, each time without success. Only when, their patience exhausted, the commissioners referred the matter to the Treasury did Davison begrudgingly and unhelpfully reply,

> [I] have to acquaint you that my accounts for stores provided for the Barrack Department, and the cash received have been regularly delivered into the Barrack office, and have been finally examined, approved and the balance paid, which said accounts will no doubt be produced to you by Lieut General DeLancey, and further that it is not in my power to furnish any other accounts than those already delivered.

It was a mistake. Herries and Bragge, now thoroughly suspicious, asked the attorney-general to introduce a bill giving them the necessary powers to compel Davison to surrender his books to them.

The Davisons, meanwhile, were struggling beneath the most profound grief. Just two weeks earlier, on 2 November, Alexander Horatio, their youngest son, had died 'of water in the head' while staying at Broadstairs. He was six years old and the second of their children to die. 'The dear remains were put into a shell within a leaden coffin,' Davison miserably wrote, 'and enclosed in an oak coffin, covered with superfine French grey cloth, with appropriate ornaments, with an engraved plate screwed upon it.' Alexander's body left on its forlorn journey to Northumberland on 19 November, the same day Davison dashed off his brusque reply to the special commissioners. A week later, 'at ¾ past three o'clock on Thursday afternoon 27ᵗʰ November', the body was interred in the elegant neo-classical vault that Davison had built for his family in the graveyard of the church at Kirknewton.

The loss of his son deeply affected Davison, plunging him into that fatalistic depression which had followed the deaths of Maurice Nelson and his brother George. Earl Nelson, who saw Davison the day before he left for Northumberland, thought he

looked 'very much cut'. It was in this dejected state that Davison
returned to London to be greeted by the publication of the 'Third
Report of the Commissioners of Military Enquiry'.

The report was damning; the accusations against Davison
were now out in the open. He stood charged not only with enjoying the interest on immense sums of public money but also with
failing to account properly for his coal prices. 'The wealth that this
man accumulated at the expense of the public', the *Annual Register*
observed that year, 'must have been immense, nor was he at any
pains to shade it from the public's eye but on the contrary, seemed
desirous to display it to the utmost splendour and magnificence.'
The attack on his reputation appalled Davison. Like Alexander
Trotter at the Navy Office before him, Davison was forced to
resign as treasurer to the Ordnance, a position he had held for just
a year. More galling still, William Marsh's friend Joseph Hunt
resumed his former position. De Lancey wrote Davison a lengthy
letter of support castigating the commissioners' 'malicious insinuations'.

On 2 February 1807 Davison's obfuscation over his
accounts was raised in the House of Commons by Lord Archibald
Hamilton, a vigorous opponent of corruption. Lord Henry Petty,
the chancellor of the exchequer, referred Hamilton to the continuing inquiry by Herries and Bragge. The government's
equivocation only spurred on Davison's many detractors in the
press. 'Copley', acidly commented *The Times* on 4 February,

> and the other eminent Artists have commenced the undertaking
> of the Davison Gallery of Historical Paintings, which seems now
> likely to be completed, not exactly with the delicate touches of
> their magic pencils, but with the ruder and rougher pound
> brushes of those equally eminent designers in their way, SIR
> ARTHUR PIGOTT, SIR SAMUEL ROMILLY, and others, who if less skilled
> in the management of drapery, will give a pretty fair specimen
> of the effect of the long robe.

In a sign of his growing alarm, Davison forwarded De Lancey's letter exonerating him to the lords commissioners at the Treasury, although as the former barrackmaster-general was also in deep trouble this was unlikely to help his cause. 'To many of your Lordships', he reminded them, 'I have the honor of being personally known, and you are probably all acquainted with the part which I have taken upon occasions of great national emergency; circumstances to which I advert, not in palliative of any misconduct, if misconduct be imputable to me, but circumstances which I should hope would render misconduct less probable.'

The initial shock past, Davison energetically set about defending himself. He launched a high-profile campaign of vindication centred on the publication of his own 'Observations' on the report, a tactic used successfully by Sir Home Popham during his feud with Benjamin Tucker in 1803. Davison opened his 'Observations' by bitterly complaining that the commissioners had unfairly depicted him 'as the public spoiler, as the man who had basely sacrificed every consideration of honour and good faith to the most boundless rapacity'. Seventy pages later, after responding in detail to all the issues raised in the report, Davison played his trump card:

> Engaged in the service of the Public, I have never thought it enough to escape censure; my object has uniformly been to merit praise. By the exertions of zeal, I have endeavoured to go far beyond the limits of duty, and am proud to state, that I have rendered services to my Country, which have been required by the acknowledgement of a PITT, and the friendship of a NELSON.

The attorney-general's bill requiring Davison to surrender his cash account produced, noted Herries and Bragge, a 'very great and sudden alteration' in his conduct. Account books started arriving from St James's Square, albeit still very slowly. The noose was drawing in. In April 1807 Davison and his principal clerk John Bowering were summoned and questioned. Then, on 28 May,

Herries and Bragge quizzed John Allen – the apprentice clerk who in 1802 had been compelled by Bowering to counter-sign false receipts in George Watson's name disguising the supply of bedding to the barracks from Davison's factory. When asked why his name was on the receipts, Allen admitted that he had been 'persuaded' to sign them: 'principally by Mr Bowering and the reason assigned was that Mr Davison could not be both Buyer and Seller'. Davison was instantly recalled. Why, he was asked, were receipts for the supply of over £50,000 worth of goods signed by Watson and Allen to 'personate tradesmen supplying goods to you and sign receipts for money they never received'?

'It being the rule in all public offices that receipts must be attached to bills of parcels,' replied Davison, 'and particularly in the Barrack Office, and as I could not make out a bill to myself, the easiest method was for the bills to be made out to me by one of the clerks in Bedford Street house, and consequently a receipt signed by that clerk.'

There was worse to come. 'On these we find a commission of 2½% is charged and allowed you on examination of your accounts by the Barrack accountant, how do you explain this?' Almost by chance, Herries and Bragge had stumbled on the one irregularity that Davison could not explain away. He had plainly charged an agency commission on goods made in his own factory, something he had categorically denied doing when he was examined under oath in December 1805. Nonplussed for a moment, Davison feebly explained that this mistake had already been noticed by his clerk and that the barrack office had been credited 'on accounts not yet delivered in'. In a flash the commissioners, scenting blood, reminded Davison that he had assured them in his letter of 19 November that all his accounts with the barrack office were closed. Where were the credits he spoke of?

On 5 June Herries and Bragge reported their dramatic find to the lords commissioners at the Treasury. 'Your Lordships', they gravely concluded, 'may think it necessary to require the opinion of his Majesty's Attorney and Solicitor General.' The two investigators probed deeper before delivering their final report in October, when their conclusions on the whole business of barrack supply under De Lancey's control were scathing – not least in respect of the vague and haphazard way in which the barrackmaster-general had employed Davison in the first place. De Lancey was disgraced but he was not indicted. The severest criticism was reserved for Davison. His crimes were manifest. Not only had he illegitimately charged agency commission totalling more than £1,300 on goods supplied by himself to the barracks, but his profit margin on those goods was as high as 19 per cent, far higher than that of his competitors. More damning still – and this was the topical issue which galvanized public opinion strongly against Davison – he had enjoyed the use of about £60,000 a day in public money for ten years, earning himself almost £30,000 in interest.

The report dismissed all Davison's excuses out of hand. He described himself, commented Herries and Bragge, as an 'agent on commission', but to them he appeared to be 'a character for which we can find no name as it is neither Merchant, Tradesman, Manufacturer nor Agent'. Davison could vociferously complain that his factory prices were still lower than others, which they were, and he might bemoan that the interest had been calculated using 'a mode of computation rarely resorted to by the most rigid creditor and certainly not consistent with the accustomed liberality of government', but he knew the damage was done. Unlike the shenanigans at Ilchester, in this crime there was no honour. His fate was sealed.

While the attorney-general hesitated over what to do with Davison, the press renewed its assault. The *Courier* blamed the delay in Davison's prosecution on the 'many persons of rank, talent, and consideration in the country' who owed him money. *The Times*, stung by an accusation that it was 'sparing peculators and their retainers', revealed on 28 December that Davison had been spotted going to Yarmouth with Sir Home Popham:

which information we immediately communicated to our readers and the public, and shall be excessively careful in future of noting the actions, naming the companions, and tracing the travels of this said Mr DAVISON, *till he is brought to justice . . . Nothing can acquit, in our mind, the late Ministers, the present Ministers, all Ministers and all public men, from some degree of implication in his supposed guilt, but the rivalship of zeal which they exhibit in placing him before a jury of his country.*

Stung by the clamour raised against him, Davison tried to head off his prosecution by meeting with Herries and Bragge to explain himself. When this failed, the commissioners reporting that 'all Mr Davison's arguments and conclusions are grounded on false premises', he made a last-ditch appeal to the lords commissioners at the Treasury. In a letter 'seeking to exculpate himself', Davison complained about the 'misapprehension arising from an imperfect knowledge of the circumstances of my conduct'. He assured the lords commissioners that he had ordered Bowering to credit the barrack office as soon as he heard about the wrongly charged commission. He could hardly be blamed if his clerk had failed to do as instructed. He then tried to turn the argument around by pointing out that, even with the agency commission, his own goods were still cheaper than those of the suppliers he had been using. The arrangement, though clumsy, had not only saved public money but had in fact prevented him earning a higher commission by supplying more expensive goods. To support his petition, Davison enclosed a letter from De Lancey confirming their informal (possibly verbal) agreement in 1797 to allow him to bolster the barrack office supplies from his own factory. He also enclosed letters from other government contractors who charged commission on their own goods. 'I cannot but feel', Davison concluded, 'how deeply my character and future happiness are involved in the result of your lordships' investigation.'

It was all too late. *Rex* v. *Alexander Davison* opened in Westminster Hall on 8 December 1808 before the lord chief justice Lord Ellenborough and a specially selected jury of forty-eight men. Davison faced thirty-six counts of defrauding the king by means of falsified vouchers to a value of £1,323 7s 8¾d. The charges related to goods worth £52,935 11s 2d supplied from the factory in Bedford Street between December 1797 and June 1802.

'Keep up your spirits as well as you can,' wrote Emma,

& remember poor Lord Melville what he suffered, yet I hope to see him rise again as you will yet & the world will be convinced that you merited thanks instead of condemnation & you will yet be assured rise higher in the minds of good people from the very prosecution *& unjust* persecution *you have met with – at present the great object will be for every friend of yours to put their shoulders to the wheel for this* I want to get Mr Rose to act so that as there is to be a sentence *that the attorney general &* vindictive Ellenborough *may at least show a little mercy.*

The 'vindictive' Ellenborough was renowned for his severe manner and sarcastic wit. On entering court, he had the disconcerting habit of blowing out his cheeks 'like a war horse'. To add insult to injury, Ellenborough was a resident of St James's Square. The prosecution was led by Sir Vicary 'Vinegar' Gibbs, the attorney-general, a dwarfish man with a prominent hooked nose. 'Plain in his wig, he was ugly out of it,' commented one observer; 'there was an asperity in his countenance and manner that was very repulsive.' The main thrust of Gibbs's argument, which was hard to counter, was that by supplying goods to the barrack office himself Davison was denying the public the checks and balances they should have expected of an agent. By charging commission on his own goods, Davison had a vested interest not only in charging a high price himself but in sourcing the most expensive goods from his competitors as a comparison.

Davison was defended by Robert Dallas. This was undoubtedly

a compliment to the lawyer's skills, because Dallas had led the prosecution at Taunton. Dallas' appointment, however, was more likely to have been influenced by his success in defending Warren Hastings, the governor-general of India, during another high-profile trial in Westminster Hall twenty years earlier. Alongside Dallas was Davison's solicitor, 'Morpeth Dick' Wilson. Dallas built his defence around the casual agreement made between De Lancey and Davison in 1797 when the barrackmaster-general gave Davison permission to supply goods from his own factory. It was not unreasonable, Dallas argued, for Davison to charge a commission on his own goods because his duties as agent of supply extended far beyond those of a normal supplier to include packing, shipping and delivering the goods to the barracks. Dallas also drily observed that had Davison intended to defraud the barrack office, he would have been a 'driveller and idiot' to involve any of his junior clerks in the conspiracy.

The defence's principal witness was Oliver De Lancey, no doubt grateful not to be in the dock himself. De Lancey recalled the change to Davison's terms in 1797 but, under cross-examination by Gibbs, conceded that he had not explicitly authorized Davison to charge commission on his own goods. De Lancey was followed into the witness box by John Allen, the young clerk who had signed the false receipts, and John Bowering, Davison's principal clerk, who had asked him to do it. Mungo Sheddon, the manager of the clothing factory, would doubtless also have been called, had he not died just weeks before the trial. A number of character witnesses were then called. These included Davison's childhood friend John Cowley, his family banker William Smart and his first patron in the City, Robert Hunter. A buzz went around the packed spectator stands as Lord Moira strode into court. The minister stated that the defendant's conduct was at all times 'strict and punctual [and] strictly delicate in refusing emoluments which he might have claimed'. Sir Evan Nepean considered Davison 'a very honest and honourable man . . . incapable of committing a fraud', while Sir Andrew Snape Hamond, the comptroller of the Navy

Office, thought him 'the last man in the world that would have attempted anything of the kind'.

Their warm words did little good. Early in February 1809, for the second time in his life, Davison heard a jury pronounce him guilty. Sentencing was postponed to allow affidavits to be submitted on Davison's behalf. In the meantime he was sent back to the King's Bench, from where, in a last-ditch effort to avoid a heavy punishment, he hurriedly issued another pamphlet. This one took the form of a 'concise statement' of his defence 'for the information of his friends'. One of those friends, perhaps his staunchest, was Emma: '*your sun is not sett,*' she assured him. Emma visited the King's Bench with Horatia when she could, distributed the pamphlet and urged James Perry, the editor of the influential *Morning Chronicle*, to support Davison in his newspaper. 'My heart bleeds for you,' she wrote, after hearing of the verdict, '& I assure you that ill as I am, if I was sure I could serve you . . . I would venture barefooted to show you my grateful Heart . . . ever ever ever *amen amen amen* as your dear friend Nelson used to say.'

James Harrison, a hack journalist who had written a partisan biography of Nelson for Emma, was sent into the King's Bench to interview her friend. 'Harrison who goes in to every coffee house & travels in the stage & was in Westminster Hall yesterday will tell you peoples opinion of you & your unjust prosecution . . . you will yet come off well in spite of all party faction & cabal . . . you must also keep my letters secret.' She went on to express what Davison must have been thinking: 'if he had lived, alas, you would not have been thus persecuted nor your unhappy but grateful Emma left to weep & neglected by almost all but you'.

In the hope of reducing, or even of avoiding, a prison sentence, Davison voluntarily paid over £18,000 into the Treasury: a sum, he claimed, equal to the whole commission he had earned supplying goods to the barrack office over the years. Ellenborough was not impressed. 'This is by no means a sufficient expiation of your offence,' he boomed when Davison returned to Westminster Hall on 27 April. Judge Grose then pronounced sentence:

for this offence therefore, founded in a dishonourable thirst of lucre, in a breach of public trust and confidence, aimed at the vitals of the state, and affecting the interests of all ranks of persons . . . this Court, taking into consideration the sum you have already paid, and the imprisonment you have already suffered, orders that you be committed to his Majesty's gaol of Newgate, and be there imprisoned for twenty-one calendar months.

Newgate prison, which squatted near Fleet Street, overshadowed by the dome of St Paul's, was a loathsome place. One unfortunate inmate described it as 'hell above ground'. For seven hundred years the prison had been a byword for death and depravity. By 1809 the prison held 486 prisoners within a space no larger than half an acre. Many were awaiting transportation to Botany Bay or their execution on the scaffold outside the prison gates. The arrangement of the buildings was simple. There were two windowless, brick-built blocks. The Common Side was for debtors, the poorest prisoners and the condemned; the Master's Side was reserved for those who could afford to pay for a little comfort and their food. For a fee of two guineas, however, and another ten shillings a week for the use of a barrack bed (seven shillings if shared), a prisoner could rent lodgings with the prison-keeper's family in State Side. State Side had twelve rooms holding up to four prisoners each. Unlike the King's Bench, prisoners could not buy out their room-mates to secure their privacy. The rooms, which were about 15 feet square, were allocated according to status. Prisoners in State Side were allowed to buy candles, food, beer and liquor, but were not allowed to visit each other's rooms. They were locked up from eight in the evening until eight in the morning.

These were the conditions in which Davison lived for almost the next two years. For a Northumbrian, it was torture. His only contact with the open (nowhere was fresh) air was to be had pacing up and down a very narrow outdoor corridor where

A view of the variety of people that Davison would have encountered inside Newgate prison.

he was continually jostled by other prisoners. He survived on the visits of Harriett and the children; as his second incarceration was far more shameful than his first, his more glamorous and aristocratic friends are unlikely to have made the trip to Newgate Street as they once had to the King's Bench. No letters of Davison's survive from this period. But even in these cruelly reduced circumstances he was not inactive, embarking on a scheme to lend money to the only man in London with a lower reputation than his own.

On the eve of the regency, the prince of Wales owed Davison over £11,000. To avoid any embarrassing disclosures of this indebtedness, the prince tried to secure, perhaps even extend, the debt against a selection of royal jewels probably belonging to his estranged wife, Princess Caroline. The sensitive negotiations were led by the prince's lawyers, Charles Bicknell and William Adam. Several meetings were held with Davison during August and September 1809 and, after tortuous discussions, the terms were agreed. The prince would personally seal the jewels into a case which would be delivered into Davison's care, though presumably not at Newgate. In return Davison would extend the debt for a further three years at 5 per cent interest. If the prince defaulted, Davison reserved the right to sell the jewels at auction. At the last moment it seems the government caught wind of this scheme and blocked it, clearing the debt with Davison and brokering a more respectable deal for the prince with Coutts' bank. Pawning the princess of Wales's jewels to a convicted criminal in Newgate prison was scandalous, even by the prince's own dissolute standards.

Davison was no doubt quite happy with this outcome, for the trial had taken a heavy toll on his finances. In November 1810 he was forced to mortgage Swarland Hall to the duke of Northumberland for £25,000. His own reputation in tatters and his businesses in disarray, Davison concentrated on salvaging his family's status by securing positions for his sons; and he was to have considerable satisfaction in seeing them prosper. In 1813

Percy, then a captain in the 18th Hussars, went to India with Lord Moira, the new governor-general of Bengal. Percy later allowed Nelson's letters to his father to be published by Sir Nicholas Harris Nicolas in his seven-volume *magnus opus*, *The Dispatches and Letters of Vice Admiral Lord Nelson*. Despite Sir Nicholas' urgings and his promise that he would print only those 'which you have no dislike to give to the world', Percy was slow in delivering the letters, most of which had to be included as an appendix to volume VII of the work in 1846. Sir Nicholas was particularly keen to include Nelson's letters to Davison before 1798, expressly asking Percy for them in December 1844. For some reason the letters were not forthcoming; possibly they were lost or with another member of the family at the time. This gap leaves Nelson's surviving correspondence with Davison beginning abruptly 'My dear Friend' in May 1797, fifteen years after they first met. Percy died in 1849.

William was bought a commission in the army after leaving Eton in 1806. Intriguingly, a William Davison is listed as unsuccessfully contesting the parliamentary seat of Milbourne Port the same year. Perhaps his father did not abandon his hopes of a political dynasty after all. In 1809 William went with his regiment, the 2nd Foot or 'Queen's Own', on the ill-starred expedition to the island of Walcheron, on the River Scheldt in Holland. The operation achieved little and ended in disarray, with more than four thousand troops dying from a cocktail of malaria, typhoid, dysentery and cholera. Sir Home Popham was the driving force behind the expedition, and though it turned so sour he displayed great personal skills of navigation during its course. 'Walcheron fever', which stalked the British army for years to come, thankfully spared William. He returned to embark on 'a tour of pleasure, information and improvement' to the Mediterranean and Middle East, accompanied by three aristocratic friends from his regiment: Lord Morfus, Lord Valentia and the Hon. Mr Burrell. The party was accompanied by 'experienced draughtsmen for the purpose of taking views of the different places of note and every ruin of antiquity'; in due course, Lord

Valentia would publish an account of the tour. From prison, Davison watched proudly as William enjoyed all the pleasures of a privileged upbringing that he himself had been denied.

William sailed on 1 November 1810, clutching letters of introduction including a number from Sir Sydney Smith to 'the different courts in his favour'. Sir Sydney, a freemason friend of Davison, Popham and Fulton, was a flamboyant naval officer who, following his exploits in Syria during 1799, defending Acre from an army led personally by Bonaparte, enjoyed a reputation – helped by his eccentric behaviour and dress – not unlike those later imperial heroes Gordon of Khartoum and T. E. Lawrence. For his efforts in the Middle East, Smith, like Nelson, had earned himself a *chelengk* from the sultan of Turkey.

William also had strict instructions to pay a visit to an old family friend who was now postmaster in Gibraltar. 'With him', his father wrote, 'you would find yourself at home and at ease.' At first Chevailler 'had no recollection' of the elegant young man standing in front of him. But when William delivered a letter from St James's Square, *Victory*'s former steward 'burst into tears with joy . . . with one breath asking 100 questions'. Over the next few days, before leaving to sail further up the Mediterranean, William spent many hours with his father's faithful old servant talking over the 'old times'. After Trafalgar, Earl Nelson had grudgingly employed his brother's steward until at least March 1806, when Chevailler demanded his wages. Irritated, the earl referred his brother's servant to Davison:

> at the same time I told him plainly that I thought he had no right to more than six months. Neither do I think he deserves it, as he has never been near us, & given us no assistance whatever in dividing the wines & other things which came from on board the Victory . . . you will recollect my Brother made him a present of above £40 last September.

Chevailler was still in London in September 1806, when he signed for his £4 12s 6d share in the £300,000 granted to veterans of the battle by the government, but he did not collect his prize money of £1 17s 6d the following April, indicating that he might already have left England. The position of postmaster at Gibraltar was an important one, responsible for managing the post to and from the ships in the Mediterranean. The place must surely have been secured for Chevailler through Davison's influence at the Navy Office. No doubt it afforded the former steward a peaceful and a comfortable end to his eventful life – if not a very rewarding one, for Davison's accounts show that Chevailler owed him money at least up to 1816. Chevailler was not the only man among his former shipmates in *Victory* to join the list of those indebted to Davison: even William Bunce, the ship's carpenter, left a bond at St James's Square for £100 six months before Trafalgar.

On William's return from his continental tour, Davison secured for him the place of aide-de-camp to the duke of Cambridge, the king's third son and governor of Hanover. William travelled out to Germany in early 1815. Although he missed the battle of Waterloo in June, he saw Wellington and the wounded in Brussels a few weeks later. News of the battle reached London on 21 June when Major Henry Percy, clutching Wellington's dispatches and four captured French Eagles, clattered into St James's Square to interrupt the prince regent's supper at number 16. It was a scene reminiscent of Chevailler's dash into the square ten years before bearing news of the arrival of *Victory* after Trafalgar. William eventually returned to England as a colonel, and with the knighthood denied his father.

The last years of Alexander Davison's life were beset by financial problems. On his release from Newgate in 1811 he ill-advisedly pursued the Treasury for £17,000 he claimed he was owed from the coal business. The Treasury counter-sued for over £40,000, a sum which included interest on the £30,000 Davison had earned while holding public money as agent of supply to the barrack office. When Davison indignantly refused to pay in August 1814, the attorney-general threatened him with bankruptcy. In a deal which protracted rather than resolved the dispute, Davison remortgaged Swarland Hall to the Treasury. He was also forced to borrow £10,000 from Philip Rundell, the maker of the Egyptian Club swords. The dispute took another twelve years to resolve, each side vigorously standing its ground. In the process it was revealed that in the ten years he had acted as the agent for the barrack office, which was only one strand of his business, Davison had received over £1,300,000 in payments from De Lancey for goods and commission, the equivalent of about £65 million today. In a rare surviving letter to her husband, Harriett blamed the 'humbugging' of the lawyers for his saga with the Treasury, accusing them of keeping him in 'perpetual hot water year after year to fill their own pockets'.

'I trust and hope events however unpleasant they may appear in perspective may turn out better than you expect,' she wrote in 1824:

> rely upon that Divine power, which has so often miraculously aided you in the hour of trial and given you fortitude & strength to support you through them and extricated you through difficulties which no human foresight could have anticipated, let us then pray in the present instance that he will not withdraw his goodness but enable you to struggle a little longer with those distressing and overwhelming transactions which have so often occurred and may the almighty of his infinite mercy ultimately make you carry off triumphant over your tormenting enemies.

After Davison took his case to court the Treasury was forced to take notice of some credits on his account and the ex gratia payment he made in 1809 while trying to stave off imprisonment. This reduced the charge to a little over £12,500, and Davison contrived to shave a further £1,000 from it by complaining to Lord Liverpool, the prime minister, that the Treasury's 5 per cent rate of interest was unfair. By this stage Davison needed every penny, for his long-running quarrel with the Treasury had taken place against the backdrop of another grave financial crisis. His bank, which had limped along for years, finally crashed in June 1816, owing £120,000. Only the intervention of the rival bank of Coutts saved Davison and his fellow partners from public humiliation or, as Middleton put it in a letter to his mother, 'the disgrace of our being gazetted through the realm, as a parcel of insolvent adventurers'. On 24 August a circular was sent to Davison & Co.'s few remaining customers informing them that their accounts were moving to Coutts, owing to 'the declining state of the health of some of the partners, added to some difficulties arising out of the peculiar situation of the times'. The deal with Coutts, however, did not absolve the partners of Davison & Co. of their liabilities, nor did it stop the recriminations and years of litigation over accusations of forgery and misappropriation of funds.

Hastings Middleton, who calculated that his family had already sunk more than £100,000 into the bank, bitterly regretted inheriting his partnership from his father: 'the pill was gilded . . . instead of inheriting a patrimony, I embraced ruin, alas!' He placed the blame for the disaster wholly on Davison. 'As a set off against the aid Mr Davison's presumed affluence afforded the Stratford Place Firm,' he wrote to William Leake, the bank's solicitor, who later found himself accused of colluding with Davison,

> the actual damage the new establishment sustained, from the unparalleled circumstance of it's Premier, being twice incarcerated, and every session of Parliament publicly quoted by name as a government creditor, may be justly opposed . . . that the effect of such stigmas were not chimerical, a reference to the sundries book, at the period of the punishments, will most satisfactorily show. I may truly add also that, even admitting the vast advantages the House derived in the first instance, from it's association with Mr Davison, for a series of years past, such advantages were withheld, with more than avaricious tenacity and above all,

through the last eighteen months of the commercial existence of the House. It was a matter of absolute surprise, not to say miracle, how it's doors were kept open, until the usual hour of shutting (five o'clock) for the truth of this fact I appeal to yourself, as well as to your knowledge, that Mr Davison was himself fully aware of the posture of affairs, and remained so perfectly supine, and insensible under it, as to admit a doubt of his sanity of mind! . . . As to his state of health being regarded as precarious I can only say, that, for one half of the ability to bustle about, and take exercise that he, to my certain knowledge, at this moment possesses, I would consent and cheerfully consent, never to desire to be more convalescent.

Venting his anger may have relieved Middleton's feelings, but it did not save the 'elegant' contents of his house in Charles Street from auction: they went under the hammer on 16 September 1816, three days before the bank's premises on Pall Mall were sold.

As so often before, John Wedgwood was bailed out by his brother Josiah. Josiah had predicted the calamity earlier in the year when he noticed that Davison and Noel had each withdrawn £15,000, 'as if scrambling to get as much as they could from the wreck'. As the longest-serving partner, Sir Gerard Noel's liabilities were enormous: almost £100,000. He was in no mood to pay. 'I have this moment information by the light of a circular letter', he wrote to Coutts on 23 August 1816,

that the affairs of Messrs Davison & Co are to be transfer'd to you; I take the liberty to acquaint you . . . that I have supported that House to the utmost of my power, & what income may remain to me — is trifling in bulk to the exigencies of the House . . . I add further, for your guidance, that nothing but legal compulsion will extort one shilling from me to sustain it further . . . my eldest son will do what he pleases but I advise him against paying any attention to their overtures.

His lordly attitude did not save Noel. A month later his estate in Rutland was sold off at the George inn in Stamford.

It was only a matter of time before Davison, too, received a knock on the door. On 25 August the auctioneer Charles Fairbrother wrote to Matthew Vizard, the lawyer handling the transfer to Coutts: 'It is impossible from the short time I have been allowed to look over the House in St James Square (the property of Alexander Davison Esq) to give you a correct estimate but I should consider the Freehold Premises, Furniture, library of books, Plate, Jewels, China, Collection of Paintings &c [to be] about fifty thousand pounds.' Davison claimed the contents had cost him 'upwards [of] £53,000' – about £2.6 million in today's terms (only £500,000 more than a handful of his relics would fetch in 2002).

By now the sale was unavoidable. The litigation with the Treasury had still to be settled, Swarland Hall was mortgaged to the hilt and few of Davison's personal debtors looked likely to settle. Moira had gone to India owing £11,000, Emma had died owing £1,200, Popham owed £6,000, and even the dependable Sir Evan Nepean was £50 in debt to his friend. To make matters even worse Davison, the agent for the battle of the Nile, owed £2,000 in unpaid prize money. It was a humiliating downfall.

'The Entire Property of ALEXANDER DAVISON, Esq.' took six months to catalogue and fourteen days to sell. The inventory opens a window into number 9 St James's Square. The sale began at noon on Monday 21 April, 1817 with twenty-four silver tablespoons, ending almost a thousand lots later with Zanetti's folio book *Greek and Roman Statues from the Originals*. In between came Davison's silver, his linen, his medals; his 'curious and valuable' watches (including one 'formerly the property of John Wilkes'), his jewels, his 'matchless' snuff boxes, his antique gems, his 'beautiful' seals, his 'magnificent' china; his 'curious' arms (including a sword 'worn by Oliver Cromwell' and no fewer than five pairs of duelling pistols); his Etruscan vases and 'superb' statuary; his enamels, miniatures, prints and paintings; and, for the final six days, his 'splendid collection of books'. Each time the hammer fell, another nail was hammered into the coffin of his status. Only Harriett's jewels escaped.

Davison could not afford to be sentimental, and many relics of Nelson were included in the sale. Ten Nile medals were offered, six in bronzed copper and four in silver, along with two china mugs by the Derby factory painted with the medal; the statuary urn; the Flaxman bust of Nelson; a wax model of Nelson by Samuel Percy; and endless books and prints on the admiral and his monuments. Although the purse escaped, the 'Nelson cenotaph' appeared on the fourth day.

> Lot 418: An OR-MULO CENOTAPH to the memory of the late Lord Nelson, surmounted by EIGHTY-FOUR GUINEAS, which are supported by four weeping Figures – THE GUINEAS WERE IN HIS LORDSHIP'S POCKET WHEN HE WAS KILLED AT THE BATTLE OF TRAFALGAR.

The cenotaph was sold to a Mr William Joy of Cheam in Surrey. It was admired at the Great Exhibition in 1851 before being sold again in December 1877, this time at Christie's, for £128 2s 0d. Fittingly James Griffin, the new owner, lived in Portsmouth, close to Victory. In 1923 the cenotaph was bought for £367 10s 0d by Lady Llangattock for her collection of Nelsonian memorabilia. In 1953 it was stolen from the Monmouth museum and, although it was later recovered, the guineas were lost for ever, having been broken off by the thief and allegedly sold for £100 in Bermondsey market.

The miniature of Emma for which Davison had paid her £200 in 1812 sold for 153 guineas. Another 'EXQUISITE MINIATURE of Lady Hamilton, with her hair and initials at the back, worn by the Immortal Nelson at the time of his Death', made only twenty-five guineas. Many of Davison's closest friends joined Nelson on the block. Among paintings by Stubbs, Gainsborough, Wouvermans, Devis and George Morland were portraits of Robert Mathews, Home Popham and Lord Moira.

The diamond anchor jewel which was the glittering key to the discovery of Alexander Davison's collection of Nelson treasures. Was this the 'brilliant anchor' repaired for Emma Hamilton by her jeweller John Salter?

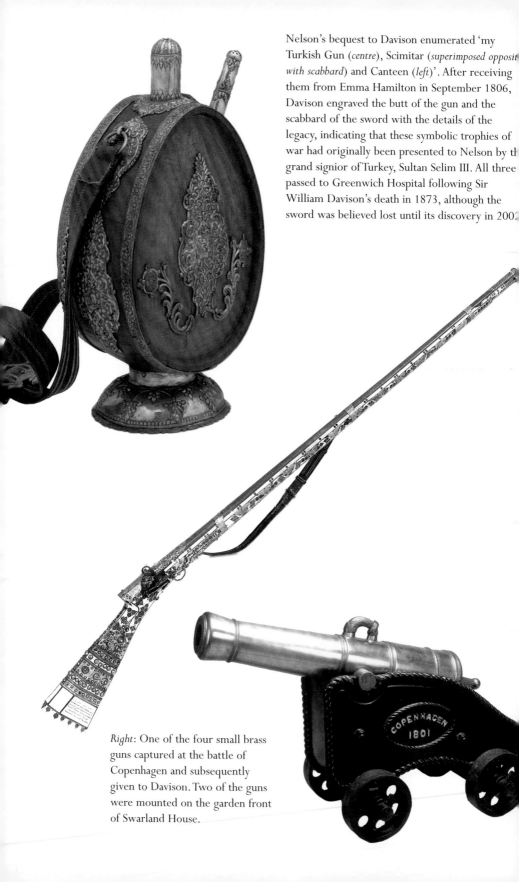

Nelson's bequest to Davison enumerated 'my Turkish Gun (*centre*), Scimitar (*superimposed opposit with scabbard*) and Canteen (*left*)'. After receiving them from Emma Hamilton in September 1806, Davison engraved the butt of the gun and the scabbard of the sword with the details of the legacy, indicating that these symbolic trophies of war had originally been presented to Nelson by the grand signior of Turkey, Sultan Selim III. All three passed to Greenwich Hospital following Sir William Davison's death in 1873, although the sword was believed lost until its discovery in 200[?]

Right: One of the four small brass guns captured at the battle of Copenhagen and subsequently given to Davison. Two of the guns were mounted on the garden front of Swarland House.

Alexander Davison as Lieutenant-Colonel of the Loyal Britons in a painting by Arthur William Devis of 1808. Davison is ostentatiously wearing Nelson's sword, bequeathed to him three years before.

Stephen Langton, Archbishop of Canterbury, shewing to the Barons of England, in the Abbey of St Edmund at Bury, the Charter of Liberties that had been granted by King Henry the First, and on which the Great Charter of King John was subsequently founded, painted by Arthur William Devis (*c.*1806) for Davison's gallery of history paintings. The barons were represented by their living descendants, including the duke of Northumberland, Earl Moira and Lord Erskine, who had defended Davison at Taunton (*see key on page 335*).

The Coal Contractor, or a New Way of supplying Government WHOLESALE by the BUSHEL.

Above: 'The Coal Contractor, or a New Way of supplying Government WHOLESALE by the BUSHEL': a satirical cartoon published 'by an Honest Scotchman' in February 1806 as pressure mounted for Davison to explain his dealings with the barrack office. Note the picture gallery behind the caricature of Davison at his desk and the admiral's hat and sword hanging on the wall in a scathing comment on his well-publicized friendship with Nelson.

Right: Davison's granddaughter and the keeper of the purse: Rosalie Davison, painted by Hermann Winterhalter in 1874.

Opposite page: The obelisk erected by Davison at Swarland after Trafalgar, 'not to commemorate the public virtues and heroic achievements of Nelson, which is the duty of England; but to the memory of a private friendship'.

ENGLAND EXPECTS EVERY MAN TO DO HIS DUTY

VICTORY 21ST OCTOBER 1805.

NELSON.

WHICH IS THE DUTY OF ENGLAND
BUT TO THE MEMORY OF PRIVATE FRIENDSHIP
THIS ERECTION IS DEDICATED BY
ALEXANDER DAVISON

Sotheby's

EST.1744

Sotheby's, London,
Monday 21 October,
2002: the purse is about
to begin a new chapter
in its remarkable story.

Richard Westall's *Melancholy*, which hung in Harriett's bedroom, was left unsold. Davison's collection of bespoke historical paintings survived until 28 June 1823 when they were offered by Mr Stanley at his rooms in Maddox Street, Hanover Square, with singular lack of success.

'My pictures had a bad sale,' Davison reported to William afterwards;

> they were chiefly bought in and which occasioned me much trouble vexation and pecuniary inconvenience — since the sale Lord Liverpool has bought the Chatham picture for £900, not half it's value, it was so very large I could do nothing with it — I shall by degrees get rid of the others — but they cause me much plague . . . no one was ever more sick of a place than I am of London and care not were I never to see it again.

After the auction the mansion in St James's Square, once the hub of Nelson's world, was sold to the duke of Northumberland; he died soon afterwards, leaving it to his son, the 3rd duke, to enjoy.

There was still Swarland, where Davison could shoot, ride and tackle the 'finny tribe' in the River Tweed. On summer days there were rides in the chaise with Elizabeth and Doddy, and afternoons spent idly watching Harriett tying her vines or examining her apple trees for 'what is called American blight'. The struggle was over — but he could not entirely escape, even here. Did anyone dare show him the note found one day by the obelisk to Nelson beside the Great North Road?

> Can Honour grace a mean and sordid mind,
> Though lightly veiled in courtly ostentation,
> Can Patriot worth a kindred spirit find,
> With the vile swindler of a freeborn nation,
> Shall Nelson's name thy character defend
> Debased mind, and base calumniator
> The liberty is gross, to call the Hero friend,
> Of a convicted, public peculator.

Local tradition attributed the cruel verse to Sir Walter Scott, who must have frequently passed the monument on his way between Edinburgh and London. If so it was a most unfriendly, if not unlikely, gesture from a fellow freemason.

Both twins were home for Christmas 1825, the cause for a great family celebration. All the estate workers and their families were invited to sit down to beef and plum pudding, washed down with strong ale and punch. At dusk the 'roaring' of the brass cannons given to Davison by Nelson after the battle of Copenhagen heralded 'as grand and brilliant display of fireworks as, perhaps, was ever seen in the North of England'. Several hundred spectators gathered on the Battle Park to watch. The following day, the horses were unharnessed from Davison's carriage and he was pulled by his estate workers through the village of Felton, accompanied by the local band, all the people 'anxious to testify their respect and gratitude to their generous benefactor'.

Davison did not entirely abandon London. He took lodgings in the Strand, then at 9 Pounell's Terrace in Lambeth, a world away from St James's Square. It was here, late one Monday evening three months after the fireworks at Swarland, with a glass of cherry brandy by his side, that he wrote a codicil to his will. In the codicil, which was never proved, he divided the remnants of his once great fortune equally and equitably among Harriett and his four surviving children. Percy, his eldest son, would receive just one-twelfth more than the others. He was in reflective, confessional mood as he explained why he did so. His family, he wrote,

> are all alike in sweetness of temper and affection and but for them I should years ago [have] sunk into my grave. I have to regret the sad, unjust, and persecuted spirit shown against me, [that] have reduced considerably my pecuniary concerns and which I am miserable to think will reduce that property I so laboriously and honestly gained . . . where I have failed I do not accuse myself of want of exertion nor of economy — for many years

*have I even deprived myself of many little indulgences — as to
expense and what is generally considered extravagance I have very
many years totally excluded from my house. I never kept a woman
nor did I ever gamble in my life, I name these because it has been
formerly hinted I was guilty of both indiscretions. They little
know me that attributed such a violent charge against me. My
wife and my fascinating family were ever uppermost in my mind,
and never imagined that I could do too much for their elevation,
prosperity and happiness.*

Eight months later, on 24 November 1826, Harriett died,
aged fifty-six. Her loss was a terrible sadness for her much older
husband. Davison, his indomitable spirit intact, lived on for three
more years, depriving 'the worms of Newton Church yard yet a
while of a feast tho' I had little left upon me to gratify them'. He
continued his trips to town, seeing the dentist, visiting his optician
in Coventry Street and having his hair cut and dressed in Mill
Street. Then, clutching a packet of souchong tea, bottles of lavender water and the *John Bull* newspaper, he would return to his
modest lodgings, across the river from the City and the great
dome of St Paul's.

EPILOGUE

THE DAY OF THE auction dawned. As they had once before, people came to watch Davison's belongings being sold – so many people, in fact, that another saleroom had to be opened at Sotheby's to accommodate them. This time, however, there was no sense of humiliation, only one of excitement, even celebration. Selling his collection in 1817 had destroyed Davison's reputation; the things he left behind would now resurrect it. The forgotten contents of his red morocco box, which had lain dormant for two hundred years, have flooded light into the darker recesses of Nelson's private life, revealing hidden loyalties and long-forgotten rivalries. The papers have completed Fanny Nelson's rehabilitation in the eyes of Nelson's biographers as a woman of equal stature to her bitter rival Emma Hamilton. In the words of Tom Pocock, the authority on Nelson who described the discovery of Davison's archive as the most significant relating to the admiral's life for more than a century, the women's letters 'open a window on to their shared lives that has been shut for two centuries'. Then there were the belongings – things they felt and breathed on; things (Pocock again) 'touched by the hand of history'. They have given us a fleeting physical intimacy with the now distant world that those remarkable people inhabited.

Davison's collection was catalogued into ninety-three lots.

For me, however, the success of the auction hinged on just one: Lot 79, 'Lord Nelson's Purse when Killed'. I had blindly estimated the purse, within minutes of first seeing it at the castle, at £60,000 to £80,000, though there was simply no auction market benchmark for such a relic. Its sale was uncharted territory for me, and for Sotheby's. Today, the twenty-one Georgian gold coins the purse contained are worth about £2,000; any price beyond that would be the value of its history. Too fragile to touch and difficult to display, the purse needed a buyer with vision, a person with the means to pursue and cherish a historical romance. At ten o'clock on the morning of 21 October 2002, Trafalgar Day, I was still uncertain we had found such a person, despite all the press attention in the purse's discovery. I knew too that if there was any doubt whatsoever in the authenticity of the purse, or in the story of its extraordinary odyssey, it would never be worth more than the gold it held. The result of the sale would be a judgement not only on the purse but also on me. With the glare of the world's media on the sale, the prospect of a very public personal disaster filled me with real dread. By the time I opened the auction – 'Lot one: two autograph letters by Maurice Nelson excitedly sending news of the victory of the Nile' – I was convinced the purse would fail to sell. To make matters worse, it was on display beside me on the rostrum, a constant reminder of the coming catastrophe.

The saleroom had an electric atmosphere and prices were strong from the start, yet throughout my mind was riveted to Lot 79, which approached as steadily as the British fleet at Trafalgar. Lot 19, the Derby wine-coolers with their as yet unexplained symbols, sold for almost £95,000, twice the expected price. The diamond anchor, the key to the discovery, sold for £160,000. Simple address leaves written by Nelson, no more than autographs, were selling to souvenir-hunters for up to £5,000 each, ten times the estimate. Normally I would expect to sell about a hundred lots an hour; yet so great was the competition for the physical remains of Davison's friendship with Nelson that over two hours had passed before I reached Lot 78: 'a seven barrelled flintlock goose rifle by Henry Nock'. In mint condition, the gun sold for £42,000. Davison's papers reveal he paid £40 for it on 21 July 1796.

There was then a palpable tension in the room as, with a deep breath, I announced the next lot. Camera lights came on and Sotheby's staff picked up telephones to talk to clients. This could mean serious interest – or simple eavesdropping by people unable to attend the sale. I paused, allowing the room to settle and the hubbub of anticipation to die away. The purse was about to take a step into the unknown, possibly changing ownership for only the second time since it was taken from Nelson as he lay dying in *Victory*. I had a sense of him watching at my shoulder.

I asked for £40,000. No-one moved. I asked again. The staff on the telephones ignored my pleading glance. I avoided the gaze of the owners sitting in the room. I could do nothing without a bid. Bewildering thoughts of disaster, which had been circling me for weeks, began crowding in. I felt the silent sympathy of the hundreds of people in front of me. With the purse's and my fate apparently sealed, I asked a final time, hoping my voice didn't betray the desperation I was feeling. Then, from somewhere among the sea of heads in front of me, a blue plastic bidding paddle was thrust firmly into the air, indicating real intent. Then another. Unable to hold back any longer, two clients on the telephones prompted bids. My spirits soared: not only was I now sure the purse would sell, but there was competition for it! Weeks of tension fell away. For the first time I began to enjoy, even to relish, the occasion. We moved smoothly up in increments of £5,000, effortlessly passing the critical hurdle of £60,000. At £100,000 I stepped up to £10,000 bids. At £200,000, £20,000 bids. There we stalled before ending, in a burst of applause, at £240,000. Taking into account Sotheby's fee, Nelson's purse had sold for £270,650. I had barely recovered my breath before Nelson's sword achieved an even higher price, selling for £336,650.

The purse remained in the saleroom until the end of the

auction, although to me it was already gone. From that day to this I have not seen it or touched it again. Having helped it on its way through history, relinquishing the purse caused me a surprising feeling of loss.

There was always the likelihood that Davison's collection would be irretrievably scattered around the world after the auction. And so it proved. Nelson, like Winston Churchill, is one of the few British historical figures who command an international following. Moreover, the discovery of his relics overseas prevented the British government blocking their export. Happily, however, after a valiant public appeal, the National Maritime Museum secured Fanny's letters to Davison for £138,650, ensuring that the single most important archive of papers in the auction will remain available to scholars in Britain. Appropriately, the Royal Naval Museum at Portsmouth, the custodian of *Victory*, secured William Chevailler's letters. More satisfying still, the British Library purchased many of Davison's private papers, confirming him as a figure of historical importance in his own right. These papers are now kept alongside no fewer than ninety volumes devoted to Nelson in the library's manuscript collection. With these few exceptions, everything else, from the diamond anchor to the Derby wine-coolers, is strewn around the world, the thread that bound them together irreparably snapped. Nelson's sword will never be reunited with its scabbard at the National Maritime Museum, although at least three lucky children – my own – stole a brief, thrilling opportunity to grasp it before it vanished again. It is to be hoped that one day the sword, and Nelson's purse, will re-emerge to cast their mesmerizing spell again.

Regret at the dispersal of the collection – and this, rather than any sense of jubilation, was the feeling I had as the saleroom emptied – should be tempered by the thought that Davison would not have shared it. He was an avid, even reckless, supporter of the principle of free trade, the primacy of the market and the sanctity of private ownership. Davison did, however, prize British history. Indeed, he built a gallery to celebrate it. No doubt he would have shared the thoughts of historian Andrew Roberts who, writing in the *Daily Mail* before the auction, remarked on the 'heavy and painful irony' if, on 'Trafalgar Day itself, these great British artefacts leave the very shores their original owner gave his life to defend'. In a quirk of fate linking those two illustrious families of the north, a year after Davison's descendants sold their Nelson treasures at Sotheby's the nation paid £22 million to prevent the current, 12th, duke of Northumberland selling an Italian picture to an American institution. Is a painting by Raphael worth a hundred Nelson purses to the British people? In an ideal world both would be saved. However, the Raphael remains at the National Gallery in London (with eight others), while Nelson's purse continues its extraordinary journey. Its sale, like the two men who have owned it, was controversial; yet its gloriously unexpected reappearance at the dawn of the twenty-first century proves that, even in our unideal, sceptical world, there is still room to dream.

APPENDIX I
THE PURSE

NELSON OWNED A 'miser' or 'stocking' netted silk purse. Among the most popular everyday types, stocking purses were often knitted by amateur needlewomen for their loved ones; in fact, by the 1790s there was a craze for doing so. Green silk was favoured as the colour was traditionally symbolic of love. In chapter 4 of *Vanity Fair*, Becky Sharp is discovered knitting a green silk purse 'for anyone who wants a purse'. Becky uses her activity to ensnare Jos Sedley, who 'before he had time to ask how . . . was actually seated *tête-à-tête* with a young lady, looking at her with a most killing expression; his arms outstretched before her in an imploring attitude, and his hands bound in a web of green silk, which she was unwinding'. The sexual possibilities suggested by the intimate nature of a purse, in its use and shape, would have been recognized by Thackeray's readers. A fragment of needlework by Emma Hamilton survives at the National Maritime Museum, but it seems far more likely that the purse was knitted for Nelson by Fanny. She would have seen the task of making such a highly personal item as the proper responsibility of a wife and as a demonstration of her domestic skills. If so, Fanny possibly purchased the necessary silk, or 'twist', from Thomas Gardom, who owned a shop on St James's Street which specialized in 'Purse-Twist, Tassels and sliders'.

Stocking purses were owned by men and women alike. This print after The sailor's orphans or Young Ladies subscription *by William Bigg clearly shows an example in use.*

The intriguing suggestion that the blood on Nelson's purse might be John Scott's came from a correspondent to *The Times* shortly after the sale of Davison's collection was announced in July 2002. It is well documented that Nelson fell on the spot where Scott had been killed a short time before. As stocking purses were generally worn looped over the waistband of a gentleman's breeches, Nelson's purse may very well have been stained with blood when he fell on the quarterdeck. The small gunshot wound to Nelson's shoulder is unlikely to have caused the stain, as it would have bled little and would have been quickly staunched. Alternatively, the purse might have been stained when the wounded Nelson reached the appalling conditions of the orlop deck. Another correspondent to *The Times*, Dr Ann-Mary Hills, pointed out that after Nelson was stripped, his uniform coat was rolled up and used as a pillow for another wounded officer beside him, one Midshipman Westphal. Dr Hills, who has made a study of Nelson's health, suggested that 'to find the accurate source of the blood on the newly discovered purse, DNA samples would be required from descendants of Nelson, John Scott and Westphal'. Dr Hills was not alone in suggesting that the bloodstain should be tested. In a further letter to *The Times*, John Munday, a former curator of the National Maritime Museum, called for a DNA 'doctor'. Such a man was Dr Peter Lamb, who very kindly offered to examine the purse at the government's Forensic Science Laboratory at Huntingdon. Unfortunately, however, the blood-staining was centuries outside the scope of non-intrusive testing. Any comprehensive investigation of the stain, or attempt to recover DNA from it, would require either the removal of material from the purse or the application of chemicals to it, both of which were unthinkable, particularly for so little gain. For the time being, the bloodstain on the purse keeps its mystery, as it should.

Another purse once claimed to have belonged to Nelson. Item number 3168 at the Royal Naval Exhibition held at Chelsea Hospital in May 1891 was catalogued as a

Small blue silk netted purse *with mouth at one end, opening with two metal pins, finished with ball ends of pearl (one ball missing). The other end of the purse is ornamented with a single ball of pearl of larger size. A sliding ring of ivory would keep the contents of the purse in their place. This purse belonged to Vice-Admiral Lord Nelson and was constantly used by him. It was removed from his dead body by Captain (afterwards Sir T. M.) Hardy in the cock-pit of the Victory immediately after Nelson's death, on October 21st, 1805, and was retained by Captain Hardy as a memento. The purse at that time contained a gold guinea, which has since been lost. The purse continued in the Hardy family until some years ago, when it was purchased by the present owner.*

Apart from this rival purse's doubtful provenance, its complete lack of documentary evidence and the known sequence of events after *Victory* reached England, it seems impossible that Hardy would have taken anything belonging to Nelson 'as a memento' after the battle, particularly money. The purse emerged again at an exhibition of Nelson relics at the Royal United Services Institution in 1905 (this time accompanied by another purse said to have belonged to Captain Hardy), before eventually disappearing into the reserve collection of the National Maritime Museum. It can be dismissed as belonging to that breed of fakes, forgeries and impostors which flourished in the years after Trafalgar. As early as 1846, Sir Nicholas Harris Nicolas, the editor of Nelson's letters and dispatches, complained in *The Times* about 'the manufacture of Nelsonian relics, swords, buckles &c'. The universal fascination with Nelson's purse, redolent of fetishistic qualities, suggests that interest in anything proven to have belonged to the admiral, far from diminishing as the years pass, is still growing.

THE SALE

...Sotheby's Press Release Monday 21 October 2002...
**NELSON COLLECTION RAISES £2.1 MILLION ON
TRAFALGAR DAY**
*Historic archive saved for the nation by the National
Maritime Museum*

THE LAST historic collection directly associated with Admiral Horatio Lord Nelson ever likely to appear on the market sold for a staggering £2,130,029 at Sotheby's in London today – Trafalgar Day – Monday, October 21, 2002. The total is more than three times the pre-sale estimate.

The collection belonged to Alexander Davison, Nelson's friend, treasurer and closest advisor, and included an astonishing group of precious objects, arms and swords, papers and relics with direct provenance to Nelson. Amazingly, it has remained unknown to the world for almost 200 years. Speaking after the sale Sotheby's specialist, Martyn Downer said: 'This has been a thrilling journey of discovery that has culminated in this fabulous result. It is not only a testament to the abiding fascination with Nelson shared around the world, but also to the extraordinary friendship that Nelson had with his friend, Alexander Davison.'

Half an hour before the auction the saleroom was so packed that an adjacent gallery was opened up to alleviate congestion. The first lot to draw gasps from the saleroom was lot 13 – Davison's Egyptian club sword – which sold for £270,650 (est: £60,000–80,000). Next up, a diamond brooch shaped as an anchor and bearing the initials 'H.N' sold for £160,650 (est: £100,000–150,000). The brooch, which was believed to be a personal gift to Lady Hamilton from Nelson, was modelled for the occasion by an Emma Hamilton look-a-like. Moments later, the much-awaited bloodstained purse that Nelson carried on the day of the battle of Trafalgar sold for £270,650 (est: £60,000–80,000). The purse still contained the 21 gold coins that Nelson placed in it on the morning of his death.

The highest price of the day was paid for Lord Nelson's scimitar, which achieved £336,650, far surpassing its pre-sale estimate of £60,000–£80,000. The sword was believed lost by scholars and it was not until Sotheby's carried out further research that the sword was matched with its original scabbard now displayed in the National Maritime Museum, on loan from Greenwich Hospital in London.

A remarkable archive of 72 previously unknown and highly revealing letters to Davison from Lady Nelson were saved for the nation today when they were purchased by the National Maritime Museum, London, for £138,650 (est: £50,000–80,000). The series throws new light on the personality of Frances Nelson, the hero's wronged and virtually forgotten wife. Another letter, this time written by Nelson's lover, Emma Hamilton, after the battle of Trafalgar sold for £31,070 against an estimate of £9,000–12,000. In it, she pours out her heart to Davison about the loss of her beloved Nelson.

An important pair of previously unrecorded presentation wine coolers in Derby porcelain made to commemorate the Battle of the Nile sold for £94,650. The pair was estimated at £40,000–60,000.

NOTES ON SOURCES

ABBREVIATIONS

ADC	'Nelson: The Alexander Davison Collection', sale catalogue, Sotheby's, London, 21 October 2002
ANQ	*Archives nationales du Québec*
AQC	*Ars Quatuor Coronatorum*
BL Add.	British Library Additional Manuscripts
BL Eg.	British Library Egerton Manuscripts
EXTON	Exton papers, Leicestershire Record Office
MON	Llangattock papers, Monmouth
Morrison	*The Hamilton and Nelson Papers*
Naish	*Nelson's Letters to his Wife*
Nicolas	*Dispatches and Letters of Vice-Admiral Lord Viscount Nelson*
NLS	National Library of Scotland
NMM	National Maritime Museum
PRO	Public Record Office
RA	Royal Archives
RNM	Royal Naval Museum, Portsmouth

For full titles and publication details of these and other works referred to below, see the bibliography.

UNLESS OTHERWISE STATED, Nelson's letters to Davison are printed in Nicolas; Nelson's correspondence with his wife, and other family letters, are in Naish; Nelson's letters to Emma are printed in Morrison. Fanny Nelson's letters to Davison, formerly ADC Lot 85, are now all in NMM DAV/2. Emma Hamilton's letters to Davison are in BL Add. 40739 (1804–06) and NMM LBK/7 (1806–14). Davison's letters to Nelson are in BL Add. 34908 and NMM CRK/3; those in ADC Lot 70 are now in an overseas private collection.

Throughout the text I have transcribed letters and contemporary documents without amendment, except for minor adjustment of spelling and punctuation where necessary to clarify – especially in the 'stream-of-consciousness' style favoured by Emma Hamilton.

CHAPTER I

Beatty, Burke and Alexander Scott all left accounts of Nelson's death. The description of events before the battle began, however, is my own. Chevailler's mission to London can be pieced together using letters from Earl Nelson (BL Add. 34992 fo. 41) and Emma Hamilton to Captain Hardy, and those from the earl (ADC Lot 90, now BL Add. 79200 fo. 9) and Hardy (NMM MSS 52/044) to Davison and to Emma (Pettigrew, *Memoirs*, vol. 2, pp. 549–50). Harriet Blackwood's letter to Emma from Portsmouth revealing that Hardy held papers of Nelson's that 'will prove highly gratifying and satisfactory to you' is printed by Pettigrew, *Memoirs*, vol. 2, p. 549. *Victory's* log is PRO ADM 51/4514. A copy of George Rose's letter to Emma assuring her of his help is printed in his diary (Harcourt, ed., *Diary and Correspondence*). Davison's library has been re-created using the catalogue to the auction of the contents of St James's Square in 1817. Nelson's last letter to Davison was ADC Lot 76. PRO PRIS 7/23 reveals that Arthur William Devis was released from the King's Bench prison on 28 November 1805. Nelson's autopsy was recorded by Beatty and reported to Earl Nelson by Alexander Scott (BL Add. 34992 fo. 39). The ball that killed Nelson is in the Royal Collection at Windsor Castle; his bloodstained uniform is at the NMM. Details of the meetings in Clarges Street and St James's Square can be gleaned from Haslewood's correspondence with Earl Nelson in NMM MSS 80/050. The wrapper for Nelson's pocket book was ADC Lot 77. It is now in a private collection. The book itself is in the National Archives at the Public Record Office. Tyson's 'list of the sundries in the trunk sent from the Victory by Capt Blackwood and opened 16 Decr 1805' is BL Add. 34992 fo. 52. Before noting the value of the larger 'leather' purse, Tyson turned the inventory over and scrawled a quick calculation of its contents on the back. Davison's 'confidential' letter to the prince is RA GEO/40496. A copy of the prince's reply was ADC Lot 81; it was also reproduced by Fitzgerald, *Life of George the Fourth*. The document entitled 'Money, Coins in Lord Nelson's Pocket Purse &c when killed' was found in the purse two hundred years later. Gaps where text is lost on the original have been filled on my own supposition. It is known, for instance, that Nelson carried a 'red case' for his private papers when at sea. In August 1801 he complains to Emma, in a letter printed in Pettigrew, *Memoirs*, vol. 2, p.150, that his servant had forgotten to bring on board *Medusa* at Harwich 'my red case . . . there's £200 in it, and all my papers'. Nicolas prints Nelson's last will and eight subsequent codicils (including the final one) in full in vol. 7, pp. ccxxi–ccxl. The wrapper for a previously unrecorded codicil dated 2 May 1804 was found among Davison's papers (ADC Lot 68). It may have once held a copy of a codicil dated 7 April in which Nelson bequeathed £100 a year to Maurice Nelson's 'widow' Sukey, the annuity to be held in trust by Davison.

CHAPTER III

Alexander Davison left a brief two-page journal of his movements from his arrival in London in April 1767 until he reached Quebec in May 1773. This was in ADC Lot 92; it is now BL Add. 79200 fo. 29. The journal is supplemented by the discovery, in May 2004, of a letter book containing transcripts of over eighty letters written to him by his family during the same period. Hancock, *Citizens of the World*, gives a vivid picture of the life of an eighteenth- century London merchant. The Davison family pedigree is examined in vols 7 and 9 of Reid et al., eds, *A History of Northumberland*. The lower town of Quebec is much as it was when Alick arrived, though the cul-de-sac harbour where he, and later Nelson, stepped ashore has been filled in to form a car park and ferry terminal. Rue Côte-de-Montaigne is, however, as perilous as ever. The Maison Chevalier, on the old quay, gives a good impression of life inside the house of a prosperous merchant. Number 13 rue St Pierre stands in stony anonymity. Burt, *The Old Province*, is a good guide to the early years of the British in Quebec. Many of Alick's friends and rivals are in the *Dictionary of Canadian Biography* (gen. ed. G.W. Brown). George Davison has qualified for a separate entry ahead of his brother, presumably because of his services to Canadian agriculture. Like his merchant peers, Alick was very litigious while in Canada. This habit has left a useful paper trail of his activities in the records of the court of common pleas at the ANQ. The entertaining story of Alick's visit to the American colonies is revealed, for instance, in ANQ-Québec TL 18/1501. Hugh Percy's letters to his father from Boston are printed in De Fonblanque, *Annals of the House of Percy*, vol. 2. Alick's role in the defence of Quebec in November 1775 is revealed in Thomas Ainslie's *Journal of the Most Remarkable Occurrences in Quebec, since Arnold Appear'd before the Town on the 14th November 1775* (in Cohen, ed., *Canada Preserved*). The orderly books of Captains Anthony Vialar and Robert Lester of the British Militia give occasional glimpses of Davison during his brief military career. Details of Mary Simpson's family and early life can be gathered from the *Quebec Gazette* and from the journal and letter books of her cousin James Thompson, the surveyor-general at the garrison and masonic deputy grand master of Quebec. These are preserved at ANQ-Québec P450 (Literary and Historical Society of Quebec Collection) 1960-01-544/1. *Albemarle*'s log covering Nelson's visit to Quebec is PRO ADM 51/24. Haldimand's secret correspondence with London over the summer of 1782 is in BL Add. 21705. His letter confirming Nelson's departure for New York is BL Add. 21716 fo. 3. Nelson's letter to his father on leaving Canada ('I have not had much success in the prize way, but it is all in good time') is BL Add. 34988 fo. 33. The letter is also printed in Nicolas, vol. 2. Captain Worth's peremptory order to Nelson to join him at Bic 'without a moment's delay' is at BL Add. 21800 fo. 344. Nelson's request for a pilot to steer *Albemarle* in the 'gulph of St Lawrence' is BL Add. 21800 fo. 342. Nelson's brief stay in Quebec and his friendship with Alick were explored in the 1994 BBC radio drama *Post Captain at Quebec*. In the drama, Davison is given a Tyneside accent, although he is more likely to have spoken in the softer north Northumbrian dialect.

CHAPTER IV

Davison's chambers at Lincoln's Inn were identified by Dr Cliff in 'Alexander Davison's chambers'. Examination of the surviving records at Lincoln's Inn reveals the extent of the remarkable network of legal and professional associates that Davison had formed by the 1780s and that would support him throughout his career. His letter of thanks to Haldimand for the award of the contract to supply the Indian presents is in BL Add. 21705. Haldimand's praise for the quality and condition of the presents on their arrival in Quebec is in BL Add. 21716 fo. 99. His proposal to Lord North that Davison ('a merchant of eminence & whose conduct and attachment to His Majesty's government I have experienced ever since my arrival in the Province') should fill the next vacancy on the legislative Counsel is in BL Add. 21716 fo. 70. The governor's recommendation that the Davisons should be awarded the lease for the king's posts is at BL Add. 21718 fo. 5. Davison's ebullient letter to his father written from Poole in May 1785 was in ADC Lot 92, now BL Add. 79200 fo. 31. The struggle for the leases to the king's posts is played out in Haldimand's papers in BL Add. 21718–36. Haldimand recorded his private thoughts on the affair, and on the Davisons, in French in his diary, which is at BL Add. 21890–2. A translated version was published in full in *Report on Canadian Archives*. Notes on Davison's later bitterly contested court case with Dunn & Co., which reveal fascinating detail on the king's posts, are in ANQ TP7/123 and ANQ TP. 18/3386. The certificate which Davison received upon becoming a master mason was published in C. O. Davison, *Davison, Alexander and his Descendants*. Davison's comments about his partner John Lees are in a letter to Haldimand in BL Add. 21737 fo. 349. Davison's letter to Thomas Parry of the East India Company outlining his plan to make the best use of *Daedalus*' voyage to New South Wales was in ADC Lot 92; it is now BL Add. 79200 fo. 33. His key role in the establishment of the convict colony emerges from Bladen and Britton, eds, *Historical Records of New South Wales*. Davison discusses the cost of freight to Botany Bay in a letter to George Chalmers at the Office of Trade in BL Add. 38227 fo. 207. George Matcham's letter revealing a hitherto unsuspected early contact between Davison and Nelson's family is reproduced in Bladen and Britton, eds, *Historical Records of New South Wales*, vol. 1, part 2, pp. 590–1. Davison's interesting correspondence with Lieutenant Governor John Simcoe is in Cruikshank, ed., *Correspondence*. Maitland's letters are in a private collection. The duke of Northumberland's comments about the Portuguese playing 'fast and loose' are quoted by Davison in a letter to Nepean at PRO FO 95/8/8. Davison's appointment as commissary-general to Lord Moira's army is at PRO WO58/166. PRO T64/121 is his meticulously kept letter book recording his correspondence with Charles Long, the secretary to the Treasury, from November 1793 to May 1796. The letters deal with the minutiae of the commissariat's work: everything from the cost of horses for the Royal Artillery (26 guineas each) to the supply of liquor to the men in the military hospital at Southampton ('3 pints per man per day'). PRO AO 3/233 reveals the subsequent ten-year struggle Davison had with the Treasury to close the commissariat's accounts, which were riddled with irregularities. Payments totalling more than £10,000 from the commissariat to Lord Moira remained unaccounted for as late as 1808. A fascinating series of letters written by Maurice Nelson to Sukey from Exeter and Cowes is preserved in NMM CRK/22/HAM/81. Henry Angelo witnessed the appalling scenes which followed the arrival of Lord Howe's prizes after the 'Glorious First of June'. He commented that the British shot appeared to have ripped through the French ships 'like that of a ploughshare on the earth': *Reminiscences*, vol. 2, p. 221. Angelo was accompanied by his friend the artist Thomas Rowlandson, who made a number of drawings of life on the south coast during Davison's time there. General De Lancey's letter inviting Davison to be agent of supply to the barrack office is reproduced, together with Davison's reply, in *The Third Report of the Commissioners of Military Enquiry*. Life at Swarland House has been re-created using papers in a private collection. These include Davison's strict instructions to his servants. The delightful church of St Mary-the-Virgin in Langley, where the body of little Harriett Davison was interred, is unchanged, though the village has been submerged by modern development. The impressive Gosling monument is in the chancel. Beside it is the 'Family vault of Alexander Davison 1796'. An inscription reveals that William Davison inspected the vault in 1855 following which, it seems, he removed his sister's remains to Northumberland.

CHAPTER V

Davison's comments about the political and military situation in early 1797 were to Simcoe. Details on the Percy Tenantry are in the Northumberland papers at Alnwick and on microfilm at BL M309 fo. 178. Maurice Nelson reports his return to the Navy Office in BL Add. 34988 fo. 208; his comment about 'artful people behind the curtain' is in the same letter. The machinations of the so-called 'Armed Neutrality' against Pitt's administration are exposed in the Northumberland papers (M309 fos 182–207) and in Aspinall, ed., *Correspondence of George, Prince of Wales*. Maurice's expectation that his brother would do the right thing regarding the prize agency after the battle of St Vincent is at BL Add. 34988 fos 208–9. In the same letter Maurice announces his reinstatement at the Navy Office, though he complains that William Marsh (a member of the Navy Board) tried to block the appointment: 'he might at least have been a silent spectator'. Nelson's reply to Davison's overt request for the agency (the earliest surviving letter between the two men) is in Nicolas, vol. 7, p. cxxxviii. Dundas' praise for Nelson after the battle of the Nile is in BL Add. 34907 fo. 394. His revealing comments to the first lord are in Spencer, *Private Papers*, vol. 4, pp. 186–7. Maurice's excited note to Davison upon first hearing of the victory was in ADC Lot 1. Davison's appointment as Nelson's agent after the battle of the Nile is printed in Nicolas, vol. 7, p. clxi, alongside the brusque letter Nelson wrote his brother informing him of the decision. Intriguingly, the original letter to Maurice, which is BL Eg. 2240 fo. 21, came to the British Library with Davison's papers. Maurice's hurt reaction to his brother's rebuff is in BL Add. 34988 fo. 282. Nelson's apology is in MON E604. Davison's elation at his engagement is evident in his letter of thanks to Nelson at BL Add. 34907 fo. 426. Davison's clumsy suggestion of bribing a commissioner at the Navy Board is mentioned by Maurice in a letter to his brother in BL Add. 34988 fo. 333. A large quantity of papers concerning the prize money for the battle of the Nile, including revealing material on the jostling of the other agents for a share in the lucrative business, was found in Davison's collection. They were bought as ADC Lot 2 by the National Maritime Museum. They are now in NMM DAV/3. Much of Davison's correspondence with Nelson about Nile prize money issues, including discussion about the ships destroyed after the battle, is in BL Add. 34908. Davison's letter announcing his idea of making a medal and distributing prints after the Abbott portrait of Nelson is in BL Add. 34908 fos 188–9. The print was published on 19 December 1798. The king 'said he thought it very like'. The declaration of the Nile captains that they were forming themselves into the 'Egyptian Club' and their resolution to present Nelson with a sword are at BL Add. 34907 fo. 142. The development of the Nile medal can be followed in the correspondence between Davison, Budge and Boulton preserved in the Boulton & Watt archives at the Birmingham Central Library (*Industrial Revolution*, 1st ser.; available on microfilm from Adam Matthew Publications Ltd). Mary Simpson's letter to Robert Mathews is quoted by Pocock in *Nelson's Women*; their marriage is recorded in the register of St George's Church, Hanover Square.

CHAPTER VI

Saumarez' letter of support to Davison was ADC Lot 2, now NMM DAV/3/3. Of all the Egyptian Club captains, it seems Berry and Saumarez were the closest to Davison. Orde's tetchy query later regarding Davison's suitability as a prize agent is in Pettigrew, *Memoirs*, vol. 2, p. 81. Davison's anxiety about the various 'insinuations' which greeted his appointment is revealed in his letter book from 1798, which was ADC Lot 70 and is now in a private overseas collection. The description of the (now lost) piece of plate Davison presented to Nelson after the battle of the Nile was ADC Lot 15; another copy is in NMM CRK/3. Davison's uncomfortable annotation informing Nelson of Fanny's intention to travel to Naples ('excuse a woman's tender feelings') is on a letter at BL Add. 34908 fos 260–1. The comments of the master of *Lady Nelson* were in ADC Lot 92 and are now at BL Add. 79200 fo. 39. 'The Derby porcelain Manufactory Agency Warehouse' was at number 21 Henrietta Street on the corner of Bedford Street. According to its advertisements in the *Morning Herald*, the warehouse offered the 'usual stock of extensive variety of Dinner, Dessert, and Tea Services, Cabinet ware of every description, Flower Pots &c; of the Derby Manufacture only, and at the lowest prices'. Details of Davison's collection of Derby porcelain are taken from the 1817 sale catalogue of the contents of St James's Square. By family tradition his Derby 'nautical service', which was ADC Lots 31–49, was a gift to him from Nelson. Fanny's gentle reprimand to Josiah is in BL Add. 34988 fo. 302. Davison's offer to be 'general agent' for 'the king of Naples and his followers' is added as a postscript in a letter to Nelson at BL Add. 34909 fo. 194. He formally presents the medal as a token of his 'respect' to Nelson in a letter at BL Add. 34909 fo. 387. Davison reports the confirmation (from William Huskisson) of the East India Company's £10,000 award to Nelson in BL Add. 34911 fo. 105. In a rare surviving letter to Fanny written in September 1798 at BL Add. 34908 fo. 27, Davison suggests that the £10,000 be left in trust with himself and Lieutenant Locker until Nelson's return to England. Sir Peter Parker's letter thanking Davison for 'your most elegant present, *to me invaluable*' was ADC Lot 10. Nelson's letter of thanks on behalf of the 'brethren of the Nile' is in Nicolas, vol. 7, p. clxxxix. Grenville's request for medals is in BL Add. 34912 fos 162–3. In the same letter Davison proudly announces the birth of Nelson's namesake and encloses a copy of the circular soliciting subscriptions for the naval pillar. His displeasure at the delay to the distribution of the Nile prize money caused by the missing muster books to *Alexander*, *Goliath* and *Zealous* is in BL Add. 34913 fos 56–7. Confirmation of the delivery to St James's Square of 'the sword ordered by your captains intended for you as a present from them in commemoration of the Glorious 1st Augt 1798' is a postscript to BL Add. 34913 fo. 69. The despatch of the sword to the Mediterranean in *Superb* is mentioned in the *Naval Chronicle* vol. 2, 1799, p. 441. Surviving correspondence in Davison's papers from Thoresby Hall (formerly ADC Lot 92, now BL Add. 79200 fos 65–8) suggests that he was familiar with the estate, and therefore presumably with the Nile pyramid.

CHAPTER VII

The goings-on at Bedford Street have been re-created from Howell, *Cobbett's Complete Collection of State Trials*, the *Third Report of the Commissioners of Military Enquiry*, and inquiry documents and correspondence held at the Public Record Office. Wilkinson's fatal comments about Davison's 'suspicious disposition' are in PRO TS11/684. Edington's tip-off to the Treasury is reproduced as appendix no. 25 in the *Third Report*. Davison confirms he has accepted a vice-presidency for Nelson in the 'Asylum' in BL Add. 34911 fo. 105. The 1803 summary of his assets shows that Davison held £500 worth of shares in Drury Lane at the time. He responded generously to the petition for funds to rebuild the theatre after it was destroyed by fire in 1809, a copy of which was found among his papers and is now at BL Add. 79200 fo. 69. By 1816, the year Sheridan died, Davison held almost £4,500 worth of shares in the new Drury Lane theatre. The glittering dinner party at St James's Square was reported by the *Sun* on 16 April 1800. The scathing remarks of the *Roi d'armes* were in ADC Lot 92, now BL Add. 79200. A copy of Huskisson's 1796 declaration of his intent to represent Morpeth as MP by renting land (at £300 a year) from Davison in the constituency is preserved at BL Add. 38759 fo. 34. Earl St Vincent's outrage at Nelson's bid for the Spanish prize money was clearly evident in ADC Lot 26, now in a private collection. Davison's opinion of the earl's memorial was in ADC Lot 29. Fanny quotes Davison's comment 'I shan't lose one farthing . . .' in a letter to her husband in Naish p. 556. Davison's jubilant cry: 'he is coming home . . .' is in Morrison, vol. 2, p. 103. The fateful meeting between Fanny and Emma at Nerot's hotel is well played by Vivien Leigh and Gladys Cooper in Alexander Korda's 1941 film *That Hamilton Woman!* 'Nilus: an ode on the Battle of the Nile' is at BL Add. 34990 fo. 95. Nilus (the dog) strayed soon after Nelson gave him to Emma. Despite an advertisement in the *Morning Herald* and the offer of a one guinea reward, he was never seen again. Rundell & Bridge's estimate for the plate voted to Nelson by Lloyd's after the battle of the Nile was in ADC Lot 24; the bill itself was ADC Lot 25. The 'strong iron-bound wainscot chest' is on display at the Royal Naval Museum, Portsmouth. Nelson's order for Davison to arrange a 'man party' is at BL Eg. 2240 fo. 33. The dinner Davison held in Nelson's honour was reported on 1 December in the *Morning Herald* and *Morning Chronicle*. The careful list Fanny prepared of her husband's Nile gifts is now with her letters to Davison at the NMM. An inventory of Nelson's belongings in store with James Dodds and of the wines in the cellar of St James's Square in March 1801 is at BL Add. 34990 fo. 10. Earl St Vincent's prediction to Nepean that 'much brouillerie' would greet Nelson on his return to London is cited by Keate, *Nelson's Wife*, p. 191. The earl's caustic remark regarding Nelson's dash around every painting studio in London is quoted in Walker, *The Nelson Portraits*, p.120. Nelson's reception at court is recorded in George Rose's diaries (Harcourt, ed., *Diaries and Correspondence*, vol. 1, p. 219). Details on Nelson's split from Fanny can be gleaned from the various legal papers sold in ADC Lot 86. Harrison, *Life of . . . Nelson*, claims that Davison was given charge of the Nelsons' separation. Nelson's last conversation with Fanny before leaving for Torbay is printed verbatim by Clark and M'Arthur, *The Life of Admiral Lord Nelson*, vol. 2, p. 380. Perhaps it was reported by Davison, who heard it from Fanny. Emma's ironic sympathy for Fanny was in a letter sold from the Bullock Collection in ADC Lot 229. Martha Lady St Vincent's letter remarking on Nelson's strained appearance was in ADC Lot 30. St Vincent's remarks to Nepean are in NMM AGC J/6. Nelson's stinging riposte is in BL Eg. 2240 fo. 53. The earl's plan to clear up the 'flagrant abuses' in the navy was revealed in a letter to the duke of Northumberland in Bonner Smith, *Letters of . . . the Earl of St Vincent*. Nelson's note to Davison to seek advice before risking the short journey out to *San Josef* is in BL Eg. 2240 fo. 47. Nelson's list of his Nile jewels, where he mentions the 'Star from Gr^d S^r', is at BL Add. 34988 fo. 380. An inventory of the Nile service of silver made by Rundell & Bridge is at BL Add. 34990 fos 7–9. For Harriett Davison's tour of *St George* see Pettigrew,

Memoirs. Bjelajac, in *Washington Allston*, points out that Flaxman, the sculptor chosen to prepare the memorial to Miller, was 'steeped . . . in Masonic mysticism'. The receipt for Davison's clandestine purchase, on Nelson's behalf, of Romney's painting of Emma from James Christie was in ADC Lot 50. Fraser, in *Beloved Emma*, has identified the picture as *Lady Hamilton as St Cecilia*.

CHAPTER VIII

The estimate from Rundell & Bridge for 'an addition of Plate to Lord Nelson's service' after the battle of Copenhagen was ADC Lot 52. Davison's 'most secret' appeal to Earl St Vincent on Maurice Nelson's behalf was in ADC Lot 26. His affronted reply to Nelson's implication that he was abusing his position is printed in Naish, pp. 573–4. Edmund's discreet enquiry about Maurice's marital position is in NMM HAM/82. Nelson christens Sukey as an 'honor'd wife' in BL Eg. 2240 fo. 87. Davison's tentative approach to Fanny after her split from Nelson, 'I have long wished to write to you', is in Naish, p. 588. Edward Parker's reports to Davison from Deal, including his revealing remark about 'that B——' Lady Hamilton, were in ADC Lot 53. Davison's bleak reaction to news of the boy's death is in Morrison, vol. 2, p. 171. Gamlin, *Nelson's Friendships*, suggests that Horatia was Parker's child by an unknown mother, adopted by Nelson. Notice of Davison's instructions to his bankers to pay Nelson whatever he needs is printed in Morrison, vol. 2, p. 171. The debate in the House of Lords on the peace terms with the French is reported in Cobbett and Wright, eds, *Cobbett's Parliamentary History of England*, vol. 36. A letter from Davison to Huskisson arranging the shipping of supplies to the Cape Colony in January 1798 is at BL Add. 38735 fo. 1. His receipts for payments totalling more than £55,000 for the goods are at BL Add. 38769 fos 337 and 470. Henry Dundas' brother, Francis, was acting governor of the Cape colony from 1798 to 1799. The best description of Merton Place is by Warwick, 'Here was Paradise'. A glimpse of Maurice Nelson's 'old black servant James Price' is in Gérin, *Horatia Nelson*, p. 47. Emma returned from Naples in 1800 with her own black female servant ('from Egypt, a Negress, about 20 years of age') who was subsequently christened Fatima Emma Charlotte Nelson Hamilton. Fanny's letter to her husband, returned to her with Davison's devastating annotation, is in MON. It is printed in Naish, p. 596.

CHAPTER IX

Query no. 24 is buried within PRO TS/11/681/2162. Davison's casual attempt to correct the error is revealed in Bowering's later testimony (see *Third Report of the Commissioners of Military Enquiry*). The clandestine meetings to discuss the plan to bribe the voters at Ilchester have been reconstructed using evidence given to the parliamentary select committee appointed to investigate the election and from Davison's trial papers, which are in PRO TS11/726. Details on Robert Mathew's career are taken from the *Dictionary of Canadian Biography* (gen. ed. G. W. Brown). Davison's continued close contact with Mary and Robert in London (dining with them '*en famille*') is revealed in a letter to Sir Robert Barclay, a mutual friend living in Clapham who would become one of Emma's self-appointed trustees. The birth of the Mathews' son, and Mary's hopes that he might aspire to an Irish earldom, are revealed in family correspondence at ANQ-Québec P450 1960-01-544/1. Emma's furious complaint about 'that *vile* Tom Tit' was in Lot 231 of the Calvin Bullock collection (Christie's, *The Calvin Bullock Collection*). The affecting note written by Nelson upon hearing of his father's death, with Emma's practical annotation, was ADC Lot 62, now in a private collection. William Nelson's comments about Davison's 'sharpness' are in Morrison vol. 2, p. 190. An entertaining account of the 1802 Ilchester election has been left in the diary of a local clerk (and blue party supporter) called Neast Greville Prideaux. A transcript is at the Somerset Record Office in DD/SAS FA 185. Manners' intemperate appeal to the voters appeared in *The Times* on 21 June 1802. Thomas Plummer's correspondence with his son is in the Clarendon papers on deposit at the Bodleian Library, Oxford, MSS Clar. dep.c.362/1. Southey mentions the election in his spoof travelogue *Letters from England* (by 'Don Manuel Alvarez Espriella'). PRO TS11/726 contains the election poll book and a copy of the voter's oath ('I . . . do swear, I have not received . . . any sum or sum of money, office, place or employment, *gift or reward . . . in order to give my vote at this election . . .*') Manners became MP for Ilchester after the 1802 election was declared void, although he was subsequently unseated himself for corruption. He was later 'committed to prison . . . for cutting down a man's trees and beating him when he complained'. Edington's letter accusing De Lancey and Davison of corruption is printed as appendix no. 25 in *The Third Report of the Commissioners of Military Enquiry*. Manners' petition regarding his suspicion of foul play at the Ilchester election was read in parliament on 29 November 1802, as noted in *Journal of the House of Commons*, 1802, vol. 58, p. 29.

Nelson's speech on St Vincent's naval bill is reported in Cobbett and Wright, eds, *Cobbett's Parliamentary History of England*, vol. 36, p. 1143. The commissioners' report on prize agency was the fourth in their long-running and wide-ranging inquiry into: 'Irregularities, Frauds, or Abuses, which are or have been practised by persons employed in the several Naval Departments'. It can be found in *Parliamentary Papers* 1802–3, IV.

CHAPTER X

Lady Bessborough gives a good account of Paris during the peace of 1802–3 in Granville, ed., *Lord Granville Leveson-Gower: Private Correspondence*, as does Bertie Greatheed in his journal (Bury and Barry, eds, *An Englishman in Paris*). Davison's letter to Nelson, written *in extremis* at Calais, is printed in Pettigrew, *Memoirs*, vol. 2, p. 282. Moira's poetic denunciation of the government is in Cobbett and Wright, eds, *Cobbett's Parliamentary History of England*, vol. 36, p. 1171. The king's private secretary, Lord Pelham, was charged by Nelson with seeking royal approval for Davison's appointment as his proxy at the installation ceremony for the Order of the Bath together with 'his humble request that your Majesty would confer the honor of a knighthood upon Mr Davidson [sic] for that purpose'. The submission is printed in Aspinall, ed., *Later Correspondence of George III*. The king, however, clearly felt strongly enough about Davison's unsuitability for the role to respond in person to William Marsden. The royal snub is printed by Hibbert, *Nelson: A Personal History*, p. 324n. The note that Nelson scrawled to Davison in Marsden's office is at BL Eg. 2240 fo. 171. Nelson's instruction for Davison to pay Emma £100 a month as an allowance is at BL Eg. 2240 fo. 161. Moira's letter to Nelson following the decision to instigate proceedings against Davison is quoted by Russell, *Nelson and the Hamiltons*, p. 287. Surviving parish records for Three Rivers from the eighteenth century contain countless Chevaliers, Chevalliers and Chevaillers. The best candidate for Nelson's steward is Louis Chevallier, born in 1766. William Chevailler appears in *Victory*'s muster as 'Henry Louis Chevalier', indicating that he may have tactfully anglicized his name. John Scott's moving correspondence with his wife Charlotte is in NMM AGC/36/3. Nelson's comment to Emma regarding the unfit state of *Victory* is quoted by Eyre Matcham, *The Nelsons of Burnham Thorpe*, p. 208. Nelson was familiar with Gardner, having attended the admiral's successful hustings in Covent Garden during the Westminster election the year before. Hardy's letter of apology to Davison following the misunderstanding over the *Orion* prize is at BL Eg. 2240 fo. 181. Charles Davison Scott was not the only child within Nelson's circle of friends named for his agent. In 1805 George and Kate Matcham christened their ninth, short-lived, child William Alexander. A number of witnesses left accounts of life in *Victory* before Trafalgar. John Scott paints a vivid picture in a letter to Charlotte which was published in *The Times* on 29 September 1923. The officers' diet is taken from a shopping list Nelson sent Davison on 23 October 1803 at BL Eg. 2240 fo. 190. An annotation by Davison indicates that he sent the goods out to the Mediterranean in *Argo* on 26 December. Nelson's reaction to Davison's 'damned electioneering scrape', dated 3 June 1803, is at BL Eg. 2240 fo. 176. Details of Davison's business with the barrack office are taken from PRO TS/11/681/2162 and from the appendices to *The Third Report of the Commissioners of Military Enquiry*. Davison's 1803 assessment of the 'state of my affairs' reveals that since buying Swarland in 1795 he had spent over £30,000 on land in Northumberland, raising his rental income to £2,500 a year. The negotiations leading to Davison's partnership in Edwards & Co. can be followed in EXTON MSS 3214. Davison's sanguine assurance to Minto that all would be well while Nelson remained at sea, 'I am sorry to find the Toulon ships are greater in number than we had reason to believe, tho' our Nile hero tells me it would be an agreeable disappointment were they to come out,' is in NLS MSS 11195 fo. 155. Detail on the Loyal Britons, including Davison's original application to the marquis of Titchfield for permission to form the regiment and a copy of its 'Rules and Regulations', are in DP6/12/38/1–27 at the Nottinghamshire Records Office. Nelson confirms the reluctant surrender of his proxy to Moira in a letter to Davison printed by Pettigrew, *Memoirs*, vol. 2, p. 343. He reports Moira's reassurance to Davison about how the proxy would be used in a letter to Emma in Morrison vol. 2, p. 241. A copy of Nelson's letter written to Davison 'on the eve of battle' off Toulon on 10 February 1804 was in ADC Lot 70: 'our fleet is healthy, our men spirited, our commanders brave and judicious – and for our numbers the finest fleet in the world'. Scott's concerned report to Marsh about the prize agency is reproduced in Gamlin, *Nelson's Friendships*, vol. 1, p. 350; Nelson's reply to Marsh's cautious enquiry in vol. 1, p. 353. His extraordinary letter to Emma about a subject which was clearly preoccupying him by early 1804 is printed in Pettigrew, *Memoirs*, vol. 2, p. 336.

CHAPTER XI

Mention of little Horatia's outing to the theatre with the Davisons is in a Nelson family letter in NMM/9292, cited by Pocock in *Nelson's Women*, p. 205. The court documents for Davison's trial in Taunton are in PRO TS11/726. Reports on the assizes are taken from the *Bath Chronicle* for 12 April 1804 and *Bath Journal* for 16 April 1804. Moira's appeal to McMahon for help in mitigating Davison's sentence is printed in Aspinall's *Correspondence of George, Prince of Wales*, vol. 4, p. 533. The conditions of life inside the King's Bench prison can be discovered from the *Report from the Select Committee Appointed to Inquire into the State of the King's Bench, Fleet and Marshalsea Prisons . . .* Nelson's comment to Emma, 'he always told me; "I know my ground"', is in

Pettigrew, *Memoirs*, vol. 2, p. 392. Nelson's letter of sympathy to Davison at 'the distressing intelligence of your sentence' is BL Eg. 2240 fo. 213. Nelson's letters to Davison in prison were not made available to Nicolas, indicating understandable Davison family discomfort at the sensitive nature of this period. Davison's disappointment when Emma failed to visit him in prison is in a note printed by Pettigrew, *Memoirs*, vol. 2, p. 425. Davison's replies to Emma's complaints about his interference in the works at Merton are in BL Add. 34989 fos 53–4. A copy of George Templer's speech at the emergency meeting of his banking partners on 21 July 1804 is at EXTON 3214/40/29. Nelson's not unreasonable attitude to the bank's failure – 'Why should my all go to save a parcel of people that I never saw or care a farthing about?' – is in a letter to Emma printed by Pettigrew, *Memoirs*, vol. 2, p. 419. Nelson's 'want of the needful' is in a note to Davison dated 17 August 1804 at BL Eg. 2240 fo. 217. Fulton's outraged appeal to Davison after the government dropped him was printed by Philip in *Robert Fulton*, p. 174. Nelson quotes Chevailler's request to leave *Victory* in a letter to Davison in Nicolas, vol. 5, pp. 475–6. Chevailler's letters to Davison, which were ADC Lot 72, are now in RNM MSS 2002/76. Davison's resigned reply to Emma's impatient demand for news of Nelson's return in October 1804, 'we cannot command the winds', is printed in Morrison, vol. 2, p. 247.

CHAPTER XII

Nelson's letter to Moira is printed in Nicolas, vol. 6, p. 310. Scott's attempts to counter Davison's influence on Nelson, and his clandestine deals with Cutforth and Wilkie, are revealed in a letter book of the secretary's at the RNM. Collingwood's lordly dismissal of Davison's approach is in NMM MSS 52/44. Nelson's letter to Haslewood, in which he complains that the French were 'leading me a dance', was Lot 206 in the Calvin Bullock collection. The poem Emma sent Davison is printed in *Memoirs of Lady Hamilton*, p. 352. Susannah Bolton's sighting of Fanny at Bath is in Russell, *Nelson and the Hamiltons*, p. 343. The letter she wrote in July 1805 is in Naish, p. 604.

Parliament's 'touchstone' with the people over corruption in the public departments is quoted by Creevey (Maxwell, ed., *The Creevey Papers*, vol. 1, p. 34). Charlotte Nelson's account of the 4 June festivities at Eton is in Gérin, *Horatia Nelson*, p. 87. A copy of the programme for *Ad Montem* in 1805 was found in Davison's papers; it is now BL Add. 79200 fo. 94. Nelson's comment to Haslewood about his proxy is in Pocock, *Horatio Nelson*, p. 310. His letter to Moira recalling the proxy is in Pettigrew, *Memoirs*, vol. 2, p. 425. Leake's desperate appeal to Davison, with the bank teetering on the edge of ruin, is in EXTON 3214/633. The letter Nelson wrote Davison the week before Trafalgar, the last to his friend, was ADC Lot 76. The letter was available to Nicolas but was not included in the archive of Nelson letters sold to the British Library by Sir William Davison's executors in 1873, signifying its especial importance.

CHAPTER XIII

The letter Mary wrote to James Thompson, her cousin in Quebec, on the morning of Nelson's funeral is at ANQ-Québec P450 (Literary and Historical Society of Quebec Collection) 1960-01-544/1. Thompson's son, who was staying with the Mathews at the time, commented that 'Col & Mrs M. are in very low spirits for Ld Nelson's death'. The events of Thursday 9 January, 1806 have been reconstructed using contemporary newspaper accounts, the very full report in the *Naval Chronicle* vol. 15 and the assessments of Jenks, 'Contesting the Hero', and White, 'Nelson's Funeral'.

CHAPTER XIV

The heartbreaking letter Emma wrote Davison after hearing the news of Nelson's death was ADC Lot 80; it is now in a private collection. Her uncharitable view of Davison as a 'Dirty vile groveler' is printed in Russell, *Nelson and the Hamiltons*, p. 355. Nelson's promise that Emma would receive the sultan's star after his death as a '*memento of friendship*' is in Pettigrew, *Memoirs*, vol. 1, p. 428. Sixty-two mourning rings were ordered from Salter on Earl Nelson's and Haslewood's instructions. A list of the recipients (who included Emma, Davison,

Marsh and the recently widowed Mrs Scott) is at BL Add. 34988 fo. 412. BL Add. 34992 fo. 80 shows that Nelson had died owing Salter £65 for unspecified jewellery, presumably gifts to Emma and Horatia. A brief statement of Nelson's capital on his death, showing he had paid off his debt to Davison, is at BL Add. 34992 fo. 77.

The diamond anchor was ADC Lot 67. No bill remains for the marble bust Flaxman made of Nelson for Davison after Trafalgar, though the sculptor charged Earl Nelson £189 for a similar one in 1809 (BL Add. 34992 fo. 299). The resolution of Emma's self-appointed trustees is printed in Morrison, vol. 2, p. 961. Davison's last recorded letter to Emma, 'could my wishes prevail, you would soon very quickly be relieved from every unpleasant sensation', is at NMM DAV 52/044. Her cry 'I was Queen of Naples *for seven years*' was in a letter she wrote Davison in November 1805 which was ADC Lot 80. Earl Nelson's perfidious offer of help is in BL Add. 34989 fo. 55. His complaint to Davison about 'secret insinuations' is BL Add. 34992 fo. 197. His attempt to include the date of the battle of Trafalgar in his calculation of the interest owing for the late payment of his lavish government grant was in ADC Lot 90, now BL Add. 79200 fo. 4. William Davison mentions going to the fair in Hyde Park with his father in his journal, which is in a private collection. He also recorded a dinner held at St James's Square on 23 June 1814 to mark the disbanding of the Loyal Britons following the treaty of Paris. Charlotte Scott's memorial to the king after her husband's death, supported by William Marsh, is printed in Dawson, *The Nelson Collection at Lloyd's*. Captain Durham's report on the meeting at Gibraltar to decide the prize agent for Trafalgar, together with Davison's subsequent complaint to Collingwood that he had been promised the role before Nelson died, are in NMM DAV 52/44. Collingwood's reply to Emma's enquiry about the captains' decision is in a private collection. Details of the extraordinary grant made by parliament to the victors of Trafalgar are in RNM 1983/1062. The triumphant procession of the Buenos Aires gold was reported by the *Morning Chronicle* on 22 September 1806. William Marsh's letter of outrage at Davison's appointment to the Ordnance is at MON E175. 'Aristides' wrote two letters to *The Times* (19 November and 19 December 1805) querying Davison's management of the naval pillar subscriptions. 'Verax' wrote on 27 December. Davison replied on 22 January 1806. The presence of the freemasons at the unveiling of the column erected in Nelson's memory at Yarmouth is noted by Yarrington, *Commemoration of the Hero*, p. 147. The inventory of 'the contents of Mahony [*sic*] chest of drawers', giving a glimpse of Nelson's purse sixty years after Trafalgar, is in a private collection. The most likely candidate for 'the *Gold* nile medal worn by the immortal Nelson when he fell' was ADC Lot 8, which was mounted to be worn. ADC Lot 8 also showed slight surface discolouration as a result of condensation within its glass mount, further evidence perhaps of its eventful history. A silver Nile medal and the 'gold snuff box made from the mast of the victory Lord Nelson's flagship at the battle of Trafalgar on which he was killed' was alongside the purse and medal in the chest of drawers in 1866. The box would be ADC Lot 87, selling for £57,360. Davison told Matthew Boulton after Trafalgar (in a rare comment on his feelings at his friend's death) that 'only the loss of my ever to be lamented bosom friend the immortal Nelson, prevented me issuing to the world one of the handsomest medals (under your direction) yet ever seen by the public'. The auction catalogue for Emma's belongings in 1813 reveals that similar snuff boxes were made after the battle of the Nile from wood taken from the wreckage of the French flagship *L'Orient*. The letters of acceptance from the artists Green approached on Davison's behalf were reproduced in *Descriptive Catalogue of the Series of Pictures . . .* Of the known current whereabouts of the pictures, Wilkie's *Alfred* is in a private collection, *The Death of the Earl of Chatham* by John Singleton Copley was presented to the Tate Gallery, London by the earl of Liverpool in 1830; and *The Fatal Wounding of Sir Philip Sidney* by Benjamin West is at the Woodmere Art Museum, Philadelphia. Davison owned at least one other painting by the young David Wilkie, called *The Clubbist*, which was originally painted to illustrate a story by Oliver Goldsmith in Leigh Hunt's collection of *Classic Tales*. The painting was catalogued as 'A small Cabinet picture of a Country Club' in Davison's 1817 auction, selling for £21 10s 6d. Apparently unaware that it had been sold, Wilkie approached Davison in April 1826 asking to borrow *The Clubbist* so that he could arrange for it to be engraved. Though the two men were never close (in his letter Wilkie had to remind Davison that he painted 'Alfred for your gallery'), the artist did take the trouble to visit his patron in Newgate in 1809. James Clarke's letter to Davison thanking him for co-operating in the production of *The Life and Services . . .* is in BL Eg. 2240. Nelson might have acquired the French sabre that would eventually pass to Davison in similar circumstances to a sword he mentions in a letter to Captain Berry at BL Add. 34908 fo. 279, written after the battle of the Nile: 'Galway gave me the sword which I forwarded to Prince Leopold, but I have the one which you brought me down the cockpit which you shall have.' Perhaps Berry (who was back in England) refused the sword, or Nelson forgot about it and this is the very sword that Davison received six years later. A weapon captured at the battle of the Nile would certainly be of sufficient symbolic importance to both men. Davison left instructions to his executors in his will dated 30 June 1827, a copy of which is at PRO PROB11/1763, that the sabre, gun and canteen should remain with his descendants at Swarland in perpetuity. However, his son William, who died without a legitimate male heir, was unable to honour his father's wishes. In addition to his bequest to the Royal Greenwich Hospital, William desired that 'the various autograph letters of the late Lord Nelson to my late father in my possession at my death' should be offered for sale to the British Museum. The letters, now in BL Eg. 2240, were duly purchased from Sir William's estate on 24 May 1873.

CHAPTER XV

Davison's examination by the commissioners of military enquiry on 6 December 1805 is printed in appendix no. 4 of their report. Herries and Bragge's dogged investigation of Davison can be followed in PRO TS/11/681/2162. Davison left details of Alexander Horatio Nelson Davison's death and funeral in a brief genealogical account of his family which was ADC Lot 92 and is now BL Add. 79200 fo. 109. Alexander's death hurt Davison badly. In 1801 he had revealed his hopes for the boy in a proud letter he wrote Nelson: 'your god son is the finest Boy I ever saw, *seventeen* years hence he will be looking to you for promotion'. Earl Nelson's remark to Haslewood that Davison looked 'very much cut' is in NMM HAS/1. Davison's 1809 trial is reported in full in Howell, *Cobbett's Complete Collection of State Trials*, vol. 31. Details of the negotiations for Davison's loan to the prince of Wales are in RA GEO 31557–31566. Davison's efforts to settle his sons into respectable military careers are revealed in a private collection of family papers. He advised them to keep close to the duke of Northumberland's sons – 'I wish you would keep up . . . a correspondence with both . . . it is of the highest importance' – and reprimanded them when they failed to meet their obligations: 'I fear it is too often the practice with young military men moving from one place to another to leave (*disgracefully* so) trifling debts.' Two letter books of William Davison's, which date from his tour of the Mediterranean and describe his meeting with Chevailler, are now at BL Add. 79200A and BL Add. 79200B. In 1990 documents relating to Davison's convoluted financial situation after his release from prison were discovered within a property formerly on the Swarland estate. Two letters from Philip Rundell to Davison, dated May and June 1824, in which the old jeweller calls in his loan are in BL Add. 79200 fos 80–2. A very small number of letters from Harriett Davison to her husband remain in the family's possession. Details on the dramatic and acrimonious collapse of Davison & Co. are taken from the archives of Coutts' Bank, MSS 4864/4867. Davison sent his profuse thanks to Sir Edward Antrobus, the senior partner of Coutts, as soon as he heard that Antrobus had agreed to take over his bank, thereby sparing his family from 'the most woeful calamity'. Davison assured him that all his old customers would transfer their balances to Coutts, enclosing, as an example of their loyalty, a letter from Lord Bridport (who had married Nelson's niece Charlotte in 1810), who promises to do so on condition he was allowed to occasionally 'overdraw to a small amount'. Hastings Middleton's opinion on the fiasco is preserved in the Middleton papers at the City of Westminster archives centre. The *New Biographical Dictionary* reported the auction of Davison's collections in 1817 thus: 'At the sale of his effects at his town house it was shown how those brilliant stars, that shine only for a moment, under the smiles of government, dispose of their wealth. More table clocks, watches, seals and trinkets, were sold than would stock a considerable dealer, and the sum he must have spent on these trifles exceeds belief, as they sold at public auction for what may be considered as an ample fortune' (vol. 1, p. 310). If Sir Walter Scott was the author of the poem that appeared on the obelisk at Swarland, he was equally scathing after Lord Moira died. 'Poor old honour and glory is dead,' Scott wrote in his journal on 22 December 1826. 'He was a man of very considerable talents but had an overmastering degree of vanity of the grossest kind. It follows, of course, that he was gullible. In fact the propensity was like a ring in his nose, into which any rogue might put a string. He had a high reputation for war, but it was after the petti-fogging hostilities in America, where he had done some clever things. He died, having the credit, or rather having had the credit, to leave more debt than any man since Caesar's time. £1,200,000 is said to be the least. There was a time when I knew him well, and regretted the foibles which mingled with his character, so as to make his noble qual-ities sometimes questionable, sometimes ridiculous. He was always kind to me. Poor Plantagenet.' Moira died on board *Revenge* off Naples on 28 November 1826, aged seventy-one. He was buried on Malta, of which he was governor at the time of his death. Moira left instructions that before his body was interred his right hand should be cut off and preserved until the death of his wife, when it was to be placed in her coffin. A statue of Moira by Flaxman is in the Memorial Hall, Calcutta. Henry Dundas died on 28 May 1811. An obelisk was erected to his memory at 'Dunira', his highland retreat, while a column was raised in St Andrew's Square, Edinburgh. The duke of Northumberland died on 10 July 1817, shortly before an 83-foot col-umn dedicated to him by his tenants was completed at Alnwick. Material on Davison's last years is taken from papers which remain in his family's possession, among which is a press report describing the festivities at Swarland over Christmas 1825. Davison died at Brighton on 10 December 1829, aged seventy-nine. On 29 December his body was interred between the coffins belonging to his wife and son within the family vault at St Gregory's church, Kirknewton.

In the entry he prepared on Davison for the *New Dictionary of National Biography*, Professor Harry Dickinson identifies him as the inspiration behind Frederick Marryat's fictional character Alexander Willemott who, during the Napoleonic wars, had been 'a large contractor with government for army clothing and accoutrements'. In 'The Way to Be Happy', a short story written in 1840 to illustrate the moral of 'cutting your coat according to your cloth', Marryat charts Willemott's decline from the grandeur of Belem Castle, where 'everything was on the most sumptious and magnificent scale', to Brighton, where, 'in a respectable but not fashionable part of this overgrown town', the army contractor ends his days in greatly reduced circumstances. Willemott's downfall is caused by 'a change of government, a demand for economy, and the wording of his contracts having been differently rendered from what Willemott had supposed their meaning to be'. It was surely no coincidence that Marryat, who witnessed Nelson's funeral procession as a child and whose father had been a merchant in the City of London, wrote 'The Way to Be Happy' on his return from a trip to North America which included a visit to Quebec. In the story, Willemott is sanguine about his fate, his words strangely echoing those Davison himself wrote in 1826: 'Although I have been a contractor, I have a good conscience . . . and, further, I have made it a rule as I have been going down hill, to find reasons why I should be thankful, and not discontented . . . it is not a loss of fortune which will affect your happiness as long as you have peace and love at home.'

BIBLIOGRAPHY

LETTERS AND PRIMARY SOURCES

Annual Register

Aspinall, A., ed., *The Correspondence of George, Prince of Wales, 1770–1812*, 8 vols (London, 1963–71)

—— *The Later Correspondence of George III*, 5 vols (Cambridge, 1962–70)

Bonner Smith, D., ed., *Letters of Admiral of the Fleet the Earl of St Vincent whilst First Lord of the Admiralty*, 2 vols (London, 1922–7)

A Catalogue of a Splendid Collection of Pictures, by British Artists, the Subjects Taken from English History; Painted Expressly for Alexander Davison, Esq. Which Will Be Sold by Auction, by Mr. Stanley . . . On Saturday the 28ᵗʰ of June, etc. (London, 1823)

Christie's, *The Calvin Bullock Collection: Napoleon, Nelson and their Time* (London, 8 May 1985)

Cobbett, W. and Wright, J., eds, *Cobbett's Parliamentary History of England*, 36 vols (London, 1806–20)

Cruikshank, E. A., ed., *The Correspondence of Lieut. Governor John Graves Simcoe, with Allied Documents Relating to his Administration of the Government of Upper Canada* (Toronto, 1923)

Davison, A., *A Reply to the Committee of Military Enquiry Respecting Barrack Supplies* (London, 1807)

Descriptive Catalogue of the Series of Pictures . . . on . . . History of England, Painted by British Artists for Alexander Davison (London, 1807)

Garlick, K. et al., eds, *The Diary of Joseph Farington*, 16 vols (New Haven, 1979–98)

Gentleman's Magazine

Granville, Countess Castilia, ed., *Lord Granville Leveson-Gower: Private Correspondence 1781–1821*, 2 vols (London, 1917)

Hansard, T., ed., *Parliamentary Debates from the year 1803 . . .* (41 vols, 1812–20)

Harcourt, L. V., ed., *The Diaries and Correspondence of the Rt. Hon. George Rose*, 2 vols (London, 1860)

Howell, T. J. H., ed., *Cobbett's Complete Collection of State Trials and Proceedings for High Treason and other Crimes and Misdemeanours from the Earliest Period to the Present Time*, 33 vols (London, 1809–26)

Hughes, E. A., ed., *The Private Correspondence of Admiral Lord Collingwood* (London, 1957)

Industrial Revolution: A Documentary History, 1st ser.: *The Boulton & Watt Archive and the Matthew Boulton Papers from Birmingham Central Library*, part 10 (Marlborough, 1994)

Journals of the House of Commons

London Directories (various)

London Gazette

Maxwell, Sir Herbert, ed., *The Creevey Papers* (London, 1904)

Morning Chronicle

Morning Herald

Morrison, A., *The Hamilton and Nelson Papers*, 2 vols (privately printed, 1893–4)

Naish, G. P. B., ed., *Nelson's Letters to his Wife and other Documents, 1785–1831* (London, 1958)

Naval Chronicle, 40 vols (1799–1819)

Nicolas, N. H., ed., *The Dispatches and Letters of Vice-Admiral Lord Viscount Nelson*, 7 vols (London, 1846)

Parliamentary papers:

Report from the Select Committee Who Were Appointed to Try and Determine the Merits of the Petition of Sir William Manners, Bart., Complaining of an Undue Election and Return for the Borough of Ilchester (Somerset) (1802–3), vol. iv, pp. 509ff.

The Fourth Report of the Commissioners of Naval Enquiry on Prize Agency (1802–3), vol. iv, pp. 249ff.

The Tenth Report of the Commissioners of Naval Enquiry on the Treasurer of the Navy (1805), vol. ii, pp. 125ff.

The Third Report of the Commissioners of Military Enquiry on the Barrackmaster-general's Office (1806–7), vol. ii, pp. 201ff.

Report from the Select Committee Appointed to Inquire into the State of the Gaol of Newgate . . . (1813–14), vol. iv, pp. 249ff.

Report from the Select Committee Appointed to Inquire into the State of the King's Bench, Fleet and Marshalsea Prisons . . . (1814–15), vol. iv, pp. 531ff.

The Quebec Almanack for the year 1792

Quebec Gazette

St James's Square . . . *The Entire Property of Alexander Davison, Esq. A Catalogue of the Superb Service of Plate* . . . *Porcelain* . . . *Gems* . . . *Books* . . . *Pictures* . . . *Which Will Be Sold by Auction, by Mr Farebrother* . . . *21ˢᵗ April, 1817, and Fifteen Following Days, etc.* (London, 1817)

Spencer, Earl, *Private Papers of George, Second Earl Spencer, First Lord of the Admiralty 1794–1801*, 4 vols (London, 1913–24)

The Times

Upton, L. F. S., ed., *The Diary and Selected Papers of Chief Justice William Smith, 1784–1793*, 2 vols (Toronto, 1963–5)

FURTHER READING
The Army

Brett-James, A., *Life in Wellington's Army* (London, 1972)

Bryant, Sir Arthur, *The Years of Endurance 1793–1802* (London, 1942)

Fortescue, Hon. Sir John, *History of the British Army*, 13 vols (London, 1899–1930)

Glover, R., *Peninsular Preparation: The Reform of the British Army 1795–1809* (Cambridge, 1963)

Guy, A. J., ed., *The Road to Waterloo: The British Army and The Struggle against Revolutionary and Napoleonic France, 1793–1815* (London, 1990)

Heythornthwaite, P. J., *The Armies of Wellington* (London, 1994)

Art, Relics and Monuments

Barrell, J., *The Dark Side of the Landscape: The Rural Poor in English Painting, 1730–1840* (Cambridge, 1981)

Beresford, Rear-Admiral Lord Charles, and Wilson, H. W., *Nelson and his Times* (London, 1897–8)

Christie Manson & Woods, *Relics of Lord Nelson, the Property of General Lord Bridport, London 12th July 1895*

Cunningham, A., *The Life of Sir David Wilkie*, 3 vols (1843)

Dawe, G., *Life of George Morland* (London, 1904)

Dawson, W. R., ed., *The Nelson Collection at Lloyd's* (London, 1932)

Foster, V., *Bags and Purses* (London, 1982)

Gilbey, Sir Walter., *George Morland: His Life and Works* (London, 1907)

Jenkins, I. and Sloan, K., *Vases and Volcanoes: Sir William Hamilton and his Collection* (London, 1996)

McCarthy, L., *Remembering Nelson* (privately printed, 1995)

Mace, R., *Trafalgar Square: Emblem of Empire* (London, 1976)

McKay, W. and Roberts, W., *John Hoppner RA: A Catalogue Raisonné* (London, 1909)

Marriot, L., *What's Left of Nelson* (Shepperton, 1995)

May, W. E. and Annis, P. G. W., *Swords for Sea Service*, 2 vols (London, 1970)

Milford Haven, Marquis of, *British Naval Medals* (London, 1923)

Pavière, S. H., *The Devis Family of Painters* (Leigh-on-Sea, 1950)

Pollard, J. G., 'Matthew Boulton and Conrad Küchler', *Numismatic Chronicle and Journal of the Royal Numismatic Society*, 1970, vol. 10, pp. 259–309

Royal Naval Exhibition 1891: Official Catalogue and Guide (London, 1891)

Royal United Services Institution: *Catalogue of the Exhibition of Nelson Relics in Commemoration of the Centenary of the Battle of Trafalgar* (London, 1905)

Strong, R., *And When Did You Last See your Father? The Victorian Painter and British History* (London, 1978)

Von Erffa, H. and Staley, A., *The Paintings of Benjamin West* (New Haven, 1986)

Walker, R., *The Nelson Portraits* (Portsmouth, 1998)

Warwick, P., 'Here was Paradise', *The Trafalgar Chronicle* (The 1805 Club), 1994, vol. 4

White, C., ed., *The Nelson Companion* (Gloucestershire, 1995)

Yarrington, A., *The Commemoration of the Hero, 1800–1864: Monuments to the British Victors of the Napoleonic Wars* (New York, 1988)

Economic, Social and Political Background

Angelo, H., *Reminiscences of Henry Angelo with Memoirs of his Late Father and Friends . . .*, 2 vols (London, 1904 edn; 2nd edn publ. 1828)

Ashton, T. S., *An Economic History of England: The Eighteenth Century* (London, 1955)

Baker, N., *Government and Contractors: The British Treasury and War Supplies, 1775–1783* (London, 1971)

Bladen, F. M. and Britton, A., eds, *Historical Records of New South Wales*, 7 vols (Sydney, 1892–1901)

Bury, J. P. T. and Barry, J. C., eds, *An Englishman in Paris, 1803: The Journal of Bertie Greatheed* (London, 1953)

Byrne, R., *Prisons and Punishments of London* (London, 1989)

Chapman, J. H. and Armytage, G. J., eds, *The Register Book of Marriages Belonging to the Parish of St George, Hanover Square, in the County of Middlesex*, 4 vols (London, 1896–7)

Colley, L., 'Whose Nation? Class and National Consciousness in Britain, 1750–1830', *Past and Present*, no. 113, 1986, pp. 97–117

—— *Britons: Forging the Nation, 1707–1837* (New Haven, 1992)

Cookson, J. E., 'The English Volunteering Movement of the French Wars: Some Contexts', *Historical Journal*, vol. 32, 1989, pp. 867–91

—— *The British Armed Nation, 1793–1815* (Oxford, 1997)

Dasent, A., *The History of St James's Square and the Foundation of the West End of London* (London, 1895)

Derry, J. W., *Politics in the Age of Fox, Pitt and Liverpool* (Basingstoke, 1990)

Dickinson, H. T., *Liberty and Property: Political Ideology in Eighteenth Century Britain* (London, 1977)

—— ed., *Britain and the French Revolution 1789–1815* (London, 1989)

—— *The Politics of the People in Eighteenth Century Britain* (London, 1995)

—— 'Popular Loyalism in Britain in the 1790s', in E. Hellmuth, ed., *The Transformation of Political Culture: England and Germany in the Late Eighteenth Century* (Oxford, 1990)

'Don Manuel Alvarez Espriella' [R. Southey], *Letters from England*, 3 vols (London, 1807)

Doty, R. G., *The Soho Mint and the Industrialization of Money* (London, 1998)

Elmsley, C., *British Society and the French Wars, 1793–1815* (London, 1979)

—— 'The Home Office and its Sources of Information and Investigation, 1791–1801', *English Historical Review*, vol. 94, 1979, pp. 532–61

Floud, R. and McCloskey, D., eds, *The Economic History of Britain since 1700* (2 vols), vol. 1: *1700–1869* (Cambridge, 1981)

George, M. D., *London Life in the Eighteenth Century* (London, 1996)

Hancock, D., '"Domestic bubbling": Eighteenth-Century London Merchants and Individual Investment in the Funds', *Economic History Review*, vol. 47, no. 4, 1994, pp. 679–702

—— *Citizens of the World: London Merchants and the Integration of the British Atlantic Community, 1735–1785* (Cambridge, 1995)

Hellmuth, E., ed., *The Transformation of Political Culture: England and Germany in the Late Eighteenth Century* (Oxford, 1990)

Langford, P., *A Polite and Commercial People: England 1727–1783* (Oxford, 1989)

Morí, J., *Britain in the Age of the French Revolution, 1785–1820* (Harlow, 2000)

Murray, V., *High Society: A Social History of the Regency Period* (London, 1998)

A New Biographical Dictionary of 3000 Contemporary Public Characters, British and Foreign, of all Ranks and Professions, 3 vols (London, 1825)

Pocock, T., *The Terror before Trafalgar* (London, 2002)

Porter, R., *English Society in the Eighteenth Century* (Harmondsworth, 1990)

—— *Enlightenment: Britain and the Creation of the Modern World* (London, 2000)

—— with Rousseau, G. S., *Gout: The Patrician Malady* (New Haven, 1998)

Reid, A., et al., eds, *A History of Northumberland*, 15 vols (Newcastle upon Tyne, 1893–1940)

Rudé, G., *Hanoverian London 1714–1808* (London, 1971)

Schwartz, R. B., *Daily Life in Johnson's London* (Madison, 1983)

Sparrow, E., *Secret Service: British Agents in France, 1792–1815* (Woodbridge, 1999)

Stevens-Cox, J., *A History of Ilchester, the Ancient County Town of Somerset* (Ilchester, 1958)

Summerson, J., *Georgian London* (New Haven, 2003)

Thorne, R. G., *The House of Commons 1790–1820*, 5 vols (London, 1986)

Weiner, Margery, *The French Exiles 1789–1815* (London, 1960)

Emma Hamilton

Constantine, D. J., *Fields of Fire: A Life of Sir William Hamilton* (London, 2001)

Foreman, A., *Georgiana, Duchess of Devonshire* (London, 1998)

Fothergill, B., *Sir William Hamilton, Envoy Extraordinary* (London, 1969)

Fraser, F., *Beloved Emma: The Life of Emma Lady Hamilton* (London, 1986)

Gérin, W., *Horatia Nelson* (Oxford, 1970)

Memoirs of Lady Hamilton; with illustrative anecdotes of many of her friends and distinguished contemporaries (London, 1815)

Tadmor, N., *Family and Friends in Eighteenth-Century England: Household, Kinship and Patronage* (Cambridge, 2001)

Fanny Nelson

Copeland, E. and McMaster, J., eds, *The Cambridge Companion to Jane Austen* (Cambridge, 1997)

Gordon, J., *The Little Duchess: The Story of Lord Nelson's Wife* (Stanewood, Devon, 2002)

Keate, E. M., *Nelson's Wife* (London, 1939)

Lincoln, M. and White, C., 'Kiss Me, Horatio', *History Today*, vol. 53, no. 11, 2003

Pocock, T., *Nelson's Women* (London, 1999)

Vickery, A., *The Gentleman's Daughter:Women's Lives in Georgian England* (New Haven, 1998)

White, C., 'The Wife's Tale: Frances, Lady Nelson and the Break-up of her Marriage', *Journal for Maritime Research*, October 2003

Freemasonry

Ars Quatuor Coronatorum, Transactions of Quatuor Coronati Lodge No. 2076 (London, 1884–)

Bjelajac, D., *Washington Allston, Secret Societies and the Alchemy of Anglo-American Painting* (Cambridge, 1997)

Brown, A., 'The Gregorians in Norfolk', *Ars Quatuor Coronatorum*, vol. 69, 1956, pp. 127–32

Hamill, J., 'The Earl of Moira, Acting Grand Master 1790–1813', *Ars Quatuor Coronatorum*, vol. 93, 1981, pp. 31–48

Jacobs, M., *Living the Enlightenment: Freemasonry and Politics in Eighteenth Century Europe* (London, 1991)

MacNulty, W. K., *Freemasonry: A Journey through Ritual and Symbol* (London, 1991)

Milborne, A. J. B., 'The Provincial Grand Lodge of Quebec, 1759–1792', *Ars Quatuor Coronatorum*, vol. 68, 1952, pp. 15–36

Money, J., 'Freemasonry and the Fabric of Loyalism in Hanoverian England', in E. Hellmuth, ed., *The Transformation of Political Culture: England and Germany in the Late Eighteenth Century* (Oxford, 1990)

Proctor, A., 'Was Nelson a Freemason?', *Ars Quatuor Coronatorum*, vol. 12, 1899, pp. 109–10

Ridley, J., *The Freemasons* (London, 1999)

Waite, A. E., *A New Encyclopaedia of Freemasonry*, 2 vols (London, 1921)

Webb, J., *Horatio, Admiral Lord Nelson:Was He . . . a Mason?* (Hersham, 1998)

The Navy

Gutridge, T., 'Aspects of Naval Prize Agency 1793–1815', *The Mariner's Mirror*, vol. 80, no. 1, 1994, pp. 45–53

Hill, R., *The Prizes of War: The Naval Prize System in the Napoleonic Wars, 1793–1815* (Stroud, 1998)

Kemp, P., *Prize Money: A Survey of the History and Distribution of the Naval Prizefund, etc.* (Aldershot, 1946)

—— *The British Sailor: A Social History of the Lower Deck* (London, 1970)

Lincoln, M., *Representing the Royal Navy: British Sea Power, 1750–1815* (Aldershot, 2002)

Pool, B., *Navy Board Contracts 1660–1832: Contract Administration under the Navy Board* (London, 1966)

Pope, D., *Life in Nelson's Navy* (London, 1981)

Rodger, N. A. M., *The Wooden World: An Anatomy of the Georgian Navy* (London, 1986)

Tracy, N., ed., *The Naval Chronicle: The Contemporary Record of the Royal Navy at War* (London, 1998)

NELSON
Life

Clarke, J. S. and M'Arthur, J., *The Life of Admiral Lord Nelson, KB from his Lordship's Manuscripts*, 2 vols (London, 1809)

Coleman, T., *Nelson: The Man and the Legend* (London, 2001)

Eyre Matcham, M. E., *The Nelsons of Burnham Thorpe* (London, 1911)

Gamlin, H., *Nelson's Friendships*, 2 vols (London, 1899)

Gardiner, R., ed., *The Campaign of Trafalgar* (London, 1997)

Harrison, J., *The Life of the Right Honourable Horatio, Lord Viscount Nelson*, 2 vols (London, 1806)

Hibbert, C., *Nelson: A Personal History* (London, 1994)

Lathom Browne, G., *The Public and Private Life of Horatio, Viscount Nelson* (London, 1891)

Moorhouse, E. H., *Nelson in England: A Domestic Chronicle* (London, 1913)

Oman, C., *Nelson* (London, 1947)

Orde, D., *Nelson's Mediterranean Command* (Edinburgh, 1997)

Pettigrew, T., *Memoirs of the Life of Vice-Admiral Lord Viscount Nelson*, 2 vols (London, 1849)

Pocock, T., *The Young Nelson in the Americas* (London, 1980)

—— *Horatio Nelson* (London, 1987)

Russell, J., *Nelson and the Hamiltons* (London, 1969)

Tracy, N., *Nelson's Battles: The Art of Victory in the Age of Sail* (London, 1996)

Vincent, E., *Nelson: Love and Fame* (New Haven, 2003)

White, C., *The Nelson Encyclopædia* (London, 2002)

Death and funeral

Beatty, Sir William, *The Authentic Narrative of the Death of Lord Nelson* (London, 1807)

Gatty, A. and Gatty, M., *Recollections of the Life of the Rev. A. J. Scott, DD* (London, 1842)

Jenks, T., 'Contesting the Hero: The Funeral of Admiral Lord Nelson', *Journal of British Studies*, 2000, vol. 39, no. 4, pp. 422–53

Navy Chronicle, 1806, vol. 15, pp. 222–35

An Official and Circumstantial Detail of the Grand National Obsequies at the Public Funeral . . . Nelson (London, 1806)

White, C., 'Nelson's Funeral', in R. Gardiner, ed., *The Campaign of Trafalgar* (London, 1997)

Personalities

Cliff, K. S., 'Alexander Davison's Chambers: A Mystery Solved', *The Nelson Dispatch*, 2000, vol. 7, part 1, pp. 41ff

Davison, C. O., *Davison, Alexander and his Descendants* (1998)

De Fonblanque, E. B., *Annals of the House of Percy, from the Conquest to the Opening of the Nineteenth Century*, 2 vols (London, 1887)

Dictionary of National Biography

Doran, W., *Memoirs of the Life of the Late Philip Rundell Esq.* (London, 1827)

Ehrman, J., *The Younger Pitt*, 3 vols (London, 1969–96)

Fay, C. R., *Huskisson and his Age* (London, 1951)

Fitzgerald, P., *Life of George the Fourth* (New York, 1881)

Fry, M., *The Dundas Despotism* (Edinburgh, 1992)

Kelly, L., *Richard Brinsley Sheridan: A Life* (London, 1997)

Melikan, R. A., *John Scott, Lord Eldon 1751–1838: The Duty of Loyalty* (Cambridge, 1999)

Melville, L., ed., *The Huskisson Papers* (London, 1931)

Philip, C. O., *Robert Fulton: A Biography* (New York, 1985)

Popham, H., *A Damned Cunning Fellow: The Life of Rear-Admiral Sir Home Popham* (Cornwall, 1991)

Reid, L., *Charles James Fox: A Man for the People* (London, 1969)

Saunders, J., 'A Portrait of Alexander Davison and his Friendship with Nelson', *The Nelson Dispatch*, April 2003, vol. 8, part 2, pp. 81–107

Turner, M. J., *Pitt the Younger: A Life* (London, 2003)

Warner, O. M. W., *The Life and Letters of Vice-Admiral Lord Collingwood* (London, 1968)

Wedgwood, B. and Wedgwood, H., *The Wedgwood Circle, 1730–1897: Four Generations of a Family and their Friends* (London, 1980)

Quebec

Bosher, J. F., *The Canada Merchants 1713–1763* (Oxford, 1987)

—— *Men and Ships in the Canada Trade 1660–1760* (Ottawa, 1992)

Brown, G. W., gen. ed., *Dictionary of Canadian Biography* (Toronto, 1966–)

Burt, A. L., *The Old Province of Quebec* (Minneapolis, 1933)

Cockloft, J., *Cursory Observations Made in Quebec, Province of Lower Canada, in the Year 1811* (Toronto, 1960)

Cohen, S. S., ed., *Canada Preserved: The Journal of Captain Thomas Ainslie* (Toronto, 1968)

Gale, G., *Historic Tales of Old Quebec* (Quebec, 1920)

Haldimand, General, private diary (in French with a translation, printed in full) in *Report on Canadian Archives*, 2nd ser., vol. 8, 1889, pp. 125ff

Lambert, J., *Travels through Lower Canada etc.* (London, 1810)

LeMoine, J. M., *The Chronicles of the St Lawrence* (Montreal, 1878)

—— *Picturesque Quebec: Quebec Past and Present* (Montreal, 1882)

McIlwraith, J., *Sir Frederick Haldimand* (Toronto, 1904)

Neatby, H., *Quebec: The Revolutionary Age, 1760–1791* (Toronto, 1966)

Vialar, Captain Anthony and Lester, Captain Robert, orderly books, in Literary and Historical Society of Quebec, *Historical Documents*, 7th ser., 1905, pp. 155–265

Young, K., *Kin, Commerce, Community: Merchants in the Port of Quebec, 1717–1745* (New York, 1995)

FILM AND FICTION

Korda, Alexander (dir.), *That Hamilton Woman!* (1941)

Marryat, F., Captain, 'The Way to Be Happy', in *Olla Podrida* (London, 1840), vol. 3, pp. 150–64

Sontag, S., *The Volcano Lover* (London, 1993)

Unsworth, B., *Losing Nelson* (London, 1999)

Weir, Peter (dir.), *Master and Commander: The Far Side of the World* (2003)

ACKNOWLEDGEMENTS

It took many people at Sotheby's to help Nelson's purse find a new home. Without them there would have been no auction and no book. This excellent team included Dr Peter Beal, Melissa Charles, Philip Howell, Andres White Correal, Marion Gloekle and Heinrich von Spreti. Tom Del Mar deserves a special mention for successfully, albeit briefly, reuniting Nelson's sword with its scabbard at the National Maritime Museum – after I was defeated by the task. Heartfelt thanks as well to Marcus Linell for his unfailing encouragement and wise counsel. Richard Pearson's photography of the collection, much of which is illustrated here with the kind permission of Sotheby's, was outstanding.

My grateful thanks to Peter Robinson of Curtis Brown for suggesting to me the idea of writing this book and for giving me the confidence to tackle it, and to the brilliant people at Transworld for making it a reality. They include Patrick Janson-Smith, Bill Scott-Kerr, Sheila Lee, Laura Sherlock, Katrina Whone, Vivien Garrett and my editor Doug Young, who patiently and with great good humour steered me through the whole exhausting process. It was a pleasure to watch Gillian Somerscales copy-edit the text with such great skill.

Grateful acknowledgement is due to Her Majesty the Queen for allowing me permission to study the details of Davison's loan to the prince of Wales held by the Royal Archives at Windsor, to the duke of Northumberland and the trustees of the Northumberland estates for permission to cite correspondence between Davison and the second duke, to the earl of Clarendon for the use of the Clarendon papers at the Bodleian Library, Oxford, and to the trustees of the British Museum for access to, among others, the Nelson papers and the Haldimand papers in the British library.

I was met with great kindness wherever the trail left by Nelson's purse led me. In Canada I should like to thank Eileen Reid Marcil and especially Pierre Louis Lapointe of the Archives nationales de Québec. Pierre gave me invaluable help in uncovering the surprising number of papers which Davison left behind in Quebec. In Northumberland my thanks go to Matthew Festing for his hospitality and enthusiastic help, Susan Collingwood-Cameron, Captain Francis Widrington, Ian and Carol Rogerson and to Alan and Vera Vaggs. After years of almost single-handedly keeping Davison's flame flickering, Vera took a keen interest in my work, generously allowing me to use her considerable research into his life, which included a detailed study of the battle park at Swarland.

In London I would like to thank Tracey Earl, the archivist at Coutts' Bank; Mark Dennis, curator of the library and museum of freemasonry; Martin Ford, the assistant curator of the museum at the Royal Hospital Chelsea; Theresa Thom, the librarian of Gray's Inn; Guy Holborn, the librarian of Lincoln's Inn; Lynda McLeod of Christie's Archives; Rina Prentice, Daphne Knott and Kiri Ross-Jones of the National Maritime Museum, Greenwich, and Jenny Grant of Regus, who very kindly gave me a fascinating tour of Davison's former home in St James's Square. James Morton, of Morton and Eden, gave expert advice on Davison's medals before they were sold and tried in vain to explain the complexities of eighteenth-century coinage to my post-decimalization brain.

I am also indebted to Pamela Clark, the registrar of the Royal Archives; Matthew Sheldon of the Royal Naval Museum, Portsmouth; Andrew Helme, the curator of the Nelson Museum, Monmouth; Linda Bankier at the Berwick-upon-Tweed Record Office and to the staff of the National Archives of Scotland; the National Library of Scotland; the City of Westminster Archives Centre; the London Library; the National Army Museum, the Northumberland Record Office; the Public Record Office at Kew; the Bodleian Library, Oxford; the Somerset Record Office; the Nottinghamshire Record Office; and the Leicestershire Record Office. I would especially like to thank the staff in the tea-room of the University Library, Cambridge who sustained me whilst I was writing this book.

Many people gave me their time, help and, in some instances, permission to use material from their collections. They include Flora

Fraser, Clive Richards, Toby and Frances Lyons, Peter and Susan, May Woods, Nicholas Tromans, Edgar Howard, Barbara Burman, Edward Schmidt, P. C. Laskaridis, Colin White and Professor Harry Dickinson who, at the outset, pointed me in the right direction by allowing me a sneak preview of his entry on Davison for the *New Dictionary of National Biography*. I am indebted to them all.

In particular, I owe a great deal to Kate Williams, who is currently preparing a life of Emma Hamilton for publication by Hutchinson. Kate read the early drafts of *Nelson's Purse,* gave invaluable guidance throughout and was unfailingly patient in helping me to complete the book.

Above all, my love and thanks to my wife Sam – to whom *Nelson's Purse* is dedicated – for her unwavering support and encouragement despite losing me to the eighteenth century for two years. Finally I wish to apologize to my children – who groan at the mention of Nelson – for their prolonged neglect. When asked, my nine-year-old daughter once wearily commented that I knew everything about Nelson down to the colour of his underpants. Not true – very far from it – but I have a good idea of what was in his purse.

PICTURE ACKNOWLEDGEMENTS

All images marked SPL are reproduced by courtesy of Sotheby's Picture Library

Text Illustrations
National Portrait Gallery Picture Library: viii; SPL: 14, 35, 39, 179, 306-7; National Maritime Museum: 18, 86, 119, 122 bottom, 179, 300, 332; English Heritage/photo National Portrait Gallery Picture Library: 70; photo Mark Dalton/private collection: 122 top, 335; copyright of The United Grand Lodge of England: 124, 177; British Museum, Department of Prints and Drawings: 256: Guildhall Library Print Collection © Corporation of London: 261, 301, 351; by courtesy of the Nelson Museum Monmouth: 206, 328; Norfolk Nelson Museum, Great Yarmouth: 324; courtesy of the Yale Center for British Art, Paul Mellon Collection: 370

Colour Sections

Alexander Davison's despatch box: SPL

View of Quebec from Pointe de Lévy by Benjamin Fisher, between 1785 and 1796, watercolour on paper, 38.1cm x 56cm. Collection Musée national des beaux-arts du Québec, acc. no 2003.273. Photo Jean-Guy Kérouac. Purchased with the support of the Minister of Canadian Heritage under the authority of the Cultural Property Export/Import Act; oil sketch of Davison by Lawrence: photo Jen Fong/private collection; Royal Exchange London: Guildhall Library Print Collection © Corporation of London; Rigaud portrait of Nelson: © National Maritime Museum

Duke of Northumberland: collection of the Duke of Northumberland; Lord Moira: copyright of The United Grand Lodge of England; HRH William Henry, Duke of Clarence: Army and Navy Club, London/www.bridgeman.co.uk; Henry Dundas: © The National Portrait Gallery Picture Library; Prince of Wales: Wallace Collection, London/www.bridgeman.co.uk

Watercolour of Swarland House; portrait of Percy and William Davison; Lemuel Abbott's portrait of Alexander Davison: all photos Mark Dalton/private collection

Fanny's seal: SPL; portrait of Fanny Nelson: © National Maritime Museum

The Battle of the Nile by Thomas Luny, c.1800: SPL

Davison's Egyptian Club sword; the Nile wine coolers; Davison's medal for the battle of the Nile obverse and reverse: all SPL

St James's Square in the late eighteenth century: city of Westminster Archive Centre, London, UK/Bridgeman Art Library/www.bridgeman.co.uk; map of St James's, Westminster, in 1755: city of Westminster Archive Centre, London UK/Bridgeman Art Library/www.bridgeman.co.uk; letter-wrapper addressed to Davison in Nelson's hand: SPL; St James's Square today: photo Mark Dalton

Nelson by Heinrich Füger, 1800: © National Portrait Gallery Picture Library; Merton Place, Surrey: Nelson Museum, Monmouth; Sipson House: photo Mark Dalton; pastel drawing of Emma

Hamilton by J.H. Schmidt, 1800: © National Maritime Museum

Revd Edmund Nelson by Sir William Beechey, 1797: © National Maritime Museum; autograph letter from Nelson: SPL

Nelson by Lemuel Abbott, 1798: © National Maritime Museum

The Prize Agent Refusing To Give Money by Thomas Rowlandson: © National Maritime Museum; John Jervis Earl St Vincent by John Hoppner, c.1800: SPL; Davison's note: SPL; Earl St Vincent's medal: SPL

The Death of Lord Nelson by Benjamin West, 1806: Walker Art Gallery/National Museums, Liverpool

The Death of Nelson by Arthur William Devis, 1807: © National Maritime Museum; Nelson's purse: SPL

Nelson's burial in St Paul's Cathedral, engraving by J. R. Hamble: Guildhall Library Print Room © Corporation of London

Diamond anchor: SPL

Turkish gun, canteen, miniature cannon and scabbard for sword only: all © National Maritime Museum; sword: SPL; portrait of Alexander Davison: SPL/private collection

Stephen Langton, Archbishop of Canterbury, shewing to the Barons of England... by Arthur William Devis: photo Mark Dalton/private collection

The Coal Contractor: © British Museum, Department of Prints and Drawings; Rosalie Davison by Hermann Winterhalter, 1874: photo Mark Dalton/private collection; obelisk at Swarland and detail of inscription: SPL

Sotheby's, London, 21 October 2002: SPL

Endpapers: coloured plan of the battle of Trafalgar, published by Robert Dodd, November 1805 © National Maritime Museum

INDEX

Davison, Jane (cousin) 76
Davison, Katty (sister) 47, 51, 52, 175, 198
Davison, Meg (sister) 52
Davison Noel, Templer & Co. 27, 243–5, 270–2, 294–5
Davison, Percy (son) 290–1, 353–5, 362
Davison, Rosalie (granddaughter) 34, 329
Davison, William (son) 229–30, 290–1, 353–5, 362
Davison & Co. (bank) 242–3, 357–8
De Lancey, Oliver 92, 108, 109, 207–8, 209
  commission of military inquiry 338–9, 342–3, 345, 348
 fraud accusations 222, 289–90
Defiance (Capt. Phillip Durham) 151, 278, 317
Derby porcelain 137–9, 157
Devis, Arthur William 20–2, 262, 330–1, 334
dinner party for Nile victory 163, 165
dinner service, Nile 163, 185
Dodds, James 160, 165, 187, 200, 222
dog bought for Lady Hamilton 162
Dreadnought (Capt. John Conn) 284
Dundas, Capt. George 281
Dundas, Henry (later Viscount Melville) 79, 80, 82, 88, 95, 115
  battle of Nile medal 120, 121
  forced out of office 288–9
  and 'infernals' inventions 273
  meets Davison in Wimbledon 278–81
  returns to power 263
Dunn, Thomas 72, 73, 76

East India Company 48, 80, 81, 146, 147, 211, 244
Edington, Robert 154, 221–2, 339
Egyptian Club 113, 130, 135, 141
  distribution of prize money 150–1
  Miller's monument 181
  presentation sword 148–9, 337
Erskine, Thomas 258–9
Eton College 290–1
Euryalus 4, 16, 292

Faden's map shop (London) 174
Farington, Joseph 102, 331

Ferdinand IV, king of Naples 141, 144, 147
Field, Sukey *see* Nelson, Sukey
Flaxman, John 33, 181
Fox, Charles 82, 103–4
France
  and American colonies 61, 62
  émigré guerrilla troops 91–2, 94–6
  French Revolution 81, 83–4, 89, 227
  French ships as prizes 132–3
  French and Spanish fleets join at Cadiz 292–3
  peace treaty 201–2, 209, 215, 230
    English visit Paris 227–9
  royalist agents 89, 91
  war with England 83–4, 101–2, 198, 225
    second war 232, 234, 238
freemasonry 56–7, 74, 84, 96, 120
  at height of Davison's career 155
  battle of Nile medals 121, 122–3, *122*, 125, 126, 144
  Nelson's regalia lost 177
  wine-coolers 138
French Party (Canada) 61, 71
Fulton, Robert 272–4

Gear, Mr (building manager) 212
George III, King 91, 105, 143, 224, 263
George, Prince of Wales 24, 26, 27–8, 47, 312
  links with Davison 156–7, 352
  Moira and Northumberland 84, 104–5
  and Whigs 238
Gibraltar 285, 290
gifts *see* present-giving
Goldsmid, Abraham 27, 309
Goliath 141
Gosling, Harriett *see* Davison, Harriett
Goslings & Sharpe 147, 223
Graham, James 218, 220
Graham, Sir Robert 257
Grant, William 72, 73
Green, Valentine 330
Grenville, Lord 145
guns, small brass 223–4, 362

Haldimand, Frederick 61, 62, 65, 77, 79
  dispute over leases to Davisons 71–5
  and Robert Mathews 128
Halsted, John 57, 58, 59, 90

Plan of the ATTACK by LORD NELSON